System Assurance

System Assurance
Beyond Detecting Vulnerabilities

Nikolai Mansourov

Djenana Campara

AMSTERDAM • BOSTON • HEIDELBERG • LONDON
NEW YORK • OXFORD • PARIS • SAN DIEGO
SAN FRANCISCO • SYDNEY • TOKYO
Morgan Kaufmann Publishers is an imprint of Elsevier

Morgan Kaufmann Publishers is an imprint of Elsevier.
30 Corporate Drive, Suite 400, Burlington, MA 01803, USA

Library of Congress Cataloging-in-Publication Data
A catalog record for this book is available from the Library of Congress.

British Library Cataloguing in Publication Data
A catalogue record for this book is available from the British Library.

ISBN: 978-0-12-381414-2

Printed and bound in the USA
11   12   13   10   9   8   7   6   5   4   3   2   1

To our children Maja and Alexander

Contents

Foreword

At the turn of the last century, *Time–Life* magazine picked Johannes Gutenberg's invention of the printing press as the most important invention of the second millennium. Their pick outranked many other inventions that have changed humankind. Anesthesia and vaccinations that have revolutionized the medical field, automobiles and airplanes that have increased mobility, and even the electric light that has powered countless social changes all ranked below Gutenberg's invention, which allowed the great expansion of literacy.

The concept of interchangeable parts in the printing press was what made the press adaptable and such a revolutionary change. Previously, books were hand copied and could easily take a year's labor to produce, making their cost prohibitive to all but a few. Gutenberg didn't invent printing or movable type. Printing had been around for many thousands of years. Movable type had been in existence for well over a thousand years before Gutenberg. Although he did invent the process for mass-producing movable type and is credited with introducing movable-type printing to Europe, his most significant contribution, and the one for which he was recognized, was tying all of these pieces together into a revolutionary new use that imparted incredible social change.

Nearer to the interests of the readers of this book are computers, which ranked well below Gutenberg's invention on the Time-Life list. This is not surprising, for computers only appeared at the twilight of the last millennium and their impact is just starting to be felt. We've only experienced a tiny portion of the changes that computers are bringing to the world. Every day new adaptations and uses for computers are rapidly changing our world. But, as with any rapid and revolutionary change, there is a dark side. Computers can be usurped by attackers, and the code on which we depend for our safety and privacy can have flaws that make the code operate in unintended or unexpected ways.

Many security professionals are attempting to make the use of computers more secure. Dr. Nikolai Mansourov and Ms. Djenana Campara's contributions to the OMG Software Assurance Ecosystem and their work on the supporting standards described in this book are providing the basis for a revolutionary change in the way knowledge about software is determined and demonstrated. From this knowledge, the potential exists for gaining a deep understanding of the software and identifying potential vulnerabilities.

One of the major strengths of the Ecosystem is the fact that it is based on internationally developed and recognized standards. The standards-based approach allows for components of the Ecosystem to be exchanged for other components for reasons such as being able to process a different computer language or for better performance. This approach provides for the interchange of the components similar to the process invented by Gutenberg and used to create most of the products we use today. In a similar way, the interchangeability offered by the

Ecosystem has the potential to drastically change how weaknesses in software are identified and evidenced.

The standards on which the SwA is based are, by necessity, not trivial. Through this book, Nick and Djenana have provided a good introduction to these underlying standards and how they fit together to form the SwA EcoSystem. I applaud Dr. Mansourv and Ms. Campara as they continue their contributions to the essential task of making computing safer and more secure for the world.

Dr. Larry Wagoner

Preface

Claude Langton: But I haven't heard anything about a murder.
Hercule Poirot: No, you would not have heard of it. Because, as yet,
it has not taken place. You see, if one can investigate a murder before
it happens, then one might even, well, a little idea … prevent it?
Agatha Christie, *Poirot: The Wasp's Nest*

System assurance is a bit like detective work: Most of the time is spent "out in the streets" gathering evidence—interviewing potential witnesses or searching for a promising cigarette butt. Gathering evidence is important. The evidence contributes to understanding the situation ("facts of the matter"). Evidence drives the investigation ("follow the facts"). Remember, some detective time is spent on planning the investigative actions. Finally evidence is used to present the case in front of the judge and the jury.

System assurance investigates the presence of security vulnerabilities in our systems. Vulnerability is any characteristic of the system that allows an attacker to commit cybercrime. A vulnerability may be something that is built into the system, intentionally or unintentionally, or something that was omitted from the system. A vulnerability may be an incorrectly designed protocol. Often, a vulnerability is very specific to a particular class of systems, while the same behavior is normal for other systems. It is much like we instruct little kids, as when we admonish: "Do not talk to strangers," while talking to a stranger is a normal behavior for a salesperson. So, a vulnerability is anything that makes a cybersystem susceptible to abuse— anything that leads to the insecurity of the system.

System assurance is like a forensic investigation performed before a cybercrime has been committed. However system assurance gathers evidence to support a much more comprehensive contention that "the system will not allow a certain crime to be committed, guaranteed." System assurance is one of the processes that is required to make our systems safer and more secure, and more resilient to cybercrime. The risks to cybersystems are very real, and before a new system is put into operation these risks must be understood and accepted. Eventually the public needs to understand and accept the risks they face when using the cybersystems. So, the persons and corporations responsible for launching new cybersystems, the regulatory organizations, and the public are the "jury" in front of which the safety and security of systems ought to be argued. System assurance is about making a clear, comprehensive, and defendable case about the safety and security of a system, to build confidence that the system is safe and secure to operate, and is free from vulnerabilities. Delivering system assurance case means communicating it to the "jury" and opening it up for critical questions by which one builds confidence.

An assurance case is more than a series of claims. Confidence must be justified by evidence. Many things can be gathered as evidence to support claims about the safety and security of systems, and some kinds of evidence offer stronger support than others. For example, a statement from a reputable security expert, such as "I believe that this voting machine is secure," may be convincing. On the other hand, a statement from an experienced ethical hacker, saying that "I could not get into this system after 5 days of attacking it," may be even more convincing as it is based on some concrete investigative actions that are directly related to the system of interest rather than on an unqualified expert opinion. What makes the second statement more convincing than the first one is knowledge of the system of interest.

It may seem that the defender community has more knowledge of the systems and is in a good position to prevent vulnerabilities by considering security from the beginning, resulting in resilient systems. However, defenders do not always have sufficient knowledge. Systems include commercial components, legacy components, open-source components, all of unknown security posture and pedigree. Systems of such mixed origins are increasingly vulnerable to defects and subversion. So even when security is considered from the beginning of the system's life cycle, many unknowns exist that are often outside of the developers' control. Also, engineers of systems are not in a good position to anticipate possible vulnerabilities that enable cyberattacks, because they lack the "attack perspective," if not the "criminal mentality," that is required to design abuse of the systems that they are trained to build. In addition, system knowledge turns out to have a short shelf life. Knowledge of the system dissipates and even "walks away" as developers change projects. So the code, often the machine code, becomes the only reliable source of knowledge that needs to be rediscovered.

Let's face it: Hackers often know more about our systems than we do. Elite hackers study our systems incessantly and find ingenious ways to abuse them "for fun and profit." What makes cybercrime an issue is that attackers succeed in sharing this knowledge among themselves and make it available to larger criminals circles, who are more interested in using knowledge of vulnerabilities more for profit than for fun. What makes cybercrime a bigger concern is that the community of attackers can be large and dispersed among all corners of the world, across jurisdictions. Attackers are not only sharing their knowledge of vulnerabilities, but are also making it repeatable and affordable by "weaponizing" it, turning into scripts that require little technical skills to use. The new reality is that the malware that exploits vulnerabilities in our systems is feeding organized crime and is becoming the foundation of a large criminal industry.

Both attackers and defenders favor automated code analysis tools for detecting vulnerabilities. However, here lies a fundamental problem: While attackers are okay with the ad hoc, hit-and-miss vulnerability detection, these methods are not well suited for defenders, who need to be meticulously systematic in understanding risks and designing security mechanisms. Therefore we focus our attention on the field of system assurance as the systematic and justified investigation of the security posture.

How can cyberdefense be made systematic, repeatable, and affordable? The solution is in working together to accumulate common cybersecurity knowledge and build automated capabilities that enable defenders to leverage their advantages and to move significantly ahead of the attackers. There are several aspects to building these collaborative capabilities. First, there is a need for standard protocols for assembling analysis tools that can address the complexities of modern systems. There are often limits to what one company or one security researcher can accomplish, which often leads to limitations, inefficiencies, and compromises in the solutions. There is a need for a larger market of interoperable components, like Lego blocks, supplied by multiple vendors, from which robust analysis solutions can be assembled. Second, there is a need for standard protocols to accumulate and exchange cybersecurity content. Yes, in order to be repeatable and affordable, cybersecurity content, including vulnerability knowledge, must be machine-readable and available to the defenders. In other words, there is a need for an ecosystem of tools as well as machine-readable content for assurance.

We titled the book *System Assurance: Beyond Detecting Vulnerabilities* because the content for systematic, repeatable, and affordable cyberdefense goes beyond knowledge of vulnerabilities and includes knowledge of the system, knowledge of risks and threats, knowledge of security safeguards, as well as knowledge of the assurance argument, together with the corresponding evidence answering the question why a system is secure. In other words, it is easy to claim that a system is not secure when at least one potential vulnerability is detected and presented as evidence. However, if no vulnerability were detected, does that really mean that the system is secure? Not really. It still requires convincing argument and evidence to that end, including the argument that the tool was applied correctly, that there are no gaps in the understanding of the particular code dialect, that no code was dropped, and so on. System assurance tools go beyond detecting vulnerabilities—such provide evidence to support the claim that the system is secure.

We are privileged to actively participate in several cybersecurity communities that are tackling this agenda. One of these communities is the Object Management Group (OMG)—an international, open membership, not-for-profit computer industry consortium with a mission to develop enterprise integration standards. Our book describes the OMG Software Assurance Ecosystem—a common framework for discovering, integrating, analyzing, and distributing facts about your existing software systems. Its foundation is the standard protocol for exchanging system facts, defined as the OMG Knowledge Discovery Metamodel (KDM). In addition, the Semantics of Business Vocabularies and Business Rules (SBVR) defines a standard protocol for exchanging security policy rules and assurance patterns. Using these standards together, the cybersecurity community can accumulate and distribute machine-readable cybersecurity content and bring automation to protect systems. Finally, the assurance argument is represented as machine-readable content, defined by the forthcoming OMG standard called the Software Assurance Case Metamodel. We describe a unique system assurance methodology that fully utilizes the OMG Software Assurance Ecosystem standards and involves an Integrated System Model, a common representation that is used for system analysis and evidence gathering.

The key to the OMG Software Assurance Ecosystem is the so-called Common Fact Model—a formal approach to building common vocabularies for information exchange, uniform XML interchange formats, and fact-oriented integration.

The book covers a lot of ground. The first part of the book provides an introduction to cybersecurity knowledge, the need for information exchanges for systematic, repeatable, and affordable cyberdefense, and the motivation for the OMG Software Assurance Ecosystem. Then we discuss the nature of system assurance and its difference for vulnerability detection and provide an introduction to the forthcoming OMG standard on Software Assurance Cases. We describe an end-to-end methodology for system assurance in the context of the OMG Software Assurance Ecosystem that brings together risk analysis, architecture analysis, and code analysis in an integrated process that is guided and planned by the assurance argument. The methodology presented in the book is based on the FORSA methodology (Fact-Oriented Repeatable System Assurance) from KDM Analytics.

The second part of the book describes various aspects of cybersecurity knowledge that are required for building cybersecurity arguments. This knowledge includes system knowledge, knowledge related to security threats and risks, and vulnerability knowledge. Finally we describe the new form of cybersecurity content— machine-readable vulnerability patterns. When describing the elements of cybersecurity knowledge, we use the SBVR notation to outline the parts of the common cybersecurity vocabulary developed using the Common Fact Model approach and the SBVR standard.

The third part of the book provides an overview of the protocols of the OMG Software Assurance Ecosystem. First, we discuss the details of the Common Fact Model approach. Then we describe linguistic models and the OMG Semantics of Business Vocabularies and Rules (SBVR) standard. Finally, we describe the OMG Knowledge Discovery Metamodel (KDM). Further details of the OMG standards can be found by reading the specifications themselves.

The fourth part of the book provides an illustration of other material by means of an end-to-end case study. Basically, Chapter 12 provides some fragments of an end-to-end system assurance project by illustrating the steps of the System Assurance Methodology, defined in Chapter 3, the Integrated System Model, and the Assurance Case.

The book also includes an online appendix, with additional details on gathering evidence to the assurance case using the Integrated System Model. The appendix is aimed at a technical audience and contains screenshots of the KDM Workbench tool from KDM Analytics. That's why we decided not to include this material in the main part of the book.

This book is designed and intended for anyone who wants a more detailed understanding of what the field of system assurance is, how to argue the security posture of a system, and how to perform a comprehensive security assessment.

The audience for this book includes security professionals who want a more in-depth understanding of the process of architecture-driven security assessment, of building security assurance cases, and of systematic methods of gathering security evidence.

Security professionals will benefit from this book by becoming familiar with the standard-based system assurance methodology that includes process and technology. The information contained in this book provides guidance to the OMG Knowledge Discovery Metamodel, the Common Fact Model, and related standards that will help develop interoperable solutions as well as contribute cybersecurity content that can enable solutions from multiple tool vendors. This can be particularly appealing to security researchers at the universities as well as open-source developers, as more and more components of the OMG Software Assurance Ecosystem become available as open-source projects.

Assurance labs will find this book useful as it provides blueprints for integrating multiple commercial tools into a powerful and highly automated assessment solution, by utilizing the Knowledge Discovery Metamodel and the Common Fact Model approach.

Security tool vendors will learn how to utilize the Ecosystem through simple import/export bridges to plug into end-to-end solutions and in this way expand their market.

Security service consumers will also benefit from reading this book. In addition to being the recipient of better, cheaper, faster, and more comprehensive security assessments, security service consumers will gain an understanding of the common pitfalls of vulnerability detection that is not supported by a clear and defendable argument.

System stakeholders will benefit from reading this book, which will help them to understand the framework for open-standard, collaborative cybersecurity. In that way they can choose best-in-the-class tools for their needs and request additional capabilities to be developed by vendors. This will provide motivation to tool vendors and security researchers to engage in efficient collaborations that are essential to making our systems more secure in the face of cyberattacks.

Why hackers know more about our systems

We live in a world comprised of systems and risk.
—**Clifton A. Ericson II, Hazard Analysis Techniques for System Safety**

Throughout history, each technological advance has inevitably become the target of those who seek to subvert it.
—**David Icove, Computer Crime**

1.1 OPERATING IN CYBERSPACE INVOLVES RISKS

To be effective during an operation, organizations need to be agile, mobile, and robust with a flexible service-oriented user experience. Delivering this need means relying heavily on Web and Internet services technology that enables organizations and their clients to synergistically work together by automating end-to-end information exchange processes for seamless collaboration and operation of fully automated information systems that work 24/7 without human intervention. However, along with these enhanced information exchange capabilities come significant security, privacy, and regulatory concerns and challenges.

Cyber criminals have also undergone a remarkable transformation as they exploit the global scale and connectivity of cyberspace and convergence of services onto the Internet, where a significant amount of financial and business transactions are taking place [Icove 1995]. Cyber criminals evolved from lone hackers driven by curiosity and the desire to make a point about the freedom of information into sophisticated, transnational networks of organized criminals who commit large-scale online crimes for significant profit. Over the past three decades, hackers managed to accumulate an arsenal of cyber attack methods. According to the Inquiry into Cyber Crime, performed by the Australian Parliament [Australia 2010], cyber crime "operates on an industrial scale and has become an increasingly important issue for the global community."

Furthermore, cyber-warfare became a reality that cannot be ignored since the 21st century battlefield includes not only the corn fields, deserts, mountain passes, and pine woods, but also the virtual communities in cyberspace along the information highways and back-roads supported by computers and mobile phones, and the miles of fiber optic cables, copper wires, the numerous network equipment boxes, and the very airwaves of the electromagnetic spectrum [Carr 2010]. This includes the nations' critical infrastructure and enterprise information systems, all the way down to the desktops and laptops in businesses and homes. The critical infrastructure is composed of many sectors that are in every nation's core industries—chemical, telecommunications, banking and finance, energy, agriculture and food, and defense—and bring us the services on which we all depend—water, postal and shipping, electrical power, public health and emergency services, and transportation. Each sector is extremely complex and to varying degrees is dependent on all the others.

Cyberspace and physical space are increasingly intertwined and software controlled. Each of the *systems* can affect our safety and security, and they have a unique design and a unique set of components; additionally, they contain inherent hazards that present unique mishap *risks*. We are constantly making a trade-off between accepting the benefits of a system versus the mishap risk it presents. As we develop and build systems, we should be concerned about eliminating and reducing mishap risk. Security services need to be seamlessly integrated into this new environment in order to assist civilian management and military commanders in recognizing the new information security threats posed by Web and Internet services-enabled activity, calculating the residual risk, and implementing appropriate security countermeasures to maintain order and control. Some risks are small and can be easily accepted, while other risks are so large that they must be dealt with immediately. While the trust side of the security equation has received a great deal of attention in the world of security, this growing reliance on Web and Internet services raises security issues that cannot be mitigated by traditional authentication processes. Although it remains important to know whether to trust information, it is becoming imperative to verify that there is no threat-related activity associated with this information.

Developing effective approaches to verify that systems operate as intended, that information can be trusted with confidence, and that no threat-related activity would follow is a key component in achieving systems security posture needed to defend against current and future attacks.

In particular, as mentioned in the 2008 OCED/APEC report, malware threat "is increasingly a shared concern for governments, businesses, and individuals in OECD countries and APEC economies. As governments rely evermore on the Internet to provide services for citizens, they face complex challenges in securing information systems and networks from attack or penetration by malicious actors. Governments are also being called on by the public to intervene and protect consumers from online threats such as ID theft. The past five years have indeed brought a surge in the use of malware to attack information systems for the purpose of gathering information, stealing money and identities, or even denying users access to essential electronic resources. Significantly, the capability also exists to use malware to disrupt the functioning of large information systems, surreptitiously modify the integrity of data, and to attack the information systems that monitor and/or operate major systems of the critical infrastructure" [OECD 2008].

1.2 WHY HACKERS ARE REPEATEDLY SUCCESSFUL

Hackers seem to know more about our systems than we do. Does this sound strange to you? Shouldn't we—the designers, developers, implementers, administrators, and defenders—have the "home advantage"? Yet hackers keep finding means of taking over our systems. New security incidents are reported weekly, while software vendors are reacting to the incidents by issuing patches to their products. The industry seems to be trying to catch up with the hackers, hoping that the "good guys" will discover *vulnerabilities* quicker than the "bad guys" so that the software builders can patch systems before incidents happen.

For now let's assume that a "vulnerability" is a certain unit of knowledge about a fault in a system that allows exploiting this system in unauthorized and possibly even malicious ways. These faults are primarily caused by human error, poor requirements specifications, poor development processes, rapidly changing technology, and poor understanding of threats. Some faults are introduced deliberately through the supply chain and slip through into delivered systems due to poor development and acquisition processes. The industry came to the realization that with traditional system security engineering, error-free, failure-free, and risk-free operation is not usually achievable within acceptable cost and time constraints over the system life cycle [ISO 15443].

So why do attackers know more about our systems than developers and defenders? They are more efficient in discovering knowledge about our systems and are better at distributing this knowledge throughout their communities. How do hackers *discover* knowledge? Hackers relentlessly study our systems and invent new ways to attack them. Some hackers have the advantage of having access to the details of the entire development process of a system they attack and knowledge of the systems that have already been put into operation. Hackers study the source code whether they can obtain it by legal or illegal means, especially for the critical proprietary and network-based systems. But hackers also study machine code and study systems by interacting with them, where no code is required. Hackers take advantage of:

- The fact that systems are often built from commercial off-the-shelf components, including a small number of the base hardware and software platforms;
- Time flexibility – they are usually not constrained in their analysis of our systems, even though such analysis may be quite time-consuming, and;
- Vulnerable legacy systems – a vast majority of systems are still legacy systems developed with lax security requirements.

However, what makes attackers extremely efficient is extensive *knowledge sharing*. Since this is an important aspect for consideration in a defenders community, let's examine how knowledge sharing is done.

Attackers vary in their knowledge and capability. It is an exaggeration to say that *every* attacker knows more about *every* system than *any* defender or developer of that system. In the attacker community, individuals have different skills and play different roles: there are few highly skilled security researchers (known as the "elite hackers"), and a larger number of less skilled attackers (known as the "script kiddies"). However, the attacker community—a nebulous assembly of groups of like-minded individuals—is very efficient in using computer communications, and social networks to share knowledge. In fact, the hackers of the early days started as the enthusiasts of the emerging computer technology, communications, and networking. Attackers have been able to accumulate significant amounts of knowledge on how to attack systems. In addition, there are individuals who transform the theoretical knowledge of the attacks into the attack scripts and tools—attack knowledge is rather practical, and tools do play a critical role in attacking cyber systems. So, theoretical knowledge is transformed into automated attack weapons that require little technical skills. Attackers are willing to share, not just their knowledge, but also their tools and "weapons," which become available to the individuals who are willing to launch attacks. As a result, an efficient *ecosystem* emerges, which amplifies the results of a few highly skilled hackers, and feeds a larger number of less skilled but highly motivated criminalized attackers. Hackers may not be systematic in what they do, but they succeed in *industrializing* their knowledge.

A large part of modern attack weapons is known as malware. According to an earlier cited OECD report [OECD 2008], malware is a general term for a piece of software inserted into an information system to cause harm to that system or other systems, or to subvert them for use other than that intended by their owners. Malware can gain remote access to an information system, record and send data from that system to a third party without the user's permission or knowledge, conceal that the information system has been compromised, disable security measures, damage the information system, or otherwise affect the data and system integrity. Different types of malware are commonly described as viruses, worms, trojan horses, backdoors, keystroke loggers, rootkits, or spyware. Malware shrinks the time between the discovery of vulnerabilities in software products and their exploitation and makes cyber attacks *repeatable*, which undermines the effectiveness of current security technologies and other defenses.

The skills within the defender community also vary greatly from the elite security researchers (who are sometimes hard to distinguish from the elite hackers) all the way to the administrators of home computer systems. However, the defender community lacks efficiency in their knowledge sharing due to too many barriers designed to retain competitive edge, expand market space, enhance offerings, etc.

1.3 WHAT ARE THE CHALLENGES IN DEFENDING CYBERSYSTEMS?

Defense of cybersecurity systems involves understanding the risks, managing the vulnerabilities, adding safeguards, and responding to the incidents. The foundation of this understanding is *knowledge* related to (1) *what* are you defending, (2) what are you defending *against*, (3) what are *vulnerabilities* you need to mitigate and

(4) what *safeguards* are included. Defense is conducted throughout the entire life cycle of the system. While long-term strategy involves better security engineering to develop more secure systems, the cyberdefense community needs to defend *existing* systems by adding safeguards in the form of patches to existing system elements, adding new security components, improving security procedures, improving configurations, and providing training.

1.3.1 Difficulties in understanding and assessing risks

Over many years the industry and the defense organizations have been developing in-house and third party approaches to evaluate and measure security posture of systems. Although significant progress has been made in understanding and documenting "what" needs to be evaluated together with expected results (e.g., Common Criteria [ISO 15408]), the lack of efficient approaches that address the "how" component made these evaluation methods underutilized. Currently, vendors who hope (or have hoped) to have their software systems certified are influenced by the slogan "Fewer is Better." The fewer the security requirements to evaluate, the better their chances for success, and the process will be faster and less costly. This is a key reason why many systems are not being evaluated for environments requiring high robustness.

Understanding and assessing risks of the systems in cyberspace is a very challenging task. There is a whole industry that has been trying to crack this challenge for some time, and for that reason, it is important that we understand what the influencers of the challenge are by examining how systems are being developed and managed throughout their life cycles, and by examining the systems' complexities. Examining the key development trends and their management will give us a better understanding of areas that are necessary to cover in security evaluation approaches.

The system complexity trends have been impacted by a rapid pace of software evolution as new technologies and supported feature sets continue to introduce ever greater levels of complexity to an already complex system of networked and autonomous software components.

1.3.2 Complex supply chains

A majority of development trends make it very difficult to assess security posture of systems, making the software and the processes for developing and acquiring software a material weakness. Some of the key trends include:

1. Heavy reliance on COTS/Open Source products further impacted by globalization trends where modern software development and supply chain support are becoming increasingly distributed worldwide. What at first might seem a great trend for producing low-cost systems quickly can turn into a nightmare for businesses where these systems are deployed. By outsourcing, using developers from foreign and unevaluated domestic suppliers, or using supply chain

components often developed with a focus only on functionality for the lowest possible price without regard to its resistance to attack makes our businesses exposed and vulnerable to attacks. For these reasons, assessing the security posture of systems needs to go beyond evaluating the software application; it needs to include evaluation of the software supply chain, the development process, and pedigree of the development team to address growing concerns regarding the ability of an adversary to subvert the software supply chain and insiders' attacks.

2. Enhancements of legacy systems, since there was a vast amount of useful, deployed, operational legacy software developed at the time when security requirements were more relaxed. These legacy software systems still represent an enormous commercial value, and therefore, there is a growing need to prolong their lifespan through maintenance efforts, and to enhance them to accommodate new market requirements and governmental regulations. However, as an existing system gets larger and more complex, its design *erodes*, which hinders system comprehension, compromises architectural integrity, and decreases maintenance productivity. This creates severe problems moving forward. The system becomes more defect-prone and at the same time, it becomes resistant to enhancement. In this situation, any attempt to retrofit secure coding practices in order to stop security erosion of the system would just aggravate the issue— it would produce a large number of changes and the associated risk from the unforeseen impact these changes introduce into the software could be so overwhelming that it would impact the business of the organization. These costly and risky methods are never implemented. As a consequence, very often quick fixes are introduced with many shortcuts and only a partial investigation for possible "weak links." New functionality is usually "shoehorned" into the preexisting architecture in a response to yet another security panic, which further compromises the security of the system. So the big question is: "How can we assess the security posture of such a system?"

3. Another key trend is increasing migration to net-centric environments and service-oriented architectures. The assessment must provide assurance that software components can be trusted to interact securely without supervision considering the following:

    * Noncompliance with open standards and protocols. Complex protocols could be considered overkill or redundant, so altering some of the steps might seem a good idea at the time. Although normal operations might not be impacted, it could certainly jeopardize the security guarantees the protocol offers.
    * Vulnerabilities associated with Web service configuration files. Web services are designed to provide greater flexibility to application platforms; however, this comes with security challenges since complexity in service configuration files might lead to mistakes that become vulnerabilities in the service.
    * Software vulnerabilities. Very often the legacy software that originally was not designed to operate on a network is integrated into a network-centric system. Suddenly, a flood of code vulnerabilities are exposed, making the entire system more vulnerable.

1.3.3 **Complex system integrations**

"As the complexity of a particular system can be viewed as the degree of difficulty in predicting the properties of the system if the properties of the system's parts are given" [Weaver 1948] it will greatly influence evaluation methodology and should play a key component in risk assessment and management.

We all agree that the current software systems are larger and continue to grow in sheer size and complexity. Very rarely does a software development project start from a clean sheet of paper. More than half of all code written today is based on enhancements and maintenance of existing functions. More often than not, new features or functionality on top of an existing code base is a large, complex piece of software that has evolved into conflicting or challenging designs that often resists evolution and/or bug fixes. Furthermore, market consolidation brings the challenge of integrating these components into net-centric systems from mergers and acquisition activities, making an existing system even larger, more complex, and harder to comprehend. The system's structure includes interconnected software components that were developed using differing methodologies, a variety of technologies, and under varying constraints and assumptions. At the same time, the documentation of such systems is never up-to-date and the information available is largely folk- or judgment-driven in nature and difficult to access. The only thing trusted to be an up-to-date source is the code itself; however, comprehension of such a code is further obscured by uncontrolled use of multiple programming languages, allowing developers to freely express themselves in more artistic ways. This causes the lack of control over software architecture, leading to erosion of the initial structural concepts of the system, increasing a system's complexity even more. This is a major source of latent security defects that assessment should uncover.

1.3.4 **Limitations of system assessment practices**

The majority of system assessments primarily focus on assessing and evaluating the development process and a product's documentation, rather than the formal artifacts. Formal security analysis is rarely performed and can be characterized at the most as opportunistic. Although the development process provides a structured way of developing the system, and as such, greatly influences security posture of the system, it still only provides a single data point to corroborate the system security, leaving some major assessment methodology gaps such as:

- **Assessment information obtained informally** – Assessment information is usually collected through interviews and documentation sampling, providing results that can be subjective, and therefore not likely repeatable.
- **Reliance on documents that might not be up-to-date** – The product's documentation, even if kept up-to-date, is typically manually generated and intended for manual review, leading to a very subjective interpretation not necessarily reflecting properties of an implemented system's artifact.
- **Lack of formal traceability between obtained information and system artifacts** – Obtained information is usually not well "connected" to the system

artifacts and as the result fails to detect the real vulnerabilities and does not offer ways to improve security posture and our confidence in it.

System development usually follows one of several development processes: waterfall, iterative (e.g., agile, Rapid Application Development (RAD), Capability Maturity Model (CMM), Model Driven Architecture (MDA)), or some custom process. Besides providing a structured way to develop the product, it also provides a framework for establishing multi-segmented *traceability* by connecting high level policy to objectives, requirements, design specification (captured as document or prototype), and implementation of system artifacts. However, once a product is fully developed, that structure is often dissolved, creating a traceability gap between requirements and the corresponding system artifacts. Because of this traceability gap the current assessment approaches resist automation, and as the result the formal analysis of the artifacts is either skipped entirely, or at some rare occasions substituted by a very laborious and costly application of formal methods applied to manually developed models. Neither approach addresses software supply chain and pedigree of the development team.

Recently, with development of new technologies in the area of white-box and black-box vulnerability detection it became possible to automate some of the security testing for software and networked systems. Although a very powerful, cost-effective way of examining formal artifacts, the results are not conclusive when determining trustworthiness of the system. This is due to issues associated with the way these technologies are implemented in commercial tools and how these tools are applied on the given system. Let's examine these technologies and tools in more detail.

1.3.5 Limitations of white-box vulnerability detection

There are two types of security testing methods: white-box testing and black-box testing.

White-box testing is based on knowledge of the system internals derived directly from the code (source or binary). The white-box testing is associated with testing of the software and has inside-out focus, targeting particular constructs, statements, code paths, or code sections. A technology used in security white-box vulnerability testing is known as *static analysis* and is commercialized in source and binary code analyzer tools. The promise of this technology is the 100% coverage of all code paths in the system. However, tools implementing this technology have several weaknesses producing inconclusive evidence of a system's trustworthiness.

1. **Lack of complete system coverage** – The tools provide some capabilities with proprietary and limited functionality, with each tool providing value only in subsets of the enterprise application space causing the need to use more than one static analysis tool to combine their strengths and avoid their weaknesses. As mentioned in the recent comparison of static analysis tools performed at NSA [Buxbaum 2007] *"Organizations trying to automate the process of testing software for vulnerabilities have no choice but to deploy a multitude of tools."* Since current source/binary code analysis tools offer little interoperability, it is

costly to evaluate, select and integrate the set of tools that provide an adequate coverage for the breadth of languages, platforms, and technologies that typical systems contain. Findings in one vulnerability report are not necessarily aligned with the pattern and condition of the vulnerability and therefore, reports from two tools for the same vulnerability many not be the same. For example, the evidence for buffer overflow vulnerability is scattered throughout the code: it involves a buffer write operation, a data item being written, another place where the buffer is allocated, and yet another place where the length of the buffer is calculated. There is a code path that allows an attacker to exploit the buffer overflow by providing some input into the application. In addition, a buffer overflow may be caused by another problem, such as an integer overflow. All this evidence has to be considered and reported in a single buffer overflow report using a common vocabulary and structure. Failure to use a common reporting standard leads to a situation where it is hard to merge reports from multiple vulnerability detection tools and achieve a significant improvement in the overall report quality, because the lack of interoperability and the common vocabulary makes it hard to 1) select the vulnerability that is reported by multiple tools; 2) for a given vulnerability, estimate the coverage of the same vulnerability pattern throughout the entire system; and 3) get coverage of the system by the multitude of tools.

2. **Lack of aid in understanding the system** – Vulnerability detections tools do not aid the team in understanding the system under assessment, an activity that is required for the evaluation team to make a conclusion about a system's trustworthiness, as well as to detect vulnerabilities that are specific to the system under evaluation—the knowledge that cannot be brought by the off-the-shelf vulnerability detection tools.

An automatic static analysis tool goes through the code, parses it, analyzes it, and searches for patterns of vulnerabilities. As a result, the tool produces a report describing the findings. As part of this process, a great deal of detailed knowledge of the system is generated because finding vulnerabilities requires a fine-grained understanding of the structure, control, and data flow of each application. However, as soon as the report is produced, this detailed knowledge *disappears*. It can no longer be used to systematically reproduce the analysis or to aid the assessment team to understand the system. It is only the list of vulnerabilities that they are provided with. A similar situation occurs during compilation. A compiler generates large amounts of fine-grained knowledge about the system, only to be discarded as soon as the object file is generated.

However, a consistent approach to representing and accumulating this knowledge is critical for a systematic and cost-efficient security evaluation, because not only do all code analysis capabilities need to share this knowledge, but also any inconsistencies in addressing the basic knowledge of the system will lead to bigger inconsistencies in derived reports.

An exploitable vulnerability is a complex phenomenon, so there are multiple possibilities to report it in a multitude of ways. The industry of vulnerability detection tools is still immature. There is no standardization on the nomenclature of vulnerabilities or on the common reporting practices, although several community efforts are emerging.

It is easy to make a case for the multi-stage analysis where a particular vulnerability detection capability is just one of the "data feeds" into the integrated system assessment model.

- **First**, the original vulnerability analysis has to be augmented with additional assessment evidence, which is usually not provided by an off-the-shelf tool. For example, such evidence can be collected from people, processes, technology, and the environment of the system under evaluation. In addition, in a large number of situations, the findings from the automatic vulnerability detection capabilities need to be augmented by the results of the manual code reviews or evaluations of formal models.
- **Second**, there is a gap between the off-the-shelf vulnerabilities that an automatic tool is looking for and the needs of a given system with its unique security functional requirements and threat model. Usually there are not enough inputs for an automatic tool to detect these vulnerabilities, so these analyses need to be performed. The inputs that are required for the additional vulnerability analysis are similar to the original analysis. This knowledge may include the specific system context, including the software and hardware environment in which the application operates, the threat model, specific architecture of the system, and other factors.
- **Third**, other kinds of analysis in the broader context of systems assurance needs to be performed, in particular, architectural analysis, software complexity metrics, or penetration (black-box) testing.

In order to obtain a cohesive view of the security application, software evaluation teams often need to do painful point-to-point integrations between existing vulnerability detection capabilities and tools. Rarely do organizations choose this path.

3. **Massive production of false positives and false negatives** – There are some fundamental barriers to comprehensive code analysis, which leads to limitations of the vulnerability detection tools, and subsequently, to false negative and false positive report findings. In order to analyze a computation, all system components have to be considered, including the so-called application code, as well as the runtime platform and all runtime services, as some of the key control and data flow relationships are provided by the runtime framework, as the computation flows through the application code into the runtime platform and services and back to the application code. Application code alone, often written in more than one programming language, in most cases does not provide an adequate picture of the computation, as some segments of the flow are determined by the runtime platform and are not visible in the application code. For example, while a large number of control flow relationships between different activities in the application code are explicit (such as statements in a sequence, or calls from a statement to another procedure), some control flow

relations are not visible in the code, including the so-called callbacks, where the application code registers a certain activity with the runtime framework (for example, an event handler or an interrupt handler) and it is the runtime framework that initiates the activity. Without the knowledge of such implicit relationships, the system knowledge is incomplete, leading to massive false positive and false negative entries in the report. While numbers of generated false negatives are unknown, the numbers of generated false positives are staggeringly high and "weeding" through a report to identify true positives is a costly process, causing limited use of such tools. To reduce the number of false reports some tools simply skip situations where they can not fully analyze a potential vulnerability within a short timeframe.

1.3.6 Limitations of black-box vulnerability detection

Black-box testing, otherwise known as dynamic testing, is designed for behavioral observation of the system in operation. It has outside-in focus, targeting functional requirements. The activity includes an expert simulating a malicious attack. Testers almost always make use of tools to simplify dynamic testing of the system for any weaknesses, technical flaws, or vulnerabilities. Currently tools in this area are categorized based on their focus of specific areas they are targeting. These areas include *network security* and *software security*, where software security is comprised of database security, security subsystems, and Web application security.

- *Network security* testing tools are focused on identifying vulnerabilities in externally accessible network-connected devices. This activity is performed by either placing packets on the wire to interrogate a host for unknown services or vulnerabilities, or by "sniffing" network traffic to identify a list of active systems, active services, active applications, and even active vulnerabilities. In this case, "sniffing" is considered less intrusive and performs a continuous analysis effort while packet injection techniques produce a picture of the network at a given point in time. The strengths and weaknesses related to network security tools could be characterized as follows:
  - Packet injection techniques
    - Strengths: can be used independent of any network management or system administration information making a much more objective security audit of any system or network and providing accurate information about which services are running, which hosts are active, and if there are any vulnerabilities present.
    - Weaknesses: since scanning takes a long time and is intrusive, this type of scanning is performed less often where most solutions opt to reduce the number of ports scanned or the vulnerabilities checked, leading to undiscovered new hosts and a variety of vulnerabilities. In addition, due to restrictive security polices, it is very common for network security groups in large enterprises to be restricted from scanning specific hosts or networks, causing many vulnerabilities to be missed.

- Sniffing techniques
  - Strengths: minimal network impact and time needed for scan (scan can be running 24/7).
  - Weaknesses: for host or server to be scanned, it needs to communicate on the network, which might lead to discovery of the presence of a server at the same time a probing hacker does.

Both techniques deal with very complex log files and they need expertise to interpret them; however, most network administrators do not have sufficient experience and expertise to either properly discern false positives or set priorities for what security holes should be fixed first, which might lead to some critical vulnerabilities not being addressed in time.

In summary, weaknesses of each technique leads to a number of false positives and false negatives, making assessments costly ("weeding" through false positives) and not so assuring (not knowing what has been missed).

Techniques used in black-box *software security* testing are known as penetration testing. A penetration test uses a malicious attacker behavior to determine which vulnerabilities can be exploited and what level of access can be gained. Unlike network security tools, penetration tools generally focus on penetrating ports 80 (HTTP) and 443 (HTTPS). These ports are traditionally allowed through a firewall to support Web servers. This way they can identify Web applications' and Web services-based applications' vulnerabilities and misbehaviors.

Here are some characteristics of a typical penetration test:

- Strength: A relatively small toolset is needed and serves as a good starting point for more in-depth vulnerability testing. High degree of information accuracy when vulnerability is reported.
- Weaknesses: High number of false negatives and some false positives. Penetration testing works only on a tightly defined scope, such as Web applications and database servers as a less structured process (at least during the system exploration and enumeration phases), which leads to the conclusion that this technique is as good as the tests they run. Penetration technique does not provide the whole security picture, especially for systems that are only accessible via the internal network, and it can be time sensitive. These weaknesses can cause many vulnerabilities to be missed (high number of false negatives) and some server responses could be misinterpreted, causing false positives to be reported.

However, recent developments in the technology areas of System Assurance offer the most promising and practical way to enhance a vendor's ability to develop and deliver software systems that can be evaluated and certified at high assurance levels while breaking the current bottleneck, which involves a laborious, unpredictable, lengthy, and costly evaluation process. These breakthrough technologies bring automation to the system assurance process.

This book provides technology guidance to achieve automation in system assurance.

1.4 WHERE DO WE GO FROM HERE?

A system assessment must discover security vulnerabilities in the system of interest. Majority of current assessment practices are relatively informal and very subjective. Due to difficulties caused by development trends and systems' complexities, they focus primarily on evaluating the development process and a product's documentation rather than formal artifacts. Security testing is rarely performed and can be characterized at the most as opportunistic. The only exception is evaluation methodology for high robustness, at which point formal methods are applied to assess a system's formal artifacts. However, this process is laborious and costly, the key reasons why most systems are not being evaluated in this way. For all these reasons, it is becoming increasingly difficult to establish or verify whether or not software is sufficiently trustworthy, and as complications will likely continue to evolve, a new approach needs to be developed to provide credible, repeatable, and cost-efficient ways for assessing a system's trustworthiness and for managing assurance risks; an approach that will still give us systematic and methodical system coverage in identifying and mitigating vulnerabilities.

Having in mind the internal complexity of the system and complexity of development trends and development environment, the only way to achieve this new approach is by implementing *automated model-driven assessment.*

Over the years, we have followed uptake of model-driven development where more and more new features, applications, and even systems are modeled in an implementation-independent way to express technical, operational, and business requirements and designs. These models are prototyped, inspected, verified, and validated before design is implemented. In a majority of the cases, once design is implemented, models and their prototypes are discarded. The reason is that throughout the implementation process, some of the designs are changed due to various reasons (e.g., impact of chosen implementation technologies) and going back to update models and prototypes to keep them current is expensive. In other words, trusted traceability is broken.

If we are able to regenerate trusted models directly from the only up-to-date system artifact, which is code itself, we would be able to recreate a process where models could be assessed and evaluated in a very practical, systematic, and cost-effective way. To achieve this goal of reestablishing trustworthy models, the following needs to be addressed:

1. Knowledge about a system's artifacts belonging to system of interest is captured and represented in a unified way, ensuring discovery and unified representation of system artifacts at the higher level of abstractions (e.g., design, architecture, and processes) without losing traceability down to the code.
2. Knowledge connecting high level requirements, goals, or policies with system's artifacts that implemented them is rediscovered and captured, providing end-to-end traceability.

3. Threat knowledge is collected, captured, and managed in relation to system's artifacts identified as system inputs.
4. Vulnerability knowledge is understood, captured, and managed in the form of standardized machine-readable content. To be successful in communicating with an IT or network systems and engineering groups, knowledge of vulnerabilities is crucial.
5. Standard-based tool infrastructure is set up that would collect, manage, analyze. and report on required knowledge and provide higher automation in achieving the ultimate goal by integrating a large set of individual tools to offset their limitations and weaknesses and integrate their strengths.

1.4.1 Systematic and repeatable defense at affordable cost

Consequently, this approach would create *confidence* in the security posture of systems. By regaining knowledge of our systems, and accumulating the knowledge of the attackers and their methods, we would be able to reason about the security mechanisms of our systems and clearly and articulately communicate and justify our solutions. This involves a clear and comprehensive game plan, which anticipates the possible moves of the opponent and uses the home advantage and the initiative to build a reasonably strong defense.

It is the nature of cybersecurity to provide a reasonable, justifiable answer to the question of whether the *countermeasures* implemented in the target system adequately *mitigate all threats* to that system. This answer is what is sometimes called the *security posture* of the system. Evaluating security posture requires detailed *knowledge,* in particular, the knowledge of the factors *internal* to the system, such as the system boundaries, components, access points, countermeasures, assets, impact, policy, design, etc., as well as the factors that are *external*, such as threats, hazards, capability and motivations of the threat agents, etc. As *vulnerability* can be described as a situation where a particular threat is not mitigated, this would mean that there exists a possibility of an *attack*, waiting for a motivated attacker to discover this situation, and execute the attack steps.

Answering the cybersecurity question is not easy due to the *uncertainty factor.* There is a great deal of uncertainty associated with any external factors, but there is uncertainty associated with the internal factors too, because our knowledge of the complex target system is not perfect. There may be some uncertainty about the impacts of the incidents to the business and even about the validity of the security policy. In a slightly different sense, there is uncertainty about the behavior of the system, but this uncertainty is only related to the current state of our knowledge, and can be removed (at a certain cost) by analyzing the system deeper.

Two disciplines, security engineering and risk assessment, address the cybersecurity question from different perspectives. **Security engineering** addresses this question in a practical way by selecting the countermeasures and building the target system. It emphasizes building the system rather than communicating the knowledge about the system, although some design documentation may be one of the outputs of a solid engineering process. Security engineering often uses "tried and tested" solutions based on "best practices," and selects countermeasures from catalogs. This pragmatic approach avoids analysis of threats and their mitigation by the security architecture, so justification is often done by reference to the recommended catalog of countermeasures. A clear, comprehensive, and defensible justification of the system's security architecture ought to be one of the mainstream activities of security engineering; however, there is little evidence that this is being done, in part because of the mismatch in the qualifications required for systems engineering, system validation, and verification on one hand, and the security validation, verification, and assurance on the other hand. It is not uncommon to push some uncertainty to the market as the system is released and patched later as the vulnerability is found by someone else and reported back to the engineering team.

Risk assessment is usually considered to be part of management and governance of the system. Risk assessment answers the cybersecurity question by evaluating the system. Usually there are two points in the system life cycle when such evaluation takes place: one as early as possible, right after the countermeasures have been selected, and the other one as late as possible, when the entire system has been implemented, and it is ready to be put into operation. The decision-making process of risk assessment involves analyzing the threats to the system, the countermeasures, and vulnerabilities. The emphasis of risk assessment is to identify the risks that need to be managed, and not to communicate the knowledge about the system. Neither is a clear, comprehensible, and defensible justification of the system's security architecture a mainstream activity of risk assessment. The nature of the risk assessment is that it identifies problems—not justifies that the available solution is adequate.

Risk assessment provides a probabilistic approach to dealing with uncertainty in our knowledge about the system. Lower end varieties of risk assessment teams offer a "best practice" approach, often based on the 'best guess." This works, because risk assessment is a pragmatic discipline, which generates the list of risks to manage and the list of recommendations of new countermeasures that would lower the risk. Since risk assessment is part of the ongoing risk management, any miscalculations can be addressed as more operational data becomes available. Risk assessment provides input to engineering, which evaluates the recommendations and implements them.

As you can see, justifying system's security posture, and communicating this knowledge in a clear, comprehensive, and defensible way, is not addressed by either security engineering or risk assessment. Engineering builds solutions. Validation and verification justify that the solution corresponds to the requirements, objectives, and policy. Risk assessment looks for problems, identifies them, and justifies significance of their existence. Risk assessment also recommends mitigating solutions. On the other hand, assurance is considered by many as an optional activity that is applicable only for a limited number of high-profile systems where high security and safety is a "must have," such as in nuclear reactors. The reason is the perceived high cost of assurance activities. However, it is important to note that assurance closes some gaps in both security engineering and risk analysis.

The Information and Communication Technology (ICT) security community refers to "Assurance" as confidence and trust that a product or service will function as advertised and provide the intended results or the product or service will be replaced or reconditioned. It refers to the security of the product or service and that the product or service fulfills the requirements of the situation, satisfying the Security Requirements.

The Cybersecurity Assurance community expands this Assurance description to explicitly talk about vulnerabilities. The National Defense Industrial Association (NDIA) Engineering for System Assurance Guidebook [NDIA 2008] defines "Assurance" as "justified measures of confidence that the system functions as intended and is free of exploitable vulnerabilities, either intentionally or unintentionally designed or inserted as part of the system at any time during the life cycle." This new definition, besides arguing positive properties, "does functions as intended," adds a need for arguing negative properties, and "does not contain exploitable vulnerabilities," which requires more comprehensive assurance methods. This book describes a framework for implementing comprehensive assurance for cybersecurity with emphasis on automation.

The Cybersecurity community more often refers to "Assurance" as "System Assurance" or "Software Assurance" (emphasizing importance of vulnerabilities in software itself). According to the Cybersecurity community, the system assurance as a discipline studies the methods of justifying cybersecurity. It is a systematic discipline that focuses on how to provide justification that the security posture is adequate. System assurance develops a clear, comprehensive, and defensible argument for security of the system. In order to support the argument, concrete and compelling *evidence* must be collected. One of the sources of evidence is system analysis. System assurance deals with uncertainty through a special kind of *reasoning* that involves the architecture of the target system. Instead of a never-ending process of seeking more and more data to eliminate the fundamental uncertainty, system assurance uses the *layered defense* considerations to address the unknowns. Needless to say, the assurance argument benefits from the available knowledge related to both the external and the internal factors of cybersecurity.

The reasoning provided by the system assurance discipline is used both in the context of engineering as well as risk assessment. System assurance is a form of systematic, repeatable, and defensible *system evaluation* that provides more detailed results than a traditional "best-practice" approach. The key difference of the system assurance approach and traditional risk assessment is that assurance justifies the claims about the security posture of the system. Assurance is a direct way to build confidence in the system. Deficit of assurance can be directly transformed into the requirements for additional countermeasures. On the other hand, while evidence of risks, produced by detecting vulnerabilities, can also be transformed into countermeasures, it does not build confidence in the system, because the absence of vulnerabilities makes only a weak indirect case about the security posture of the system. This is why we need system assurance. This is why we need to move beyond detecting vulnerabilities.

The answer to weaponized exploits and malware is to automate security analysis, automate checklists involved in threat and risk analysis and use the assurance case as a planning tool for establishing defense in depth.

From the system assurance perspective, deficiencies in the argument indicate defects in the defense. Particular points in the architecture of the system that prevent us from building a defensible assurance argument are the candidates for the engineering to fix. The new, improved mechanisms will directly support the assurance argument and, at the same time, improve the security posture of the system.

Collecting evidence for assurance, in particular within the layered defense argument, is more demanding on the depth and accuracy of the system analysis and the accuracy of the corresponding data.

1.4.2 **The OMG software assurance ecosystem**

An **ecosystem** refers to a community of participants in knowledge-intensive exchanges involving an explicit and growing shared body of *knowledge* and corresponding automated *tools* for collecting, analyzing, and reporting on the various facets of knowledge, as well as a *market* where participants exchange tools, services, and content in order to solve significant problems. The essential characteristic of an ecosystem is establishment of knowledge *content* as a product. An ecosystem involves a certain communication infrastructure, sometimes referred to as "plumbing," based on the number of knowledge-sharing protocols provided by a number of knowledge-management tools.

The purpose of the ecosystem within a cybersecurity community is to facilitate collection and accumulation of cybersecurity knowledge needed for assurance, and to ensure its efficient and affordable delivery to the defenders of cybersystems, as well as to other stakeholders. An important feature of the cybersecurity knowledge is separation between the *general* knowledge (applicable to large families of systems) and *concrete* knowledge (accurate facts related to the system of interest). To illustrate this separation, a certain area at the bottom of the ecosystem "marketplace" in the middle of Figure 1 represents concrete knowledge, while the rest represents general knowledge. Keep in mind that "concrete" facts are specific to the system of interest, so, the "concrete knowledge" area represents multiple local cyberdefense environments, while the "general knowledge" area is the knowledge owned by the entire cyberdefense community. The icons titled "defender," "inspector," and "stakeholder" in Figure 1 represent people interested in providing assurance of one individual system. Basically, this is your team.

The OMG Software Assurance Ecosystem defines a stack of standard protocols for the knowledge-based tools, including knowledge discovery tools, knowledge integration tools, knowledge transformation tools, knowledge provisioning and management tools, and knowledge delivery tools.

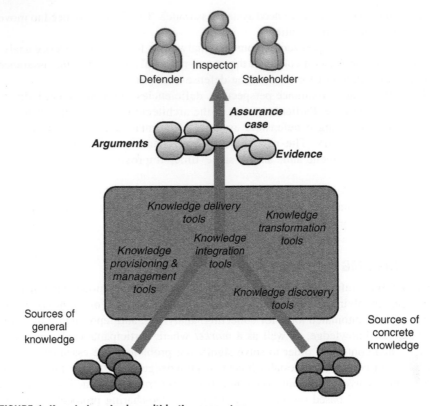

FIGURE 1 Knowledge sharing within the ecosystem

1.4.3 Linguistic modeling to manage the common vocabulary

The key requirement for knowledge exchange between tools in the ecosystem is a common, agreed upon vocabulary that represents the *conceptual commitment* of the participants. However, much of the computer security information gathered and disseminated by individuals and organizations cannot currently be combined or compared because a common vocabulary has yet to emerge in the field of computer security. Numerous individuals and organizations regularly gather and disseminate information related to computer security. This information describes security events, as well as the characteristics of computer and network systems. Unfortunately, much of this computer security information cannot be combined without significant manual effort because the terms currently used in the field of computer security tend to be unique to different individuals and organizations.

Devising a common vocabulary for cybersecurity is the first logical step in the industry evolution from proprietary, in-house, stovepipe solutions to efficient and collaborative cybersecurity ecosystem that can take advantage of the economies of scale. Established standard vocabulary brings several tangible benefits and justifies the efforts required. Indeed, at the heart of any security assessment project there is a need to manage and integrate multiple pieces of information from different sources. Standard vocabulary decouples producers of cybersecurity knowledge from the consumers of knowledge and the distribution channels, and consequently opens up the market of efficient tools that can take advantage of the economies of scale. A single coherent picture that is both accurate and comprehensive enough is necessary to reason about the security of the system and to build a defendable assurance case. Knowledge-based systems and services are expensive to build, test, and maintain. Several technical problems stand in the way of shared, reusable, knowledge-based systems. Like conventional applications, knowledge-based systems are based on heterogeneous hardware platforms, programming languages, and network protocols. However, knowledge-based systems pose special requirements for interoperability. Such systems operate on and communicate using machine-readable knowledge content. They ask queries and give answers. They take "background knowledge" as an input and exchange derived knowledge. For such knowledge-level communication, we need conventions at three levels: knowledge representation format, communication protocol, and specification of the content of shared knowledge. Standard knowledge representation formats and communication protocols are independent of the content of knowledge being exchanged or communicated. A common language is used for standardization of the knowledge content. In general, agreeing upon a vocabulary for a phenomenon makes systematic studies possible. In particular, standardization of the cybersecurity vocabulary brings the following benefits:

- A common language for intrusions and vulnerabilities enables us to compile statistics, observe patterns, and draw other conclusions from collected intrusion and vulnerability data. This process will extend our knowledge of the phenomenon, provide an efficient way to close the knowledge gap with attackers, and will make it possible to strengthen systems against intrusions using this knowledge.
- An established taxonomy would be useful when reporting incidents to incident response teams, such as the CERT Coordination Center. It could also be used in the bulletins issued by incident response teams in order to warn system owners and administrators of new security flaws that can be exploited in intrusions.
- If the common language included a grading of the severity or impact of the intrusion or the vulnerability, system owners and administrators would be helped in prioritizing their efforts.

A common language is a *linguistic model* of a domain that is used to compose complex statements about the domain. The foundation of a linguistic model is a vocabulary. From a finite, well-defined vocabulary one can compose a large number of coherent sentences. A body of formally represented knowledge is based on a *conceptualization*: the objects, concepts, and other entities that are presumed to exist in some area of interest and the relationships between them. A conceptualization is an abstract, simplified view of the world that we wish to represent for some purpose. Every knowledge base, knowledge-based system, or knowledge-level agent is *committed* to some conceptualization, explicitly or implicitly. That is one reason why vocabulary, rather than format is the focus of linguistic models. The set of objects that can be represented by the statements of a linguistic model is called the universe of discourse. This set of objects, and the discernable relationships among them, are reflected in the vocabulary as a set of *terms*. In such a vocabulary, definitions associate the names of objects and concepts in the universe of discourse with human-readable text describing what the names are meant to denote, and formal rules that constrain the interpretation and well-formed use of these terms.

Pragmatically, a common language defines the vocabulary with which queries and assertions are exchanged among participants of the ecosystem. Conceptual commitments are agreements to use the shared vocabulary in a coherent and consistent manner. The agents sharing a vocabulary need not share a knowledge base; each knows things the other does not, and an agent that commits to a conceptualization is not required to answer all queries that can be formulated in the shared vocabulary. In short, a commitment to a common vocabulary is a guarantee of consistency, and supports multiple implementation choices with respect to queries and assertions using the vocabulary. A vocabulary serves a different purpose than a knowledge base: a shared language need only describe a vocabulary for talking about a domain, whereas a knowledge base may include the knowledge needed to solve a problem or answer arbitrary queries about a domain. Knowledge base includes concrete and specific operational facts.

Linguistic models include the following three important parts:

- Representation of the things in the domain, also known as taxonomy. Taxonomy focuses on the noun concepts. Landwehr et al. made the following observation in his work on a cybersecurity taxonomy: "A taxonomy is not simply a neutral structure for categorizing specimens. It implicitly embodies a theory of the universe from which those specimens are drawn. It defines what data are to be recorded and how like and unlike specimens are to be distinguished" [Landwehr 1994]. Taxonomy does not resist automation if it supports definitions that can be interpreted as queries into an appropriate knowledge base. Unfortunately, several taxonomies already proposed in the field of cybersecurity resist automation. The art of making discernable definition involves careful selection of the characteristics that are aligned with the conceptual commitment.
- Representation of the relationships in the domain. Nouns alone are insufficient for constructing rich statements about a domain. Connections between nouns are generally expressed using verbs and verb phrases that relate appropriate terms. These noun and verb combinations are called sentential forms and are the basic blocks that permit complex sentences to be made about the domain.
- Mechanism for constructing statements in the vocabulary of noun and verb concepts. In addition to the vocabulary of terms and sentential forms, a linguistic model must include the mechanism for combining them into meaningful statements.

1.5 WHO SHOULD READ THIS BOOK?

This book is designed and intended for anyone who wants a detailed understanding of how to perform system security assurance in a more objective, systematic, repeatable, and automated way. The audience for this book includes:

- Security and security assessment professionals who want to achieve efficient, comprehensive, and repeatable assessment process, and
- Security consumers interested in a cost-effective assessment process with objective results. Security consumers include the personnel in the following roles within the organization: technical, program/project, and security management.

Bibliography

The Parliament of the Commonwealth of Australia, House of Representatives, Standing Committee on Communications (2010) *Hackers, Fraudsters and Botnets: Tackling the Problem of Cyber Crime*. The Report of the Inquiry into Cyber Crime. Canberra, Australia. ISBN 978-0-642-79313-3.

Buxbaum, P. (2007). All for one, but not one for all. *Government Computer News,* March 19, 2007. http://gcn.com/Issues/2007/03/March-19-2007.aspx.

Carr, J. (2010). *Inside Cyber Warfare,* O'Reilly & Associates, Inc. Sebastopol, CA.

Icove, D., Seger, K., & VonStorch, W. (1995). *Computer Crime: A Crime Fighter's Handbook*. O'Reilly & Associates, Inc. Sebastopol, CA.

ISO/IEC 15443-1:2005 *Information Technology – Security Techniques – A Framework for IT Security Assurance. Part 1: Overview and Framework*. (2005).

ISO/IEC 15408-1:2005 *Information Technology – Security Techniques – Evaluation Criteria for IT Security Part 1: Introduction and General Model*. (2005).

Landwehr, C., Bull, A. R., McDermott, J., & Choi, W. (1994). A taxonomy of computer program security flaws. *ACM Computing Surveys, 26*(3), 211–254.

NDIA, *Engineering for System Assurance Guidebook*. (2008).

OECD. (2008). *Malicious Software (Malware). A security threat to the Internet economy, Ministerial Background Report*. DSTI/ICCP/REG(2007)/5/FINAL.

Weaver, W. (1948). Science and complexity. *American Scientist, 36*(4), 536.

Confidence as a product

2

The words of some men are trusted simply on account of their reputation for caution, judgment, and veracity. But this does not mean that the question of their right to our confidence cannot arise in the case of all their assertions: only that we are confident that any claim they make weightily and seriously will in fact prove to be well-founded, to have a sound case behind it, to deserve—have a right to—our attention on its merits.
—Stephen Toulmin, The Uses Of Argument

2.1 ARE YOU CONFIDENT THAT THERE IS NO BLACK CAT IN THE DARK ROOM?

When assessing security posture of the system, concept of location is very important in achieving confidence that the system is secure to operate. In other words, it is confidence that every system location is visited and evaluated, all locations in the system are found to be protected from identified threats, and no location is found to be vulnerable.

Importance of location for achieving confidence is best illustrated through the following example, "How to find a black cat in a dark room?"

As we all know, it is hard to find a black cat in a dark room, especially if we are not sure that the cat is there. Searching through a large space, for example, the size of a skyscraper, can take a long time and may be quite costly. For that reason, many skyscraper managers would decide to wait for the cat to become hungry, at which point it will show up by itself. Security risk assessment is often a lot like that, too.

But what is the process of finding the cat? First, we have to make some assumptions: We are going to look for a live cat, not a stuffed animal cat nor a photo of a cat nor any other form or shape like a cat. Second, we need to clarify the scope: What are the confines of the room in which we are going to look for the cat. The outcome of the exercise of finding something (for example, finding a cat) within the given confines involves determining the location of the object. There are two possible situations that we need to be aware of: 1) there is at least one cat in the room; and 2) there are no cats in the room. So, how do we find a cat? We perform some search activity; For example, we take a net and try to catch the cat. When we have caught something (and identified the location

System Assurance: Beyond Detecting Vulnerabilities. DOI: 10.1016/B978-0-12-381414-2.00002-6

of this object), we need to know that this object is indeed a cat (and not a chair, or a hat, or a rat). The object must feel like a cat, look like a cat, and behave like a cat.

So, it is the *essential characteristics* of the object that we need to focus on in order to conduct the search. In our example, we will focus on the following four groups of characteristics:

- Characteristics of being a cat: cat has a tail, cat has pointy ears, cat meows, cat runs after mice, cat likes milk, cat has very large eye sockets, cat has a specialized jaw, cat has seven lumbar vertebrae.
- Characteristics of being a living thing: thing breathes, thing has temperature, thing eats food, thing makes sound, thing has smell, thing moves from one location to another.
- Characteristics of being in the room: location of thing is inside room, thing enters room, thing is not at location that is outside room.
- Characteristics of being: it has color, it has weight, it has height, it has length, it can be located, it is at a single location at any given time.

From this perspective, not all *facts* about cats are equally useful for our search. It is clear that we need to focus on the *discernable* characteristics, the ones that we can incorporate into our search procedure. For example, the following facts involving cats are not relevant to search: cats are believed to have been domesticated in ancient Egypt; the word "cat" is derived from the Turkish word "qadi"; cats are valued by humans for companionship; cats are associated with humans for at least 9500 years. A discernable characteristic gives an objective and repeatable procedure to say if some location is occupied by a cat or not.

The need of finding a black cat in the dark room can be motivated by several subtly different scenarios, each of which determines a different desired outcome of the search. Here are three scenarios:

1. Justify that there are five black cats in the room
2. Justify that there is no black cat in the room
3. Justify that there will be no black cats in the room for the next 12 months

In the first scenario, we located five black cats. In presenting a set of five locations, we make an implicit *claim* that each location contains a black cat. So each location has to pass the "contains a black cat" test. We assume that cats are not removed from their locations. It could have been ten or more black cats in the room but we found five and claimed there are five black cats. How can a bystander be confident in the outcome of our search? First of all, we must convince her that there are no false reports (e.g., the dark brown cat). Validating the claim that "a given location contains a black cat" requires systematic application of the set of the essential characteristics. A critical bystander may question our way of identifying a black cat and may ask us to produce the evidence for each cat that we claim. But, how do we know that there were no more than five black cats in the room? How important is it to know if there are *only* five black cats?

In the second scenario, the experience of our search is used to justify the claim "there is no black cat in the room." This second scenario is different because, at least at the first site, no explicit location is produced, otherwise the fact of finding a location containing a black cat becomes a counter evidence to the claim. The two claims are quite different, too. In the first scenario, we made a *positive* claim that "there is a location in the room that contains the black cat." In the second scenario, we make a *negative* claim that "there is no black cat in the room." However, let's be clear; this claim is also about locations. This claim says that "No one location in the room contains a black cat."

Validating the negative claim that "there is no black cat in the room" goes beyond search, because it requires additional evidence gathering activities to justify the claim. This claim raises many critical questions: How thorough was the search? (Did you visit all corners of the room? Did you look under the couch?) What exactly did you see during the search? Did you see any cats at all? And how did you know that what you found was not the cat? Justification of this claim requires more evidence than in the first scenario involving a positive claim.

There are two ways we can build justification of our claim. The "*process-based*" assurance produces evidence of compliance to the objectives of the search. This brings confidence that the search team performed its duties according to the statement of work. For example, we agreed that the search team will put a bowl of milk at the entrance of the room and will call the cat by saying "Kitty-kitty-kitty" at least three times. The advantage of the "process-based" assurance is that it always deals with a positive claim, so the evidence is, in most cases, some sort of record of performance. For example, as evidence, the search team brings us a movie, demonstrating that they have indeed performed the required steps and no black cat showed up. The evidence directly supports the claim that the required steps have been performed. The benefit of the "process-based" assurance approach is that it is aligned with the statement of work and that it requires direct evidence of compliance. The statement of work provides the argument framework for the justification and guides the evidence collection, so when the consumer of the assurance believes in the statement of work, he is very likely to be convinced by the corresponding evidence.

On the other hand, the "*goal-based*" assurance requires an argument to justify the original negative claim, in our case the claim "there are no black cats in the room." The evidence collected by the search team must support this argument. Goal-based assurance addresses the critical questions head-on.

Design of an argument requires some *planning*. The concept of "location" introduced earlier turns out to be essential for reasoning about the search, as the evidence collecting procedure associated with the argument deals with locations. Locations with similar characteristics that suggest common search tactics are often arranged into "*zones*," or "components." Zones usually have *entry points*, where cats and other things may enter and exit. Each zone constrains the *behaviors* that can occur within that zone. The patterns of locations determine the patterns of behaviors that may take place in these locations (see Figure 1).

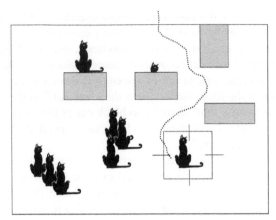

FIGURE 1 The room with black cats

In the world of systems, it is the *architecture* that provides a language for describing different locations within a system. Each component determines some pattern of behaviors (for example, the movements of cats through the room to their hiding places, or the flow of data packets through the web server). Behavior rules are based on certain *continuity of flow*: Cats do not simply appear at a given location, and the same principle applies to the flows of control and data through software in cyber systems.

Let's assume that the room has three different zones presented in Figure 2. Zone A has one entry point, and we learned that it is some sort of revolving door not friendly to cats. Also, Zone A does not have any other features; it is one open, empty space, with no hiding places. Zone B has only one entry point that is suitable for cats. Zone B has some additional features inside where cats could hide. Zone C has an entry point and we learned that this entry point is claimed to be unsuitable for cats to enter.

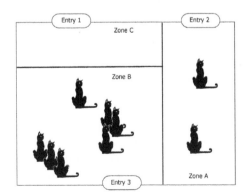

FIGURE 2 Zones within the room

Characteristics of locations determine the *structure* of the argument. For example, the knowledge of the zones from Figure 2 determines the strategy to justify that a black cat is not in the room. We justify separately that a cat is not in each zone. For Zone C, we need to check that the entry point is indeed unsuitable for cats to enter Zone C. Then we need to check that there are indeed no other entry points to Zone C. We request these two checks and use the reports as evidence to justify the claim that "there are no black cats in Zone C." To be precise, we justify the first sub-claim, "the entry point to Zone C is not suitable for any cat to enter the zone," using the first report as evidence. We may further support the claim by indirect evidence to the credibility of the person performing the report. The evidence in support to the second sub-claim, "Zone C has only one entry point," is provided by the second report. Again, we may want to supplement this evidence by the side argument, justifying the credibility and thoroughness of the analysis method. The top claim is justified by the argument that if a zone has a single entry point that is not suitable for any cat, then it is not possible that a cat enters the zone, and therefore, the zone does not contain a cat, and therefore, does not contain any black cat. This claim is justified by the two sub-claims rather than directly by evidence (see Figure 3).

The same argument is not defendable when applied to Zone A, because the entry points to Zone A may be suitable for a cat. The definition "is not friendly to cats" does not imply "not suitable for cats to enter the zone beyond the

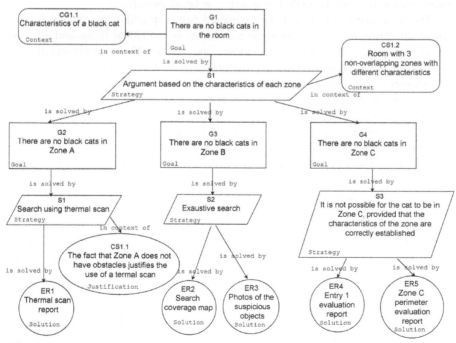

FIGURE 3 Assurance case for Scenario 2—there is no black cat in the room

reasonable doubt," so we need a different strategy. We can still check that there are no other entry points to Zone A; we can check that the gates repel cats most of the time, while leaving a remote possibility that a cat may have gotten through. This leaves some uncertainty, so we cannot fully justify the claim. To cover the deficit of assurance, we can make an additional check. For example, based on the assumed characteristics of Zone A, we could use a thermal scanner. If the scan did not report any objects with a temperature higher than 20 degrees Celsius, we can use this as evidence to support the claim that "there are no cats in Zone A." The consumer of our assurance case may still not be convinced: What if the thermal scanner is malfunctioning? What if there are some places that are hidden from the scanner? We could further request an additional check. We could let a dog into Zone A and observe that the thermal scan was showing the dog, that the dog was moving around Zone A, and that the dog did not bark. These reported facts can be added as further evidence to address the critical questions of the reviewer and justify the claim that "there are no cats in Zone A."

Zone B does not share the assumptions we made for Zone A, which warranted the use of the thermal scan. We need a different strategy to support the claim that "there are no cats in Zone B." We could do an exhaustive search of Zone B and produce the testimony and photos as evidence that the search party has indeed visited all locations in Zone B and that no location contained a cat at the time of the search. The argument should also describe the measures that prevented a cat to roam within the Zone B while the search was being performed.

The next step is to present the assurance case explicitly, in a visual format, where all claims and all assumptions are shown as individual icons and all links between claims, sub-claims, and evidence are visible. Visual representation of the assurance case adds to the clarity of the argument and encourages review of the assurance case, which facilitates its consumption.

The knowledge of the architecture of the room helped us design the argument that involves a different search strategy for each zone, taking advantage of the individual characteristics of each zone. The design of the argument determined the evidence gathering during the execution of the search.

Now let's consider the third scenario: "there will be no black cats in the room for the next 12 months." Here the outcome is a pure claim; for example, "the risk of a cat entering the room within the next 12 months is made as low as reasonably practicable." Again, this is a claim about all locations: "no location in the room has high risk of a cat entering that location within the next 12 months." There is a further difference from our second scenario. In the previous scenario, the "no location" claim referred to the past events—one of the implicit assumptions in the "no black cat in the room" scenario is bounded with a certain timeframe: "no location in the room contained the cat at the time of search." In the "will be no black cats in the room" scenario, we are interested in a future timeframe.

As we extend the timeframe from "here and now" to cover a future period of time, we need to change the justification approach. It does not make sense to justify this claim by the characteristics of a single search. Instead, the justification of the claim comes from the characteristics of the *risk mitigation countermeasures* that we apply. In particular, we would like to claim that the countermeasures were set up in such a way that no location in the room will contain a cat. The assurance scenario also involves a "no location" claim, and to justify this claim, we must produce the *evidence* of the countermeasures and their efficiency. For any complex claim, the connection between the evidence and the claim is no longer trivial, and required an *argument* that contains a number of intermediate sub-claims and additional warrants.

Let's see how this approach works for the "will be no black cats scenario." Again we use a different argument for each zone, taking advantage of the unique characteristics of each zone (see Figure 4). The previous argument for Zone C is applicable to the assurance scenario, because one can reasonably assume that if an entry point is not suitable for any cat to enter Zone C now, it will not be suitable for those cats in the future, so Zone C is sealed, free from "cat encounters."

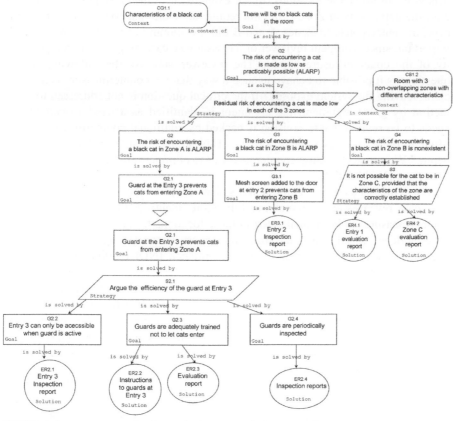

FIGURE 4 Assurance case for Scenario 3—there will be no cat in the room

However, the arguments for Zone A and B are no longer applicable, because they both involved a single search, which was sufficient for justifying claims about the events-to-date, but not sufficient as a guarantee for future events. In other words, a one-time search is not a sufficient countermeasure, as cats may enter the room after the search is over. This argument leaves too much "assurance deficit."

In order to design the assurance argument, we need to check to see if the system has any features that mitigate the risk, or modify the system and add some countermeasures. For example, we could recommend a security guard at the entry point to Zone B. In the "assurance scenario," a guard is a countermeasure against cats entering Zone B, as well as the evidence collection mechanism—we can take a testimony from the guard that no cats entered Zone B within the last three hours, which would support the claim that there is no cat in Zone B. Each countermeasure must be associated with an evidence collecting mechanism, because in order to justify the claim, we need to understand that the countermeasure was actually working.

The concept of *location* is important for the selection of countermeasures, as they are associated with particular locations based on the characteristics of the behaviors around these locations (in our example, near the entry points). In particular, the entry point in Zone C did not require an additional countermeasure; however, the entry points to Zones A and B did. Positioning of the countermeasure is important, since a diligent reviewer of the assurance case may identify the possibility of the countermeasure bypass. The reviewer may ask the following critical question: Is it possible to behave in such a way that the countermeasure is not efficient, leaving the system exposed? If the critical question is not addressed to satisfaction by given argument, the argument is identified as a *weak argument* that needs to be revised where revision is backed by additional countermeasures identified through risk assessment activity. This simple idea is called "defense in depth." We can keep adding countermeasures to eliminate any remaining undesired behaviors [NDIA 2008].

Assurance is an architectural activity that identifies locations where an assurance case reveals weak argument, and therefore, identifies the need for additional countermeasures to be implemented in these locations to mitigate the risk. Assurance evidence usually takes the form of a report demonstrating the presence of a countermeasure and the proof of its performance [NDIA 2008], [ISO 15026], [SSE-CMM 2003].

The weak argument leads to a weak assurance case, which leads to low level confidence that the system is not vulnerable. From the architecture perspective, it is important to realize that there is a certain location associated with the vulnerability. How do we know where the vulnerability zone is? This zone is determined by the combination of the threat and inadequately addressed system's exposure through either the missing or inadequate countermeasure or implemented vulnerability. For example, in the black cat example, the vulnerability area for Zone B is located around the entry point to Zone B where a cat can enter. The exposed area, which is the zone in which an unmitigated threat is possible, is the entire Zone B.

The assurance scenario is more complex than the previous ones because it involves timeframes and the relationships between threats and countermeasures. It raises more critical questions: What are the countermeasures? For each countermeasure, what particular threat behaviors does it mitigate? (Did we consider all possible ways cats are getting into the room? Did we consider all possible locations that cats can hide in the room? For each given location, how do we know that there is no cat there?) A critical person may ask how do we know that the countermeasures are indeed in place? How do we know that they will still be there and efficient in the next 12 months?

Traditional detection of vulnerabilities is to some extent similar to the first scenario: A team of experts looks at the system and identifies five problems. They may argue why the identified problems are risky (why we should believe that a situation passes "the cat test"). However, there is a gap between opportunistic approach in finding vulnerability and assembling defensible assurance arguments that all vulnerabilities are identified. We can also say that scenarios 2 and 3 produce *more knowledge* than scenario 1. In particular, scenario 1 produces knowledge about five locations in the room where cats were claimed to be found, while scenario 2 provides knowledge about *all* locations in the room. Scenario 3 provides knowledge about all locations and about the countermeasures, and connects countermeasures to the characteristics of all locations in the room over the desired period of time. We also say that scenarios 2 and 3 produce *more confidence* than scenario 1 because they provide justification to the claims.

2.2 THE NATURE OF ASSURANCE

There is a great deal of confusion surrounding the term "assurance," especially in the area of cyber security, as this is a relatively new area. There is a general understanding that some "assurance" has to accompany a system, however, there is no consensus for which of the several disciplines that are involved in building a system is best positioned to perform "assurance." As the result, several of these disciplines mention assurance, often in passing, but there does not seem to be a single champion. As a result, various parts of assurance are fragmented across several handbooks, often using conflicting viewpoints and terminology. None of the disciplines focus on assurance or are positioned to handle convergence of assurance of both safety and security properties of cyber systems and their material extensions.

For example, the International Security Engineering Association (ISSEA) promotes the discipline of Security Engineering to address the goals of understanding security risks associated with an enterprise, providing security guidance into other engineering activities, establishing confidence in the correctness of security mechanisms, and "integrating the efforts of all engineering disciplines and specialties into a combined understanding of the trustworthiness of a system."

According to ISSEA, security engineering interfaces with many other disciplines, including Enterprise Engineering, Systems Engineering, Software Engineering, Human Factors Engineering, Communications Engineering, Hardware Engineering, Test Engineering, and System Administration. Security engineering is divided into three basic areas: risk assessment, engineering, and assurance [SSE-CMM 2003]. Such partitioning, however, may lead one to believe that assurance is something specific to security engineering. Yet, assurance has been developed in the context of safety engineering for many years [Wilson 1997], [Kelly 1998], [SafSec 2006].

There is an area of Quality Assurance that is developing its own arsenal of methods and techniques, related to validation, verification, and testing, usually with the emphasis on products.

Finally, the ISO/IEC standard 15026, "System and Software Assurance," treats assurance as common for safety and security, as this standard "...provides requirements for the life cycle, including development, operation, maintenance, and disposal of systems and software products that are critically required to exhibit and be shown to possess properties related to safety, security, dependability, or other characteristics. It defines an assurance case as the central artifact for planning, monitoring, achieving, and showing the achievement and sustainment of the properties and for related support of other decision making." [ISO 15026]

A common topic to assurance for safety and security is the emphasis on analysis of the engineering artifacts, rather than development of the engineering artifacts, and especially a common methodological framework for analyzing design artifacts and implementing artifacts. Of course, engineering discipline requires analysis to evaluate alternative designs; however, validation and verification activities, including testing, is considered a separate specialty. In the area of software engineering, there is a significant emphasis on engineering *new* systems; some attention to validation and verification activities, including testing; however, very little attention to the analysis and modification of already *existing* code, also known as maintenance engineering.

So, system assurance deserves a status of a stand-alone engineering discipline in order to focus on these common topics. This discipline can then interface with system security engineering and safety engineering to provide guidance for arguing safety or security.

In order to provide a clear picture, detailed interactions between system engineering, risk analysis, and assurance need to be considered.

2.2.1 Engineering, risk, and assurance

System engineering and system assurance are intimately related. To assure a system means to demonstrate that system engineering principles were correctly followed to meet the security goals. However, "good" system engineering as it is commonly understood does not guarantee that the resulting system will have the necessary level of system assurance. The need for providing additional guidance for system assurance is based on the rapid evolution of threats and changes in the operating environments of systems. The assurance of systems has usually been relegated to various processes as part of a broader systems engineering strategy. For example, discussion and validation of requirements is performed to ensure a consistent program definition and architecture. Testing and evaluation are done to ensure that the developed system meets its specifications and the requirements behind them. Various organizational audits and assessments track the use of systems engineering principles throughout the program's life cycle, to ensure that organizational performance is a function of good practice. Because of the complexity and nature of the evolving threats, however, it is important to plan and coordinate these practices and processes, to keep the threat in mind across the system's life cycle. System assurance cannot be executed as an isolated business process at a specific time in the program's schedule, but must be executed continuously from the very earliest conceptualization of the system to its fielding and eventual disposal.

Today, the risk management process often does not consider assurance issues in an integrated way, resulting in project stakeholders unknowingly accepting risks that can have unintended and severe financial, legal, and national security implications. Addressing assurance issues late in the process or in a nonintegrated manner may result in the system not being used as intended, or in excessive costs or delays in system certification or accreditation. Although assurance does not provide any additional security services or safeguards, it rather refers to the security of the product or service and that the product or service fulfills the requirements of the situation, and satisfies the Security Requirements. This may appear to be a less than important aspect at first sight, particularly when the cost of providing or obtaining assurance is factored in. However, it should never be forgotten that, while assurance does not provide additional security services or safeguards, it does serve to reduce the *uncertainty* associated with vulnerabilities, and thus, often eliminates the need for additional security services or safeguards. Risk management must consider the broader consequences of a failure (e.g., to the mission, people's lives, property, business services, or reputation), not just the failure of the system to operate as intended. In many cases, *layered defenses* (e.g., defense-in-depth or engineering-in-depth) may be necessary to provide acceptable risk mitigation.

The System Security Engineering Capability Maturity Model (SSE-CMM) developed by ISSEA [SSE-CMM 2003], considers risk assessment, engineering, and assurance as key components of the process that delivers security and, although these components are related, it is possible and useful to examine them separately. The risk assessment process identifies and prioritizes threats to the developing product or system, the security engineering process works with other engineering disciplines to determine and implement security solutions, and the assurance process establishes confidence in the security solutions and conveys this confidence to stakeholders (see Figure 5).

The Risk Assessment – A major goal of security engineering is the reduction of risk. Risk assessment is the process of identifying problems that have not yet occurred. Risks are assessed by examining the *likelihood* of the threat and

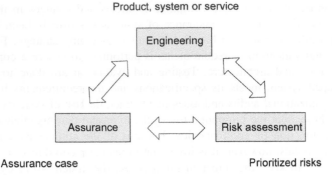

FIGURE 5 Interdependency—risk, engineering and assurance

vulnerability and by considering the potential *impact* of an unwanted incident. Associated with that likelihood is a factor of *uncertainty,* which will vary dependent upon a particular situation. This means that the likelihood can only be predicted within certain limits. In addition, impact assessed for a particular risk also has associated uncertainty, as the unwanted incident may not turn out as expected. Because the factors may have a large amount of uncertainty as to the accuracy of the predictions associated with them, planning and the justification of security can be very difficult. One way to partially deal with this problem is to implement techniques to detect the occurrence of an unwanted incident.

An unwanted incident is made up of three components: threat, vulnerability, and impact. Vulnerabilities are properties of the asset that may be exploited by a threat and include weaknesses. If either the threat or the vulnerability is not present, there can be no unwanted incident and thus no risk. Risk management is the process of assessing and quantifying risk, and establishing an acceptable level of risk for the organization (see Figure 6). Managing risk is an important part of the management of security.

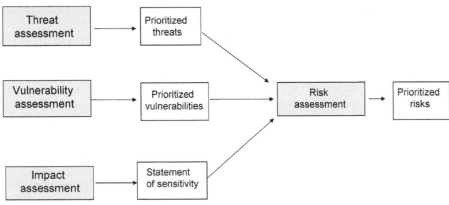

FIGURE 6 Incident components: threat, vulnerability, and impact

Risks are mitigated by the implementation of *safeguards*, which may address the threat, the vulnerability, the impact, or the risk itself. However, it is not feasible to mitigate all risks or completely mitigate all of any particular risk. This is in large part due to the cost of risk mitigation and to the associated uncertainties. Thus, some residual risk must always be accepted. In the presence of high uncertainty, risk acceptance becomes very problematic due to its inexact nature. One of the few areas under the risk taker's control is the uncertainty associated with the system.

The Engineering – Security engineering is a process that proceeds through concept, design, implementation, test, deployment, operation, maintenance, and decommission. Throughout this process, security engineers must work closely with the other system engineering teams. This helps to ensure that security is an integral part of the larger process, and not a separate and distinct activity. Using the information from the risk process described above, and other information about system requirements, relevant laws, and policies, security engineers work with the stakeholders to identify security needs. Once needs are identified, security engineers identify and track specific requirements (seeFigure 7).

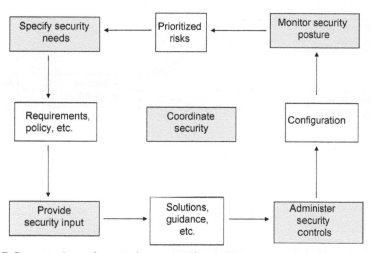

FIGURE 7 Process of creating solution to security problem

The process of creating solutions to security problems generally involves identifying possible alternatives and then evaluating the alternatives to determine which is the most promising. The difficulty in integrating this activity with the rest of the engineering process is that the solutions cannot be selected on security considerations alone. Rather, a wide variety of other considerations, including cost, performance, technical risk, and ease of use must be addressed. Typically, these decisions should be captured to minimize the need to revisit issues. The analyses produced also form a significant basis for assurance efforts.

Later in the life cycle, the security engineer is called on to ensure that products and systems are properly configured in relation to the perceived risks, ensuring that new threats do not make the system unsafe to operate.

The Assurance – Assurance provides a very important element when performing a security risk assessment and during the risk management phase of determining if additional safeguards are required and if so, whether they are implemented correctly by engineering. Although assurance does not live in isolation, we can distinctly talk about assurance life cycle, assurance requirements, assurance infrastructure, assurance stakeholders, assurance management, and assurance specialized expertise (see Figure 8). For this reason, there is a need to treat assurance as a stand-alone discipline and as such, it is explored in detail throughout the book.

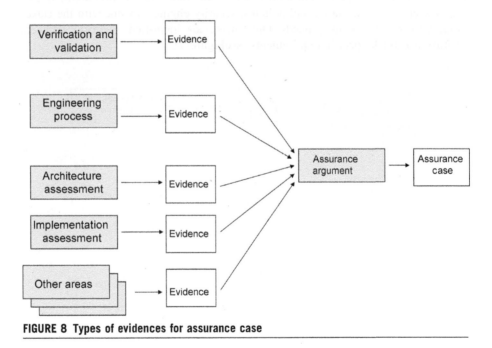

FIGURE 8 Types of evidences for assurance case

2.2.2 Assurance case

The umbrella component in system assurance is "assurance case," which is defined as a reasoned, auditable *argument* created to support the contention that a defined system will satisfy particular requirements, along with supporting *evidence*. This structured approach allows for the documentation of all relevant information that can be analyzed to validate if the application is meeting the set objectives, which lends itself to a *repeatable* process that allows you to go back and review the information to justify any decisions made based on the results of the assessment. It also aids the collection of supporting evidence at different points over time, providing the ability to analyze trends in both risk and trustworthiness [Toulmin 1984, 2003], [Kelly 1998], [NDIA 2008], [ISO 15026].

The purpose of assurance case is to convince *stakeholders*, such as system owner, regulators, or acquirers, about certain properties of the system that are not obvious from system descriptions. Thus, a security assurance case is about confidentiality, integrity, and availability of information and services provided by the systems in cyberspace. In other words, assurance case is the documented assurance (i.e., argument and supporting evidence) of the achievement and maintenance of a system's security. It is primarily the means by which those who are accountable for the mission, system, or service provision, assure themselves that those services are delivering, and will continue to deliver, an acceptable level of security.

Assurance case was developed by the safety community, primarily in the UK where it has been mandated by a number of legislations as the means to argue about safety of systems [Kelly 1998], [Wilson 1997]. Assurance case is necessary for regulators, as the main objective of regulation of certain activity is to ensure that those who are accountable for the security discharge their responsibility properly followed by an adequate means of obtaining regulatory approval for the service or project concerned.

The development of an assurance case is not an alternative to carrying out security assessment; rather, it is a means of structuring and documenting a summary of the results of such an assessment and other activities (e.g., simulations, surveys, etc.), in a way that a reader can readily follow the logical reasoning as to why a change or ongoing service can be considered safe and secure.

Procurers of critical computer-based systems have to assess the suitability of implementations provided by external contractors. What an assessor requires is a clear, comprehensible, and defensible argument, with supporting evidence that a system will behave acceptably.

The designers of a system will obviously take security requirements into account, but the satisfactory design and implementation of such requirements does not manifest itself clearly in the models and artifacts of the development process; for example, one cannot look at a development process and assume a system's reliability and security.

A contractor may provide the assessor with a large amount of diverse material on which to make their assessment. They may provide a formal specification of the system and a design by refinement. They may produce hundreds of pages of carefully crafted fault tree analysis. They may place great emphasis on the coverage and success of the system testing strategy. Each of these sources may provide a useful line of argument or a key piece of evidence, but individually they are insufficient grounds for an assessor to believe that a system is acceptably secure.

Also, individual analyses models are likely to be based on a number of underlying assumptions, which are not easily captured in the model itself. There will always be issues that cannot be captured in any specific analysis model; principal amongst these is the justification of the model itself.

What an assessor requires is an *overall argument* bringing together the various strands of reasoning and diverse sources of evidence in the form of an assurance case, which makes clear the underlying assumptions and rationale. An effective assurance case needs to be a clear, comprehensive, and defensible argument that a system will behave acceptably throughout its operations and decommissioning.

There is a need for analysis models and artifacts to derive measures of security, reliability, etc., to make the properties manifest and controllable.

A structured account of these analyses models is usually presented to the appropriate regulatory authority as an assurance case.

An assurance case consists of four principal elements: objectives, argument, evidence, and context. *Security* case will emphasize security objectives, namely confidentiality, integrity, and availability. To assure security, the systems owner has to demonstrate that security objectives are addressed. The security argument communicates the relationship between the evidence and objectives and shows that evidence indicates that objectives have been achieved. Context identifies the basis of the argument. Argument without evidence is unjustified and therefore, unconvincing. Evidence without argument is unexplained—it can be unclear that (or how) security objectives have been satisfied. [Eurocontrol 2006]

Requirements are supported by claims. Claims are supported by other (sub) claims. Leaf sub-claims are supported by evidence. The structured tree of sub-claims defines context for argument.

2.2.2.1 Contents of an assurance case

A good assurance case should include at least the following [Eurocontrol 2006]:

- **Claim** – what the assurance case is trying to show—this should be directly related to the claim that the subject of the assurance case is acceptably secure.
- **Purpose** – why is the assurance case being written and for whom.
- **Scope** – what is, and is not, covered.
- **System Description** – a description of the system/change and its operational and physical environment, sufficient only to explain what the assurance case addresses and for the reader to understand the remainder of the assurance case.
- **Justification** – for project assurance cases, the justification for introducing the change (and therefore potentially for incurring some risk).
- **Argument** – a reasoned and well-structured assurance argument showing how the aim is satisfied.
- **Evidence** – Concrete, agreed-upon, available facts about the system of interest that can support the claim directly or indirectly.

- **Caveats** – all assumptions, outstanding security issues, and any limitations or restrictions on the operation of the system.
- **Conclusions** – a simple statement to the effect that the claim has been satisfied to the stated caveats.

2.2.2.1.1 Assurance claims

Assurance case involves one or more Assurance Claims (from here on referred to as "claims"). Each claim is phrased as a proposition and presents a statement about a desired result, objective, or point of measure that is important to assess and understand; it is answered as true or false. A typical system assurance claim is a safeguard effectiveness statement – a claim that a particular security control adequately mitigates certain identified risks. The characteristics of claims can be summarized as follows:

- Claims should be bounded.
- Claims should never be open-ended.
- Claims should be provable.

In particular, the claim statement should involve discernable facts, such that they can be recognized with confidence among the available facts about the subject of the assurance case, at least in principle, even if the evidence gathering involves some complex analysis that will derive additional intermediate facts. When forming claims, the answers on the following questions could be helpful:

- What statements would convince us that the claim is true?
- What are the reasons for why we can say that the claim is true?

2.2.2.1.2 Assurance arguments

The role of an assurance argument is to succinctly explain the relationship between an assurance claim and an assurance evidence, and is used to clearly describe how a claim is justified:

- How evidence should be collected and interpreted; and
- Ultimately, what evidence supports the claim.

Assurance Arguments (from here on referred to as "argument") assist in the claim structure build-up and can be viewed as a strategy for substantiating bigger goals or high-level claims by decomposing an assurance claim into a number of smaller sub-claims. While evidence is the set of available, agreed-upon and undisputed facts about the system of interest, assurance argument addresses the conceptual distance between the available facts and the claim statements, for example, when the claim involves analysis, or when the available facts needs to be accumulated because none of them provides direct support to the claim.

Decomposition is repeated until there is no need for further simplification since the claim can now be objectively proven. End results of this divide-and-conquer strategy are sub-claims that do not need further refinement and could be viewed as a contractual agreement on how evidence will be collected and how much of evidence is required:

- When evidence is considered missing?
- What level of evidence collecting is required?

These sub-claims form the set of measurable goals for collecting evidence.

A typical assurance case requires decomposition of the top claims into several levels of sub-claims that are eventually supported by evidence. In some cases, a single assurance argument may be used to support multiple assurance claims.

An assurance argument can be constructed based on an evaluation and testing of the product. This approach is often used for security-related products, particularly under the Security Evaluation or Common Criteria scheme, ISO/IEC 15408-1:2005 [ISO 15408], [Merkow 2005]. In this case, the assurance argument is based upon the Protection Profile of the product and the Evaluated Assurance Level achieved.

Assurance arguments can be constructed in many other ways and drawn from many different sources. In the examples given previously, the assurance arguments have been based upon:

- Testing and evaluation of the product or service;
- The reputation of the supplier;
- The professional competence of the engineers performing the work; and
- The maturity of the processes used.

Other sources that could be used include:

- The methods used in the design of the product or service;
- The tools used in the design of the product;
- The tools used in the performance of the service; and
- Many other potential sources.

All of the above can be used to support the assurance claim. Which strategy is used in a particular instance largely depends upon the needs of the assurance recipient and how they will make use of the assurance case associated with the product or service.

2.2.2.1.3 Assurance evidence

The assurance evidence are the concrete facts that were collected in support of a given claim or sub-claim. For each claim, agreed upon collection techniques are used to capture the evidence.

All assurance components are interdependent as they together demonstrate in a clear and defendable manner, how the agreed-upon, readily available facts support meaningful claims about the effectiveness of the safeguards of the system of interest and its resulting security posture.

It is important to note that although assurance does not add any additional safeguards to counter risks related to security, it does provide the confidence that the controls that have been implemented will reduce the anticipated risk.

Assurance can also be viewed as the confidence that the safeguards will function as intended. This confidence is derived from the properties of correctness and effectiveness. Correctness is the property that the safeguards, as designed, implement the requirements. Effectiveness is the property that the safeguards provide security adequate to meet the customer's security needs. The strength of the evidentiary support to the claims is determined by the required level of assurance.

2.2.2.2 Structure of the assurance argument

Goal-Structuring Notation (GSN), developed by the University of York in the UK, provides a visual means of setting out hierarchical assurance arguments, with textual annotation and references to supporting evidence [Kelly 1998], [Eurocontrol 2006].

The structured approach of GSN, if correctly applied, brings some rigor into the process of building assurance arguments and provides the means for capturing essential explanatory material, including assumptions, context, and justifications within the argument framework. Figure 9 shows, in an adapted form of GSN, a specimen argument and evidence structure to illustrate the GSN symbology most commonly used in assurance cases (see also Table 1).

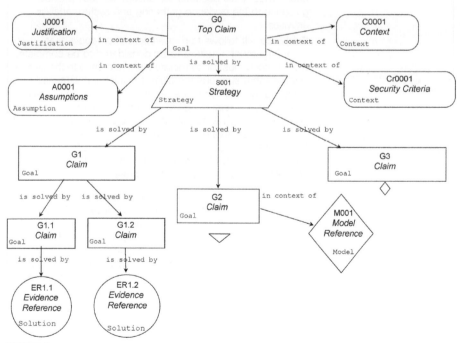

FIGURE 9 Assurance case presented in Goal-Structuring Notation

Table 1 Goal-Structuring Notation Components

G0 *Top Claim* Goal	**Claim** – A claim should take the form of a simple predicate—i.e., a statement that can be shown to be only true or false. Goal-Structuring Notation (GSN) provides for the structured, logical decomposition of claims into lower-level claims. For an argument structure to be sufficient, it is essential to ensure that, at each level of decomposition: the set of claims covers everything that is needed in order to show that the parent claim is true; there is no valid (counter) claim that could undermine the parent claim. In Figure 9, for example, if it can be shown that the claim G1 is satisfied by the combination of claims G1.1 and G1.2, then we need to show that G1.1 and G1.2 are true in order to show that G1 is true. If this principle is applied rigorously all the way down, through, and across a GSN structure, then it is necessary to show only that each argument at the very bottom of the structure is satisfied (i.e., shown to be true) in order to assert that the top-level claim has been satisfied. Satisfaction of the lowest-level claims is the purpose of evidence. Unnecessary (or misplaced) claims do not in themselves invalidate an argument structure; however, they can seriously detract from a clear understanding of the essential claims and should be avoided. In GSN, claims are often called goals because the assurance case provides guidance to the evidence gathering and system analysis activities.
ER1.2 *Evidence Reference* Solution	**Evidence** – It follows from the information above that, for an argument structure to be considered to be complete, every branch must be terminated in a reference to the item of evidence that supports the claim to which it is attached. Evidence therefore must be: appropriate to, and necessary to support, the related claim — spurious evidence (i.e., information which is not relevant to a claim) must be avoided since it would serve only to confuse the agreement sufficient to support the related claim – inadequate evidence undermines the related claim and consequently all the connected higher levels of the structure.
S001 *Strategy* Strategy	**Argument** – Strategies are a useful means of adding "comment" to the structure to explain, for example, how the decomposition will develop. They are not predicates and do not form part of the logical decomposition of the claim; rather, they are there purely for explanation of the decomposition. In GSN, argument is often referred to as strategy, since it explains the decomposition of a claim into sub-claims, and therefore, describes the strategy of assurance.

Continued

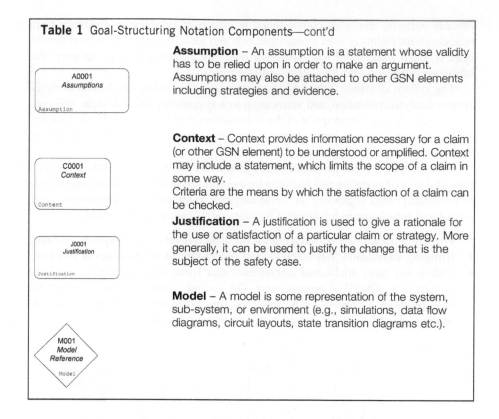

Table 1 Goal-Structuring Notation Components—cont'd

Assumption – An assumption is a statement whose validity has to be relied upon in order to make an argument. Assumptions may also be attached to other GSN elements including strategies and evidence.

Context – Context provides information necessary for a claim (or other GSN element) to be understood or amplified. Context may include a statement, which limits the scope of a claim in some way.
Criteria are the means by which the satisfaction of a claim can be checked.

Justification – A justification is used to give a rationale for the use or satisfaction of a particular claim or strategy. More generally, it can be used to justify the change that is the subject of the safety case.

Model – A model is some representation of the system, sub-system, or environment (e.g., simulations, data flow diagrams, circuit layouts, state transition diagrams etc.).

2.3 OVERVIEW OF THE ASSURANCE PROCESS

An assurance process involves several *activities* that analyze a system and produce an assurance case for the consumption of the system stakeholders. The assurance case is the enabling mechanism aimed to show that the system will meet its prioritized requirements, and that it will operate as intended in the operational environment, minimizing the risk of being exploited through weaknesses and vulnerabilities. It is a means to identify, in a structured way, all the assurance components and their relations. As previously stated, those components are presented as claims, arguments, and evidence, where claims trace through to their supporting arguments and from those arguments to the supporting evidence. System assurance is not something radically new; on the contrary, it provides a repeatable and systematic way to perform risk assessment and system analysis, which are established engineering disciplines [Landoll 2006], [Payne 1993]. System assurance also provides guidance to the validation and verification activities as they are performed against the system, as well as against the processes of the risk assessment. Once the assurance assessment is completed, risk assessment can be performed. This process starts by reviewing claims found in breach of compliance. Evidence from noncompliant claims is used to calculate risk and identify course of actions to mitigate it. Each stakeholder will have their own risk assessment—e.g., security, liability, performance, and regulatory compliance.

The system assurance is the way to communicate the findings of the risk analysis, system analysis, validation, and verification in a systematic, rational, clear, and convincing way for the consumption of the stakeholders (see Figure 10). The key to system assurance is management of knowledge about the system, its mission, and its environment.

Besides that, system assurance, through the use of its components, presents a powerful way of modeling and assessing trustworthiness in a more formal way (degree of formalism varies depending on use of narrative arguments versus well-structured, formalized sub-claims as arguments); it brings significant value in area of:

- Providing traceability between high-level objectives/policies to system artifacts;
- Bringing automation, repeatability, and objectivity to the assessment process;
- Unlike any other traditional assessments that focus on particular view of the system (e.g., CMMI = process view, QA testing = technical view) assurance case provides a cross-domain view, bringing all system components such as functional, architectural, operational, and process together.

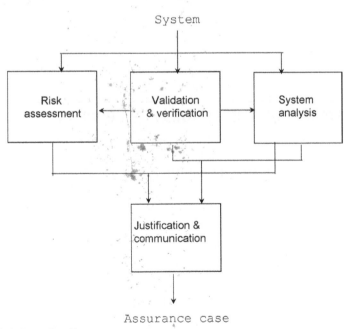

FIGURE 10 Information flow

2.3.1 **Producing confidence**

System assurance provides coordinated guidance for multidisciplinary, cross-domain activities that generate facts about the system, and use these facts as evidence to communicate the discovered knowledge and transform it into confidence. The aim of the end result is to achieve the acceptable measures of system assurance and manage the risk of exploitable vulnerabilities.

The confidence produced using this formal approach can be viewed as *product* due to the following characteristics:

- Measurable – confidence can be measured with results expressed as achieved confidence level of high, medium, or low. Achieved levels are based on findings from system analysis activities.
- Acceptable – the methods that produced the confidence are clear, objective, and as such, acceptable to consumers.
- Repeatable – every time confidence is produced using the same "acceptable" methods on the same set of system artifacts, it would result in the same "confidence level."
- Transferable – measured level of confidence produced by acceptable and repeatable methods is transferable to its consumers; and as such, confidence can be packaged together with a system as its attribute.

2.3.2 **Economics of confidence**

Today, most of assessment activities that make up assurance processes are informal, subjective, and manual due to lack of comprehensive tooling and agreed-upon assurance content in machine-readable form, which makes assessment approaches resist automation. Less automation means a laborious, unpredictable, lengthy, and costly assurance process.

The good example would be the Common Criteria (CC) Evaluation Assurance Process [ISO 15408], [Merkow 2005]—IT system certification process of commercial products that will be deployed in the government environment. CC Evaluation Assurance Levels (EAL1 through EAL7 numerical rating) of an IT system reflect at what level the system was tested to verify if it meets all of its security requirements. The intent of the higher levels is to provide higher confidence that the system's principal security features are reliably implemented, focusing on covering development of product with a given level of strictness, and only higher EALs involve evaluation of formal system artifacts (EAL 5 – to EAL 7), leading to a costly and laborious evaluation process.

In 2006, the US Government Accountability Office (GAO) published a report on common criteria evaluations that summarized a range of costs and schedules reported for evaluations performed at levels EAL2 through EAL4 [GAO-06-392 2006] that is summarized in Figure 11.

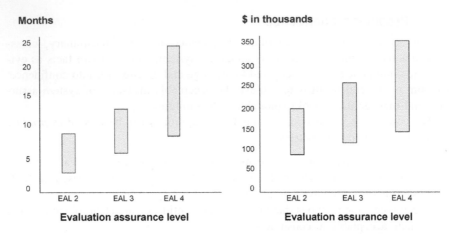

Source: GAO analysis of data provided by Common Criteria NIAP Laboratories (2006)

FIGURE 11 Summarized cost of Common Criteria Evaluation

While certification cost for EAL1 through EAL4 is measured in hundreds of thousands of dollars, EAL5 through EAL7 is measured in millions of dollars. For example, EAL 7 of OS Separation Kernel can cost up to $5M and last up to 2.5 years—not so practical to be applied across all systems.

Automation in security assurance would be game changing.

Bibliography

Eurocontrol, Organization For The Safety of Air Navigation, European Air Traffic Management, *Safety Case Development Manual,* DAP/SSH/091. (2006).

ISO/IEC 15026 *Systems and Software Engineering – Systems and Software Assurance,* Draft. (2009).

ISO/IEC 15408-1:2005 *Information Technology - Security Techniques - Evaluation Criteria for IT Security Part 1: Introduction and General Model.* (2005).

Toulmin, S. E. (1984). *An Introduction to Reasoning.* New York, NY: Macmillan.

Toulmin, S. E. (2003). *The Uses of Argument.* New York, NY: Cambridge University Press.

Kelly, T. P. (1998). *Arguing Safety – A Systematic Approach to Managing Safety Cases.* University of York, PhD Thesis.

Landoll, D. J. (2006). *The Security Risk Assessment Handbook.* New York, NY: Auerbach Publications.

Merkow, M. S., & Breithaupt, J. (2005). *Computer Security Assurance Using the Common Criteria.* Clifton Park, NY: Thompson Delmar Learning.

NDIA, *Engineering for System Assurance Guidebook.* (2008).

Payne, C. N., Froscher, K. N., & Landwehr, C. E. (1993). Toward A Comprehensive Infosec Certification Methodology, Center for High Assurance Computing Systems Naval Research Laboratory. In *Proc. 16th National Computer Security Conference* (pp. 165–172). Baltimore MD: NCSC/NIST.

ISSEA (2003). *SSE-CMM Systems Security Engineering – Capability Maturity Model, 3.0* http://www.sse-cmm.org/index.html.

Wilson, S. P., Kelly, T. P., & McDermid, J. A. (1997). Safety Case Development: Current Practice, Future Prospects. In: *Proc. Safety of Software Based Systems - Twelfth Annual CSR Workshop*. York, England.

SafSec (2006) *Integration of Safety & Security Certification. SafSec Methodology: Standard*. Dobbing, B., Lautieri, S., (Eds), Praxis High Integrity Systems, UK.

GAO-06-392 (2006) U.S. Government Accountability Office. *Information Assurance*. National Partnership Offers Benefits, but Faces Considerable Challenges. March 2006, Washington, DC.

How to build confidence

- *Would you tell me, please, which way I ought to go from here?*
- *That depends a good deal on where you want to get to.*
- *I don't much care where. . .*
- *Then it doesn't matter which way you go.*
- *. . .As long as I get somewhere, Alice added as an explanation.*
- *Oh, you're sure to do that, said the Cat, if you only walk long enough.*

—Lewis Carroll, Alice in Wonderland

If words of command are not clear and distinct, if orders are not thoroughly understood, the General is to blame. But if his orders are clear, and the soldiers nevertheless disobey, then it is the fault of their officers.

—Sun Tsu

3.1 ASSURANCE IN THE SYSTEM LIFE CYCLE

Defense of a cyber system should embrace the entire system life cycle [ISO 15288], [NDIA 2008]. When planning activities in the system life cycle, organizations usually aim at identifying the main security needs of the system as soon as possible after an Operational Concept has been developed. This initial assessment of the security implications of the system serves as the basis for developing a Security Management Plan in which detailed security activities are specified. It should address, among other things, what the project is seeking to achieve (e.g., to deliver benefits in capacity, performance, safety, and/or security), the possible impact on security (in general terms only, since a security assessment would not have been started at this stage), the criteria for deciding what is "secure" in the context of the project and, in broad terms, the strategy for demonstrating security. Security Needs are transformed into Security Objectives, and subsequently, into the Security Requirements (see Figure 1).

Initial Assurance Argument. Building on the security needs, the Initial Assurance Argument should be as complete as possible and at least sufficient to provide a set of goals for the security management plan to address. It also provides the starting point and framework for the development of the Project Assurance Case, although it needs to be recognized that the initial view of what the assurance

System Assurance: Beyond Detecting Vulnerabilities. DOI: 10.1016/B978-0-12-381414-2.00003-8

argument should look like may need to change, depending on the results of the subsequent security assessment.

Security Management Plan specifies the security activities to be conducted throughout the system life cycle and the responsibilities for their execution.

Security Assessment. System assurance is delivered through a coordinated sequence of actions, some of which are performed throughout the system life cycle, and produce process-based evidence including the records of performing the assurance activities, the results of the corresponding verification and validation activities; while others are performed during the evaluation of the system and produce product-based evidence, including the evaluation of the process-based evidence and independent system evaluation. The three main phases of system assessment (referred to as TRA, PSA and SSA below) provide much of the evidence needed for the system security assurance case, as follows:

- **Threats and Risk Assessment** (TRA) produces security objectives to limit the likelihood of incidents as well as limit the impact of incidents, such that the associated risk would be acceptable, including recommendations of the additional security controls, [Swiderski 2004], [Howard 2003], [Sherwood 2005], [NIST SP800-30], [RCMP 2007].
- **Preliminary System Assessment** (PSA) produces assurance that the design of the system adequately mitigates the identified threats and produces security requirements and desired assurance levels for the system elements.
- **System Security Assessment** (SSA) produces assurance that the security requirements are met in the implemented system and that risk is acceptable.

Implementation and Integration covers all the activities needed in order to bring the new/modified system—the subject of the Assurance Case—into operational service.

Transfer into Operation of the new/modified system would normally be subject to a risk assessment and mitigation for this phase itself (part of the project assurance case) and be concluded by finalization and regulatory approval of the project assurance case.

Operational Security Service is necessary because most, if not all, of the preceding security assessment work is predictive in nature. It is therefore important that further assurance of the security is obtained from what is actually achieved in operational service. If the operational experience differs significantly from the results of the predictive security assessment, it may be necessary to review and update the system assurance case.

Figure 1 illustrates the outline of the system life cycle processes and their contribution to assurance.

The ultimate objective of the end-to-end assurance is to justify that the system is secure during the operation. The multi-phased approach when assurance is built into the system life cycle accumulates evidence as the system is being developed. The phases are summarized as follows. First, the the TRA phase identifies security threats and produces security objectives, which define the meaning of being secure

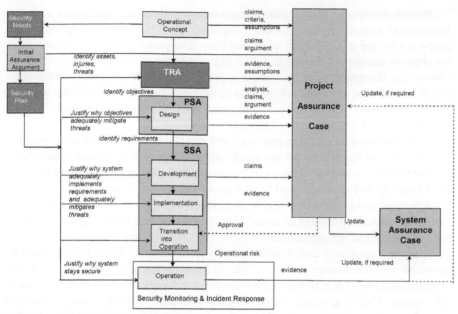

FIGURE 1 Assurance and assessment

for the system of interest. Second, the PSA phase provides justification that the system is *designed* to be secure. The benefit of producing the initial assurance argument early in the system life cycle is that any weak arguments can be identified early and channeled to system engineering activity in the form of the recommendations of additional safeguards. Third, the SSA phase provides the justification that the system is *built* to be secure. The evidence for the SSA phase must be derived from the system itself, rather than from any design documents that describe the system. The evidence for the SSA phase supports several *positive* claims; for example, the evidence that the system implements selected safeguards, as well as *negative* claims; that no behavior bypasses a safeguard; and that no unmitigated vulnerability exists. It is advisable that the SSA assurance case includes considerations for the entire supply chain assurance, from assurance of the acquired components to the assurance of the delivery and installation of the system, as there are multiple ways to introduce vulnerabilities (either intentional or unintentional) into the operational system. Fourth, the operational security service is assured in part by the assurance of the designed administrative rules and procedures at the SSA phase, and in part by performing additional security assessments during the operation phase. The operational assessment provides further evidence to the system assurance case, justifying the claim that the system *stays* secure during the operation. Finally, any change to the system (for example, a patch to one of the system elements, a hardware replacement, change in the operating environment, or change of personnel) may require an additional assurance.

System development processes of requirement definition, requirement analysis, architecture design, implementation, integration, and transition into operation are addressed by the initial project assurance case. The project assurance case defines the security baseline of the system. This first assurance case is predictive in nature (shows that the operation of the system is predicted to be secure). This initial project assurance case is subsumed into the system assurance case, together with the results of security audits, surveys, and operational monitoring (to show that, up to that point in time, it actually has been secure).

A system assurance case is produced and maintained in order to show that the ongoing, day-to-day operations are secure and that they will remain so indefinitely. Changes to the systems or changes to the operational environment need to be managed securely and assured by additional project assurance cases.

A system owner may also decide to produce a project assurance case when a particular substantial change to an existing security-related service/system (including the changes to the operational environment) is to be undertaken.

A project assurance case would normally consider only those risks created or modified by the change and rely on an assumption (or evidence from the corresponding system assurance case) that the prechange situation is at least tolerably secure. Project assurance cases are used to update, and are usually subsumed into, the system assurance case. The system assurance case, updated periodically, provides the reference to *all* operational risks accepted by the system owner and provides an important safeguard that small risks accumulated over time do not aggregate into unacceptable risks.

Continuous assurance is achieved when the system assurance case is a living document that is updated throughout the entire system life cycle. The OMG Assurance Ecosystem emphasizes management of the system assurance case in the form of an *integrated system model*, which maintains the traceability links between the security needs, security objectives, security requirements, the corresponding assurance claims and their implementation in the system, and makes incremental project assurance cost efficient and affordable.

3.2 ACTIVITIES OF SYSTEM ASSURANCE PROCESS

Let's look at the distilled system assurance process presented as a cross-section of various activities of the system life cycle, and consider these activities according to their logical dependencies regardless of the technical process at which they are performed, and regardless of how these steps are incorporated into the project process of the system life cycle.

As described earlier in this chapter, an ideal assurance process should be integrated into the overall system engineering process as *continuous assurance* in order to efficiently plan the common activities between risk management, system assurance, and system engineering; provide timely recommendations to engineering;

and capture the facts as soon as they are produced to avoid costly rediscovery. However, in reality, many organizations perform a third-party security assessment as a one-time activity prior to the transition into operations, or even during the operations phase.

In the context of cybersecurity, the assurance process and the corresponding examples are necessarily biased towards the software and network assurance, because both the desired and the undesired behavior of cyber systems are largely determined by the software components, although the methodology presented here is applicable not only to the technical aspects of security, but to administrative and physical aspects as well.

Further, the OMG Assurance Ecosystem facilitates the fact-oriented approach in which assurance facts and evidence are managed as elements of an integrated model, based on a persistent fact-based repository. The benefit of managing assurance is so that a minor delta project assurance can be performed in the context of the repository in the most efficient way, by physically reusing the existing facts about the system. Later in Chapter 9 we describe the technical details of this approach.

The objective of the assurance process is to understand the security posture of the entire system and to transform this knowledge into justified confidence for the stakeholders through a clear, comprehensive, and defendable assurance case that supports the claim that the system functions as intended and is free of vulnerabilities, either intentional or unintentional. The generic phases of the assurance process are presented at Figure 2.

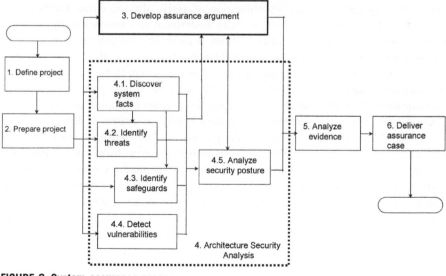

FIGURE 2 System assurance process

In summary, this process produces justification of the following two key claims: Adequate security requirements are defined to mitigate all identified threats and the implemented system satisfies them.

Project definition. The main output of this phase is the Statement of Work (SOW) for the security assessment. This document is critical to the success of the project because it captures the agreement between the producers and the consumers of the assurance case regarding the objectives of the assessment, its scope, rigor, and, consequently, the budget. The SOW provides the administrative framework for all subsequent phases. In case of a third-party security assessment, this includes signing the legal contract [Landoll 2006], [Miles 2004], [Cunningham 2005].

Project preparation. This phase involves selecting the assessment team, the introduction of the team to the organization being assessed, and setting up the tool infrastructure for evidence collection and analysis. The main output of this phase is the baseline *system model* that is used throughout the entire system assurance project to manage and analyze facts about the system being assessed and its environment.

Assurance argument development. This phase involves development of the assurance claims, structured into a systematic and defendable assurance argument. While overlaps exist between the architecture security analysis phase of system assurance and traditional risk analysis, system architecture design, and validation and verification activities, systematic evidence collection guided by a defendable assurance argument is unique to the system assurance process. Architecture security analysis within an *integrated system model* is a characteristic of the fact-oriented system assurance.

Architecture security analysis and evidence gathering. This phase involves discovering system facts, and identification of assets, threats, vulnerabilities, and safeguards within the scope of the security assessment and analysis of the *security posture*. Architecture security analysis phase is *guided* by the argument structure of the assurance case. However, the architecture security analysis phase is executed in parallel with assurance case development so that the system facts, threats, and safeguards contribute to the structure of the assurance case. It is important to note that identification of assets, threats, and safeguards is usually done as part of the risk management process, so (depending on how system assurance is integrated into the system life cycle) at a minimum, the preexisting knowledge of assets, threats, and safeguards is made available to the system assessment team, and is imported into the integrated model for assurance. If this information does not exist at assessment time, it will be re-created in this phase; otherwise, preexisting information will be validated in great details. Each activity of the architecture security analysis phase includes built-in verification and validation mechanisms that contribute to assurance evidence. The rigor of evidence gathering is determined at the project definition phase. As the outcome of the architecture security analysis phase, an *integrated model* of the system under assessment is created.

Analyze evidence. At this phase the evidence is analyzed in the context of assurance case to identify weak and unsupported claims. The identified claims are flagged as possible vulnerabilities. This information is passed to risk management activity for risk analysis and possible mitigation solution. Identified mitigation solution might involve engineering and modification of the assurance case for additional assessment. The architecture-driven assurance case is well-aligned with building defense-in-depth solutions. The claims that turned out to be unsupported due to uncertainty are linked to a certain zone within the system architecture and therefore provide concrete guidance for adding defenses to better protect this zone. This iterative process between engineering, risk management, and assurance further contributes to confidence building.

Assurance case delivery. This phase concludes the system assurance project. The assurance case is presented to the system stakeholders, often in the form of a certification document package.

The sections that follow will describe all phases in more detail.

3.2.1 Project definition

Phase 1. "Define project" addresses the initial engagement between the producers and the consumers of the assurance case. The system assessment project is initiated by the project "sponsor," usually the program management authority responsible for the system being assessed, or the accreditation authority responsible for authorizing the operations of the system. The project sponsor defines the success of the project in terms of framework within which the assurance project is performed, the required deliverables, the quality of the deliverables, the timeframe of the project, and its budget. Detailed steps related to the project definition may vary significantly in the context of a third-party security assessment, performed during the operations, certification and accreditation of the system during the transition into operations, or the in-house continuous assurance integrated into the system development life cycle. Figure 3 illustrates the key activities.

Activity 1.1 – **Obtain initial information about the system**. At this step, the project sponsor provides the assessment team with sufficient information about the system to understand the objectives of the project and perform planning. This is the critical step of the project and usually requires multiple iterations. A sample Concept of Operations (CONOP) document as well as a full conceptual description of a sample system are illustrated in Chapter 12, Case Study.

Activity 1.2 – **Identify system boundaries**. Proper understanding of the physical as well as the logical boundaries of the system is a critical element of scoping the assurance project. This activity identifies the system to be assessed as a collection of activities within a certain operating environment under a single command or management. Assurance project may involve multiple systems in case assessment is performed for an entire organization, such as a business unit or a separate company. The physical elements of an information system include certain facilities (campuses, buildings, rooms, or some other delimited space), computer equipment (servers, workstations, mobile equipment), communication and networking equipment, as well as other equipment and connections. The physical boundaries of an

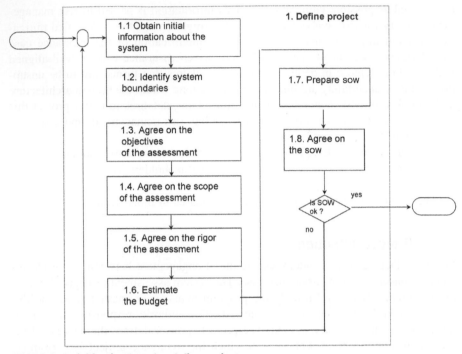

FIGURE 3 Activities in phase1 – define project

information system identify what elements are within the scope of the system and those outside of the scope.

The logical elements of an information system are the functions performed by the system. The logical boundaries of an information system identify the functions that are within the scope of the system and those functions that are outside the scope.

Further guidance to identifying the system boundaries is provided in Chapter 4.

Activity 1.3 – **Agree on the objectives of the assessment.** The primary objective of a system assurance project is to produce justified confidence in the current security posture of the system to be assessed. However, an assurance project can provide multiple specific benefits; for example, provide the justification for system modernization, produce recommendations for improved security safeguards, be part of the security checks and balances, provide an independent review of the security program, and certify the system for the authorization to operate. The real objectives need to be understood because they affect the delivery of the assurance case.

Activity 1.4 – **Agree on the scope of the assessment.** The scope of assessment is determined by the boundaries of the system to be assessed, the categories of assets, threats and safeguards to be considered during assessment. Further guidance is provided in Chapter 5.

Activity 1.5 – **Agree on the rigor of the assessment**. The rigor of assessment is determined by criteria used to evaluate evidence (the two commonly used criteria are "preponderance of evidence," when a claim is considered justified when there is more supporting evidence than counter evidence; and "beyond a reasonable doubt") and the desired thoroughness to be applied in looking for counter evidence (from sampling to exhaustive search). These considerations affect the structure of the argument in the assurance case.

Activity 1.6 – **Estimate the budget**. Rigor and scope are the two variables that determine the statement of work and subsequently the budget and time for completion of the assurance project. The use of automated tools is another contributing factor.

Activity 1.7 – **Prepare the statement of work (SOW)**. In many assurance projects, the SOW is a part of a legal agreement.

Activity 1.8 – **Agree on the SOW**. Agreement on the SOW is often an iterative process. Also, it is not unusual to have bidding for a particular project within the given objectives and scope.

Defining the scope and boundaries of the assurance case is an essential first step in the development of the assurance case. It should explain clearly:

- What the assurance case covers (and what does it not cover).
- Boundaries of responsibility with respect to managerial control and other stakeholders.
- Relationship with other assurance cases, if applicable.
- Applicability and compliance with security regulations and standards.
- Any assumptions made in defining the scope, boundaries, or security criteria.

The description of the Context usually includes:

- The purpose of the system from a security perspective.
- The interfaces with other systems, including people, procedures, and equipment.
- The operational environment, including all characteristics that may be affected and elements that are relied upon when assessing acceptable levels of security.
- A reference to CONOP that explains how the system, and the service that it supports, are intended to operate.

Security criteria are essential to the definition of what is secure in the context of the top-level Assurance Claim. Basically, there are three categories of criteria:

- Absolute – compliance with a defined target; such criteria are usually quantitative.
- Relative – relative to the existing (or previous) level of security. Such criteria may be qualitative or quantitative.
- Reductive – where the risk is required to be reduced as far as reasonably practicable. Such criteria are usually qualitative.

In general, absolute criteria are preferred since satisfaction of them does not depend on proof of past security achievement. Risk classification schemes are often used as criteria on which to base absolute arguments. It is useful to specify more than one type of criterion, and sometimes all three. For example, reducing risk as far as reasonably practicable may not be adequate on its own, since as a minimum, the risk must not increase, and reducing risk as far as reasonably practicable on its own does not ensure that this minimum is achieved.

3.2.2 Project preparation

Phase 2. "Prepare project" is the transition from defining the project, bidding, and negotiation to evidence gathering and analysis of the system. This transition involves three activities (illustrated at Figure 4): preparation of the team, preparation of the project, and establishing the baseline system model.

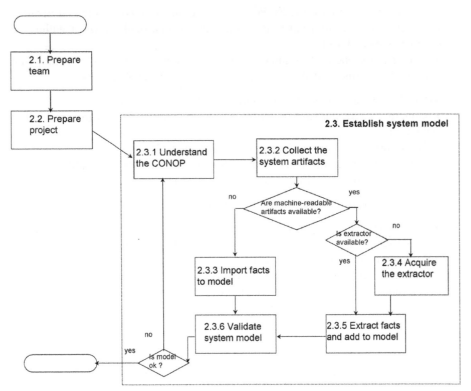

FIGURE 4 Activities in phase 2 – Project preparation

Activity 2.1 – **Prepare team**. This activity involves selection of the assessment team and introduction of the team to the organization to be assessed. The team leadership must ensure adequate expertise, experience, and skills of the members of the team, including the skills of using automated tools.

Activity 2.2 – **Prepare project**. This activity involves introduction of the assessment team to the organization to be assessed, which involves obtaining written permissions for performing assessment activities in order to comply to the legislation and organization's policy, requesting access permissions and user accounts, obtaining the licenses for the tools required for the assessment project, installing the tools, planning and coordinating the assessment activities with the customer, and scheduling interviews. The details of this phase are outside of the scope of this book.

Activity 2.3 – **Establish system model**. The objective of this activity is to collect the baseline facts about the structure and behavior of the system being assessed. The project preparation phase is characterized by the use of *automated knowledge extraction tools* to capture the bulk of accurate low-level system facts related to the structure and behavior of the system. The system model is used during the evidence gathering during the architecture security analysis phase, when the initial facts about the system are further extended and enriched to allow reasoning about the effectiveness of system safeguards and as a result, reasoning about the security posture of the system. Discovery of the system facts is guided by the standard protocol for exchanging system facts, described in Chapter 11. The exact content of the baseline system model is determined in part by the availability of the extractor tools. The need for certain system facts is in part determined by the implementation of the system. As a rule of thumb, the baseline system model should contain the network diagram of the system that enumerates all the relevant physical nodes and applications and their interconnections, and should enumerate all system artifacts, how they are used to build the system, full logical views of each application within the scope of the assessment, facts related to the runtime platform, and facts related to the user interfaces and persistent data of the system.

Activity 2.3.1 – **Understand the CONOP**. The CONOP document provides the initial guidance to the purpose of the system, the elements of the system and their roles, and provides the starting point for understanding its key artifacts. Example of the CONOP document is provided in Chapter 12.

Activity 2.3.2 – **Collect the system artifacts**. A system artifact is a tangible document created through the system development process. Examples are requirement specification documents, design documents, source code, and executables. Artifacts are sources of facts about the system. At this phase, a determination is made whether an artifact contributes to the *baseline system model*. Some system artifacts are machine-readable, meaning that they are structured documents with well-defined syntax and semantics, such as source files, executables, and XML files. Unstructured documents, such as text documents and emails, may contain useful facts about the system, but are in general significantly more difficult to process automatically. Some pieces of information may not be available as machine-readable documents; for example, the network configuration of the system or the user interface of the system. Guidance to this activity and examples of system artifacts are provided in Chapter 11, section Inventory views.

Activity 2.3.3 – **Import facts to model**. This activity deals with the pieces of information that are not available in machine-readable format. In that case, the corresponding machine-readable description is created manually and imported into the system model. Additional guidance to this phase is provided in Chapter 9 and Chapter 11 also some relevant examples are given in the online appendix. The cost of the assessment is minimized when the system model is populated using automated extractor tools. Fortunately, the trend of the modern system development is to accumulate the accurate machine-readable information throughout the system life cycle.

Activity 2.3.4 – **Acquire the extractor**. Depending on the type of the system artifacts (e.g., executable format, programming language, data definition language, runtime platform, network configuration) the assessment team should acquire the corresponding knowledge extraction tool. Extractors that are specific to the system of interest must be custom built for the purpose of the project.

Phase 2.3.5 – **Extract facts and add to model**. During this activity, the extractor is applied to the corresponding system artifacts and system facts are added to the system model. Further guidance to the fact-oriented models and fact-oriented integration is provided in Chapter 9, Common Fact Model. The outcome of this activity is a KDM view of the system of interest, according to one of the KDM viewpoints, further described in Chapter 11 (Inventory, Build, Code, Platform, User Interface, Data or Event view).

Phase 2.3.6 – **Validate system model**. Validation and verification of the system model is the critical activity for the entire system assurance project because the system model is used to manage all pieces of assurance knowledge throughout the project. Populating the system model is usually an iterative process because the initial understanding of the system and its artifacts is seldom comprehensive enough. *Evidence* to the correctness of the baseline system model is critical to the assurance case. Because of the required automation, the bulk of the justification effort can be done once through the process of certifying the extractors, which can then be reused during multiple assurance projects.

3.2.3 Assurance argument development

Phase 3 "assurance argument development" is performed in parallel with phase 4 "architecture security analysis" activities; multiple dependencies exist between these two phases: architecture facts help structure assurance case, while the assurance argument provides decomposition of the security claims and thus provides guidance to evidence collection as well as the context in which assurance evidence is interpreted.

An assurance argument is a set of claims that assert that the service or system concerned is secure. Assurance argument starts with a top-level claim about what the assurance case is trying to demonstrate in relation to the security of the system (see Figure 5). The top claim is supported by the security criteria, which define what is secure in the context of the assurance project and any fundamental assumptions on which the claim relies. The operational context of the claim is usually provided by the CONOP document.

The top claim is then decomposed into individual *safeguard effectiveness claims* and then further into lower-level claims until the bottom claims allow straightforward analysis (See Figures 5–11; Concrete example of the further goal decomposition for one property is provided in Chapter 12). Each claim in the assurance case is expressed as a predicate—i.e., a statement that can be only true or false. The set of claims at each level of decomposition is necessary and sufficient to show that the parent claim is true. The strategy explains the decomposition. Each branch of the assurance case structure is terminated in supporting evidence.

An assurance case contains claims and evidence that demonstrates:

- Validity of the architecture security analysis (evidence for claims G3, G10, G11, G12, G13, G14, G15, and G16 below)
- Mitigation of Identified Risks (evidence for claims G17, G18, G19, and G20 below)

There is a clear distinction between *product-based* (direct) and *process-based* (backing) arguments and related evidence.

Product-based evidence of the validity of the architecture security analysis is concerned with the statements that determine the security posture of the system and demonstrates that:

- All relevant undesired events have been identified.
- The potential impact of the undesired events have been categorized correctly.
- Safeguard effectiveness claims have been identified that the undesired events are acceptably mitigated.

The key issue here is to ensure that the architecture security analysis is complete— i.e., that all risks have been taken into account. It would not be sufficient to show that the safeguards mitigate risks based on an incomplete/incorrect threat and risk assessment.

Process-based evidence of architecture security analysis is concerned with the system life cycle processes and should show that:

- The security risks were determined using an established and appropriate process.
- The techniques and tools used to support the risk determination were verified and validated.
- The architecture security analysis process was executed by suitable competent and experienced personnel.

Process-based evidence is concerned with the execution of the system life cycle processes (as some of them are safeguards to certain risks), and includes evidence that:

- The methods and techniques used are appropriate and adequate for the properties of the system under consideration.
- The tools used to support the processes were verified and validated to a level appropriate for the assigned assurance level and were properly used.
- The validation and verification processes were properly and completely executed and the guidance, procedures, and standards were adhered to.

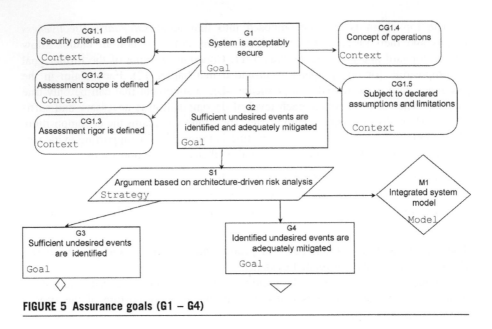

FIGURE 5 Assurance goals (G1 – G4)

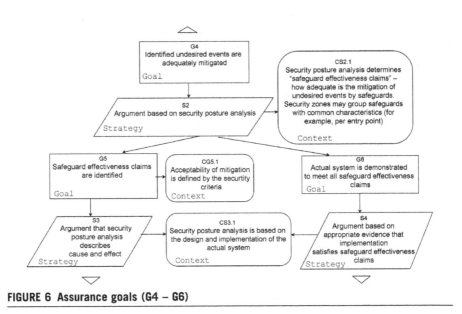

FIGURE 6 Assurance goals (G4 – G6)

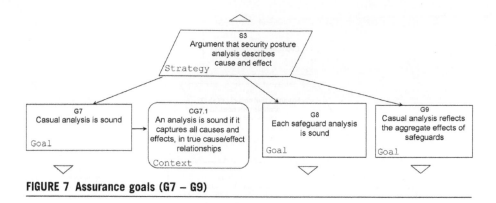

FIGURE 7 Assurance goals (G7 – G9)

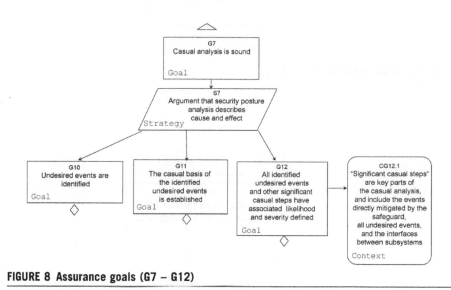

FIGURE 8 Assurance goals (G7 – G12)

3.2.4 **Architecture security analysis**

Phase 4 "architecture security analysis" uses the system model as the foundation for discovering system facts related to the architecture of the system, identifying threats and safeguards, and detecting vulnerabilities (see Figure 12). Security posture of the system is determined by the effectiveness of the safeguards against the threats (an *undesired event* is one of the components of a threat, see Chapter 5). A threat that is not mitigated by safeguards represents a *vulnerability* in the system. Some implementation vulnerabilities can be detected without the reference to the threats, either based on the prior experiences with similar off-the-shelf components, or based on known fault patterns. The remaining vulnerabilities are specific

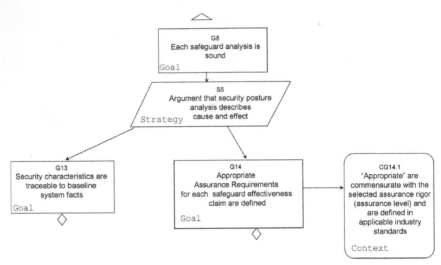

FIGURE 9 Assurance goals (G8 – G14)

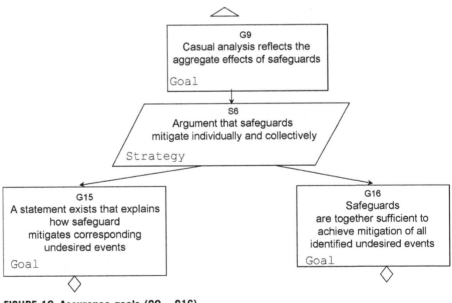

FIGURE 10 Assurance goals (G9 – G16)

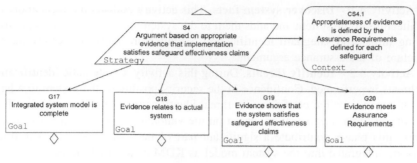

FIGURE 11 Assurance goals (G17 – G20)

to the system of interest and its threats. Vulnerabilities of all three kinds are the counter evidence to the security of the system. The rigor of the assessment determines the comprehensiveness of the vulnerability detection and security posture analysis. Any gaps in understanding the architecture of the system and the threats to the system seriously undermine the assurance of the system. Gaps in the identification of the current safeguards may lead to biased counter evidence (as some of the vulnerabilities may be mitigated by the missed safeguards).

Defense-in-depth approach is used to compensate for the uncertainty in vulnerability detection. Defense-in-depth involves additional architecture facts that identify the nested *zones* of defense, each with its own specific security claims. These zones are used to structure the assurance case (defined at Phase 3). Architecture security analysis phase is guided by the assurance case and gathers direct product-based evidence for the assurance case (see Figure 12).

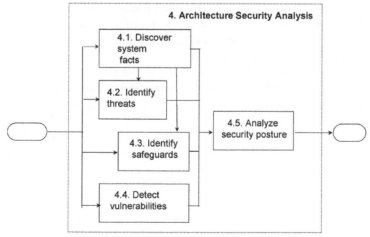

FIGURE 12 Activities in phase 4 – Architecture Security Analysis

Activity 4.1 – **Discover system facts**. This activity collects the facts about the architecture of the system and adds them to the system model. These facts are used during threat and safeguard identification. Architecture facts also determine the structure of the assurance argument.

Activity 4.2 – **Identify threats**. During this activity a systematic identification of threats is performed. Confidence in the security posture of the system to a large extent depends on the confidence in threat identification. Therefore, the justification of the threat identification, based on the validation and verification activities during this phase, contribute a significant part of the assurance case. The threat facts are integrated into the system model as KDM conceptual views.

Activity 4.3 – **Identify safeguards**. This activity identifies the safeguards. Identification of threats and safeguards can be performed in parallel for the administrative, technical, and physical areas of security. The safeguard facts are integrated into the system model as KDM conceptual views.

Activity 4.4 – **Detect vulnerabilities**. This activity identifies vulnerabilities that can be detected independently of threats or the security policy of the given system. The vulnerability facts are integrated into the system model.

Activity 4.5 – **Analyze security posture**. Analysis of the security posture is an architecture-driven activity. This activity is tightly related to the development of the assurance case (Phase 3). The outcome of this activity is the evidence for the safeguard effectiveness claims of the assurance case.

Phase 4 is the most extensive phase. Each of these activities are described in more detail in the following sections.

3.2.4.1 Discover system facts

Activity 4.1 – "Discover system facts" is part of the architecture security analysis phase. This phase extends and enriches the baseline system model with the architecture facts about the system components, their functions, system entry points, and security policy of the system, as well as the specific vocabulary of the system. These facts are integrated with the baseline facts. Further guidance to this phase is provided in Chapter 4 and Chapter 11.

The Figure 13 illustrates the key activities in this phase.

Activities 4.1.1 – 4.1.5 are performed in parallel, although activity 4.1.3 has certain conceptual dependencies on activity 4.1.2; also, activity 4.1.5 depends on activity 4.1.4.

Activity 4.1.1 – **Discover system components and add to model.** The baseline system model is expected to contain the top level system components that correspond to the physical elements, users, networks, and entire applications. This activity identifies *components* corresponding to the internal subsystems and layers, with the resolution commensurate with the scope and rigor of the assessment. System components are nested. The fact-oriented approach to architecture analysis is characterized by the use of the repository of facts to manage all pieces of cybersecurity information. Integration of architecture information to the baseline system models is achieved by establishing "vertical" traceability links from architecture components

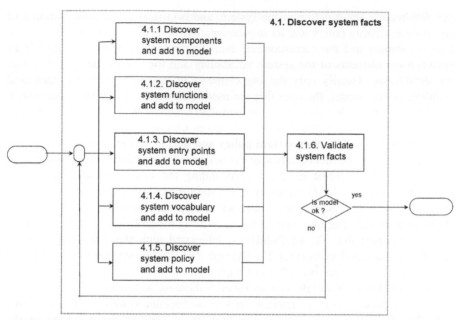

FIGURE 13 Activities in phase 4.1 – Discover system facts

to the low level system elements that implement them. Vertical traceability links are also established between the parent components and their children. Further guidance is provided in Chapter 4 and Chapter 11. Examples are provided in Chapter 12.

Activity 4.1.2 – **Discover system functions and add to model.** This activity extends the baseline model with the so-called behavior units of the system—the *functions* of the system with the resolution commensurate with the scope and rigor of the assessment. Behavior units are "first class citizens" in the system model. Similar to the system components, behavior units can be nested. Behavior units are also linked to the elements of the baseline system model by the vertical traceability links. Chapter 4 describes what are system functions and how they fit into architectural model. The outcome of this activity is the so-called behavior view (behavior facts in the KDM conceptual view), as illustrated in Chapter 11. Examples are provided in Chapter 12.

Activity 4.1.3 – **Discover system entry points and add to model.** This activity identifies and describes the entry points at the boundary of the system and adds the corresponding facts to the system model. The system model is expected to contain the elements of the system as well as the relevant parts of the operational environment; therefore, the boundary of the system and the entry point elements are located inside the repository. Further guidance is provided in Chapters 4 and 5. Examples are provided in Chapter 12.

Activity 4.1.4 – **Discover system vocabulary and add to model.** Understanding of the system vocabulary provides essential guidance to the understanding of the architecture and function of the system, and is critical to the understanding of the system security policy and its implementation. This activity identifies the system vocabulary and the corresponding facts to the system model. Vertical links between the elements of the system vocabulary and the rest of the system model are established. Usually only the key elements of the vocabulary are integrated with the system model, the ones that are used to formulate the rules of the system security policy. Further guidance is provided in Chapters 9, 10, and 11. An example of the full system vocabulary is provided in Chapter 12.

Activity 4.1.6 – **Discover system policy and add to model.** System policy provides guidance to the identification of the undesired events and consequently helps build a systematic threat model. Understanding the system vocabulary and its traceability links to the elements of the system model is the key prerequisite to transforming system policy rules into facts and integrating them with the rest of the system model. The outcome of this activity is the so-called KDM conceptual view, containing the list of RuleUnits, integrated with the rest of the system model, as illustrated in Chapter 11. Examples of the full system vocabulary and security policy rules are provided in Chapter 12.

Activity 4.1.6 – **Validate system facts.** Validation and verification of the system facts is based on the traceability links to the baseline system model. The critical element of the verification is the analysis of gaps in the coverage of the elements of the baseline system model by the architecture elements. Validation activity gathers evidence that the models are correct and complete. This activity is illustrated in the online appendix.

3.2.4.2 Threat identification

Activity 4.2 – "Identify threats" is part of the architecture security analysis phase The key activities of the threat identification process are illustrated at Figure 14. Guidance to the systematic threat identification is provided in Chapter 5. The outcome of this activity is a set of linguistic facts in the so-called KDM conceptual view that use the concepts from the risk vocabulary defined in Chapter 5. KDM conceptual views are further illustrated in Chapter 11.

3.2.4.3 Safeguard identification

Activity 4.3 – "Identify safeguards" is part of the architecture security analysis phase (see Figure 15). This activity identifies certain locations within the system that are considered security safeguards. First, the assessment team will identify the expected safeguards (based on the applicable industry catalogs of security controls, such as the NIST SP800-53 and experience), add the corresponding facts to the system model, and establish the vertical traceability links to the rest of the system model. Second, the assessment team will identify the mandatory security controls required for some regulated industries, such as the federal government, healthcare, and banking. Third, the assessment team will note any missing expected safeguards to be considered as vulnerabilities at the analysis phase. The outcome of this activity is a set of linguistic facts of the KDM conceptual view that uses the concepts from the safeguards vocabulary.

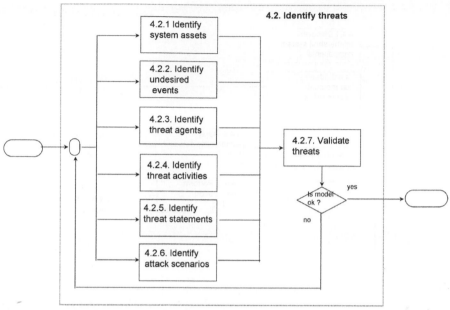

FIGURE 14 Activities in phase 4.2 – Identify threats

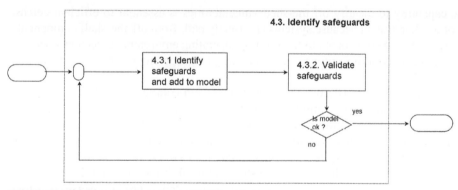

FIGURE 15 Activities in phase 4.3 – Identify safeguards

3.2.4.4 Vulnerability detection

Activity 4.4 – "Detect vulnerabilities" involves three distinct activities (see Figure 16):

- Identifying known vulnerabilities in off-the-shelf components (off-the-shelf vulnerabilities, for short)
- Detecting vulnerabilities by applying vulnerability detection tools and validating their output
- Performing penetration testing

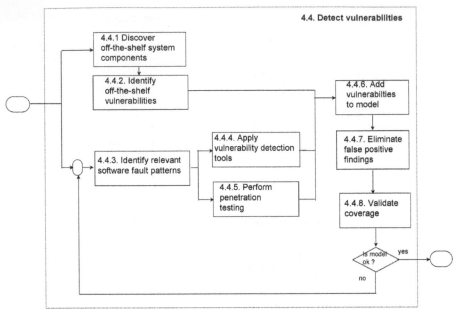

FIGURE 16 Activities in phase 4.4 – Detect vulnerabilities

The capability to identify off-the-shelf vulnerabilities is essential to efficient defense of a cyber system because systems are usually built from off-the-shelf components, especially when it comes to the run-time operating environment, such as operating systems, networking software, programming language environments, and run-time libraries.

Activity 4.4.1 – **Discover off-the-shelf system components**. During this activity, the off-the-shelf components of the system are identified, and this information is added to the system model in the form of attributes so that this information becomes available for the architecture analysis and their impact on the functions of the system and their relation to safeguards is understood.

Activity 4.4.2 – **Identify off-the-shelf vulnerabilities**. During this activity, the information about the off-the-shelf components (vendor, product, version) is used to search existing vulnerability databases to obtain the list of known vulnerabilities and their ratings, as well as other information. Further details of this process are described in Chapter 6. The information about vulnerabilities is integrated into the system model (activity 4.4.6).

The capability to detect vulnerabilities based on the known software fault patterns is important in order to deal with the technical vulnerabilities in custom-built components. There are two approaches: one is detection based on static analysis of the code (source or binary), and the second is penetration testing of the system in operation. Both detection techniques involve an up-to-date and comprehensive catalog of patterns.

Activity 4.4.3 – **Identify relevant software fault patterns**. This activity is common to static and dynamic approaches. Ideally the assessment team should have access to an up-to-date repository of patterns and a generic capability to perform static analysis and/or penetration testing. Further details of this process are provided in Chapter 7. Accumulating and sharing software fault patterns as machine-readable content for tools is one of the key characteristics of the OMG Assurance Ecosystem.

Activity 4.4.4 – **Apply vulnerability detection tools**. Several static analysis tools for automated detection of security vulnerabilities have been developed, both free, open source, and commercial. Current vulnerability detection tools usually have some pre built, proprietary set of patterns. Automatic detection of vulnerabilities by static analysis of the code is an important capability for the defense of cyber systems [Dowd 2007], [Seacord 2006]. Further details are provided in Chapter 7.

Activity 4.4.5 – **Perform penetration testing**. Penetration testing is the process of interacting with the operational system with the purpose of identifying vulnerabilities. An arsenal of testing tools is used to automate some of the operations, while the guidance from the system model or similar knowledge of the architecture and the behavior of the system usually leads to dramatic improvements in coverage, compared to the "black-box" only testing [Sutton 2007]. Details of the penetration testing techniques are outside of the scope of this book.

Activity 4.4.6 – **Add vulnerabilities to model**. The characteristic of the end-to-end system assurance approach described in this book is that all pieces of assurance information are managed in an integrated system model. Therefore, the knowledge of the vulnerabilities should be added to the system model to be used during security posture analysis.

Activity 4.4.7 – **Eliminate false positive findings**. Static analysis tools are known to generate false positive reports, so additional effort must be spent to understand the findings and eliminate false positives. The advantage of using the system model to eliminate the false positive report is that vulnerability findings are put into context of the system architecture, and that the findings from multiple vulnerability detection tools can be collated, which makes the false positive elimination process more efficient.

Activity 4.4.8 – **Validate coverage**. Vulnerability detection is the source of counter evidence for assurance. It is important to understand that there is a *gap* between vulnerability detection and assurance, since the lack of evidence of vulnerabilities (the three approaches outlined above were used but did not yield any findings after the false reports have been identified and eliminated) does not directly translate into the evidence of the lack of vulnerabilities. One particular concern is that of *coverage*: the particular engineering approach of the code of the system may create barriers for the automated tools to analyze some of the components (this is applicable both to static analysis as well as to the penetration testing). Commercial vulnerability detection tools do not provide any information about the coverage, which makes it difficult to use their findings as assurance evidence.

Managing the list of all vulnerabilities in the system is one of the critical activities of cyberdefense. Vulnerability findings could be used as guidance to mitigate the risk by applying patches to fix vulnerabilities in the off-the-shelf and custom-developed products. While it is tempting to look for an automated capability to detect vulnerabilities, the reality is that such a solution is not practically attainable for the following reasons:

1. Lack of machine-readable artifacts for many of the system elements. We assume that an automated vulnerability detection solution will systematically analyze some artifacts, such as the source code. Although software is usually the major part of the cyber systems, they include other parts, such as people, procedures, hardware, and the physical environment. Software elements are quite special, because they do involve machine-readable descriptions (which is rather trivial, since software constitutes instructions for the hardware). Ultimately, there is always some kind of code corresponding to a cyber system—even if it is the binary code for some of the software components. Worst case scenario, it is possible to extract the binary image of the software in operation, if all other forms are not available or have been lost.

2. However, other elements of the system often do not have machine-readable descriptions, short of the scanned paper documents, and even then, the difference is in how formal these documents are. Many elements of the system are described in an informal language that makes descriptions ambiguous, even for the most comprehensive descriptions. There are also cases where some system elements are simply left undocumented.

3. People and procedure elements of the cyber system would be the usual suspects for the lack of machine-readable formal description. However, this issue is more complicated. For example, many cyber systems use external third-party services. Machine-readable description of the behavior of the service may have the same rigor as the code of the software element, and yet, even the binary image of the service is usually not available.

4. Lack of machine-readable artifacts limits the usefulness of the off-the-shelf automated vulnerability detection tool because the knowledge of some of the system components is not (readily) available to the tool. This has an obvious consequence that the off-the-shelf tool cannot detect vulnerabilities in some system elements. There is, however, a less obvious consequence, that the automated tool will miss certain control- and data flows, which may drastically affect the soundness of the system analysis and result in false positives and false negatives.

5. Absence of precise vulnerability knowledge may lead to incorrect decisions in regards to vulnerabilities in the known elements. Incorrect decisions lead to false positives (a certain situation is mistakenly reported as vulnerability) and false negatives (a certain vulnerability is not reported). It is, in fact, the largest problem with utilizing an automated vulnerability detection tool. The value proposition of automatic detection is greatly undermined by the need to evaluate the reports and weed out false positives. The false negatives, on the other hand, present an even bigger problem.

6. A vulnerability detection tool does not let us know how good the detection is. This is pretty much the name of the game: an "automatic vulnerability detection tool" does just that—detects vulnerabilities and produces a report with findings. When the input data led the tool to believe that a certain situation does not satisfy its criteria of vulnerability, it is not reported. So, the detection approach lacks the assurance component by definition. And the following needs to be considered: What if the automatic vulnerability detection tool did not report any problems? Does this mean that the system is secure?

7. An off-the-shelf vulnerability detection tool is limited in its knowledge of what constitutes vulnerability. The automated vulnerability detection tool is internally programmed to look for situations that constitute vulnerability. Therefore, an off-the-shelf tool will not detect violations of specific security policies for the system of interest. Further, such a tool is only as good as the "sum of all knowledge of what is a vulnerability in the entire community"—at the time when the tool was released. This immediately raises two questions: Is this "sum of all knowledge" related to vulnerabilities captured somewhere, or is the tool limited to the "sum of knowledge of its development team?" To keep things real, the tool is supposed to detect situations that the real attackers might exploit. How much exactly does a particular development team know about the attackers and their methods? And also, how fast are new knowledge items added to the tool as the new attack vectors are identified? Attackers do evolve their methods and look for new ingenious ways to exploit systems for fun, for profit, out of hatred, and as part of the military objectives. How do you know that the knowledge content for an off-the-shelf automated vulnerability detection tool is up-to-date with the known attack weapons?

8. The collective knowledge of the vulnerabilities in the entire community is not systematic. The "vulnerability market" is the community of vulnerability researchers of various shades as several communities are interested to know vulnerabilities and substantial investment is and will be made in such knowledge; these communities are diverse and include governments, criminals, computer enthusiasts, computer incident response centers, and software vendors. The "vulnerability market" does deliver results, but they are "hit and miss."

So the use of the of-the-shelf vulnerability detection tools does not fully satisfy assurance needs for cyber systems. Therefore, it is important to systematically identify threats and analyze the effectiveness of the safeguards in order to systematically identify the vulnerabilities that correspond to unmitigated threats and policy violations.

3.2.4.5 Security posture analysis

Activity 4.5 – "Analyze security posture" is the culmination of the architecture security analysis phase. The input into the analysis is the fully extended system model, which includes the system functions, the flows of data between them, the vertical traceability links to the baseline system information, and the horizontal traceability links to the elements of cybersecurity: assets, entry points, safeguards, undesired events, and vulnerabilities. Analysis of the security posture is based on analysis of *cause and effect* (see Figures 5–11). The causes of each identified undesired event are determined by causal analysis. Identification and analysis of all possible causes of undesired events involves tracing the possible sequences of events that the system or its environment can perform, focusing on the behaviors that contribute to the undesired events. The effect of each undesired event is determined by impact analysis. An impact analysis determines all possible consequences of an undesired event within the operating environment in which the system is deployed. Cause and effect analysis requires that a systematic data flow analysis is performed on the full system model, which follows the attacker's commands and data as they flow through the entry points, parsed and acted upon, by system functions at system components, and how they interact with the system assets. For the purposes of the security posture analysis, the role of safeguards is to constrain the acceptable behaviors by filtering the commands and data in such a way that they cannot cause system failures by causing undesired events (see also Chapter 5).

The security posture analysis phase involves architecture-driven cause and effect analysis to develop the mitigation argument to demonstrate that the safeguards mitigate the undesired events.

Figure 17 illustrates a full system model. This is a Data Flow Diagram (DFD), in which system functions are represented as white circles with names. System functions are connected by data flows, represented by lines. Each system function has vertical traceability links to the baseline system elements. These links are not shown at the diagram (imagine that they go into invisible layers underneath the current one); however, these links are critical for the data flow analysis using the full system model, because they make it possible to account for all data flow paths between the system functions with full accuracy. The vertical traceability links are also critical for building the argument from the coverage perspective (to demonstrate that all low-level behaviors have been accounted for). The DFD is superimposed by several grey symbols, representing the cybersecurity elements: assets, represented by grey rectangles with names inside of them; undesired events, represented as small grey circles; entry points, represented as grey squares at the boundary of the system; and safeguards, represented as grey bars.

The prerequisite of the security posture analysis is selection of *analysis strategy*. For example, we are going to examine each entry point and all data flows originating at that entry point. The analysis strategy determines the structure of the assurance argument. Instead of selecting an entry point argument strategy, we could have selected an asset strategy, an undesired event strategy, or a safeguard strategy. Selection of the strategy is driven by the architecture facts.

Entry point EP1 involves data flows that start with function F4, continue to function F5, then branch into F8, F7 followed by F8, F6 followed by F7 and F8. The only undesired event can be produced by the function F8. This event affects asset A1. There is a safeguard SG2 associated with function F5. At this point we need to analyze the effectiveness of the safeguard SG2 against the undesired event UDE1 by demonstrating that none of the data flows downstream from the SG2 will cause UDE1.

Entry point EP2. Involved data flows that start with function F1 and continue to function F2 and F3. This branch is similar to the one described earlier, because

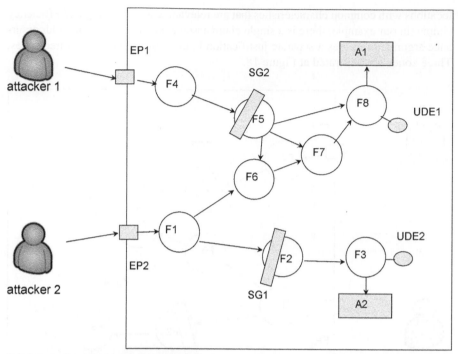

FIGURE 17 Security functional diagram

there is a single undesired event UDE2 associated with function F3, affecting the asset A2, and a single safeguard SG1 at function F2. However, there exists an additional path from the function F1 to the function F6 and further to F7 and F8. This path is a potential for attacker 2 to cause undesired event UDE1 affecting asset A1. At this point, instead of solving the safeguard effectiveness problem, we need to solve the vulnerability problem: we need to analyze that it is not possible for the commands and data from EP2 to cause UDE1. The same problem is involved in the task of eliminating false positives in vulnerability detection.

This is a very simplified illustration of the systematic security posture analysis using data flow analysis. In reality, there are usually many relationships between the safeguards and the undesired events, and in addition, there are also technical vulnerabilities identified independently at Phase 4.4. This simplified diagram illustrates an important characteristic of the analysis approach: this analysis is architecture-driven, because we partitioned the functional description of the system into several "zones" based on some common characteristics (being reachable from a certain entry point), and then further identifying several "exposed zones," such as Zone 1 (F5, F6, F7, F8), which is the zone of effectiveness for the safeguard SG2 against the undesired event UDE1; Zone 2 (F1, F2, F3), which is the zone of effectiveness for the safeguard SG1 against the undesired event UDE2; and Zone 3 (F1, F6, F7, F8), which is the zone of exposure to the undesired event UDE1. Each zone includes the architecture locations with common characteristics that are relevant to a set of safeguard efficiency claims (in our example, there is a single claim associated with each zone). Our assurance argument includes a separate justification branch for each of these three zones. Three zones are illustrated at Figure 18.

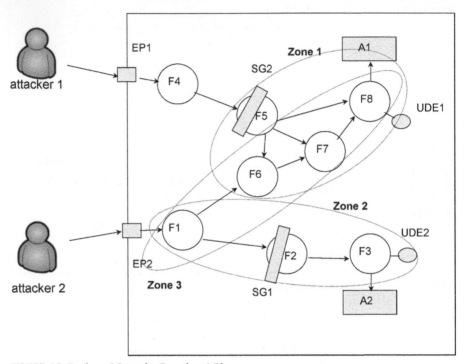

FIGURE 18 Zoning of Security Functional Diagram

Figure 19 illustrates the casual analysis for Zone 3. Event E1 directly causes the undesired event UDE1, and is associated with the function F8. Event E1 is caused by a combination of events E2 and E3, associated with function F7. Event E2 can be caused by either event E4 or event E5, associated with the function F6. Event E3 can be caused by event E6, associated with F6. Events E4, E5, and E6 are caused by a single event E7 associated with the function F1. Finally, event E7 can be caused by the event E8, which is under direct control of the attacker 2; this event is based on one of the ways the attacker can interact with our system through the entry point EP2. System behaviors that correspond to events E8-E1-UDE1 are called *attack paths* (from the external perspective) or *vulnerability paths* (from the internal perspective). The internal events E8-E1 do not cause harm by themselves; the UDE1 is the first event that is identified as undesirable. The impact analysis investigates the consequences of the event UDE1, which is a similar casual chain extending forward from UDE1, both into other functions and assets of the system

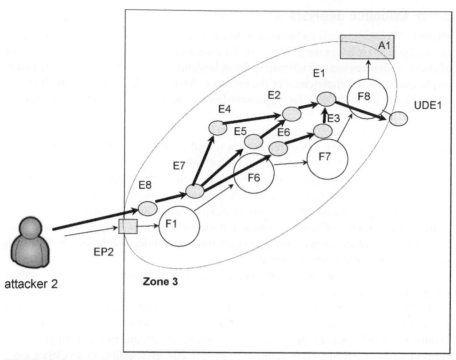

FIGURE 19 Casual analysis of Zone 3

and in its operating environment. The prerequisite of the impact analysis is that the system model enumerates all assets within the scope of the assessment. Further guidance is provided in Chapters 5.

Safeguard effectiveness argument for Zone 3 must demonstrate that the architecture of the system makes the sequence of events E8-UDE1 infeasible. While the knowledge of the causal sequence of events is the key prerequisite of the safeguard effectiveness argument, the argument itself (and the corresponding evidence) can be complicated. Deterministic casual analysis based on the systematic investigation of the data flows in the system can be approximated by considering risks. Risk is the measure of likelihood or probability of, as well as the severity of the impact associated with, a particular undesired event. Causal analysis determines the likelihood of an undesired event, while impact analysis determines the severity of the impact. Architecture-driven risk analysis determines the risk measures of the undesired events and develops the argument that demonstrates the effectiveness of the safeguards against the risk to an acceptable level, commensurate with the security criteria of the assurance case. The structure of the argument is further determined by the assurance requirements based on the selected assurance level commensurate with the selected assurance rigor.

A sample argument structure that drives the analysis of a single safeguard effectiveness claim is described in full detail in Chapter 12. The online appendix illustrates how evidence to the analysis is collected by KDM tools.

3.2.5 **Evidence analysis**

Phase 5 – "Evidence analysis" evaluates the facts gathered during the architecture security analysis phase under the guidance of the assurance argument. Evidence is the heart of every assurance case and ultimately the defendability of the assurance case depends on the quality and completeness of the evidence. Assurance Evidence is usually either derived from the system artifacts (product-based evidence) or is produced during the life cycle (process-based evidence) or involves the facts based on expert judgment, and is presented to demonstrate that the claim to which it relates is valid (i.e., the claim statement is true). Often evidence fact is a record of some sort, demonstrating that a certain event took place or that a certain relationship exists. Evidence can be diverse as various things may be produced as evidence, such as documents, expert testimony, test results, measurement results, records related to process, product, and people. Fact-oriented system assurance is characterized by using an integrated system model as the primary source of direct evidence and supporting traceability between multiple external facts that are added into the integrated system model as evidence and the core facts related to the system of interest.

A well-structured assurance argument provides clarity and defines the context for gathering evidence.

Evaluation of evidence is required for complex claims, supported by multiple pieces of direct and indirect evidence. Evaluation of evidence is a systematic procedure by which each evidence item is weighted according to the strength of its support to the corresponding claim (see Figure 20). Evaluation of evidence concerns with counter evidence to the claim.

Once confidence into collected evidence is achieved, evidentiary support is propagated to all claims of the assurance case. Identified weak and unsupported claims are flagged as possible vulnerabilities. As mentioned previously, at this stage iterative process between risk management, engineering, and assurance becomes a key to building confidence about a system's security posture and includes activities such as risk analysis, recommendation of mitigation solution, engineering mitigation solution, and assuring mitigation solution. The architecture-driven assurance case is well-aligned with building defense-in-depth solutions. The claims that turned out to be unsupported due to uncertainty are linked to a certain zone within the system architecture, and therefore, provide concrete guidance for adding defenses to better protect this zone. This iterative process between engineering, risk management, and assurance further contributes to confidence building.

3.2.6 **Assurance case delivery**

Phase 6 – "Assurance case delivery" concludes the system assurance project. The objective of the system assurance process is to gather sufficient knowledge regarding the security posture of the system and to communicate this knowledge in a clear and convincing way to the senior management in support of their risk acceptance. Usually the assurance case documentation is used as an input in a management decision to approve the transition of the system into operation, or decision to

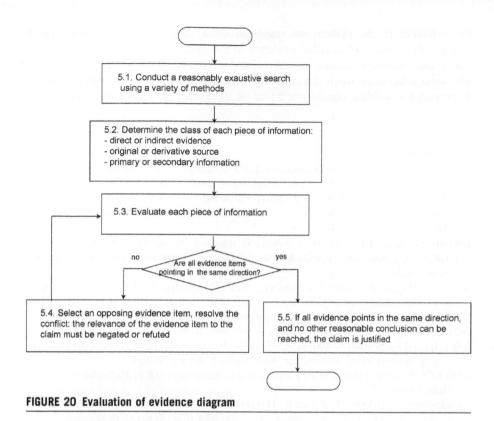

FIGURE 20 Evaluation of evidence diagram

acquire the system. The assurance case is presented to the system stakeholders, often in the form of a certification package.

The practical details of the delivery of the assurance case and the outline of the accompanying documentation vary greatly depending on the organizational context in which the system assurance is performed. The organizational context also affects the depth at which the evidence is made available to the consumer of assurance. Common scenarios include:

- Continuous assurance integrated into the system life cycle
- Independent third-party assurance during the acquisition of the system

When assurance is integrated into the system life cycle, assurance is usually delivered inside the same organization, and because of that, there are few limitations on the availability of evidence. The entire assurance case becomes a living document that is updated when modifications are made to the system during the maintenance phase.

On the other hand, assessment performed during the acquisition of the system is often performed by a trusted third-party laboratory, and the relationships between the sponsor of assurance, the organization performing security evaluation, and the producer of the system are regulated by a contractual framework, which restricts the transfer of detailed evidence to the sponsor of assurance. In this scenario, the evaluator creates an abbreviated presentation of the assurance case. The trust relation between the consumer of assurance and the evaluator becomes important for building confidence based on the abbreviated assurance case.

Bibliography

Eurocontrol (2006), European Organization For The Safety Of Air Navigation, European Air Traffic Management, *Safety Case Development Manual*, DAP/SSH/091.

Dowd, M., McDonald, J., & Schuh, J. (2007). *The Art of Software Security Assessment: Identifying and Preventing Software Vulnerabilities*. Upper Saddle River, NJ: Addison-Wesley.

Howard, M., & LeBlanc, D. (2003). *Writing Secure Code*. Redmond, WA: Microsoft Press.

Landoll, D. J. (2006). *The Security Risk Assessment Handbook*. New York, NY: Auerbach Publications.

Miles, G., Rogers, R., Fuller, E., Hoagberg, M. P., & Dykstra, T. (2004). *Security Assessment: Case Studies for Implementing the NSA IAM*. Rockland, MA: Syngress Publishing.

ISO/IEC 15288-1:2008 *Life Cycle Management – System Life Cycle Processes*. (2008).

NDIA, *Engineering for System Assurance Guidebook*. 2008.

NIST Special Publication SP800-30. (2002). *Risk Management Guide for Information Technology Systems*, Gary Stoneburner, Alice Goguen, Alexis Feringa.

CSE, RCMP. (2007). *Harmonized Threat and Risk Assessment (TRA) Methodology*. TRA-1 Date: October 23.

Cunningham, B., Dykstra, T., Fuller, E., Hoagberg, M. P., Little, C., & Miles, G. et al. (Eds.), (2005). *Network Security Evaluation: Using the NSA IEM*. Syngress Publishing.

Seacord, R. (2006). *Secure Coding in C and C++*. Upper Saddle River, NJ: Addison-Wesley.

Sherwood, J., Clark, A., & Lynas, A. (2005). *Enterprise Security Architecture: A Business-Driven Approach*. San-Francisco, CA: CMP Books.

Sutton, M., Greene, A., & Amini, P. (2007). *Fuzzing: Brute force vulnerability discovery*. Addison-Wesley, Upper Saddle River, NJ.

Swiderski, F., & Snyder, W. (2004). *Threat Modeling*. Redmond, WA: Microsoft Press.

Knowledge of system as an element of cybersecurity argument

When once your point of view is changed, the very thing which was so damning becomes a clue to the truth
—**Arthur Conan-Doyle, The Casebook of Sherlock Holmes**

Captain Hastings: Look at that, Poirot. Look at that view!
Hercule Poirot: Yes, well, views are very nice, Hastings. But they should be painted for us, so that we may study them in the warmth and comfort of our own home. That is why we pay the artist, for exposing himself to these conditions on our behalf.
—**Agatha Christie, Poirot: The Adventure of Clapham Cook**

4.1 WHAT IS SYSTEM?

The word "system" became quite common in our everyday language to the extent that there is some confusion in its usage between different communities. Indeed, this word is used rather often, as we speak of "the solar system," "a system of government," "a health system," "a system of winning poker," a "communication system," or a "weapon system," and in so doing, we imply certain *purposefulness* and some sort of *organization* imposed on various *elements* that *interact* between themselves. A system is something that involves and exhibits behavior—a set of *activities* that can be defined in terms of the manipulation of materials, energy, or information.

A standard definition of a system by IEEE: System is a collection of components organized to accomplish a specific *function* or set of functions [IEEE 610.12].

Systems are studied by the general systems theory—an interdisciplinary theory about the nature of complex organizations in nature, society, and science, and is a framework by which one can investigate and/or describe any group of elements that are functioning together to fulfill some objective (whether intended, designed, man made, or not).

A standard definition of a system from the systems engineering community: A composite, at any level of complexity, of personnel, procedures, materials, tools,

System Assurance: Beyond Detecting Vulnerabilities. DOI: 10.1016/B978-0-12-381414-2.00004-X equipment, facilities, and software. The elements of this composite entity are used together in the intended operational or support environment to perform a given task or achieve a specific production, support, or mission requirement. [Air Force 2000]

On the other hand, certain communities prefer to use the word "system" in its narrow and concrete meaning—such as a particular computer application, or a physical system, a facility with a specific geographic location that involves a certain technology to provide service. Concrete systems are procured by organizations and fielded to support organizations and their operations [DoDAF 2007]. The context in which a concrete technical system operates is referred to as an "organization," which is defined as "an organization structure with a mission." In a business community, the term "enterprise" is often used to refer to the complex socio-technical organizations designed to provide goods and services to their customers.

National Institute for Standards and Technology (NIST) equates "system" and "information system" [NIST SP 800-18] and defines "information system" as a discrete set of information resources organized for the collection, processing, maintenance, use, sharing, dissemination, or disposition of information.

Certain communities prefer to use the term "network," or "organization network" to mean a specific installation of personnel, operational procedures, technology, and physical facilities, that contain valuable information assets of the organization, in particular, the Network Rating Methodology from the National Security Agency (NSA) [Moore 2000].

The Information Technology Security community distinguishes a system, which is defined as a specific installation "with particular purpose and a known operational environment" and a product, which is defined as "a hardware and/or software package that can be bought off the shelf and incorporated into a variety of systems" [ISO 15408].

System assurance deals with man-made systems, created and utilized for the benefit of man. Cyber systems involve a combination of hardware, software, and humans. System assurance embraces the entire system life cycle from the conception of ideas through to the retirement of a system. System assurance supports the governance of systems and the processes for acquiring and supplying system products and services. Reasoning about systems for the purpose of evaluating security posture requires a common vocabulary that can be used to improve communication and cooperation between diverse disciplines and identify, utilize and manage relevant information units in an integrated, coherent fashion.

4.2 BOUNDARIES OF THE SYSTEM

The systems approach implies a *commitment* on our part to focus our attention only at the few selected *elements* (out of the entire universe), that are relevant to the particular *behavior* in question. For the systems approach to be applicable, it is important that the selected elements are discrete and identifiable. The set of elements selected as relevant to the system's behavior determine the so-called *external boundary* of the system. Systems approach involves another boundary that separates selected elements into the system and its *environment*. For a physical system, this boundary is usually the same as the scope of responsibility of the owner. A system performs its function as the result of *interaction* between its elements or subsystems. This interaction, which may be very complex indeed, generally insures that a system is not simply equal to the sum of its parts. Units of the system's behavior are the individual *functions* that are performed by the system's elements or the elements of its environment. The environment can include other systems that interact with the system of interest, either directly via *interfaces* or indirectly in other ways. The elements outside of the system boundary are only included because their interactions with the target system are relevant to the behavior of the system, therefore, any interactions between the elements of the environment of the system are usually ignored (see Figure 1).

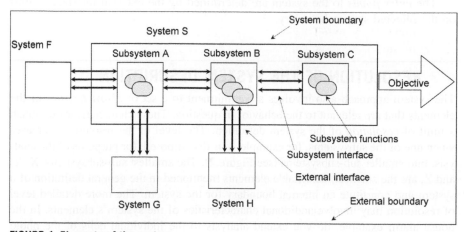

FIGURE 1 Elements of the system

System definition is based on the decision on where to draw the system's boundary. Consider a house alarm system. It includes a number of easily identifiable physical elements: several sensors, such as door/window contacts, motion sensors, glassbreak detectors, CO_2 detectors, smoke detectors, water detectors; a control panel; a siren; a lot of wires if you are using an older model; or a wireless network (some newer wireless models have sensors that wirelessly communicate to the wireless receiver of the control panel). The control panel is powered by electricity and has a 12V backup battery. Should the battery be included as part of the alarm system? A house alarm system usually includes a communicator module, which is connected to the monitoring station. What about the telephone line that is running from the control panel to the telephone jack in the wall? What about the external line that runs from the house to the telephone pole? What about the telephone switching equipment in the grey metal box down the street? Do we include the monitoring station as part of the house alarm system? What about the police department and the fire department that are alerted by the monitoring station? Should they be included as parts of the system? The decision to establish the system boundary is made on the basis of what aspect of the system behavior is of concern. For example, if the immediate concern is how to adjust the motion detector in the family room so that Charlie the dog does not activate it when he jumps on the couch, the system boundary may be closed in. However, if the problem involves the response time when the police arrive at the premises, the boundary needs to be broader.

The choice of the appropriate system boundary determines the soundness and complexity of the analysis. Selection of the system boundaries must be commensurate with the goals of the analysis. To reach certain conclusions about a system, it may be desirable to include more elements within the external boundary. This may require complex, time-consuming analysis. If the money, time, and staff available are inadequate for this task and more efficient analysis approaches are not possible, then the system boundary must be "moved in" and the amount of information expected to result from the analysis must be reduced [Vesely 1981].

The *entry points* to the system are determined by the external interfaces based on the selected system boundary.

4.3 RESOLUTION OF THE SYSTEM DESCRIPTION

The system approach also involves a commitment to a set of *characteristics* of the elements that are relevant to the behavior in question. These characteristics establish a limit of *resolution* of the system definition. The level of the resolution increases when one of the subsystems, for example B, is decomposed, for purposes of the analysis, into smaller sub-subsystems (see Figure 2). The smallest sub-subsystems, X, Y, and Z, are the smallest identifiable elements mentioned in the general definition of a system and constitute an internal boundary for the system. The more detailed level of resolution may involve additional characteristics of the system's elements. In the house alarm example, do you extend analysis to the individual cells of the photo sensor in the motion detector? What about the circuit board? Are you going to consider soldering on the circuit board? What about the molecular structure of the wires?

The limit of resolution (the internal boundary) must be established from considerations of feasibility and from the goal of the analysis. Once the limit of resolution has been established (and thus the "system's elements" defined), we assume no knowledge and are not concerned about interactions taking place at lower levels. Functions of the system elements are adjusted to the selected level of resolution to adequately describe the overall behavior of the system.

The same system can be described at various levels of resolution. In Figure 2, the interaction between subsystem B and system H (in the environment of the target system S), can be described directly at the top level of the resolution, or at a more detailed level of the protocol that involves subsystems X and Y. Functions of the subsystem B are implemented by the functions of the corresponding subsystems X, Y, and Z at a more detailed level of resolution.

We now see that the system boundary serves to delineate system *outputs* (effects of the system on its environment) and system *inputs* (effects of the environment on the system); the limits of resolution serve to define the elements of the system and to establish the basic interactions within the system.

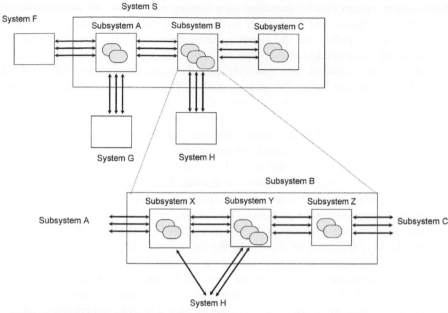

FIGURE 2 Determining system's boundaries

Cyber systems involve multiple layers of *protocols* and involve interactions between a multitude of systems; therefore, the security boundary that the owner of any given system has to be concerned about can be extremely large and complex. Vulnerabilities may occur in different components, often outside of the jurisdiction of the system's owner (and beyond his reach) or at lower levels of the protocol outside of the resolution of the original system definition. As the consequence, a rather detailed resolution of the system needs to be considered in order to understand and reduce the risk of cyber attacks.

4.4 CONCEPTUAL COMMITMENT FOR SYSTEM DESCRIPTIONS

It is important to understand that the determination of the system boundaries and limits of resolution are fundamental decisions of the system analysis. While certain elements of a system, such as the physical elements and their relationships, observable events, and the objects being exchanged are often predetermined by the corresponding *identifiable* objects in the real world, the functions of the elements are often *abstractions* introduced by the system analysis based on the selected level of resolution. In addition, certain system elements are introduced during the system analysis as *aggregations* of existing physical elements to lower the resolution and obtain a more compact and comprehensive system definition. For example, the home alarm system can be described as a sensing subsystem (an aggregation of all contacts, sensors, and detectors), a control subsystem (involving the control panel and all keypads), and the signaling subsystem (involving the siren and the communicator module and the monitoring station).

The system's elements, their characteristics, the system boundaries, and limits of resolution are defined before the security analysis begins and are adhered to during the analysis, because these elements constitute the *conceptual commitment* for the target system and the foundation of the *vocabulary* for describing any properties of the system of interest, including its security. However, in practical situations, the boundaries or limits of resolution may need to be adjusted because of information gained during the analysis, in particular, the level of resolution of some system elements may need to be increased to allow more accurate analysis. The system boundaries and limits of resolution, and any adjustments, must be clearly defined in order to facilitate information exchanges during the analysis of the system.

Now let us share a few comments, which will help put the material of this chapter into the bigger context of this book. We believe that the idea of a "conceptual commitment" is central for establishing an ecosystem for exchanging knowledge. Conceptual commitment means using a carefully preselected set of concepts (a vocabulary) to describe systems, their behaviors, security policy, safeguards, and the entire assurance case. The elements of such a preselected common vocabulary consist of nouns and noun phrases that describe individual entities/objects in the system and in any associated domains; and verbs and verb phrases that describe relationships between objects. We use a certain methodology to build discernable common vocabularies; this methodology helps identify *discernable* noun and verb concepts (this methodology is introduced in Chapter 9). Discernable concepts are important because they are unambiguous and allow maintaining traceability links to lower levels of resolution. Incidentally, the OMG Assurance Ecosystem includes standards that define how to exchange well-defined vocabularies and how to systematically transform a well-defined vocabulary into an XML schema for exchanging information about the individual objects. At the same time, the elements of the well-defined vocabulary are identifiable facts that can be stored in a database, or in a suitable fact-based repository. One of the characteristics of the OMG system assurance process is the use of the "integrated system model," which is stored in a fact-based repository. In the upcoming chapters we are going to introduce the elements of the common vocabulary for cybersecurity for the OMG Assurance Ecosystem. We will do that with varying degrees of formality, because this book is not a formal specification. This chapter will introduce the noun and verb concepts in a very informal way because we assume familiarity with the basic system engineering concepts, and also, because these concepts are, in general, well established and are used in a rather uniform way. However, keep in mind that when we are saying "identify," for example, "identify a system component," this means: use the definition of the "system component" from the common vocabulary, apply the definition to locate the corresponding object in the system of interest, and then add the corresponding facts into the integrated system model. When the objects are already known (because they were identified as part of a preexisting process in the life cycle of the system of interest), the task of "identification" is to map the existing definition to the common vocabulary and add the new facts to the integrated system model. The mapping between vocabularies is often required because different methodologies make different conceptual commitments.

When managing descriptions of the system at increasing levels of resolution, it is important to maintain the so-called *vertical traceability links* between the elements at different levels of resolution. In terms of a physical, fact-based repository, a traceability link is a particular relationship (a *fact*) in which one object is implemented by one or more other objects. For the purposes of the cost-efficient analysis, it is also important to be able to transfer the characteristics of systems, established at higher levels of the resolution, to the lower resolution descriptions (where there are fewer elements, with more abstract functions and characteristics), so that the majority of the analysis and managing of the information is done using the system description with the lower resolution. Chapter 9 provides further guidance related to managing multiple pieces of information, managing conceptual commitments, and describes the mechanisms for performing analysis at varying levels of resolution. Chapter 11 describes a standard protocol for exchanging system facts that extends the vertical traceability links all the way down to the very low-level implementation facts (such facts are discovered automatically by compiler-like tools).

The integrated system model also has the so-called "*horizontal links*," which are relationships between objects, based on the verb concepts defined in the common vocabulary. When facts from different vocabularies are integrated, for example, when we want to map a threat to a system function, we establish a physical relationship (a *fact*) between the two concepts from the two parts of the common vocabulary.

The rest of this chapter describes the elements of the common vocabulary for managing facts about the system of interest as part of the integrated system model in support of the system assurance process outlined in Chapter 3. Chapters 5, 6, and 7 describe other units of the cybersecurity knowledge used throughout the assurance process and shows how these facts are integrated with the system facts to support the security posture analysis and gathering evidence for the system's assurance case.

4.5 SYSTEM ARCHITECTURE

Knowledge about systems of concern to system assurance includes both the general knowledge of the systems theory and systems engineering, as well as specific knowledge about a particular system under assessment. System knowledge involves several *viewpoints*:

- **Hierarchy**: Systems, Subsystems, Units, Assemblies, Components, Parts, Activities, Protocols
- **Elements**: Hardware, Software, Personnel, Procedures, Entry points, Environments, Facilities, Documentation

- **Operations**: Functions, Tasks, Modes, Phases
- **Domains**: Boundaries, Zones, Organizational Boundaries, Criticality, Complexity, Security, Safety
- **Life cycle**: Activities, Enabling Systems, Supply Chain

These viewpoints are *interconnected:* a single identifiable element of a system participates in multiple relationships with other elements in other viewpoints. For example, a server participates in several hierarchies: A server *is part of* the accounting subsystem, and at the same time, it *is part of* the network of the data center unit. The accounting subsystem *is part of* the finance department hierarchy, which is in turn *part of* the organization of interest. However, the server *is owned by* a different organization, which leases it to the organization of interest. There are diverse hierarchies of elements associated with the server itself: The server *consists of* two RAID disk arrays, each with four hard disks; a processing unit, consisting of four core processors; a memory unit, consisting of four memory chips; a bus; two network controllers; and several other controllers of the peripheral devices. Another hierarchy associated with the server includes various software products *installed on* this server, including the operating system, device drivers, the transaction processing monitor, the application server, the web server, and various application programs. The server *supports* various functions, such as managing the ledger and managing the inventory; however, there are other equipment units that are also involved with these tasks, such as the database server, the network switch, the firewall, the desktop computers, etc. The server of interest *is associated with* several other hardware units that are part of the same network but that are involved in different business functions. Several personnel roles *are associated with* the server and various functions that it is involved with. The server *is located in* a certain facility. The server *supports* several interfaces (both at the logical level and at the physical level), including low levels of protocol; for example, the server supports web access over HTTP protocol, but at the same time supports TCP and IP protocols and the Ethernet protocol. The protocols *supported by* the server also constitute a hierarchy. Each of these viewpoints involves certain events and scenarios.

Life cycle processes bring another set of viewpoints to the system organization. The server *was manufactured by* another organization at yet a different location. The server *was installed by* yet another organization. A different organization *produced* the operating system. The web server software *is developed* using the open source model. A certain application program *uses* a web service provided by the human resources department of the organization of interest (which is located in a different facility in a different country). Another application *uses* a web service provided by an external organization. Most of the application software *was developed by* the personnel of the engineering department of the organization of interest, while the business objects layer *was implemented by* a contractor.

Different stakeholders of the system have specific concerns, and therefore, need different views of the system, which focus on the elements, hierarchies, and relationships that are relevant to their concerns. Facts about the system of interest are arranged into meaningful units, called *views*, which focus on a few elements and their relationships, tailored to the specific concerns of system's stakeholders. Each view is defined by the corresponding viewpoint, which describes what element types and relationship types need to be addressed by the compliant view. The viewpoint is an element of generic knowledge that is utilized as a template for building a view about the system.

Figure 3 illustrates an integrated system model that contains certain unique elements and relationships between them, including hierarchies. In particular, the model contains four types of elements (represented as circles with different shading), two types of relationships (thin and thick lines), and several overlapping hierarchies. The middle part of the figure illustrates three views of the system. Note that certain elements occur on multiple views, and that each view contains a limited selection of elements and relationships. The right part of the figure shows the viewpoints describing the views, which illustrates the rules for selection of the elements and relationships on each view. In particular, the top view only shows the white elements and how they are organized in hierarchies. It does not show black and grey elements, despite the fact that there are relationships to them. This view does not show the hierarchy of the grey elements either. The bottom two views share the same viewpoint. They focus on thick relationships between white, black, and grey elements, focusing on a certain initial element.

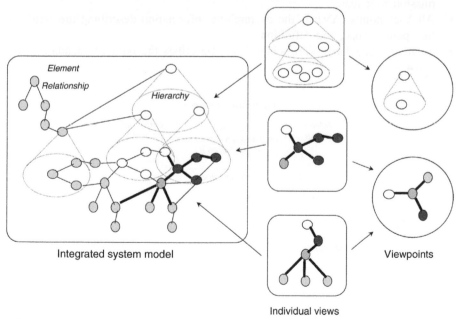

FIGURE 3 Illustration of integrated system model

ISO/IEC 42010 defines system architecture as "the fundamental organization of a system embodied in its components, their relationships to each other, and to the environment, and the principles guiding its design and evolution." The concept of views and viewpoints is central to the ISO architectural description of systems. The particular set of viewpoints is determined by a particular *architecture framework*, while the vocabulary for the system elements and their relationships is, to a large extent, specific to the system of interest.

Each viewpoint also defines a vocabulary and is thus part of the conceptual commitment for exchanging information about the system of interest.

4.6 EXAMPLE OF AN ARCHITECTURE FRAMEWORK

The US Department of Defense Architecture Framework (DoDAF) [DoDAF 2007] describes a particular set of 26 viewpoints to ensure uniformity and standardization in the documentation and communication of architecture. The 26 DoDAF viewpoints are designed to document the entire architecture, from requirements to implementation.

Viewpoints can be grouped into four categories of views (see Figure 4):

- Operational Viewpoints (OV): Focuses on the behaviors and functions describing the enterprise mission aspects.
- System Viewpoints (SV): Describes the system and applications supporting the mission functions.
- All Viewpoints (AV): Is the overarching information describing the architecture plans, scope, and definitions.
- Technical Standards Viewpoints (TV): Describes the policies, standards, and constraints.

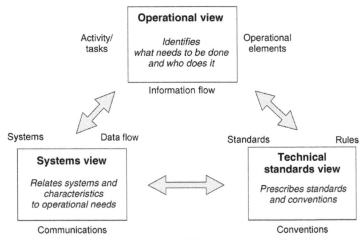

FIGURE 4 Department of Defense Architecture Framework Information Flow

Tables 1–4 illustrate the architecture views of the DoDAF. As you can see, these products represent the fundamental viewpoints described above.

Table 1 Department of Defense Architecture Framework Operational Views

Viewpoint	Framework Product	Description
High-level operational concepts graphic	OV-1	High-level graphical or textual description of operational concept
Operational node connectivity description	OV-2	Operational nodes, connectivity, and information exchange needlines between nodes
Operational information exchange matrix	OV-3	Information exchanged between nodes and the relevant attributes of the exchange
Organizational relationships chart	OV-4	Organizational, role, or other relationships among organizations
Operational activity diagram	OV-5	Capabilities, operational activities, relationships among activities, inputs, and outputs
Operational rules model	OV-6a	One of three products used to describe operational activity—identifies business rules that constrain operation
Operational state transition diagram	OV-6b	One of three products used to describe operational activity—identifies business process response to events
Operational event-trace description	OV-6c	One of three products used to describe operational activity—traces actions in a scenario or sequence of events
Logical data model	OV-7	Documentation of the system data requirements and structural business process rules of the operational view

Table 2 Department of Defense Architecture Framework System Views

Viewpoint	Framework Product	Description
System interface description	SV-1	Identification of system nodes, systems, and system items and their interconnections, within and between nodes
System communication description	SV-2	System nodes, systems, and system items, and their realized communication lay-downs

Continued

Table 2 Department of Defense Architecture Framework System Views—cont'd

Viewpoint	Framework Product	Description
System-System Matrix	SV-3	Relationships among systems in a given architecture; can be designed to show relationships of interest, e.g., system-type interfaces, planned vs existing interfaces, etc.
Systems functionality description	SV-4	Functions performed by systems and the system data flows among system functions
Operational activity to system function traceability matrix	SV-5	Mapping of system back to capabilities or of system functions back to operational activities
System data exchange matrix	SV-6	Provides details of system data elements being exchanged between systems and attributes of that exchange
Systems performance matrix	SV-7	Performance characteristics of system view elements for the appropriate time frames
Systems evolution description	SV-8	Planned incremental steps towards migrating a suite of systems to a more efficient suite, or toward evolving a current system to a future implementation
Systems technology forecast	SV-9	Emerging technologies and software/hardware products that are expected to be available in a given set of time frames and that will affect future development of the architecture
Systems rules model	SV-10a	One of the three products used to describe system functionality—identifies constraints that are imposed on systems functionality due to some aspect of systems design or implementation
Systems state-transition description	SV-10b	One of the three products used to describe system functionality—identifies responses of a system to events
System event-trace description	SV-10c	One of the three products used to describe system functionality—identifies system-specific requirements of critical sequences of events described in the operational view
Physical schema	SV-11	Physical implementation of the Logical Data Model entities, e.g., message formats, file structures, physical schema

Table 3 Department of Defense Architecture Framework Technology Views

Viewpoint	Framework Product	Description
Technical standards profile	TV-1	Listing of standards that apply to systems view elements in a given architecture
Technical standards forecast	TV-2	Description of emerging standards and potential impact on current system view elements within a set of time frames

Table 4 Department of Defense Architecture Framework all Views

Viewpoint	Framework Product	Description
Overview and summary information	AV-1	Scope, purpose, intended users, environment depicted, analytical findings
Integrated dictionary	AV-2	Architecture data repository with definitions of all items used in all products

4.7 ELEMENTS OF A SYSTEM

System description uses the following fundamental elements:

- System elements (referred to as subsystems, components, or nodes);
- Relations between the system elements (referred to as channels or interfaces);
- System functions (activities that comprise the system's behavior; functions are performed by nodes);
- Relations between the system functions (dependencies between the activities);
- Objects that are exchanged between the functions (in many cases, these are limited to information elements, but in a general system, these objects can include material objects, energy, even people, for example, when describing the National Hockey League as a system that involves exchanges between various clubs).

Systems can be described at several increasing levels of resolution. At a minimum, there are two such levels: operational and systems.

Operational viewpoints describe the tasks and activities, operational elements, and information exchanges required to conduct operations. Operational viewpoints involve the following key noun concepts:

Operational node is an element of the operational architecture that produces, consumes, or processes information. Usually an operational node represents an operational role, fulfilled by an organization or a human, and organization, or an organization type, a logical grouping of organizations, etc.

Information exchange needline represents a need for some kind of information exchange between two connected operational nodes. A needline represents a flow of information, and not a physical communications link.

Information exchange is an act of exchanging information between two distinct operational nodes and the characteristics of the act, including the information element that needs to be exchanged and the characteristics of the exchange; for example, transaction type, access control requirement, confidentiality, integrity, availability, dissemination control, protection needs, classification, and classification caveat.

Information element is the information content that is required to be exchanged between nodes. Information elements can be organized in hierarchies.

Operational activity is an action performed in conducting the operation of the enterprise.

Operational activity is performed at operational node. Activities can be organized in hierarchies. Operational capability is one or more sequences of activities.

Event is a specification of a significant occurrence that has a location in time and space. In the context of state diagram, an event is an occurrence that can trigger a transition.

State is defined as a condition or situation during the life of an object during which it satisfies some condition, performs some activity, or waits for some event.

Figure 5 illustrates the operational views and their relationships.

Systems viewpoints describe systems, services, and interconnections supporting operations. System viewpoints involve the following noun concepts.

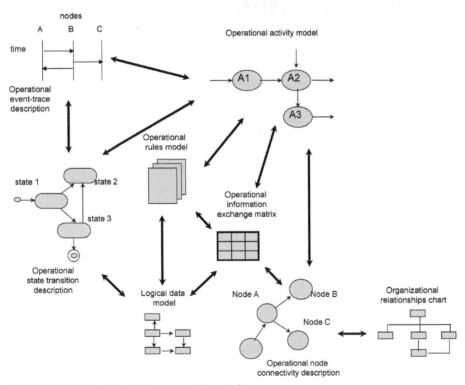

FIGURE 5 Relationships between operational views

Systems node – a node with the identification and allocation of resources (e.g., platforms, units, facilities, and locations) required to implement specific roles and missions.

System item – an element of a system, such as a hardware item or a software item.

Service – a distinct part of the functionality that is provided by a system on one side of the interface to some other system on the other side of the interface to include those capabilities to execute a business or mission process or exchange information among both machine and human users via standard interfaces and specifications.

Interface is an abstract representation of one or more communication paths between system nodes or between systems (including communication systems).

System function – a data transform that supports the automation of operational activities or information exchange.

Figure 6 illustrates the relationships between the operational and system views.

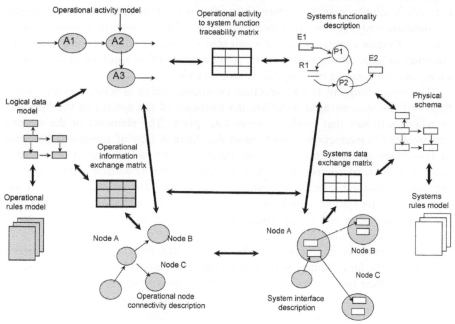

FIGURE 6 Relationships between the operational and system views

4.8 SYSTEM KNOWLEDGE INVOLVES MULTIPLE VIEWPOINTS

A system can be described from multiple viewpoints. We need to examine various viewpoints in more detail to decide which of them is more suitable to contain the *"location"* of vulnerability.

The following are the major categories of viewpoints:

- The Event Trace viewpoint
- The Structure viewpoint
- The Data Flow viewpoint
- The "Rules" viewpoint
- The State Transition viewpoint

The Event Trace viewpoint is literally the most visible one, because event flow views describe sequences of events. Events are individual, observable occurrences. What occurrence is claimed to be observable is determined by the selection of the boundaries of the system, both external and internal. Usually, events are observable at the external boundary of the system. The Event Trace view shows the system in operation, as it can be perceived by an outside observer. Event Trace view shows information exchanges between the elements of the system. Event Trace is often described as a dynamic viewpoint that represents behaviors of the system as sequences of events in the order in which they occurred in time. Certain events may occur simultaneously. Certain events that occur together (either in sequence or simultaneously) can be combined into "phases," which are often confused with "states." Certain events and event sequences (at some resolution, of course) are common to large families of systems. A debug trace of an application is an event view, and the contents of a log file is an event view.

The next viewpoint is the Structure viewpoint, which is related to the "locations" of the systems as it describes the elements of the system as the "places" in which activities that produce events take place. The elements of the system are involved in interactions, which mean that there is flow of something between various elements. The Structure viewpoint defines the participants of the interactions, which is, of course, determined by the external boundaries (the scope of the system) and the selected resolution. Some of the "places" are directly at the boundary of the system, which means they are the discrete points of interaction between the system and its environment. These elements are often referred to as the system "entry points."

Additional Structure views can be used to represent various relationships between nodes; for example, an organizational relationship chart represents organizations and their parts, roles, and other relationships among organizations.

The events are correlated with the flow of objects, although a software intensive system is mainly about the flow of information. This viewpoint can describe the flow of money, the flow of color, the flow of goods, and the flow of personnel, even the flow of service offerings, or the flow of knowledge. The Data Flow viewpoint describes how data flows between the activities of the system or between the activities and the system's environment as the system performs its function. This viewpoint emphasizes the capabilities and operational activities of the system, the relationships between activities, their inputs and outputs, etc.

Flows of data and events are determined by some rules that distinguish one system from another. The Rules viewpoint is the static viewpoint that describes the elements of the system, the events they cause, and the rules they impose on the event flow, the associated data flow, how these rules determine the possible events of the system in operation, and how the rules constrain possible behaviors, which are sequences of events. The code of a software application is an example of a Rules view.

Now we have defined all the ingredients, and we can define the concept of a *state*, which is somewhat more elusive. In general, state is defined as a *condition* or mode with regards to circumstances or with regards to form, such as structure, growth, or development. State is a very fundamental concept, but it is the least visible one, since it is an abstraction of behavior.

State corresponds to a "stable" condition of the system of interest, at a certain period of time, that is determined by the behavior of the system at the previous periods. Usually, a state can be described by a simpler subset of the behavior rules. Behavior of a stateless system does not depend on the previous periods. As opposed to the behavior *phases* (or event-based states), systems may easily have an infinite number of states. Defining vulnerabilities in terms of states should be avoided, because of the difficulties in systematic examination of all states. Viewpoints as locations of vulnerabilities are illustrated at Figure 7.

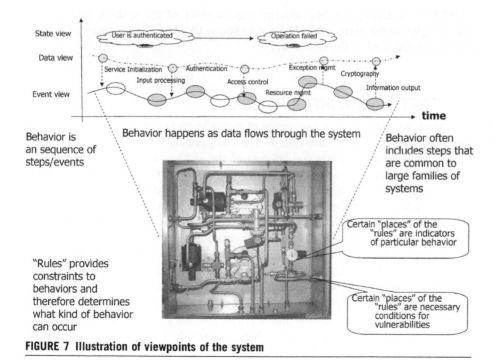

FIGURE 7 Illustration of viewpoints of the system

Additional viewpoints may be needed to address the concerns of other stake-holders of the system. For example, the Motivation viewpoint describes the objectives of the system (the ends) and the mechanisms (the means) that are used to achieve the objectives.

4.9 CONCEPT OF OPERATIONS (CONOP)

The CONOP (sometimes called ConOps) stands for the Concept of Operations. CONOP is a brief overview of a system at a low resolution. Usually, a CONOP document addresses the following questions:

- What does the system do for the organization?
- Who are the stakeholders? In particular, who are the User and other key players, such as the System Operator, the System Security Officer, etc.?
- What is the motivation for deploying the system (e.g., what current deficiencies are addressed for which the IT requirements are defined)?
- When are the main activities occurring? (the event flow view)?
- What are the main activities (decision points)?
- What are the connection points to other systems?

CONOP also defines the key security requirements of the system, such as the access rights of the users and their need-to-know. Chapter 12 illustrates a CONOP for the system used in the case study.

4.10 NETWORK CONFIGURATION

In general, a *computation* is a sequence of steps/events performed by the system or one of the activities within the system. The computation is performed by the code, which is supported by other components of the system. Code provides the constraints to computations and therefore, determines which computations can occur. For example, the computation is determined by the control flow relationships between individual activities, and further by the data flow relationships describing how individual activities act as producers and consumers of data. These relationships are the constraints for the computation (see Figure 7).

In order to analyze a computation, all system components have to be considered, including the so-called *application code*, but also the *runtime platform* and all runtime services, as some of the key control and data flow relationships are provided by the runtime platform, as the computation flows through the application code into the runtime platform and services and back to the application code. Application code alone in most cases does not provide an adequate picture of the computation, as some segments of the flow are determined by the runtime platform and *are not visible* in the application code. For example, while a large number of control flow relationships between different activities in the application code are *explicit* (such as statements in a sequence, or calls from a statement to another procedure), some control flow relations are *not visible* in the code, including the so-called callbacks, where the application code registers a certain activity with the runtime platform (for example, an event handler or an interrupt handler) and it is the runtime platform that initiates the activity. Without the knowledge of such implicit relationships, the system knowledge is not complete at a very fundamental level, leading to incomplete coverage of code analysis by vulnerability detection tools, and subsequently, to false negative and false positive report findings.

A system is a collection of activities that exchange information to achieve some common purpose. Computations occur at *system nodes* that are connected by *channels*. Following the NIST Common Vulnerability Scoring System (CVSS) [NIST IR-7435 2007], [Schiffman 2004] approach we distinguish *local channels* between system nodes deployed at the same machine, *adjacent network channels* between system nodes deployed at the same local area network, and *remote channels*. This distinction is important because it determines the class of *access* required in order to exploit vulnerability. Each system node performs *computation* to provide *services* to other system nodes or the environment of the entire system. Data interchanges use channels. We distinguish between *data at rest* (for example, databases), *data in motion* (data in the channel), and *data in use* (data flowing inside the computation) (see Figure 8).

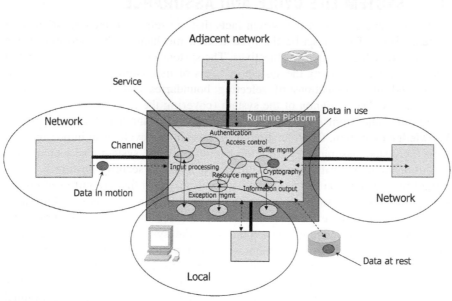

FIGURE 8 Network context for computation

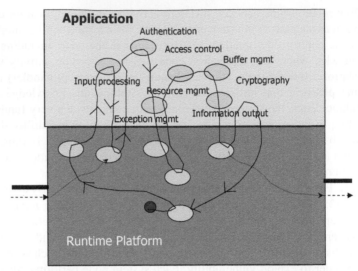

FIGURE 9 Runtime platform – the key component when assessing system

The runtime platform manages *resources* on behalf of the application. This is a very important consideration, as, in fact, many vulnerabilities are related to the usage of the resources (see Figure 9).

4.11 SYSTEM LIFE CYCLE AND ASSURANCE

So far we have addressed the system facts that are related to the *operations* of a system. These facts describe the system as a mechanism that performs some activities to achieve required objectives. The system facts addressed the common vocabulary for describing the system in terms of its components, functions, and rules, and the implications of selecting boundaries and resolutions of such descriptions. The *evolution* of the system (covering the time from conception to operations, and from operations to disposal) bring another dimension to the knowledge of system. Consideration of the system life cycle is an important concern for system assurance because the evolution of the system also includes the evolution of its security posture. Ultimately, a strong security posture is determined by organization of the system (the various rules that are enforced during the operation of the system, whether by technical mechanisms, physical mechanisms, or administrative measures). However, the confidence in the security posture involves knowledge of the evolution of the system, and claims regarding various aspects of how the system was put together. Cyberdefense measures extend to the early phases of the system life cycle: Defenders need to be confident that the desired security mechanisms are built correctly so that they are available during the operations as efficient elements of the operational defense. In order to achieve this, additional defense mechanisms are designed and added to upstream activities of the system life cycle. The *evolutionary countermeasures* are accounted for in the system assurance case together with the *operational countermeasures*. Claims about evolutionary countermeasures involve knowledge of system life cycle activities prior to operations, and sometimes also of the activities involved in the disposal of the system.

The system life cycle involves multiple activities. ISO/IEC 15288:2008, "Systems and software engineering—system life cycle processes," defines a standard framework for describing the system life cycle in terms of various activities involved in creating and utilizing systems. Collectively these activities are bringing together the elements of the future system and are imposing the required organization upon them so that the system emerges, and when launched into operation, its elements are engaged in coordinated interactions that satisfy the objective of the system. The system assurance process as described in Chapter 3 is a logical cross section of the diverse activities throughout the system life cycle organized together to systematically build confidence in the security posture of the system.

4.11.1 System life cycle stages

The system life cycle framework defined in ISO/IEC 15288:2008 [ISO 15288] focuses on the underlying essential set of characteristic life cycle *stages* that exist in the complete life cycle of any system that exists, despite a necessary and apparently limitless variety in system life cycles. Life cycles vary according to the nature, purpose, use, and prevailing circumstance of the system. However, the system life cycle activities can be arranged into several common categories, which become parts of the common vocabulary for descriptions of systems. The first such categorization is based on the evolutionary timeline. Evolution of each system can be arranged into several stages. Each stage has a distinct purpose and contribution to the whole life cycle and is to be considered when planning and executing the system lifecycle (see Table 5).

Table 5 System's Life Cycle Stages and Their Purpose

Life Cycle Stages	Purpose
Concept	Identify stakeholder's needs Explore concepts Propose viable solution
Development	Refine system requirements Create solution description Build system Verify and validate system
Production	Mass produce system Inspect and test
Utilization	Operate system to satisfy user's needs
Support	Provide sustained system capability
Retirement	Store, archive, or dispose of the system

The stages provide a framework within which enterprise management has high-level visibility and control of the project and technical processes. The stages describe the major progress and achievement milestones of the system through its life cycle; they give rise to the primary decision gates of the life cycle. These decision gates are used by organizations to contain the inherent uncertainties and risks associated with costs, schedule, and functionality when they create or utilize a system.

4.11.2 Enabling systems

Throughout the life cycle of a system of interest, essential services are required from systems that are not directly a part of the operational environment, e.g., development system, production system, training system. Each of these systems enables a certain stage of the system of interest to be conducted and facilitates progression through the system life cycle. These enabling systems contribute indirectly to the services provided by the system of interest when it is being utilized.

As with any system, each enabling system also has its *own* life cycle. Each enabling system's life cycle is linked and synchronized to that of the system of interest, specifying, in particular, when a need for it is specified during conception of the system of interest, or later, if lead times permit, and when the enabling system is operated to provide its particular service to the system of interest.

This has profound implications to the system assurance process. Some of the security controls (safeguards) for the system of interest are applied to the system of interest itself. For example, in a home security system, there is a requirement to install a sensor on every entrance door and on every glass panel of the ground floor of the building; such safeguards can often be examined during the assessment of the system of interest as they are implemented by certain artifacts within the scope of the system of interest; other requirements applied to the system of interest include administrative controls, for example, the requirement that the residents entering the building receive training regarding tailgating.

On the other hand, some of the security controls are applied to one of the enabling systems; for example, adequate testing of the door sensors by the manufacturer is applied to the production system, and adequate design of the sensors is an example of a security control applied to the development system. The system of interest, as well as any of the enabling systems, includes people, process, hardware and software elements, its own operational environment, facilities, etc. For example, system assurance may involve several physical security controls, separate for the development system facilities, production system facilities, and the facilities of the system of interest. Each system involves its own threat model. In general, each system has its own risk management process; however, from the viewpoint

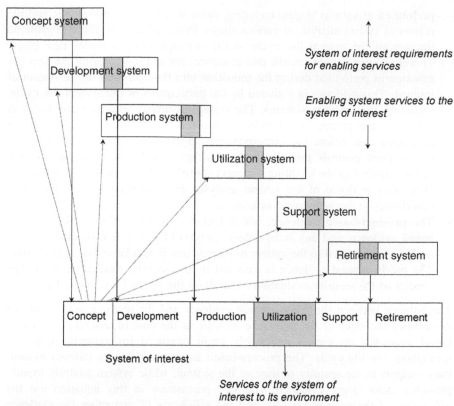

System of interest requirements
for enabling services

Enabling system services to the
system of interest

Services of the system of
interest to its environment

FIGURE 10 System of interest and supporting services from enabling system

of the system of interest, there are often contractual relations in place to deliver assurance back to the main assurance process of the system of interest, because threats to the enabling systems may have consequences affecting the system of interest (see Figure 10).

These considerations determine the *location* of the security controls and the *sources of evidence* for assurance. Security posture of the system of interest (during its operation) is affected by *all* stages of *all* enabling systems. Therefore, the security controls need to be placed to all critical systems, based on the combined threat model. The evidence for the security evaluation consists of two major categories:

- The **process-based evidence**, which includes the records of security-related activities throughout the system life cycle, including those in the system of interest and in the enabling systems; the results of verification and validation performed at various stages, including those in the enabling systems; and the results of system analysis at various stages. Process-based evidence is gathered throughout the system life cycle as the corresponding activities take place. Therefore, one cannot retrofit this evidence, for example, during the security assessment performed during the transition into the operation of the system of interest. This evidence is gathered by the participants of the system life cycle, including the enabling systems. The system assurance activities that result in gathering the process-based evidence must be planned through the system assurance case before the corresponding stages take place. The evidence of the security controls throughout the concept, development, and production phases (including the enabling systems) contribute to the process-based assurance. The evidence of the system analysis throughout the system life cycle contributes to the goal-based assurance.

- The **product-based evidence**, which includes the evaluation of the process-based evidence, and any independent analysis of the system of interest. This analysis is restricted to the system of interest and is to a large extent predictive. The product-based evidence is gathered by the security evaluation team. The verdict of the security evaluation is based on the product-based evidence.

The balance between the process-based evidence and the product-based evidence determines the rigor of the assurance as well as the cost of assurance. Process-based assurance involves a reasonably small overhead for gathering evidence throughout the life cycle. The process-based assurance provides *indirect* evidentiary support to the security posture of the system, while system analysis usually provides more *direct* evidence. The key parameters in this equation are the efficiency of the system analysis, and the efficiency of managing the evidence items and evaluating them within the context of the system assurance case.

Utilization stage enabling systems are of particular importance to assurance of the operational risk because their operational stages coexist with the operational stage of the system of interest. They include, among others, operating system, services that are utilized by the system of interest, support infrastructure, such as power supply or internet provisioning, operator training system, and user training systems. Security safeguards applied to these systems have more direct impact on mitigating the operational risk of the system of interest.

4.11.3 Supply chain

Each enabling system may itself be considered as a system of interest, having in turn its own enabling systems. For system assurance, it is important to understand the entire *supply chain organization*. It is very common that multiple components of the system of interest and its immediate enabling systems are preexisting, off-the-shelf components (for example, commercially available hardware, operating systems, programming languages and the corresponding programming environments, configuration management systems, and network equipment, to name just a few key elements of a software intensive system). Some of these components are directly integrated as parts of the system of interest, while other components contribute indirectly by enabling the development and production stages of the life cycle of the system of interest, and thus, affecting its elements. Preexisting components limit the end-to-end assurance of the system of interest because certain security controls cannot be enabled, and the corresponding evidence may not be available. Since the initial level of assurance of the preexisting components may be low (the initial assurance is the assurance case that is provided with the component), assurance must rely on the evaluation evidence resulting from the direct evaluation of the artifacts of the system of interest.

4.11.4 **System life cycle processes**

The system life cycle framework, defined in ISO/IEC 152888:2008, involves the following four groups of processes.

1. **Enterprise processes**: The enterprise processes manage the organization's capability to acquire and supply system products or services through the initiation, support, and control of projects.
2. **Agreement processes**: Establishment of agreements with organizational entities external to the organization and internal to the organization. The agreement processes consist of the acquisition process—used by acquiring organization—and the supply process—used by supplying organizations. System assurance is often an important item for agreement between an acquirer and the supplier.
3. **Project management processes**: The project management processes are used to establish and evolve project plans, to assess actual achievement and progress against the plans, and to control execution of the project through to fulfillment.
4. **Technical processes**: The technical processes are used to define the need for a system and to transform that need into an effective product, to permit consistent reproduction of the product where necessary, to utilize the product to provide the required services, to sustain the provision of those services and, when the product is retired from service, to dispose of that product.

Enterprise processes provide the *context* for the system assurance process. According to ISO/IEC 15288:2008, the enterprise processes include the enterprise management process, investment management process, system life cycle management process, and resource management process. These processes are often referred to as the *enterprise governance*.

Enterprise management produces strategic and tactical plans and objectives for system life cycle management, including quality management, assurance, and control in accordance with ISO 9001. Enterprise management is the main *consumer* of the system assurance, which contributes to the assessment of the impact of security on strategic and tactical plans to review the system life cycle policies and procedures and confirm their continuing suitability, adequacy and effectiveness, and make changes as appropriate.

The system assurance process, as it is outlined in Chapter 3, must be managed together with other life cycle processes because it consumes resources of the enterprise, and is usually considered a good investment, which enables the organization to become more competitive within a larger supply chain, and not only a "necessary evil" to satisfy the mandatory regulatory requirements [NDIA 2008].

According to ISO/IEC 15288:2008, the project management processes include the planning process, assessment process, control process, decision making process, risk management process, and configuration management process. Project management processes contain *locations* in which many important process-based administrative safeguards are applied.

The project definition phase of the system assurance process, as outlined in Chapter 3, is the point of alignment with the enterprise processes, including the determination of the objectives, the criteria, and the budget of the assurance. Assurance case enables rational decision making regarding the activities involved in achieving strong security posture of the system by identifying the actions that provide adequate justification, including the rationalization of safeguards and the corresponding arguments and evidence. Assurance case is an instrument for *rational governance* of the system life cycle activities because it identifies and justifies what safeguards will be implemented (e.g., trusted supplier selection, trusted component acquisition, programming language selection, anti-virus tool use), and what evidence must be collected to justifiably achieve the required security posture at the desired level of assurance. Assurance case development clarifies the interaction between functionality, cost, schedule, security, safety, dependability, and other attributes of the system so that the appropriate trade-offs can be made through risk management. System assurance is tightly related with the risk assessment process because the knowledge of the operational environment and the particular threats is an input to the system assurance process, where it is used to justify the efficiency of the security safeguards.

System assurance, including the assurance case development and maintenance, system evaluation, and evidence gathering is executed as part of the technical processes of the system life cycle. According to ISO/IEC 15288:2008, the technical processes include the following:

- **Stakeholder requirements definition process**: This process defines the need for a system that can provide services to users and other stakeholders in a defined environment. This is achieved by developing a model, frequently textual, that concentrates on system purpose and behavior and is described in the context of the operational environment and conditions. The stakeholder requirements identify the parties involved with the system throughout its life cycle and express their needs, wants, desires, and expectations, together with the constraints they and the operational environment impose. This involves capturing, clearly articulating, and managing the requirements of each and every stakeholder, or stakeholder class, in a form that permits continuous tracing of decisions to their needs throughout the life cycle. The Stakeholder

Requirements are the reference against which each and every resulting operational system services is validated in order to confirm that the system fulfills needs.

- **Requirements analysis process**: This process transforms the stakeholder, needs-driven view of desired system services into a technical view of required system products that could deliver those services. The resulting system requirement specifies, from the developer's perspective, what the system is required to do in order to satisfy stakeholder needs. The objective is to build a representation of future system products that will meet stakeholder needs, and that, as far as constraints permit, avoids implementation issues. The system requirements are the basis for tests that verify the conformance of a supplied system to the designers' intended solution.
- **Architectural design process**: This process synthesizes a solution that satisfies system requirements. Architectural design involves identifying and exploring one or more implementation strategies at a level of resolution consistent with the system's technical and commercial requirements and risks. From this, a design solution is defined in terms of the requirements for a complete set of technically and commercially viable components from which the system is configured. The architectural design is also a basis for planning and devising an assembly and test strategy that will detect and diagnose faults during the integration steps.
- **Implementation process**: This process implements a component required in an acquirer's system. This may be achieved by designing, making, and testing a novel component; making and testing a new component according to an existing design; or adapting and testing an existing component. The implementation process continues the design undertaken at the system/subsystem levels by performing detailed design in accordance with selected implementation technologies. The component is fabricated and/or assembled according to the selected implementation technologies. A fabricated or adapted component is tested against criteria derived from the component characteristics defined in the system requirements and possibly in an acquisition agreement.
- **Integration processes**: The verified components are assembled to create the system product specified in the system requirements.
- **Verification process**: Through assessment of the system product, verification demonstrates that its behavior and characteristics comply with its specified design requirements. Verification provides the information required to effect the remedial actions that correct failings in the realized system or the processes that act on it.
- **Transition process**: The transition process installs the verified system in its operational locations according to an agreed schedule, together with the utilization stage enabling systems (e.g., operating system, support system, operator training system, user training system), as defined in agreements, in order to establish the capability to provide the system services specified by the stakeholder needs.

- **Validation process:** The validation process is conducted to provide objective evidence that the services provided by the system when in use comply with the needs of the stakeholders and are defined in the requirements documents contained in the agreement to acquire the system. Where variances are identified, these are recorded and guide corrective actions. Since validation is a comparative assessment against needs, it also results in confirmation that stakeholders', and in particular the users', needs were correctly identified and requested; again, variances lead to corrective actions.
- **Operation and maintenance process**: The operation and maintenance process enables staffing and training personnel for operation and maintenance activities, operating the system, maintaining the system, monitoring the system and the operator-system performance, and recording problems for analysis.
- **Disposal processes:** The disposal process is applied to deactivate and remove the system from operational service, consigning it to a final condition, and returning the environment to its original or an acceptable condition. System elements are destroyed, stored, and/or reclaimed in an environmentally sound manner.

Security-related system assurance makes security considerations *visible* throughout the entire system life cycle, which allows systematic analysis of all factors contributing to the security posture of the system and planning the related activities and safeguards in a cost-efficient, timely, and consistent manner. The value of an end-to-end assurance case is that the systematic and objective development of the security argument and claims accumulates knowledge related to the security posture in a single integrated system model; extends justification to the existing risk management and security activities; and accumulates evidence from multiple sources.

4.11.5 The implications to the common vocabulary and the integrated system model

System life cycle considerations, including the stages and the technical processes, enabling systems, and the supply chain has implications to the common vocabulary for describing system facts and the organization of the integrated system model for assurance.

The integrated system model no longer has only one system boundary; it needs to include the boundaries of various enabling systems (commensurate with the selected scope of assurance). Relationships between system elements must include evolutionary relations, where an element of an enabling system creates an element of the system of interest. The integrated system model must include the organizational boundaries and attributes of the supply chain elements.

Finally, the integrated system model must be able to include the system life cycle processes and their activities in order to provide traceability links between the safeguards and the corresponding activities in the system life cycle (see Figure 11).

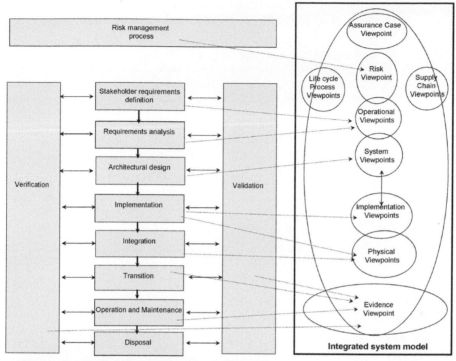

FIGURE 11 System life cycle with corresponding views

Bibliography

Air Force *System Safety Handbook*. (2000). Air Force Safety Agency Kirtland AFB NM 87117-5670.

DoD Architecture Framework. 1.5. (2007).

IEEE Std 610.12-1990 *IEEE Standard Glossary of Software Engineering Terminology Description*. (1990).

ISO/IEC 15408-1:2005 *Information Technology – Security Techniques - Evaluation Criteria for IT Security Part 1: Introduction and General Model*. (2005)

ISO/IEC 15288-1:2008 *Life Cycle Management – System Life Cycle Processes*. (2008).

NDIA, *Engineering for System Assurance Guidebook*. (2008)

Moore, A. P., & Strohmayer, B. (2000). *Visual NRM User's Manual: Tools for Applying the Network Rating Methodology*. Naval Research Lab Washington DC Center For Computer High Assurance Systems.

NIST SP 800-18 *Information Security Guide for Developing Security Plans for Federal Information Systems*. (2006).

NIST Interagency Report 7435 *The Common Vulnerability Scoring System (CVSS) and Its Applicability to Federal Agency Systems*. (2007). Mell, P., Scarfone, K., Romanosky, S.

Schiffman, M., Eschelbeck, G., Ahmad, D., Wright, A., & Romanosky, S. (2004). CVSS: A Common Vulnerability Scoring System. National Infrastructure Advisory Council (NIAC).

Vesely, W. E., Goldberg, F. F., Roberts, N. H., & Haasl, D. F. (1981). *Fault Tree Handbook*. NUREG-0492, US Nuclear Regulatory Commission.

Knowledge of risk as an element of cybersecurity argument

5

> *How infinitely good that Providence is, which has settled in its government of mankind such narrow bounds to his sight and knowledge of things; and though he walks in the midst of so many thousand dangers, the sight of which, if discovered to him, would distract his mind and sink his spirits, he is kept serene and calm, by having the events of things hid from his eyes, and knowing nothing of the dangers which surround him.*
>
> —**Daniel Defoe**, *Robinson Crusoe*

5.1 INTRODUCTION

Each new cyber system creates new opportunities and causes new risks. Knowledge of specific risks, including unique threats and undesired events related to the system of interest is critical for the system assurance process, as described in Chapters 2 and 3. Risk assessment produces an estimate of the risk of security incidents involving the cybersystem of interest. It answers the following questions:

- *What* can go wrong?
- How *bad* could it be?
- How *likely* is it to occur?

Answers to these questions produce a measure of risk that is used to prioritize risks during the risk management process. Should the management of this risk be through reduction, then the safeguard selection process provides answers to the question:

What could be done to reduce the exposure?

The key to justified cybersecurity is the connection between traditional risk assessment and assurance to create an end-to-end *argument* that the risk of security incidents during the operation of the system is made as low as reasonably practicable by implementing safeguards that are effective against the risks identified. Confidence in the security posture of the system largely depends on understanding the risks that are specific to the system. Systematic and repeatable identification of

System Assurance: Beyond Detecting Vulnerabilities. DOI: 10.1016/B978-0-12-381414-2.00005-1

risks is therefore essential for justifiable cybersecurity. While it is true to say that risks arise from *uncertainty*, justifiable cybersecurity focuses on such *components* of risk that are deterministic and predictable.

The two fundamental questions of identifying risks are "What is the risk *to*?" and "From what *sources* does the risk originate?" *Assets* are the targets of risk. *Threats* are the sources of risk. Threats are different from both *threat agents* and attacks. An *attack* is a particular scenario of how a given threat materializes and turns into a security incident. Detailed understanding of the components of cyber threats is required for making comprehensive threat statements, selecting counter-measures, and formulating clear and comprehensive claims regarding the effective-ness of these countermeasures. Knowledge of threats determines the structure of the assurance argument as described earlier in Chapter 3.

It is a common understanding that development teams that collectively have detailed knowledge of the design and implementation of the system are not well suited to identify threats. Developers focus on features, on building and creating, not on breaking things apart and finding flaws. There is a conceptual gap between what a development team knows about the system and what needs to be known about the ways the system can be attacked. In order to adequately identify threats, the risk assessment team must have comprehensive knowledge of the shady land-scape of cyber crime, the experience of the incidents and attacks. Consequently, one risk analysis team performs better than another. What matters is the security experience, including knowledge of attacks that were successful. Are the former hackers the best people to perform risk assessment? Several risk analysis text-books, especially those aiming at improving the security skills of developers, rec-ommend *brainstorming* as the method for identifying threats. Of course, at the end each team produces a set of risks to manage and provides some recommendations on additional countermeasures. Yet there is a need for justified confidence that no more threats of the same or larger magnitude exist.

Some organizations favor penetration testing as the method of assessing their secu-rity posture. The so-called 'red team' of ethical hackers may be contracted to identify security risks. However in order to be comprehensive, penetration testing depends on the same knowledge that is required to identify threats by reviewing the design and implementation artifacts. As a result, penetration testing is plagued by the same subjectivity. A more experienced team may identify more problems but nevertheless leaves open the question of what problems may still be remain unidentified.

Ad hoc methods for identifying security holes in cybersystems are sufficient for hackers; however, the risk assessment process underlying cyberdefense must be *systematic*.

So how can risk assessment be made more systematic, repeatable, and objective to provide a solid foundation for system assurance? One approach is to accumulate cybersecurity knowledge and distribute it to the defenders. Accumulating attack knowledge can make risk assessment more repeatable by applying accredited and up-to-date *checklists*, so that even an unexperienced risk analyst can be systematic in the process—for example, when a list of the key words describing the system can be used to *query* a comprehensive attack knowledge repository—and produce a credible list of threats. When such a resource is available early in the system's life cycle, many mistakes and inconsistencies in the downstream processes can be avoided. The OMG Software Assurance Ecosystem emphasizes development of the *standard protocols* for exchanging cybersecurity knowledge based on the system facts, which facilitate the transformation of cybersecurity knowledge into machine-readable *content* that can be accumulated, exchanged, and used as input into automated assurance tools. Accumulation and distribution of cybersecurity knowledge from more experienced analysts all the way down to the defenders of individual systems require more attention to the exchange standards. Cybersecurity knowledge should be systematically collected and accumulated, unlocked from the tools, and distributed from the few experts onto the larger community. This means knowledge should be turned into a *commodity*, in very much the same way as electricity was unlocked from disconnected closed-circuit proprietary systems that included production, transmission, and consumption into a normalized, interconnected "grid" that led to the explosive growth of how electricity is utilized.

Currently, there is a large knowledge gap between attackers and defenders. Collaborative cybersecurity and accumulation of cybersecurity knowledge is the starting point for closing this gap. Once collaboration in the area of cybersecurity picks up, risk assessments will become more repeatable, but will this also lead to more affordable cybersecurity? Many believe that it will. Once the cyberdefense community understands what knowledge has to be accumulated and exchanged, then standards and other protocols for communicating the knowledge will become progressively more efficient and automated tools will appear.

The complementary approach to more systematic risk assessment is through the development of an integrated *assurance case* that extends claims and arguments to the identification of threats. System assurance focuses on the justification aspect of both engineering and risk assessment. Justified identification of threats provides the foundation for selecting security countermeasures and contributes to justification of the countermeasures' effectiveness. In particular, during the identification of threats it is important that the risk assessment team provide clear and defendable justification that sufficient threats have been identified (commensurate with the selected security criteria).

Since it is prohibitively expensive—and probably impossible—to safeguard information and assets against *all* threats, modern security practice is based on assessing threats and vulnerabilities with regard to the risk each presents, and then selecting appropriate, cost-effective countermeasures. Systematic identification of threats is particularly important in justifying such a balance, which otherwise leads to unknowingly accepting high risks.

Assessing the *level of threat* is even more difficult than identifying the threat itself. The level of threat is the measure of the probability of the threat event and the measure of the associated impact. The threat and its level are often collectively referred to as an individual "risk". Without access to reliable, consistent, and comprehensive data on previous incidents, little useful guidance can be provided on the probability of the threat materializing. Several people have added that in the dynamic landscape of the cybersecurity threats and new attack methods, observation of past events is not necessarily a good guide to future accidents. Another way to access threats is to gather intelligence information related to identifying possible attackers and their capability, motivations, and plans from a network of agents, as is done in law enforcement and national security agencies. However, intelligence gathering only applies to certain types of threats and is unrealistic for most organizations. As a result, there is a tendency to base risk management on assessing *vulnerabilities* and their associated *impact*, or the level of damage that your organization would sustain if a threat event successfully exploited vulnerability. This is believed to be much easier, since both factors are within the scope of the organization. Consequently, a certain "mythification" of the concept of vulnerability occurs, as some condition that can be systematically detected in the system. The vulnerability approach is explored in more detail in Chapters 6 and 7. The current chapter focuses at deterministic strategies for systematic identification of threats as a precursor for systematic detection of vulnerabilities.

5.2 BASIC CYBERSECURITY ELEMENTS

The framework for cybersecurity is defined in several international standards and recommendations such as ISO/IEC 13335 Guidelines for the Management of IT Security [ISO 13335], ISO-IEC 15443 A Framework for IT Security Assurance [ISO 15443], ISO/IEC 17779 A Code of Practice for Information Security Management [ISO 17779], ISO/IEC 27001 Information Security Management Systems [ISO 27001], ISO-IEC 15026 Systems and Software Assurance [ISO 15026], ISO/IEC 15408 Evaluation Criteria for IT security [ISO 15408], and NIST SP800-30 Risk Management Guide [NIST SP800-30]. The following six terms—assets, impacts, threats, safeguards, vulnerabilities, and risks—describe at a high level the major elements involved in cybersecurity assurance. The terminology is based on ISO/IEC 13335. These elements are illustrated at Figures 1 and 2. Precise fact-oriented vocabulary of discernable noun and verb phrases is described in the next section.

5.2.1 Assets

The proper management of assets is vital to the success of the organization and is a major responsibility of all management levels. The assets of an organization include the following categories:

- Physical assets (e.g., computer hardware, communications facilities, buildings);
- Information (e.g., documents, databases);
- Software;
- The ability to produce some product or provide a service;
- People;
- Intangibles (e.g., goodwill, image).

Most of these assets may be considered valuable enough to warrant some degree of protection. As assessment of the risks being accepted is necessary to determine whether the assets are adequately protected.

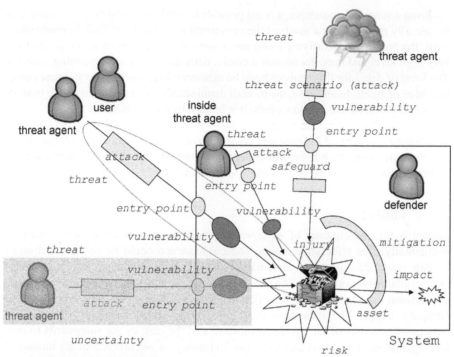

FIGURE1 Cyber attack components

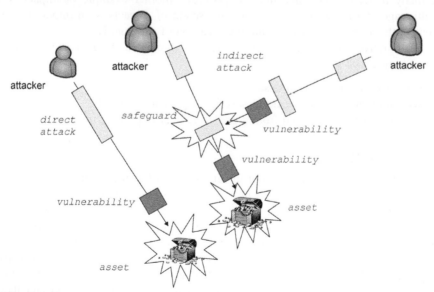

FIGURE 2 Direct and Indirect (multi-stage) attack

From a security perspective, it is not possible to implement and maintain a successful security program if the assets of the organization are not identified. In many situations, the process of identifying assets and assigning a value can be accomplished at a very high level and may not require a costly, detailed, and time-consuming analysis. The level of detail for this analysis must be measured in terms of time and cost versus the value of assets. In any case, the level of detail should be determined on the basis of the security objectives. In many cases, it is helpful to group assets.

Asset attributes relevant to security include their value and/or sensitivity.

Chapter 4 described the complex environment of the system life cycle including the multiple support systems and supply chain which must be considered for the identification of assets related to the system of interest.

5.2.2 Impact

Impact is the consequence of an unwanted incident, caused either deliberately or accidentally, that affects the assets. The consequence could be the destruction of certain assets; damage to the information system; and loss of confidentiality, integrity, availability, nonrepudiation, accountability, authenticity, or reliability. Possible indirect consequences include financial losses and the loss of market share or company image. The measurement of impacts permits a balance to be reached between the results of an unwanted incident and the cost of the safeguards to protect against the unwanted incident. The frequency of occurrence of an unwanted incident needs to be taken into account. This is particularly important when the amount of harm caused by each occurrence is low but when the aggregate effect of many incidents over time may be harmful. Another example of impact is a multi-stage attack (see Figure 2). The assessment of impacts is an important element in the assessment of risks and the selection of safeguards.

Quantitative and qualitative measurements of impact can be achieved in a number of ways, such as:

- Establishing the financial cost;
- Assigning an empirical scale of severity (e.g., 1 through 10);
- Use of adjectives selected from a predefined list (e.g., low, medium, high).

5.2.3 Threats

Assets are subject to many kinds of threats. A threat has the potential to cause an unwanted incident that may result in harm to a system or an organization and its assets. This harm can occur from either direct or indirect attack on the information being handled by a system or service, for example, its unauthorized destruction, disclosure, modification, corruption, and unavailability or loss. A threat needs to exploit an existing vulnerability of the asset in order to successfully cause harm to the asset. Threats may be of natural or human origin and may be accidental or deliberate. Both accidental and deliberate threats should be identified and their level and likelihood assessed.

Threats may impact specific parts of an organization, for example, the disruption to personal computers. Some threats may be general to the surrounding environment in the particular location in which a system or an organization exists, such as damage to buildings from hurricanes or lightning. A threat may arise from within the organization, as in sabotage by an employee, or from outside, as in malicious hacking or industrial espionage. The harm caused by the unwanted incident may be temporary, for example, a five minute loss of service due to the restart of the server, or may be permanent, as in the case of destroying an asset.

The amount of harm caused by a threat can vary widely for each occurrence. For example, earthquakes in a particular location may have different strengths on each occasion.

Threats have characteristics that provide useful information about the threat itself. Examples of such information include:

- Source, that is, insider vs. outsider;
- Motivation of the threat agent, for example, financial gain, competitive advantage;
- Capability of the threat agent;
- Frequency of occurrence;
- Threat severity;
- Threats qualified in terms such as high, medium, and low, depending on the outcome of the threat assessment

Threats to the system of interest usually include threats to the support systems and supply chain, as described in Chapter 4.

5.2.4 **Safeguards**

Safeguards (countermeasures, controls) are practices, procedures, or mechanisms that may protect against a threat, reduce vulnerability, limit the impact of an unwanted incident, detect unwanted incidents, and facilitate recovery. Effective security usually requires a combination of different safeguards to provide *layers* of security for assets. For example, access control mechanisms applied to computers should be supported by audit controls, personnel procedures, training, and physical security. Some safeguards may already exist as part of the environment or as an inherent aspect of assets, or may be already in place in the system or organization. It is important to note that safeguards can come in different shapes and forms, such as technology choosing (e.g., choosing Java over C++ programming language for implementation of system components), design decisions (e.g., no information flow from architecture component A to architecture component B), or designing and implementing protective mechanisms (e.g., authentication safeguard or adding firewall).

Safeguards may be considered to perform one or more of the following functions:

- Prevention;
- Deterrence;
- Detection;
- Limitation;

- Correction;
- Recovery;
- Monitoring;
- Awareness.

An appropriate selection of safeguards is essential for a properly implemented security program. Many safeguards can server multiple functions. It is often more cost effective to select safeguards that will satisfy multiple functions. Some examples of areas where safeguards can be used include:

- Physical environment;
- Technical environment (hardware, software, and communications);
- Personnel;
- Administration;
- Security awareness, which is relevant to the personnel area.

Chapter 4 described the complex environment of the system life cycle that involves multiple support systems and supply chain which collectively determines the set of *locations* to which safeguards can be applied. Examples of specific safeguards are:

- Access control mechanisms;
- Antivirus software;
- Encryption for confidentiality;
- Digital signatures;
- Firewalls;
- Monitoring and analysis tools;
- Redundant power supplies;
- Backup copies of information;
- Personnel background checks.

5.2.5 Vulnerabilities

Vulnerabilities associated with assets include weaknesses in physical layout, organization, procedures, personnel, management, administration, hardware, software, or information. They may be exploited by a threat agent and cause harm to the information system or business objectives. A vulnerability in itself does not cause harm; a vulnerability is merely a *condition* or set of conditions that may allow a threat to affect an asset. Vulnerabilities arising from different sources need to be considered, for example, those intrinsic to the asset. Vulnerabilities may remain unless the asset itself changes such that the vulnerability no longer applies. An example of a vulnerability is lack of an access control mechanism—a vulnerability that could allow the threat of an intrusion to occur and assets to be lost. Within a specific system or an organization not all vulnerabilities will be susceptible to a threat. Vulnerabilities that have a corresponding threat are of immediate concern. However, as the environment can change dynamically, all vulnerabilities should be monitored to identify those that have been exposed to old or new threats.

Vulnerability analysis is the examination of features that may be exploited by identified threats. This analysis must take into account the environment and existing safeguards. The measure of a vulnerability of a particular system or asset to a threat is a statement of the ease with which the system or asset may be harmed.

Vulnerabilities may be qualified in terms such as high, medium, and low, depending on the outcome of the vulnerability assessment.

5.2.6 **Risks**

Risk is the potential that a given threat will exploit vulnerabilities of an asset and thereby cause loss or damage to an organization. Single or multiple threats may exploit single or multiple vulnerabilities. We distinguish the threat as a certain multi-component state of affairs in the system, and risk, which is a certain measure associated with the threat (the level of threat).

A threat scenario describes how a particular threat or group of threats may exploit a particular vulnerability or group of vulnerabilities exposing assets to harm. The risk is characterized by a combination of two factors, the probability of the unwanted incident occurring and its impact. Any change to assets, threats, vulnerabilities, and safeguards may have significant effects on risks. Early detection or knowledge of changes in the environment or system increases the opportunity for appropriate actions to be taken to reduce the risk.

5.3 COMMON VOCABULARY FOR THREAT IDENTIFICATION

In order to systematically build assurance cases and reason about the effectiveness of security countermeasures, it is necessary to have a conceptualization of threats as something against which we build countermeasures. Such a concept must provide that knowledge of threats be aligned with the system facts and can be turned into machine-readable content able to be exchanged using a standard protocol for the purposes of system assurance. The goal of this chapter is to describe a discernable conceptualization that can support repeatable and systematic assurance and automation.

How far is the community from normalizing knowledge of cyber threats and collaborating by exchanging machine-readable documents? In 2008, the NATO report titled "Improving Common Security Risk Analysis" [NATO 2008] mentioned that the different methods used by various NATO countries such as EBIOS for France, NIST Risk Management SP800-30 and CRAMM for UK, ITSG-04 for Canada, and MAGERIT for Spain differ in their knowledge bases (assets, threats, vulnerabilities, etc.) and type of results (quantitative or qualitative), which makes it difficult or impossible to compare risk assessments when different methods have been used.

Our ability to identify cyber threats for a given system in a systematic and repeatable way depends on a common understanding of the threat theory and, in particular, understanding the *locations* that can be systematically covered during the search for threats. The cause of the incompatibilities between diverse risk assessment methodologies, reported by the NATO report, is that the definitions of threats and risks currently used in the cybersecurity community are rather high level and do not have the required precision that allows establishing traceability links to the system facts. High-level non-discernable definitions are often responsible for higher levels of subjectivity in applying a particular risk assessment methodology and for the larger variation between the outcomes, produced by different teams. The lack of discernable definitions was one of the challenges reported by the IDEAS Group during the Defense Enterprise Architecture Interoperability project [McDaniel 2008]. This issue is addressed by analyzing original vocabularies and applying the vocabulary disambiguation methodology, such as the BORO methodology (described in more detail in Chapter 9) to identify the basic discernable concepts for inclusion into the common vocabulary and establishing the mappings between the individual original vocabularies and the common vocabulary. In the rest of this chapter we use the so-called SBVR Structured English. You will recognize it by a distinctive typesetting. This notation is fully explained in Chapter 10. Chapter 9 explains the OMG Common Fact Model approach which provides guidance to building common vocabularies as contracts for information exchange including how to generate XML schema for information exchange from this notation and how it defines fact-based repositories.

5.3.1 Defining discernable vocabulary for assets

There is little disagreement between different methodologies regarding asset identification and its role in the risk assessment.

```
Asset
   Concept type:    noun concept
   Definition:      tangible or intangible things that are within the
                    scope of the system and that require protection
                    because they are valuable to the owner of the system.
                    Assets are also of interest to potential attackers.
                    Assets include but are not limited to information in
                    all forms and media, networks, systems, materiel, real
                    property, financial resources, employee trust,
                    public confidence and reputation

Asset category
   Definition:      group of assets with similar characteristics
   Concept type:    noun concept
   Note:            This is a useful abstraction, which allows knowledge
                    exchange between different systems within the global
                    cybersecurity ecosystem. Asset category creates a
                    hierarchy of assets. Various lists of asset
```

Note: `categories` are available as the so-called risk
               assessment checklists

               Usually, a distinction is made between `assets` and
               `capabilities` (a demonstrable capacity or ability to
               perform a particular `action`). `Service` is defined as a
               `mechanism` to enable access to one or more `capabilities`,
               where the access is provided using a prescribed
               `interface` and is exercised consistent with constraints
               and policies as specified by the service description.
               Service provides access to a capability (which usually
               involves assets). A system delivers services.

`Asset category` *includes* `asset category`
  Concept type: `verb concept`
`Asset category` *includes* `asset`
  Concept type: `verb concept`

The two often used top-level categories of assets are tangible and intangible assets:

- Tangible assets—concrete items;
  - Software asset—computer program, procedures, and possible associated documentation and data pertaining to the operation of a computer system;
  - Information asset—any pattern of symbols or sounds to which meaning may be assigned;
  - Interface asset—connection points relating to the systems and hardware that are necessary for the delivery of service but are not proprietary;
  - Physical assets—pretty much anything else that is concrete;
- Intangible assets—matters of attitude arising from personal perceptions, both individual and collective.

Enumeration of asset categories is an example of generic cybersecurity content that is exchanged in the OMG Assurance Ecosystem. Chapter 9 provides more details on the transformation of well-defined vocabularies of noun and verb concepts into standard information exchange protocols.

5.3.1.1 Characteristics of assets

Assets have *value*. For some assets it is possible to provide the dollar amount, for example, the cost of replacing a server in case of physical damage; however, in most cases only a qualitative estimate can be provided. Often the value of the asset is the inverse of the injury to the asset.

`value`
  Definition: `estimated worth, monetary, cultural or other`
  Concept type: `property`

```
Note:           from the vocabulary perspective this is a special noun
                concept
Note:           the methodology for evaluating an asset may vary
                greatly between different risk analysis
                methodologies and different teams
cost
  Definition:   appreciated or depreciated worth of tangible assets;
                replacement cost
  General concept:  value
asset has value
  Concept type:   is property-of-fact type
  Note:           from the vocabulary perspective, this is a special verb
                  concept
```

5.3.1.2 Security requirements (confidentiality, integrity, and availability)

Confidentiality, integrity, and availability (CIA) enable analysts to identify the importance of the affected system asset to a user's organization, measured in terms of confidentiality, integrity, and availability. That is, if an asset supports a business function for which availability is most important, the analyst can assign a greater value to availability, relative to confidentiality and integrity. According to the NIST CVSS score specification [Schiffman 2004], each security requirement has three possible values: low, medium, or high.

Some risk analysis methodologies use a more abstract measure of "criticality." However, a separate consideration of the asset's value in terms of losing its CIA is necessary as different safeguards are required to protect the asset against losing each CIA facet. When more primitive measures are selected as the base concepts, it is easier to reach agreement regarding any derived measures.

```
confidentiality
  Definition:   the attribute that an asset must not be disclosed to
                unauthorized individuals because of the resulting
                impact on national or other interests
  General concept:  sensitivity
  Note:           incident related to confidentiality is unauthorized
                  disclosure
integrity
  Definition:   the attribute that requires the accuracy and
                completeness of assets and the authenticity of
                transactions
  General concept:  sensitivity
  Note:           accuracy is related to the untampered form of the
                  asset
```

```
    Note:              incident related to integrity is tampering
availability
    Definition:        the attribute that requires the condition of being
                       usable on demand to support operations, programs,
                       and services.
    General concept:   sensitivity
    Note:              incident related to availability is interruption
                       and loss
asset has sensitivity
    Concept type:      property-of-fact type
asset evaluation
    Definition:        the process of estimating the value and the
                       sensitivities of a particular asset
    Concept type:      noun concept
    General concept:   activity
```

5.3.2 **Threats and Hazards**

Analysis of the definitions used throughout cybersecurity publications demonstrates a certain confusion in the definitions of threat and risk. In order to build a common vocabulary and provide guidance to the threat identification process in system assurance, we can draw some insights from a related body of knowledge developed within the safety community over the last five decades. The safety community has developed several systematic architecture-driven methods of identifying risks related to the safety of systems [Clifton 2005]. Architecture-driven methods focus at the concept of a *location* within one of the system *views* (as described in Chapter 4) as the basis for a systematic and repeatable system analysis.

System safety is concerned with the prevention of a safety accident, or mishap, which is defined as "an unplanned event or series of events resulting in death, injury, occupational illness, damage to or loss of equipment or property, or damage to the environment" [MIL-STD-882D]. System safety is built on the premise that mishaps are not random events; instead they are deterministic and controllable events that are the results of a unique set of *conditions* (i.e., hazards), which are predictable when properly analyzed. A hazard is a potential condition that can result in a mishap or an accident, given that the hazard occurs. A hazard is the precursor to a mishap; a hazard defines a *potential* event (i.e., a mishap), while a mishap is the *occurred* event.

In order to build architecture-driven identification of hazards, system safety considers a hazard as an *aggregate entity* that involves several basic discernable *components* (see Figure 3). The components of a hazard define the necessary conditions for a mishap and the end outcome or effect of the mishap. In system safety, a hazard is comprised of the following three basic components [Clifton 2005]:

FIGURE 3 Components of hazard

1. Hazardous element (HE). This is the basic hazardous resource creating the impetus for the hazard, such as a hazardous energy source such as explosives being used in the system.
2. Initiating mechanism (IM). This is the trigger or initiator event(s) causing the hazard to occur. The IM causes actualization or transformation of the hazard from a dormant state to an active mishap state.
3. Target and Threat (T/T). This is the person or thing that is vulnerable to injury and/or damage, and it describes the severity of the mishap event. This is the mishap outcome and the expected consequential damage and loss.

The elements are necessary and sufficient to result in a mishap, which is useful in determining the hazard mitigation:

- When one of these components is removed, the hazard is eliminated.
- When the probability of the IM component is reduced, the mishap probability is reduced.
- When the element in the HE side or the T/T side of the triangle is reduced, the mishap severity is reduced.

Hazards can be described by the so-called *hazard statements*, based on the elements of the hazard triangle. Consider the following hazard statement: "Worker is electrocuted by touching exposed contacts in electrical panel containing high voltage."

In this example all three hazard components are present and can be clearly identified as the elements of the system of interest (see Figure 4). In this particular example there are actually two IMs involved. The T/T defines the mishap outcome,

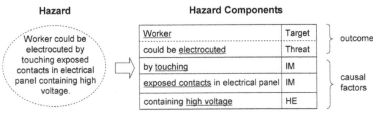

FIGURE 4 Hazard statement

while the combined HE and T/T define the mishap *severity*. The HE and IM are the hazard causal factors that define the mishap *probability*. If the high-voltage component can be removed from the system, the hazard is eliminated. If the voltage can be reduced to a lower, less harmful level, then the mishap severity is reduced.

The *causal factors* of hazards are the specific items responsible for how a unique hazard exists in a system. Hazards in system safety are unavoidable, in part because hazardous elements must be used in the system, in the same way that security threats are unavoidable because attackers have access to the system through the same channels as used by the legitimate users. Hazards also result from inadequate safety and security considerations—either poor or insufficient design or incorrect implementation of a good design, resulting from the unmitigated effect of hardware failures, human errors, software glitches, or sneak paths.

Once a potential harmful event is identified, risk is a fairly straightforward concept, where risk is defined as Risk = Probability × Severity

The mishap probability factor is the probability of the hazard components occurring and transforming into the mishap. The mishap severity factor is the overall consequence of the mishap, usually in terms of loss resulting from the mishap (i.e., the undesired outcome). Both probability and severity can be defined and assessed in either qualitative or quantitative terms. Time is factored into the risk concept through the probability calculation of an undesired event, as the duration window of "exposure" during which one of the IM exists. For example, the risk of an adversary obtaining sensitive information from a 1-minute unencrypted communication may be considered smaller than the risk of a 1-hour unencrypted communication.

Hazards and mishaps are linked by risk. The three basic hazard components define both the hazard and the mishap. The three basic hazard components can be further decomposed into major hazard *causal factor categories*, which are: (1) hardware, (2) software, (3) humans, (4) interfaces, (5) functions, and (6) the environment. Finally, the causal factor categories are refined even further into the actual specific detailed *causes,* such as a hardware component failure mode (see Figure 5).

In the area of system security, the mishaps are security incidents resulting in the loss of confidentiality, integrity, and/or availability of the assets. Some researchers explicitly add *subversion* of a system node as a separate incident type. The counterpart of the T/T component is Asset/Injury. A notable difference is that in the area of system security there is no explicit hazardous element. Instead, a typical source of security incidents is the malicious action of the *threat agent*. On the other hand, security assessment methodologies often consider natural hazards as one of the sources of threats, together with the action of intentional attackers. This demonstrates how close the two models are. Lightning is the source of high voltage (the HE component), which can cause loss of a server equipment (the T/T component). On the other hand, a hacker is the source of "attack capability" (hazardous element?) that can cause subversion of a system node running an unhardened version of Windows (asset and injury). The initiation mechanisms are practically identical between the safety and security areas, as they provide a *cause and effect link*

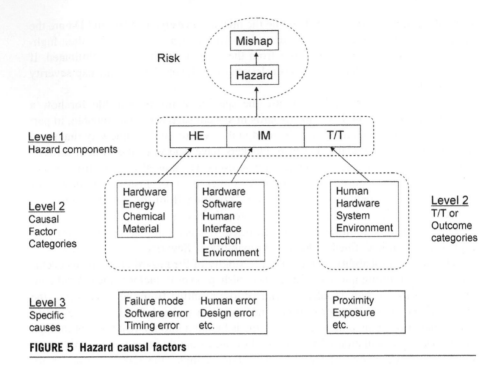

FIGURE 5 Hazard causal factors

between the hazardous element (or the threat agent) to the target and injury. The concept of an initiation mechanism is quite close to the concept of "vulnerability" that is used in system security, although there are some important differences that we will point out later. Several authors already made arguments for combined safety and security assurance, and the term *security hazard* has been used in several publications.

Note that both a safety hazard and a security threat are *deterministic entities* (like a mini system, consisting of a unique set of *identifiable* components that are traceable to the elements of the system of interest). Hazard components either exist or they do not. A mishap, on the other hand, has a certain probability of occurring, based on the probability of the initiating mechanisms, such as human error, component failures, or timing errors. The HE component has a probability of 1 of occurring, since it must be present in order for the hazard to exist.

On the other hand, in system security it is more difficult to determine the probability of the malicious actions by the attacker, and there is less statistical correlation with past historic data because attacker actions are not random and evolving.

One of the potential causes of ambiguity in the definitions of "security threat" in cybersecurity is the complex nature of both the causes and consequences of an elementary injury to an asset. This makes "security threat" a complex collection of interrelated facts, and different authors focus on different parts of this phenomenon. The complexity of the security threat can be described using a small number of elementary discernable concepts. The key is to identify an elementary "undesired event" associated with an asset—an "injury" to a specific asset. An "event" is a *discernable* concept because it is traceable to one or more statements in the code. Then a "security threat" becomes a discernable assembly of a threat agent, an entry point, an asset, and an injury. (Application of the BORO methodology, outlined in Chapter 9, shows that a "threat" is a *tuple*—a relationship between several noun concepts.) Multiple "events" can be identified as the *causes* of the "injury." Similarly, an injury event may cause further damage by causing additional injuries to other assets. Multiple attack scenarios can be associated with the same threat: An attack scenario can be described as a *path* through the causal graph. Finally, at least one of the causal events must be associated with the *entry point* of the threat.

This discernable interpretation is consistent with the terminology defined at the beginning of this chapter based on [ISO 13335]. Yet the more conservative definitions are discernable and can be traced to existing system facts, enabling the systematic recognition of threats and causal analysis of the security posture. The rest of this section provides the details of this discernable vocabulary. Figure 6 provides the necessary illustration.

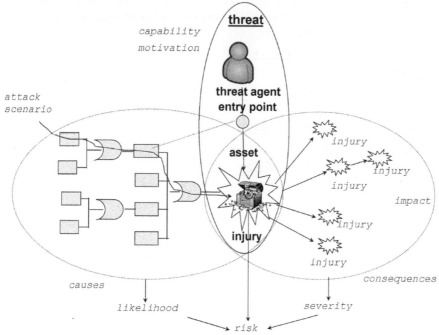

FIGURE 6 Causes and consequences of threats

5.3.3 **Defining discernable vocabulary for injury and impact**

Information security is about protecting information and information systems from unauthorized access, use, disclosure, disruption, modification, or destruction in order to provide:

1. Confidentiality, which means preserving authorized restrictions on access and disclosure, including means for protecting personal privacy and proprietary information;
2. Integrity, which means guarding against improper information modification or destruction, and includes ensuring information nonrepudiation and authenticity;
3. Availability, which means ensuring timely and reliable access to and use of information.

Certain events result in *injury*, such as "unauthorized use, disclosure, disruption, modification, or destruction of information and information systems."

injury
    Definition: the damage that results from the compromise of assets
    Note: Injury is elementary damage that can be traced to system
    Note: in non cyber scenarios a physical access to the asset may be the prerequisite of injuries to the asset
    Concept type: noun concept
    Synonym: harm
    Note: impact is non elementary, cumulative damage
injury *targets* asset
    Concept type: verb concept
injury *targets* asset category
    Concept type: verb concept
    Note: This results in generic injury checklists
threat event
    Definition: the event that results in compromise to assets
    Synonym: undesired event
    Note: threat event is an elementary event that can be traced to system
    Note: impact is a collection of threat events associated with a given initial threat event
threat event *causes* injury *to* asset
    Concept type: verb concept

```
threat event causes threat event
   Concept type:        verb concept
threat event has impact
   Definition:          the state of affairs that injuries caused by threat
                        event collectively comprise impact
```

Enumeration of possible injuries is an example of generic cybersecurity content that is exchanged in the OMG Assurance Ecosystem. Chapter 9 provides more details on the transformation of well-defined vocabularies of noun and verb concepts into standard information exchange protocols. Here are some examples in which we describe pairs of injury/asset category.

Injuries related to confidentiality: disclosure of information assets, which can be further subdivided into disclosure of data at rest, disclosure of data in motion, disclosure of data in use, and disclosure of data in facilities ("dumpster diving") and equipment (recovering sensitive information from a disposed hard drive or from a stolen laptop).

Injuries related to integrity:

- Tampering with equipment, facilities;
- Tampering with information assets;
- Tampering with service;
- Subversion of a system node.

Injuries related to availability: partial or full loss of equipment, service, information asset, facility, personnel illustrates impact statements. It shows several exemplary injuries/asset category pairs (solid lines) and then uses the dotted lines to show some impacts, portraying possible causal relationships between injuries.

The relationships shown in Figure 7 can be verbalized as follows:

- Disclosure of information causes tampering with information (e.g., when user login credentials are compromised).
- Tampering with equipment causes tampering with information (e.g., due to malfunction).
- Tampering with equipment causes disclosure of information (e.g., a telephone bug).
- Tampering with equipment causes tampering with service (both a distortion and subversion).
- Tampering with information causes distortion of service (a fancy way to say "garbage in–garbage out").
- Subversion of service causes disclosure of information (e.g., a typical spybot scenario, when a trojan installs a keylogger and exports sensitive information, such as financial account information and credentials).
- Subversion of service causes subversion of service (i.e., further service, subverting other computers on the network).

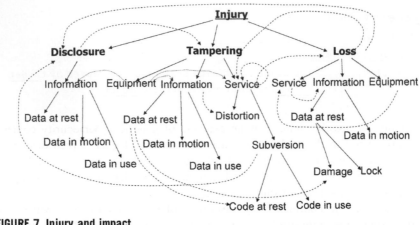

FIGURE 7 Injury and impact

- Subversion of service causes loss (of service, information).
- Loss of information causes tampering with service (e.g., when records are deleted).
- Loss of service causes tampering with service (e.g., when a protection mechanism is disabled).
- Loss of equipment causes disclosure of information (e.g., from a stolen usb stick).
- Loss of equipment causes loss of service.

5.3.4 Defining discernable vocabulary for threats

```
threat
    Definition:        a set of potential incidents in which a threat agent
                       causes a threat event to an asset using a specific entry
                       point into the system
    Concept type:      noun concept
    Note:              a threat event is the key concept. This is a specific inci-
                       dent customized for the given system. A threat event can
                       belong to several abstract groups (threat activity and
                       threat class) which provide means to manage knowledge
                       about threats and build reusable libraries of threats

threat causes injury to asset
threat activity
    Definition:        a generic group of threats with common consequences or
                       outcomes
    Example:           sabotage
    Note:              threat activity is used to build checklists of threats
```

threat event *belongs to* **threat activity**

Synonym: threat activity *includes* threat event

Necessity: threat activities *belongs to* **zero or more** threat activities

threat class

Definition: a generic group of threat activities with common characteristics

Example: deliberate threat

Note: threat class captures reusable categories of threat activities

threat activity *belongs to* **threat class**

Necessity: threat activity *belongs to* **zero or more** threat classes

threat event *is accidental*

Definition: unplanned threats caused by human beings

threat event *is deliberate*

Definition: planned or premeditated threats caused by human beings.

threat event *is a natural hazard*

Definition: threats caused by forces of nature.

Example: power failure

threat *affects* **asset**

Necessity: threat event *affects* **one or more** assets

threat agent category

Definition: a subdivision of threat activity, intended to focus on deliberate threats with common motivation or accidental threats and natural hazards with similar causal factors

threat agent

Definition: an identifiable organization, individual or type of individual posing deliberate threats, or a specific kind of accident or natural hazard

Synonym: **threat source, attacker, adversary**

threat agent *causes* **threat**

Necessity: each threat agent *causes* **at least one** threat

threat agent *belongs to* threat agent category

Synonym: threat agent category *includes* threat agent

Necessity: threat agent *belongs to* **one or more** threat agent categories

threat agent category *engages in* **threat agent activity**

Necessity: threat agent category *engages in* **one or more** threat agent activity

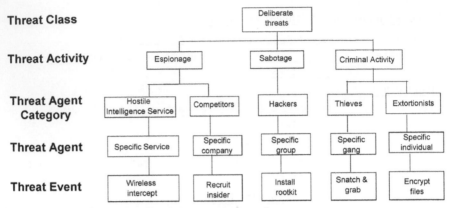

FIGURE 8 Illustration of threat and threat agent grouping

5.3.5 **Threat scenarios and attacks**

threat scenario

   Definition: a detailed chronological and functional description of an actual or hypothetical threat intended to facilitate risk analysis by creating a confirmed relationship between an Asset of value and a threat agent having motivation toward that asset and having the capability to exploit a vulnerability found in the same asset

   Note: a threat scenario occurs when a threat agent takes action against an asset by exploiting vulnerabilities within the system

threat scenario *describes* threat

   Necessity: threat scenario *describes* **exactly one** threat

attack

   Definition: sequence of actions that involve interaction with system and that results in threat event

   Note: the system must allow injury; the attack forces system into producing injury

   Note: attack may involve physical access to an asset

   Note: attack involves malicious intent

   Note: attack involves particular entry point, which is an attribute of the interactions with the system; attack may involve more than one entry point

attack *results in* injury

   Definition: state of affairs that the attack resulted in injury

Note:	the system must allow <u>injury</u>; the attack forces system into producing <u>injury</u>
Synonym:	<u>attack</u> *produces* <u>injury</u>

<u>attack</u> *has* impact

Definition:	state of affairs that attack resulted in injuries that collectively comprise impact

<u>attack</u> *targets* <u>asset</u>

Definition:	state of affairs **that** an <u>attack</u> *produces* <u>injury</u> to <u>asset</u>
Note:	there is some object that is valuable to the attacker; this is the attacker's viewpoint
Synonym:	<u>attack</u> *injures* <u>asset</u>
Note:	<u>attack</u> may impact additional <u>asset</u> as 'collateral damage'; however in order to predict attacks, it is important to understand <u>motivation</u> of the attacker

5.3.6 **Defining discernable vocabulary for vulnerabilities**

<u>vulnerability</u>

Definition:	an attribute of a <u>system</u> or the <u>environment</u> in which it is located that allows a <u>threat event</u>, or increases the severity of the <u>impact</u>
Note:	an inadequacy related to security that could permit an attacker to produce injury
Note:	an actual flaw or inadequacy related to a specific <u>safeguard</u> or a missing <u>safeguard</u> that could expose <u>employees</u>, <u>assets</u>, or <u>service delivery</u> to <u>injury</u>
Note:	a vulnerability is a characteristic, attribute, or weakness of any asset within a system or environment that increases the probability of a <u>threat event</u> occurring or the severity of its effects causing harm (in terms of confidentiality, availability, and/or integrity). The presence of vulnerability does not in itself produce injury; vulnerability is merely a condition or a set of conditions that could allow assets to be *injured by* a <u>threat agent</u>

<u>System</u> *has* <u>vulnerability</u>

Definition:	state of affairs that the <u>vulnerability</u> is an <u>attribute</u> of the <u>system</u> or the <u>environment</u> of the <u>system</u>
Note:	the fact that <u>vulnerability</u> has 'location' in the <u>system</u> is vital to systematic detection and mitigation of vulnerabilities

vulnerability *is exploited by* threat agent

Definition:	state of affairs that the attacker *performs* an attack that *results in* injury and that *is enabled by* the vulnerability
Note:	the presence of vulnerability in the system does not result in injury unless the vulnerability is exploited by the attacker in the course of interactions with the system
Note:	'exploitation' means that injury is produced by the system, where the attacker forces the system into producing such injury
Note:	attacker is a simple case of a more general concept of a threat agent that may also include forces of nature and other unintentional events known as hazards

vulnerability *enables* attack

Definition:	state of affairs that the vulnerability is involved in interactions with the system that constitutes the attack
Synonym:	attack *is enabled by* vulnerability
Possibility:	attack *is enabled by* **one or more** vulnerability

vulnerability *exposes* asset

Definition:	state of affairs that the vulnerability *enables* an attack that *produces* injury to the asset
Note:	injury to the asset is only done as the result of a successful attack; the presence of a vulnerability does not in itself result in any injury to the asset

Vulnerability-1 *exposes* vulnerability-2

Definition:	state of affairs that the vulnerability-1 enables an attack that reduces the effectiveness of a safeguard to another vulnerability-2
Note:	injury to the asset is only done as the result of a successful attack; the presence of the vulnerability-1 or vulnerability-2 does not in itself *result* in any injury to the asset
Note:	vulnerability-1 indirectly *exposes* asset; injury to asset cannot be produced by an *attack* on vulnerability-1 because it is *prevented* by safeguard, however injury may be *produced by* a combination of attack on **the** safeguard **that** *is enabled by* **the** vulnerability-2, *followed by* attack on **the** asset itself

vulnerability *has* impact
    Definition:　　state of affairs **that** the attack **that** *is enabled by* the
    　　　　　　　vulnerability *has* impact
    Note:　　　　vulnerability is associated with impact only through
    　　　　　　　an attack; this association may be quite complex, since
    　　　　　　　a particular attack may be enabled by more than one
    　　　　　　　vulnerability

vulnerability *has* severity
    Definition:　　a metric of vulnerability that enables
    　　　　　　　prioritization of vulnerabilities for the purpose
    　　　　　　　of mitigation
    Note:　　　　NIST SCAP standard called Common Vulnerability
    　　　　　　　Scoring System (CVSS) defines a standard approach to
    　　　　　　　evaluate severity of a vulnerability, called SCAP
    　　　　　　　'score'

vulnerability class
    Definition:　　a generic group of vulnerability based on the broad
    　　　　　　　security policy requirements
    Note:　　　　vulnerability class is important for managing
    　　　　　　　knowledge of vulnerabilities

vulnerability group
    Definition:　　a subdivision of vulnerability class, intended to
    　　　　　　　capture all vulnerability associated with a related
    　　　　　　　group of safeguard
    Note:　　　　vulnerability group is important for managing
    　　　　　　　knowledge of vulnerabilities

vulnerability *belongs to* vulnerability group

vulnerability group *belongs to* vulnerability class

Since vulnerabilities are key to system assurance and risk management, Chapters 6
and 7 explore this subject in greater detail.

5.3.7 **Defining discernable vocabulary for safeguards**

safeguard
    Definition:　　practices, procedures or mechanisms that reduce the
    　　　　　　　risk to personnel, assets, or service delivery by
    　　　　　　　decreasing the likelihood of a threat event, reducing

	the probability of occurrence of the threat event, or mitigating the severity of the impact of the threat event
Synonym:	countermeasure
Synonym:	security control
Note:	there are eight categories of safeguards based on their interaction with the threat agent, vulnerability or asset

safeguard *mitigates* vulnerability
  Synonym: safeguard *corrects* vulnerability
safeguard *protects* asset
Safeguard *deters* threat agent
Safeguard *detects* attack
Safeguard *prevents* threat event
Safeguard *limits* impact of threat event
safeguard *monitors* threat event
safeguard *recovers* asset
safeguard *is effective against* threat event

The "bow-tie diagram" (showing causes of the threat to the left and consequences of the threat to the right) is a useful tool to analyze safeguards. Figure 9 shows *preventing* safeguards placed at particular branches of the causal tree; *limiting* safeguards placed at particular branches on the consequence tree, a *deterring* safeguard that lowers motivation of the attacker, a *preventive* safeguard that hardens the system by eliminating an entry point (e.g., disconnecting an unauthorized modem or turning off an unused service to shrink the so-called attack surface); and a *detecting* safeguard at the bottom), which reduces the risk by limiting exposure of an injury or exposure to a vulnerability. *Corrective* safeguards may also reduce the vulnerability exposure (e.g., a spring that forces an open door to close, reducing exposure) or undo the injury (e.g., by restarting the system or restoring the lost or corrupted information from backup). Finally, detecting and *monitoring* safeguards alert defenders about the ongoing threat activities which reduces risk by reducing the window of exposure to the attack. Some safeguards raise security *awareness* and thus contribute to hardening secure operational procedures.

5.3.8 **Risk**

risk

Definition:	the measure of the probability of occurence and the severity of impact of a specific threat
Synonym:	original risk

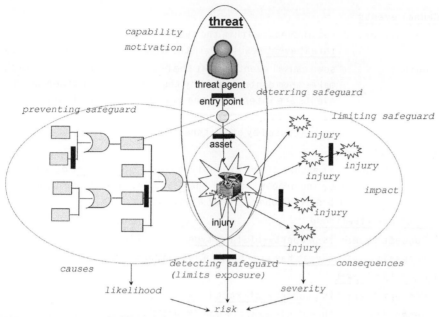

FIGURE 9 Threats and Safeguards

Note: threat event causes specified injury resulting from
              natural hazards, accidental threats, or a deliberate
              threat agent, having motivation toward an asset and the
              capability to exploit a vulnerability of the asset (or
              the system containing an information asset), to
              successfully compromise the asset. Risk is the measure
              of the likelihood of the causes of the threat and
              severity of the impact of the threat

Threat *has* risk

  Concept type: is property-of-fact type

impact

  Definition: a description of the cumulative effects on the system
                  resulting from injury to employees or assets arising
                  from a given threat event

  Synonym: Consequence

threat event *produces* injury

  Concept type: verb concept

  Necessity: threat event has zero or more injuries

  Note: threat event may produce injuries directly or
                  indirectly, the combined injuries comprises impact

Causal events

Definition: set of events within the system culminating in a given
threat event resulting in the injury to employees or assets

Note: some causal events are at the boundary of the system, which
makes them controllable by the threat agent; other causal
events are internal to the system; some causal events are
failures in system functions (that either occur naturally
or are caused by other threats)

likelihood

Definition: a measure of the probability of a threat event determined
by the probability of the causal events occurring within
the given operational environment

threat *has* likelihood

Concept type: is property-of-fact type

Necessity: threat has exactly one likelihood

threat *has* impact

Concept type: is property-of-fact type

Necessity: threat has exactly one impact

risk assessment

Definition: the process of estimating the risk of a particular threat
and the corresponding set of assets, and vulnerabilities
with confirmed relationships to each other

Risk assessment *involves* threat

Necessity: it is obligatory that risk assessment includes exactly
one threat

Synonym: threat event of the risk assessment

Risk assessment *involves* asset

Necessity: it is obligatory that risk assessment includes one or
more assets that are affected by the threat of the risk
assessment

Synonym: business object of the risk assessment

Risk assessment *involves* vulnerability

Possibility: it is possible that risk assessment includes one or more
vulnerabilities that are exploited by the threat of the
risk assessment

Synonym: vulnerability of the risk assessment

Risk assessment *involves* threat agent

Necessity: it is obligatory that risk assessment includes exactly one
threat agent that causes the threat of the risk assessment

```
Synonym:        threat agent of the risk assessment
Risk assessment calculates risk
System has risk
  Definition:   the risks of the system is the set of risk of all threat to
                the system
System has aggregated risk
  Definition:   the risk of the system is the cumulative risk of all
                threat to the system
```

The fact-oriented discernable vocabulary for threat identification allows management of the information during the threat and risk analysis process in a fact-based repository, instead of, for example, a spreadsheet, in particular, verb concepts related to "risk assessment" correspond to typical entries of a TRA spreadsheet [RCMP 2007], [Sherwood 2005]. This fact-oriented vocabulary allows the use of automated tools for risk analysis, and allows integration of the threat and risk facts into the integrated system model, as described in Chapter 3.

5.4 SYSTEMATIC THREAT IDENTIFICATION

The systematic threat identification process is essential for producing stronger claims for the assurance case and building defendable assurance arguments and evidence. One of the characteristics of the threat identification process that is specific to its use in system assurance is the set of activities that lead to assurance of the process itself, by performing verification and validation tasks, and collecting evidence that justifies completeness of the list of identified threats that all sufficient threats have been identified.

Threat identification is the cognitive process of matching the components of the threat against the multitude of system facts (available as the integrated system model, as described in Chapter 3).

Systematic, repeatable, and objective identification of threats involves the "security threat" *patterns* that utilize "security threat" components as follows:

- Use threat activity and threat agent category checklists;
- Evaluate trigger events and causal factors;
- Use asset category checklists;
- Use checklists to identify injuries to assets;
- Evaluate possible assets and injuries;
- Evaluate injury events for consequential impact;
- Evaluate system facts to systematically identify entry points.

In addition, security threat identification can use key failure state questions and evaluations of the threat-triggering mechanisms.

The discernable threat concept provides the best threat recognition resource by evaluating individually each of the four threat component categories (threat agent, entry point, asset, and injury) against the systems facts. This means, for example, identifying and evaluating all of the unique entry point components in the system design as the first step [Swiderski 2004]. Subsequently, all system assets are evaluated for injuries and undesired events, then all causal factors.

Threat agent category and threat activity checklists are examples of cybersecurity *content* that is key to the justifiable identification of the threat agents of the security threats and further evaluation of the likelihood of the threat based on the capabilities and motivations of the identified threat agent. This is similar to using the industry standard hazardous source checklists, such as explosives, fuel, batteries, electricity, acceleration, and chemicals to identify safety hazards. System components that match the elements of one of the hazard source checklists may lead to identification of a potential safety hazard in the system. In the area of cybersecurity, threat agents are external to the system, so this knowledge cannot be turned into *patterns* that can be recognized in the system facts, but they are nevertheless important for systematic threat identification. Once the four threat components have been identified, knowledge of *attack pattern* can be used to further investigate the possible attack scenarios. Accumulating and exchanging the certified machine-readable *threat agent category* and *threat activity* checklists is required for distributing cyberdefense knowledge across the defender community.

Threats can be recognized by focusing on known or preestablished undesired events (the injury to asset component of a security threat). This means considering and evaluating known undesired events within the system. By following these undesired events backward, certain threats can be more readily recognized. A similar systematic approach is used in system safety for systematic identification of safety hazards [Clifton 2005]. For example, a missile system has certain undesired events that are known right from the conceptual stage of system development. In the design of missile systems, it is well accepted that an inadvertent missile launch is an undesired mishap. Therefore any conditions contributing to this event would formulate a hazard, such as autoignition, switch failures, and human error.

Another method for recognizing threats is through the use of *key state questions*. This method involves a set of clue questions that must be answered, each of which can trigger the recognition of a threat. The key states are potential states or ways the subsystem could fail or operate incorrectly and thereby result in creating a threat. For example, when evaluating each subsystem, answering the question "What happens when the subsystem fails to operate?" may lead to recognition of a security threat. A similar approach is the foundation for the HAZOP technique for systematic safety hazard identification.

Certain threats can be recognized by focusing on known causal threat-triggering mechanisms. In cybersecurity many threats involve the control- and data-flow path from some entry point to the "point of injury," which is a particular *location* in the system capable of producing potential injury and the common safeguards in the form of data filters. In particular, this approach focuses at known safeguards and their components, and the possibilities of bypass. Similar techniques are applied in system safety. For example, in the design of aircraft it is common knowledge that fuel ignition sources and fuel leakage sources are initiating mechanisms for fire/explosion hazards. Therefore, the systematic safety hazard recognition would benefit from detailed review of the design for ignition sources and leakage sources when fuel is involved. Component failure modes and human error are common triggering modes for both safety hazards and security threats, for example, when system design indicates a human decision point used as a safeguard that mitigates a certain triggering mechanism.

Use of the integrated system model allows *automation* of several tasks of the systematic threat identification, based on the central concept of a vertical traceability link, as follows. The integrated system model contains detailed system facts (automatically derived from the system artifacts, such as binary and source code by knowledge discovery tools) as well as the high-level threat facts (identified and imported into the integrated system model, such as threat agents and asset classes). The high-level threat facts are linked to the low-level system facts through chains of vertical traceability links. Entry points, physical assets (especially the information assets and capability assets), and "points of injury" can be identified by automated pattern recognition against the detailed system facts, and then propagated to the high-level threat facts by using vertical traceability links. Similar to standard protocols for exchanging checklists for identifying external components of threats, accumulating and exchanging certified machine-readable *patterns* is required for distributing cyberdefense knowledge across the defender community. The key enabler for the exchange of cybersecurity patterns is the availability of a standard protocol for exchanging system facts, supporting traceability links, and integration of multiple vocabularies because both the facts about the system of interest (extracted by knowledge discovery tools) and the patterns must use the same protocol, the same conceptual commitment to the predefined common vocabulary. Cybersecurity patterns are further addressed in Chapter 7. The standard protocol for exchanging system facts is described in Chapter 11. The underlying mechanisms for fact-based integration of multiple vocabularies are described in Chapter 9. Finally, Chapter 10 describes the standard protocol for managing and exchanging vocabularies and defining new patterns. These components provide the foundation for the OMG Assurance Ecosystem described in more detail in Chapter 8.

5.5 ASSURANCE STRATEGIES

Let's look at threat identification in the context of the system assurance strategy. First of all, we want to stress the point that assurance is a complex collection of activities throughout the life cycle of the system that contributes to governance of the system [ISO 15288]. This determines the overall system assurance strategy, including the integration of assurance activities with other system life cycle processes and the scope of individual system assurance projects. These considerations lead to the particular structure of the assurance case, which is tailored to the governance needs of the life cycle of the system of interest. However, within the complex mosaic of system life-cycle processes, the assurance activities follow certain steps based on the logical dependencies between inputs and outputs of these steps, as outlined in Chapter 3. The central goal of the assurance case developed in Chapter 3 is the so-called *safeguard effectiveness claim*. This claim involves one or more threats. Assurance strategy provides guidance on how to manage multiple safeguard effectiveness claims within the assurance case. With this understanding, systematic threat identification involves several distinct approaches, based on the particular threat component that is identified first. Selected strategy determines the structure of the collection of threats and consequently determines the detailed structure of the assurance argument and the goal structure of the assurance activities. Although multiple approaches are possible, the following five strategies are noteworthy:

- Injury argument (structure assurance argument by injuries to assets);
- Entry point argument (structure assurance argument by various entry points into the system);
- Threat activity argument (structure assurance argument by known threat categories, threat activities, and threat agent categories);
- Vulnerability argument (structure assurance argument by known vulnerabilities and weaknesses);
- Security requirements argument (structure assurance argument by the security requirements).

5.5.1 Injury argument

Injury argument considers various *undesired events* (threat events)—failures of assets and loss of assets and how this affects the mission of the system. Undesired events can, in turn, be structured by assets and asset types. Undesired events are used to identify the "points of injury" in the system, as specific *locations* in the system views (including the structure views as well as functional views) that are capable of producing injury to identified assets, and are therefore components of one or more individual security threats. The injury argument proceeds by identifying the safeguards in relation to how each undesired event is managed (deterred, prevented, detected, and reduced, see Figure 9). The injury argument justifies the selection of the safeguards, and if the resulting justification is weak and cannot be supported by defendable evidence, recommendations for additional safeguards for the corresponding system locations can be provided as feedback to the system engineering process. The injury strategy was used in the assurance case in Chapter 3.

5.5.2 Entry point argument

Entry point argument starts with the system *entry points*. This argument is warranted by the claim that all entry points are correctly identified. Potential issues related to knowledge of the entry points include hidden entry points (through the platform); hidden behaviors (in the platform); and interaction with the platform (incomplete facts related to behavior). Accurate information about the entry points can be acquired using a bottom-up approach. This approach starts with the implementation-level system facts to identify the physical entry points based on the well-known patterns determined by the underlying runtime platform and then traces them back to the conceptual entry points using the vertical traceability links. This approach usually provides very reliable, accurate information and therefore generates defendable evidence. This claim is further supported by the side argument justifying the accuracy and completeness of the implementation-level system facts (using evidence related to the properties of the knowledge discovery tools, the activities and transparency of the knowledge discovery process used, as well as the qualifications of the personnel running the knowledge discovery tools).

The argument then addresses each entry point separately. It identifies the behaviors related to the particular entry point, builds the behavior graph, and then assesses how effective are the safeguards in mitigating the undesired behaviors. This argument does not systematically enumerate the assets and injuries. Therefore, further assurance can be produced by cross-correlating the resulting list of threats with the systematically produced list of injuries, and/or the systematic inventory of assets to produce evidence that all high-impact behaviors have been addressed.

5.5.3 Threat argument

Threat argument starts with the preexisting catalog of *threat categories* from which threats to similar systems are selected. The initial list of threats is extended by system-specific threats based on the particular mission and the corresponding environment. The list of threats can be structured by the threat classes, threat activities, and threat agent categories (as illustrated in Figure 8). Then the safeguards are identified, and their effectiveness is evaluated to understand how well they mitigate the identified threats and whether any vulnerability can be identified by detecting a particular threat that is not adequately mitigated by safeguards.

The issue with this approach is related to the fundamental uncertainty of our knowledge of threats. One can be systematic, however, and construct a reasonable threat profile that can be further improved by additionally considering assets, impacts, and vulnerabilities. Accumulating cybersecurity knowledge in the form of machine-readable checklists created and updated by experts can significantly improve the rigor of security evaluations across the defender community. Completeness of the list of threats can be justified by the use of validated checklists, use of qualified and experienced personnel, and cross-correlation of the identified threats to systematic inventory of assets and injuries, including violation of system-specific security policy. This approach is not restricted to a catalog of known vulnerabilities, so it operates more *from the first principles* and can identify violations of security policy specific to the system of interest.

5.5.4 **Vulnerability argument**

The vulnerability argument starts with known *vulnerabilities* and weaknesses and proceeds to identifying safeguards and justifying that all identified vulnerabilities are adequately mitigated by the safeguards, commensurate with the security criteria. This strategy is based on availability of the following machine-readable content:

- Known vulnerabilities in off-the-shelf system elements;
- Known patterns of the "points of injury";
- Known patterns related to the potential causal factors of threats;
- Known safeguard inefficiency patterns.

The advantage of the vulnerability-centric strategy is that it aligns with follow-up risk mitigation activities that are driven by the identified vulnerabilities. The disadvantage of this approach is that a system vulnerability is a complex phenomenon, which makes it difficult to detect systematically, with sufficient assurance. Detection of security vulnerabilities generates *counterevidence* to the security claims for the system. However, the inability to detect further vulnerabilities represents only indirect evidence in support of the security claims. Therefore the vulnerability argument needs to be supported by other considerations, outlined in this section, as well as by the backing evidence related to the qualification and experience of the personnel performing vulnerability detection; characteristics of the tools involved (static analysis tools, penetration testing tools, etc.), and the corresponding methodologies, including the coverage criteria and patterns involved. Vulnerability argument is described in more detail in Chapters 6 and 7.

5.5.5 **Security requirement argument**

When assurance activities are integrated into the technical processes of the system life cycle, as illustrated at the beginning of Chapter 3, the assurance argument is organized in a distinct three-phase collection of goals:

- Sufficient threats have been identified and security objectives have been set commensurate with the security criteria of the assurance project.
- Security requirements to system elements and system functions mitigate the threats and achieve the identified security objectives.
- The system adequately implements the identified security requirements and achieves security objectives.

With this approach the majority of the system analysis activities of the assurance process are concerned with satisfying the identified security requirements either at the design phase as part of the Preliminary Security Assessment (PSA) or at the implementation phase as part of the System Security Assessment (SSA). Knowledge of assets, injuries, and threats is used at the first phase, known as the Threat and Risk Assessment (TRA) to justify the selection of the security requirements. Note that it is important to justify that implementation achieves security objectives, rather than simply justify satisfaction of the security requirements. The simple reason is that a system has emergent behaviors (the system is bigger than the sum of its parts); in particular, new functions and new vulnerabilities could be inserted into the system as it is implemented.

5.6 ASSURANCE OF THE THREAT IDENTIFICATION

Assurance evidence for threat identification is derived primarily from the use of relevant checklists and from traceability links between the elements of the integrated system model. Individual threat identification strategies (injury argument, entry point argument, threat argument, and vulnerability argument) all provide unique perspectives on threat. Assurance of threat identification is done by cross-correlating the results of these approaches. In addition, the identified components of threats are linked to the system elements, which allows for additional cross-correlation. (If a certain system element is associated with one of the threat components, are all similar elements also associated with threat components?) An additional backing argument is based on using qualified and experienced personnel to perform threat identification.

The threat identification activity involves verification and validation tasks, as well as the assurance task. For example, in Table 1 the threat identification activity (TIA) is summarized as consisting of the following steps:

Table 1 TIA Activity Steps

TIA Step	Major Tasks	Contributions to Assurance Case
TIA Verification	Review and analyze the results of the TIA process.	Process steps completed evidence
TIA Validation	Review and analyze the Security Zones to ensure its completeness and correctness.	Process steps completed evidence
	Review and analyze the description of the operational environment to ensure its completeness and correctness	Operational environment description
	Review, analyze, justify, and document security-related assumptions about the system, its operational environment, and its regulatory framework to ensure their completeness and correctness.	Security assumptions
	Review and analyze traceability between functions, failures, threats, threat impact, and safeguard effectiveness claims.	Integrated system model is updated safeguard effectiveness claims
	Review and analyze the credibility and sensitivity of derived safeguard effectiveness claims to assumptions and risk.	

Continued

Table 1 TIA Activity Steps—cont'd

TIA Step	Major Tasks	Contributions to Assurance Case
TIA Process Assurance	Ensure that the TIA steps are applied. Ensure that assessment approaches are applied. Ensure that all outputs of the TIA steps, including the TIA verification, TIA validation, and TIA process assurance, are formally placed under configuration management. Ensure that any deficiencies detected during the TIA verification or TIA validation activities have been resolved. Ensure that the TIA process would be repeatable by personnel other than the original analyst(s). Ensure that the findings have been disseminated to interested parties. Ensure that the outputs of the TIA process are not incorrect and/or incomplete due to deficiencies in the TIA process itself.	Process steps completed evidence Integrated system model is updated Deficiency log

Bibliography

Clifton, A. (2005). *Ericson II, Hazard Analysis Techniques for System Safety.* Hoboken, NJ: Wiley-Interscience.

ISO/IEC 13335-1 *Guidelines for the Management of IT Security.*

ISO/IEC 15443 *A Framework for IT Security Assurance.*

ISO/IEC 17779 *A Code of Practice for Information Security Management.*

ISO/IEC 27001 *Information Security Management Systems.*

ISO/IEC 15026 *Systems and Software Assurance, Draft.*

ISO/IEC 15288-1:2008 *Life Cycle Management—System Life Cycle Processes.* (2008).

ISO/IEC 15408-1:2005 *Information Technology—Security Techniques—Evaluation Criteria for IT Security Part 1: Introduction and General Model.* (2005).

McDaniel, D. (2008). Analyzing and Presenting Multi-Nation Process Interoperability Data for End-Users: the International Defence Enterprise Architecture Specification (IDEAS) project. In: *Proc. Integrated EA Conference.* London, UK. http://www.integrated-ea.com.

Military Standard MIL-STD-882D, *Standard Practice for System Safety.* (2000).

NATO Research and Technology Organization (RTO). *Improving Common Security Risk Analysis. TR-IST-049.* (2008).

NIST Special Publication SP800-30. (2002). *Risk Management Guide for Information Technology Systems.* Stoneburner, G., Goguen, A., Feringa, A.

CSE, RCMP. (2007). *Harmonized Threat and Risk Assessment (TRA) Methodology.* TRA-1 Date: October 23.

Sherwood, J., Clark, A., & Lynas, A. (2005). *Enterprise Security Architecture: A Business-Driven Approach.* San-Francisco, CA: CMP Books.

Schiffman, M., Eschelbeck, G., Ahmad, D., Wright, A., & Romanosky, S. (2004). *CVSS: A Common Vulnerability Scoring System.* National Infrastructure Advisory Council (NIAC).

Swiderski, F., & Snyder, W. (2004). *Threat Modeling.* Redmond, WA: Microsoft Press.

Knowledge of vulnerabilities as an element of cybersecurity argument

6

They attack when the opponent is unprepared and appear where least expected.

—Sun Tzu, The Art of War

6.1 VULNERABILITY AS A UNIT OF KNOWLEDGE

This chapter explores the current foundation of systems assurance—vulnerability detection. In Chapter 1 we introduced the concept of a vulnerability as a specific unit of knowledge related to a fault in the system that allows exploitation of the system. In Chapter 3 we related vulnerabilities to threats and safeguards and described three major kinds of vulnerabilities:

- off-the-shelf vulnerabilities – known vulnerabilities in commercial off-the-shelf products; once detected in a particular version of the product, these units of knowledge can be stored and accumulated because the same product is used in many other implemented systems. In a given system off-the-shelf vulnerabilities can be identified without the reference to threats;
- discernable vulnerabilities – vulnerabilities that can be detected based on a known pattern, again without the reference to the specific threats to the system of interest;
- unmitigated threats – vulnerabilities that are specific to the system of interest, when a particular threat is not adequately mitigated by the safeguards implemented in the system, as well as by any other features of the system of interest. Detection of these vulnerabilities requires comprehensive analysis of the system as described in Chapter 3.

The general guidance to the identification of threats for the purpose of systematically identifying unmitigated threats was provided in Chapter 5. This chapter addresses off-the-shelf vulnerabilities. Discernable vulnerabilities are addressed further in Chapter 7. In this chapter we discuss possibility of detecting off-the-shelf vulnerabilities, and the market of the vulnerability knowledge as well as the vulnerability detection ecosystem built around the NIST SCAP standards [NIST SP800-126].

System Assurance: Beyond Detecting Vulnerabilities. DOI: 10.1016/B978-0-12-381414-2.00006-3
Copyright © 2011 Elsevier Inc. All rights reserved.

While vulnerability knowledge is one of the most important parts of the systems assurance content, it must be integrated with other knowledge in order to enable assurance. The defense community must use systematic approaches that produce justifiable confidence in the effectiveness of defense mechanisms based on the adequate knowledge of their systems. The overview of the System Assurance process was given in Chapters 2 and 3 to guide in the transition from ad hoc vulnerability detection to systematic, fact-oriented and repeatable assurance.

6.1.1 What is vulnerability?

The term *vulnerability* refers to the features of a system that make it susceptible to a deliberate attack or hazardous event. This term originates from Latin noun vulnus—**wound** and the corresponding verb vulnero—**to wound, injure, hurt, harm.** The term vulnerability is an example of one of those tricky situations where the language makes it easy to create a useful word through the process known as objectification (creating a noun from a verb or an adjective; for example, doing → deed), that refers to several intuitive situations, but the overall *extent* of which is not quite as clear. You know that a system was impacted by an attack and therefore you know that the attack on the system took place and succeeded (from the defender's perspective you see the aftermath of the attack and often miss the events that lead to the preparation of the attack). In this case, it can be concluded that the system was vulnerable to the attack at what point the word vulnerability can be used to refer to the *features* of the system that made it vulnerable to the attack or to refer to the features of all systems that make them vulnerable to a similar attack, or to refer to features of all systems that make them vulnerable to all attacks. But, what are these features? What is the reality behind them? How do we systematically find them? The intentional scope of the objectified verb or adjective can be quite large and may include features of a different nature.

An intuitive example of vulnerability is a door or window in a residential home. Here is one of the expert reports on home intrusion that can be very much applied to a software system:

Statistics tell us that 70% of the burglars use some amount of force to enter a residential home, but their preference is to gain easy access through an open door or window. Although home burglaries may seem random in occurrence, they actually involve a selection process. The burglar's selection process is simple. Choose an unoccupied home with the easiest access, the greatest amount of cover, and with the best escape routes.

Remember, the burglar will simply bypass your home if it requires too much effort or requires more skill and tools than they possess. Windows are left unlocked and open at a much higher rate than doors, while sliding glass doors are secured only by latches and not locks. Most burglars enter via the front, back, or garage doors. Experienced burglars know that the garage door is usually the weakest point of entry followed by the back door. The average door strike plate is secured only by the softwood doorjamb molding – these light-weight moldings are construction/structure flaws and are easy to break.

Good neighbors should look out for each other, detecting any suspicious activity especially around weak points. In addition, alarm systems are at the top of a home security plan and home safes are excellent protection for valuable assets in case the intruder succeeds in entering the house.

The first step in protecting your house and assets is to harden the target or make your home more difficult to enter.

The same situation is with software systems—if weak features in the software are not identified, fixed, and protected by safeguards, they turn into vulnerabilities enabling the intruder to enter the system.

The concept of "vulnerability" is a powerful *abstraction* that allows us to collectively refer to a multitude of otherwise unrelated situations, events, and things from a particular viewpoint—how these situations, events, and things enable attacks. The concept of vulnerability is useful because it provides convenient shorthand for certain sentences (for example, "the increased budget for understanding the vulnerabilities in critical infrastructure"). This concept allows consideration of the systems in isolation from the details of the attacks and attackers (as these details are not always available), as well as in isolation from the details of the victim system (as hardly any organization is motivated to publish these details). So, the concept of "vulnerability" abstracts away the relationship between the system and the attacker, which uses a particular attack vector. It considers just the attack's footprint in the system regardless of the exact identity of the attacker and even the variations of the attack actions. Some usages may become disconnected from the discernable reality and result in ambiguous and even contentious statements. The fact-oriented approach and the linguistic analysis are the tools that are used to disentangle some of these ambiguous usages. Further details of the fact-oriented approach and linguistic analysis are provided in Chapters 9 and 10.

Why is the concept of a "vulnerability" relevant to system assurance? In fact, the concept of vulnerability happens to be quite central to the current mainstream approach to systems assurance. According to NDIA [NDIA 2008], system assurance is defined as the justified confidence that the system functions as intended and is free of exploitable vulnerabilities, either intentionally or unintentionally designed or inserted as part of the system at any time during the life cycle.

This approach is based on an observation that vulnerability has a somewhat deterministic nature: It is either "designed in" or "inserted" into the system, and once it is there, it stays there. For example, an unscrupulous construction worker could tamper with the latch on the sliding door while installing it. This creates the *place* on the house that is less resistant to forced entry. This is an example of a vulnerability intentionally inserted as part of the system. The construction worker can then sell this vulnerability to a burglar. The same vulnerability can occur unintentionally and unknowingly as the result of an incident at the sliding door factory. An example of a vulnerability "designed into the system," an insecure operational procedure of the system, is the scenario when the homeowner can disarm the alarm and open the door to the burglar who shouts "Fire! Fire!" outside of the door. The first example involves the physical structure of the system, the second example involves the operating procedures and the states of the system.

From the assurance perspective, the following two questions need to be answered: "How do we systematically inspect the system for vulnerabilities?" and "How do we build confidence that the system is free from vulnerabilities?" This chapter addresses several knowledge aspects of this problem. How can we know what are all vulnerabilities? Can one produce a list of all vulnerabilities of a given system? How many vulnerabilities can a system have? Is there a finite number of them? How one can look for them?

The emphasis of this chapter is to provide a uniform view on the vulnerability knowledge so that vulnerability facts can be systematically managed throughout the system assurance process.

6.1.2 The history of vulnerability as a unit of knowledge

The notion of a vulnerability as a concrete technical defect that contributes to an attack that can be studied and cataloged (and thus the usage of the word "vulnerability" in the plural form), in short, the notion of a vulnerability as a unit of knowledge, began catching the public attention in the 1970s.

Brief analysis of the publications in the *New York Times* (see Table 1) shows the following distribution of the number of articles that mention the word "vulnerability" in singular form in comparison to the plural form "vulnerabilities".

These statistics include all articles regardless of the context in which the term "vulnerability" is used. The most frequent contexts involve politics and defense, including the famous "window of vulnerability" theme of Ronald Reagan's

Table 1: Number of Articles in the *New York Times* That Mention the Word "Vulnerability" vs. "Vulnerabilities"

Period	Singular	Plural
1900–1909	33	0
1910–1919	54	1
1920–1929	111	0
1930–1939	271	0
1940–1949	385	1
1950–1959	462	7
1960–1969	890	25
1970–1979	1884	97
1980–1989	3098	233
1990–1999	2691	396
2000–2009	3892	980

presidential campaign of 1980, which was mentioned in 181 articles in the period of 1980–1989, two articles prior to this period, and six articles after this period. Since the 1980s, the attention of the public shifted toward the social impact of the computer systems. The increasing use of the plural form indicates the interest towards individual vulnerabilities as identifiable features, that can be enumerated and catalogued.

The catalogs of computer vulnerabilities, complete with rich technical detail, became publicly available in the late 1980s. Computer Emergency Response Team (CERT) started publishing technical advisories since it was established in 1988. CERT advisories provided timely information about current security issues, vulnerabilities, and availability of exploits. The independent Bugtraq mailing list was established in 1993 to raise awareness of the security issues in commercial software products and force better patching by vendors.

The particular event that has triggered the process of consolidation of the defender community was the so-called Morris worm incident that affected 10% of Internet systems in November 1988. A few months later the Computer Emergency Response Team Coordination Center (CERT/CC) was established at the Software Engineering Institute (SEI). SEI is a federally funded research and development center at Carnegie Mellon University in Pittsburgh, Pennsylvania. The Defense Advanced Research Projects Agency (DARPA) tasked the SEI with setting up a center to coordinate communication among experts during security emergencies and to help prevent future incidents. Although it was established as an incident response team, the CERT/CC has evolved beyond that, focusing instead on identifying and addressing existing and potential threats and the corresponding vulnerabilities, notifying systems administrators and other technical personnel of these vulnerabilities, and coordinating with vendors and incident response teams worldwide to address the vulnerabilities.

Since the 1970s, the academic community began studying the flaws, errors, defects, and vulnerabilities in computer systems that lead to their failure and abuse under deliberate attacks. Cautious at the beginning, the publications of the technical details of the vulnerabilities increased in the 1990s. Since then multiple taxonomies of computer vulnerabilities have been suggested and several online databases of computer vulnerabilities have been developed, detailing over 60,000 individual technical vulnerabilities in over 27,000 software products, covering the period of 45 years.

Likely, the most well known of computer vulnerability types—the buffer overflow—was understood as early as 1972, when the Computer Security Technology Planning Study laid out the technique: "The code performing this function does not check the source and destination addresses properly, permitting portions of the monitor to be overlaid by the user. This can be used to inject code into the monitor that will permit the user to seize control of the machine." Today, the monitor would be referred to as the operating system kernel.

The earliest documented hostile exploitation of a buffer overflow was in 1988. It was one of several exploits used by the Morris worm to propagate itself over the Internet. The program exploited was a UNIX service called *finger*. Later, in 1995,

Thomas Lopatic independently rediscovered the buffer overflow and published his findings on the Bugtraq security mailing list. A year later, in 1996, Elias Levy published in *Phrack* magazine the paper "Smashing the Stack for Fun and Profit," a step-by-step introduction to exploiting stack-based buffer overflow vulnerabilities.

Since then, at least two major Internet worms have exploited buffer overflows to compromise a large number of systems. In 2001, the Code Red worm exploited a buffer overflow in Microsoft's Internet Information Services (IIS) 5.0, and in 2003, the SQL Slammer worm compromised machines running Microsoft SQL Server 2000.

Interest in the technical details of the impact of technology correlated with the successful deployment of computer networks and the subsequent rise of cyber-crime. Several other technologies have created the network phenomenon, such as railways, telegraph, and telephone, but none of them caused such interest in the discussion of vulnerabilities as computer networks, partly because none of the previous technologies, while comparable in scope, have created bigger opportunities for abuse—as well as larger impact of their abuse and failure.

On the other hand, the problem of failures in engineering systems was not entirely new. Some argue, that the knowledge of the past failures is also the key to understanding the engineering profession: "the colossal disasters that do occur are ultimately failures of design, but the lessons learned from these disasters can do more to advance engineering knowledge than all the successful machines and structures in the world" [Petroski 1992]. The failures of computer systems have been discussed since soon after the first commercial computers were introduced in 1951. Initially these discussions were driven by the military community and were focused at handling of sensitive information in time-sharing computer systems. At nearly the same time, the public started discussion of the impact of information systems and computer networks on privacy. The concepts of computer security and privacy as we know them today, appeared at least in the mid-1960s. The concept of a vulnerability of computers has been discussed since back in 1965.

At the same time, the field of safety engineering has already been developing mathematical methods for analysis of random failures in systems, namely the Failure Modes, Effects, and Analysis (since 1949) and Fault Tree Analysis Method (since 1961). The concept of *safeguards* is old and well-established in the field of systems engineering. The challenge brought by the interconnected computer systems was that of the deliberate, non-random nature of the attacks that are aimed at inducing the failures and the enormous complexity of the systems.

6.1.3 Vulnerabilities and the phases of the system life cycle

Note that a design error or even an implementation error does not by itself produce *injury* (there is no harm from a software package when it is sitting on the shelf), unless the system is actually put into operation, is performing its function, and is running. And even then, the attacker has to exercise some control over the system to cause the system to produce some injury.

The key question is, "What exactly happens during the 'exploitation of vulnerability'"? What "state of affairs" "can produce injury" and in what sense it "can be reached" by the attacker?

It is the system that produces injury during its operation. The attacker *"exploits"* the system by exercising control over the system by providing some specially crafted inputs to the system, and steering its behavior into the state where injury is produced.

The objective of system assessment is to analyze available artifacts of the system in order to systematically identify (predict) all states of the operation that may result in injury to system's assets (given a motivated and capable attacker).

A state is a certain sequence of events, part of the master sequence of events that corresponds to the overall behavior. Behavior of the system is in most cases potentially infinite (in practice; however, each behavior is always finite, because each system is at some point put into operation and usually is periodically stopped, even though some information systems run for months without interruption). The only practical way of describing infinite behavior is by considering the repeating sequences of events or states and describing them a cyclic state transition graph. This is always possible, in principle, since each system is determined by a finite set of rules (e.g., the instructions in the code), and each event in the behavior of the system is associated with a particular rule; for example, a fragment of code. One fragment of code is usually associated with multiple states. For example, the code contains an instruction: "display the price of the item," which causes the appearance of the number at the screen. Depending on the choice of the event vocabulary, this may correspond to multiple states, for example, "a positive number is displayed" and "number zero is displayed." The particular state (within the given event vocabulary) is determined by the previous behavior of the system, which in some cases may be influenced by the inputs from the attacker.

Some of the events can be described as *threat events*. Mistakes, errors, faults, or issues may be *introduced* at various stages of the system's life cycle (including the entirely incorrect requirements that the system is trying to implement). The system code has to be deployed and configured, producing the actual system ready to be put into operation. Until the system is put into operation nothing malicious can happen.

During the system's operation, there could also be errors in the operational procedures or the operator's errors that cause a threat event to occur.

Multiple publications attempt to distinguish several distinct categories of vulnerabilities. For example, it is useful to distinguish technology-related and organizational vulnerabilities:

- Technology-related is defined as any weakness that is introduced into the deployed system, whether introduced into the system code and not mitigated by the system configuration, or one introduced through the system configuration.
- Organizational is defined as any weakness in the operational procedures.

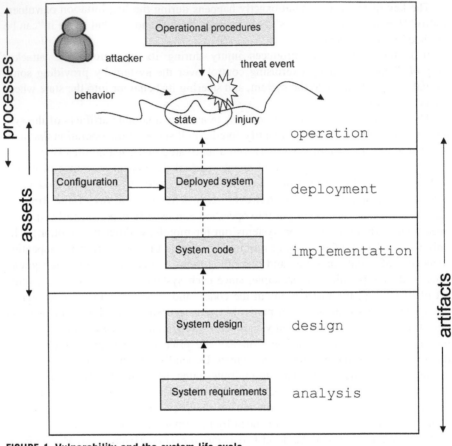

FIGURE 1 Vulnerability and the system life cycle

The *stages* at which faults can be introduced into the system are illustrated in Figure 1. This illustration is a guide for selection of the artifacts for analysis by automated tools, as well as the limitations of this approach.

6.1.4 Enumeration of vulnerabilities as a knowledge product

So, individual vulnerabilities can be enumerated. Indeed, the system (or at least an off-the-shelf component) can be identified, followed by identification of distinct *events* through which injury can be produced. A distinct kind of injury corresponds to a distinct vulnerability. For example, you may identify vulnerabilities that allow remote execution of code on the attacked computer and another group that allows leaking of files from the attacked computer. But how do we know what the distinct vulnerabilities are that allow remote execution of code? The sources of ambiguities are variations in the steps leading to "exploitation," raising the question: Are two different exploits that allow remote execution of code using the same vulnerability, or two different ones?

In order to address the ambiguities resulting from the variations in exploiting vulnerabilities, the distinguishing characteristic of the *"location"* of the vulnerability in the system code and the artifacts that are involved in producing injury can be considered. For example, a certain type of location can be defined as the offset in the executable file of the component. If two different exploits target a buffer overflow at the same location in the executable, then they use the same vulnerability. When the source code of the system is available, the location in the binary file can be substituted to the line number and position in a source file.

Distinction between vulnerability and an insecure configuration is useful when addressing the difference between the system code and deployed systems with various configurations. Vulnerability is determined by the software code, while an exposure is determined by the configuration of the system. On the other hand, an exposure is often supported by code. A very common exposure is a default password in a component, such as a router or a firewall. In some deployed systems the administrator will change the default password into a new one (hopefully, a strong password with 10 characters with lower case, uppercase, special characters and digits); however, some systems will be put into operations with the default password, in which case a vulnerability is created during the system configuration (by inaction, by not doing anything). However, this vulnerability is supported by the design of the code where either the default password is hardcoded or where the code assumes that the password is always present in the configuration file. Both situations support the inaction on behalf of the administrator. The exact location of this code is less obvious than in the case of code immediately responsible for injury, like a buffer overflow. This is a technical difficulty, but not a conceptual one. No matter how difficult it may be to establish the boundary for the authentication mechanism in the code, it is still possible to do so. Such a boundary will be part of the "location" of the exposure because the harm event here consists in passing this boundary with a default password, since obviously the attacker can download the administrator guide or try the default password. The system can have multiple configuration exposures; for example, a default administrator password and a default guest user password. These exposures have different locations, even if they use the same code for checking the password, as in the administrator password example above, the two situations will use different entry points.

To summarize, different vulnerabilities produce different kinds of injury and use different locations in the code of the system or an off-the-shelf component.

Based on these considerations, you can start accumulating technical knowledge about distinct vulnerabilities in systems.

There are three levels of technical knowledge related to vulnerabilities:

1. The knowledge that a distinct vulnerability exists in a particular system or commercial software product.
2. The knowledge of a working exploit for the vulnerability (at least one).

3. The knowledge of a pattern for the vulnerability (e.g., something that is the same for all buffer overflows regardless of where in the code or in which product they occur)

6.2 VULNERABILITY DATABASES

The Morris Internet worm incident of 1988 was the turning point, when the cybersecurity community began accumulating knowledge on the technical details of vulnerabilities in commercial software products. Since then, several public vulnerability databases were established.

A vulnerability database is supported by a so-called *Security information provider* who tracks the new vulnerabilities and publishes alerts to a wide community of subscribers. A vulnerability database is a collection of records containing technical descriptions of vulnerabilities in computer systems. Some vulnerability databases are organized as simple unstructured mailing lists where messages are posted to announce a new vulnerability and discuss it. Others are more structured collections of records, more like real databases. Most security information providers offer search capabilities and RSS feeds. Several companies are offering secondary aggregation of the alerts from multiple databases. In Table 2, we provide a snapshot (as of mid-January 2010) current vulnerability databases.

A record in a vulnerability database is the current unit of knowledge of a technical vulnerability. It contains a brief description of the issue and lists the vulnerable products, mentioning the vendor, product name, and version. Each vulnerability entry is assigned a unique identifier. Most vulnerability databases allow search by vendor and product. Each record usually includes multiple references to related information, usually vendor information, other vulnerability databases, blogs, etc. Often, vulnerability is given a rating. It is very useful and recommended to use available information (through subscriptions) for risk assessment because most implemented systems involve off-the-shelf components. Choice of which database is better or more useful should be based on information needed by a given system in a given environment with a goal of achieving the confidence in a decision being made.

As your system uses multiple off-the-shelf components, there are numerous vulnerability *facts* that are available as input to the system assurance process. The key concern is to systematically manage these facts and integrate them with other units of knowledge for your system. Below we describe the *conceptual commitment* related to the vulnerability knowledge. As you will see, different vulnerability databases provide slightly different facts, so it is important to be able to collate these facts. In the section on NIST SCAP ecosystem and its common vulnerability identifier approach we will show the first solution to this problem. Further technical guidance to the OMG fact-oriented approach to integration of all units of cybersecurity knowledge is provided in Chapter 9.

Table 2: List of Vulnerability Databases

Name	Year Established	Type	Total Number of Vulnerabilities	Total Number of Products	Total Number of Product Vendors
CERT	1988	Database	44,074		
Bugtraq	1993	Mailing list			
Internet Security Systems (ISS X-Force)	1994	Database	40,000		
Security Focus	1999	Database	37,927		3,176
CVE	1999	Naming standard	42,232		
Security Tracker	2001	Database			
Vulnwatch	2001	Mailing list			
OSVDB	2002	Database	60,706	26,577	4,414
Secunia	2002	Database	31,062	27,853	4,244
US-CERT	2003	Database	2,615		
FrSirt/ Vupen	2004	Database		20,000	8,000
NIST NVD	2005	Database	40,358	20,275	

6.2.1 US-CERT

US-CERT publishes information about a wide variety of vulnerabilities [US-CERT]. Vulnerabilities that meet a certain severity threshold are described in US-CERT Technical Alerts. However, it is difficult to measure the severity of a vulnerability in a way that is appropriate for all users. For example, a severe vulnerability in a rarely used application may not qualify for publication as a technical alert but may be very important to a system administrator who runs the vulnerable application. US-CERT Vulnerability Notes provide a way to publish information about these less-severe vulnerabilities.

Vulnerability notes include technical descriptions of the vulnerability, as well as the impact, solutions and workarounds, and lists of affected vendors. You can search the vulnerability notes database, or you can browse by several key fields. Help is available for customizing search queries and view features. You can customize database queries to obtain specific information, such as the 10 most recently updated vulnerabilities or the 20 vulnerabilities with the highest severity metric.

US-CERT also offers a subscription feed that lists the 30 most recently published vulnerability notes.

The US-CERT Vulnerability Notes Database contains two types of documents: Vulnerability Notes, which generally describe vulnerabilities independent of a particular vendor, and Vendor Information documents, which provide information about a specific vendor's solution to a problem. The fields in each of these documents are described here in more detail.

For the purpose of information consolidation between vulnerability entries from deferent databases it is useful to summarize presented information by the model in Figure 2

The diagram is a conceptual model of the US-CERT database, illustrating the noun concepts and their roles. These concepts are explained below. This is the vocabulary of concrete *vulnerability facts* that extends the generic terms given in Chapter 5.

Vulnerability ID – US-CERT assigns vulnerability ID numbers at random to uniquely identify a vulnerability. These IDs are four to six digits long and are frequently prefixed with "VU#" to mark them as vulnerability IDs; for example VU#492515. This ID is specific to vulnerability facts managed by the US-CERT database. Without standardization, such as the NIST SCAP, facts from a different vulnerability database may be difficult (or even impossible) to collate with the

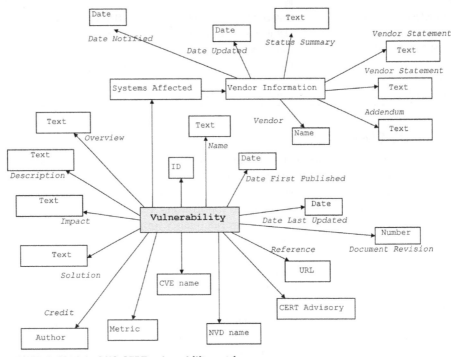

FIGURE 2 Model of US-CERT vulnerability entries

facts from US-CERT. Vulnerability is such a complex phenomenon, so it is not uncommon that two vulnerability researchers identify different states and locations as the vulnerability responsible to the same incident. The situation is further complicated by the fact that one security incident may involve multiple vulnerabilities.

Vulnerability name – The vulnerability name is a short description that summarizes the nature of the problem and the affected software product. While the name may include a clause describing the impact of the vulnerability, most names are focused on the nature of the defect that caused the problem to occur. For example, "Microsoft Explorer HTML object memory corruption vulnerability."

Overview – The overview is an abstract of the vulnerability that provides a summary of the problem and its impact to the reader. The overview field was not originally in the database, so older documents may not include this information. For example, "An invalid pointer reference within Microsoft Internet Explorer may lead to execution of arbitrary code."

Description – The vulnerability description contains one or more paragraphs of text describing the vulnerability.

Impact – The impact statement describes the benefit that an intruder might gain by exploiting the vulnerability. It also frequently includes preconditions the attacker must meet to be able to exploit the vulnerability. For example, "By convincing a user to load a specially crafted HTML document or Microsoft Office document, a remote, unauthenticated attacker may be able to execute arbitrary code or cause a denial-of-service condition."

Solution – The solution section contains information about how to correct the vulnerability.

Systems affected – This section includes a list of systems that may be affected by the vulnerability including the information about vendors. The vendor name is a link to more detailed information from the vendor about the vulnerability in question. Additional summary information is provided for each vendor as well, including a status field indicating whether the vendor has any vulnerable products for the issue described in the vulnerability note, and dates when the vendor was notified and when the vendor information was last updated.

Date notified – This is the date that the vendor was notified of the vulnerability. In some cases, this may be the date that the vendor first contacted us, or it may be the earliest date when the vendor is known to have been aware of the vulnerability (for example, if they published a patch or an advisory).

Date updated – This is when the vendor information was last updated. As vendors produce patches and publish advisories, vendor statement, vendor information, or addendum fields may be updated, affecting this date.

Status summary – This field indicates, in broad terms, whether the vendor has any products that we consider to be vulnerable. In many cases, the relationship between a vendor's products and a vulnerability is more complex than a simple "Vulnerable" or "Not Vulnerable" field. Users are encouraged to read the detailed vendor statements and to use this field only as a broad indicator of whether any products might be vulnerable.

Vendor statement – This is the vendor's official response to our queries about the vulnerability. With little more than typographical edits, this information is provided directly by the vendor and does not necessarily reflect our opinions. In fact, vendors are welcome to provide statements that contradict other information in the vulnerability note. We suggest that the vendors include relevant information about correcting the problem, such as pointers to software patches and security advisories. We are highly confident that information in this field comes from the vendor. Statements are usually PGP signed or otherwise authenticated.

Vendor information – This is information we are reasonably confident is from the vendor. Typically, this includes public documents (that were not sent to us by the vendor) and statements that are not strongly authenticated.

Addendum – The addendum section contains one or more paragraphs of US-CERT comments on this vulnerability, especially when US-CERT disagrees with the vendor's assessment of the problem, when the vendor did not provide a statement.

References – The references are a collection of URLs at our web site and others providing additional information about the vulnerability.

Credit – This section of the document identifies who initially discovered the vulnerability, anyone who was instrumental in the development of the vulnerability note, and the primary author of the document.

Date public – This is the date on which the vulnerability was first known to the public. Usually this date is when the vulnerability note was first published, when an exploit was first discovered, when the vendor first distributed a patch publicly, or when a description of the vulnerability was posted to a public mailing list.

Date first published – This is the date when we first published the vulnerability note. This date should be the date public or later.

Date last updated – This is the date the vulnerability note was last updated. Each vulnerability note is updated as new information is received, or when a vendor information document changes for this vulnerability note.

CERT advisory – If a CERT Advisory was published for this vulnerability, this field will contain a pointer to that advisory. Beginning January 28, 2004, CERT Advisories became a core component of US-CERT Technical Alerts.

CVE name – The CVE name is a standardized identificator of a vulnerability, part of NIST SCAP. CVE name is the thirteen-character ID used by the "Common Vulnerabilities and Exposures" group to uniquely identify a vulnerability. The name is also a link to additional information on the CVE web site about the vulnerability. While the mapping between CVE names and US-CERT vulnerability IDs are usually pretty close, in some cases multiple vulnerabilities may map to one CVE name, or vice versa. The CVE group tracks a large number of security problems, not all of which meet the US-CERT criteria for being considered a vulnerability. For example, US-CERT does not track viruses or Trojan horse programs in the vulnerability notes database. A sample CVE name is "CVE-2010-0249."

NVD name – The NVD name is usually the same as the CVE name. The name is also a link to additional information on the National Vulnerability Database (NVD) which is repository for the NSIT SCAP standardized content.

Metric – The metric value is a number between 0 and 180 that assigns an approximate severity to the vulnerability. This number considers several factors, including:

- Is information about the vulnerability widely available or known?
- Is the vulnerability being exploited?
- Is the Internet infrastructure at risk because of this vulnerability?
- How many systems on the Internet are at risk from this vulnerability?
- What is the impact of exploiting the vulnerability?
- How easy is it to exploit the vulnerability?
- What are the preconditions required to exploit the vulnerability?

Because the questions are answered with approximate values that may differ significantly from one site to another, users should not rely too heavily on the metric for prioritizing vulnerabilities. However, it may be useful for separating the very serious vulnerabilities from the large number of less severe vulnerabilities described in the database. Typically, vulnerabilities with a metric greater than 40 are candidates for US-CERT Technical Alerts. The questions are not all weighted equally, and the resulting score is not linear (a vulnerability with a metric of 40 is not twice as severe as one with a metric of 20).

Document revision – This field contains the revision number for this document. This field can be used to determine whether the document has changed since the last time it was viewed.

6.2.2 Open Source Vulnerability Database

This section illustrates the Open Source Vulnerability Database (OSVDB) [OSVDB].

Figure 3 illustrates the conceptual model of the OSVBD vulnerability database, focusing at the noun concepts and their roles.

Vulnerability ID – OSVDB assigns unique vulnerability ID numbers to identify vulnerability. For example, 61697.

Title – The vulnerability title is a short description that summarizes the nature of the problem and the affected software product. While the name may include a clause describing the impact of the vulnerability, most names are focused on the nature of the defect that caused the problem to occur. For example, "Microsoft IE mshtml.dll Use-After-Free Arbitrary Code Execution (Aurora)."

Description – The vulnerability title is a short description that summarizes the nature of the problem and the affected software product. While the name may include a clause describing the impact of the vulnerability, most names are focused on the nature of the defect that caused the problem to occur.

Disclosure date – This is usually the same as Public Date in US-CERT. This is the date on which the vulnerability was first published. However, as opposed to US-CERT, OSVDB tracks separately the date when an exploit was first discovered, when the vendor first distributed a patch publicly, and when a description of the vulnerability was posted to a public mailing list.

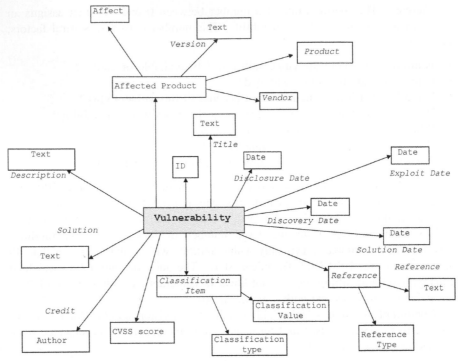

FIGURE 3 Model of OSVDB vulnerability entries

Discovery date – This is the date on which the vulnerability was posted to a public mailing list.

Exploit date – This is the date on which the an exploit was first discovered.

Solution date – This is the date in which the vendor first distributed a patch publicly.

Classification – OSVDB provides own classification of vulnerabilities. The classification is a list of items, where each pair consists of a classification type (dimension of the classification vector) and a value. For example, a classification statement for 61697 is "Location: Local/Remote, Context Dependent; Attack Type: Input Manipulation; Impact: Loss of Integrity; Disclosure: Discovered in the Wild; OSVDB: web-related."

Classification type – Classification vector is OSVDB includes the following dimensions: Location, Attack Type, Impact, Disclosure, and other.

Classification value –The classification value provides the value of a classification item on the dimension defined by the classification type. For example, Location type has the following values: Local, Remote, Dialup, Wireless, Mobile, Local/Remote, Context Dependent, and Unknown. Attack Type has the following values: Authentication Management, Cryptographic, Denial of Service,

Information Disclosure, Infrastructure, Input Manipulation, Misconfiguration, Race Condition, Other, Unknown. Impact has the following values: Confidentiality, Integrity, Availability.

Solution – The solution section contains information about how to correct the vulnerability.

Affected products – This section includes a list of vendors who may be affected by the vulnerability. OSVDB contains normalized facts about {vendor, product, version} configurations, each can be annotated as Affected, Not Affected, or Possibly Affected. Vendor names and product names are enumerations specific to OSVDB (see Table 3).

Table 3: Example of Affected Product Facts	
Affect type:	*Affected*
Vendor:	*Microsoft Corporation*
Product:	*Internet Explorer*
Version:	*6 SP1*

References – The references are a collection of URLs at our web site and others providing additional information about the vulnerability. In OSVDB, each reference is annotated with the reference type. OSVDB provides references to other major vulnerability databases, such as Security Focus, Secunia, ISS X-Force, CVE, US-CERT, Security Tracker, and VUPEN; references to exploits, such as Metasploit and Milw0rm; and references to scanner tools signatures, such as Nessus Script ID, Nikto Item ID, OVAL ID, Packet Storm, Snort Signature ID, and Tenable PVS.

Credits – This section of the vulnerability record identifies the vulnerability researcher who initially discovered the vulnerability. At the time of writing, there were 4739 contributors to OSVDB.

6.3 VULNERABILITY LIFE CYCLE

There are several events associated with vulnerability as a unit of knowledge of interest to the community: creation, discovery, disclosure, the release of a patch, publication, and automation of the exploitation. "Vulnerability life cycle" is illustrated at Figure 4. A "vulnerability life cycle" helps better understand possible sequences of events associated with a given vulnerability during its lifetime. This demonstrates above all that the off-the-shelf vulnerability knowledge is ad hoc, hit-and-miss, and must be integrated into more systematic approaches. New attacks demonstrate that hackers have knowledge of some vulnerabilities that are unknown to the product vendors and security information providers. There exist a market for vulnerability

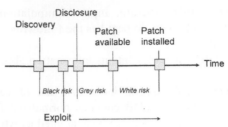

FIGURE 4 Vulnerability life cycle

knowledge where a unit of vulnerability knowledge has a price tag from several thousand US dollars to a once reported $125.000 for a previously unknown vulnerability with a reliable exploit. The usual order of events in a vulnerability life cycle is as follows [Arbaugh 2000]:

- **Creation**. Vulnerabilities are usually created unintentionally, during system development. Vulnerability is caused by an incorrect design decision at one of the phases of the system life cycle. Mistakes and bugs that are discovered and fixed during the development and testing phases are not counted as vulnerabilities, only those flaws that are released into the operations of the system. If the creation is malicious and thus intentional, discovery and creation coincide. The time of vulnerability creation can be established in retrospect, after the vulnerability is discovered.
- **Discovery**. When someone discovers that a product has security or survivability implications, the flaw becomes vulnerability. It doesn't matter if the discoverer is part of the attacker or defender community. In many cases, there is no record of the original discovery event; the discoverer may never disclose his finding. When a vulnerability is first discovered by the vendor of the product, the fix may become available simultaneously with the disclosure, or in some cases even without the disclosure, when the fix is added into a large bundle. This is why patches from vendors are scrutinized by vulnerability researchers.
- **Disclosure**. The vulnerability is disclosed when the discoverer reveals details of the problem to a wider audience. For example, vulnerability announcement may be posted to a public mailing list such as Bugtraq. As a full-disclosure moderated mailing list, Bugtraq serves as a forum for detailed discussion and announcement of computer security vulnerabilities: What they are, how to exploit them, and how to fix them. Alternatively, details of the vulnerability may be communicated to the product vendor directly. Obviously, the many levels of disclosure comprise a vast continuum of who was informed and what aspect of the vulnerability the disclosure revealed. Currently ISO/IEC is working on a standard on Responsible Vulnerability Disclosure (ISO/IEC CD 29147).
- **Correction**. Vulnerability is correctable when the vendor or developer releases a software modification or configuration change that corrects the underlying flaw.

After that, the administrator of the particular system affected by this vulnerability has the responsibility of applying the patch. Many systems for several years remain uncorrected and therefore vulnerable.

- **Exploitation**. The knowledge of the vulnerability can be expanded to the point when a particular sequence of actions is developed and tried, at least in the laboratory environment that actually penetrates at least one deployed system that uses the vulnerable product. There is a thriving community interested in successful exploits (representing various shades of penetration testers, vulnerability researchers, hackers, and criminals). Needless to say, some exploits never become public knowledge.
- **Publicity**. Vulnerability becomes public in several ways. A news story could bring attention to the problem, or an incident response center could issue a report concerning the vulnerability. Some vulnerabilities live a quiet life (never discovered, never disclosed, or disclosed only to a vendor and then quietly fixed). Disclosure to a public mailing list for the security community is a gray area. However, some vulnerabilities receive significant public attention, often because they were used by a high-profile cyber attack, or because the media picks up the story and expands it beyond the security community and the vendors.
- **Scripting**. Initially, successful exploitation of a new vulnerability requires moderate skill. However, once the steps leading to a successful exploitation are scripted, those with little or no skill can exploit the vulnerability to compromise systems. Scripting dramatically increases the size of the population that can exploit systems with that vulnerability. Further, although we use the term "scripting" in the sense of automating, this phase applies to any simplification of intrusion techniques that exploit the vulnerability, such as hacker "cookbooks" or detailed descriptions on how to exploit the vulnerability. In essence, at this point the vulnerability has been industrialized.
- **Death**. Vulnerability dies when the number of systems that can be exploited becomes insignificant because all systems at risk have been patched or retired. In practice, administrators can never patch all the systems at risk. Vulnerability creation, discovery and disclosure are casually related, so they always occur in this order. Disclosure can, however, occur almost simultaneously with discovery. After the initial disclosure, the vulnerability can be further disclosed, made public, scripted, or corrected in any order.

6.4 NIST SECURITY CONTENT AUTOMATION PROTOCOL (SCAP) ECOSYSTEM

Standardization of vulnerability knowledge by NIST SCAP [NIST SP800-126] established a larger cyber security *ecosystem*, which allows automated exchanges of content and development of vulnerability management tools that can consume this standardized content and automate the key *vulnerability management* operations for the defender community. Security Content Automation Protocol (SCAP) has been developed to help provide organizations with a comprehensive, standardized approach to exchanging vulnerability knowledge as content for automated vulnerability management tools. SCAP comprises a suite of specifications for organizing and expressing vulnerability-related information in standardized ways. SCAP can be used for maintaining the security of enterprise systems, such as automatically verifying the installation of patches, checking system security configuration settings, and examining systems for signs of compromise.

6.4.1 Overview of SCAP ecosystem

SCAP has two major elements. First, it is a *protocol*—a suite of six open specifications that standardize the format and nomenclature by which security software communicates information about software flaws and security configurations. Each specification is also known as a SCAP component. Second, SCAP includes software flaw and security configuration standardized reference data, also known as SCAP *content* (see Tables 4 and 5).

The components are grouped by type:

- Enumerations, vulnerability measurement, and scoring, and
- Expression and checking languages.

The enumerations group has nomenclatures and dictionaries for security and product-related information.

SCAP has several uses, other than automating checks for known vulnerabilities, including automating the verification of security configuration settings, and generating reports that link low-level settings to high-level requirements.

6.4.2 Information exchanges in SCAP ecosystem

The next two characteristics of the NIST SCAP ecosystem are important to list and discuss since they are responsible for SCAP success and global improvement in security vulnerability management.

First, NIST standards for SCAP allow formal compliance checking. NIST has established the SCAP Product Validation program and SCAP Laboratory Accreditation program to certify compliance to SCAP. These programs work together to ensure that SCAP products are thoroughly tested and validated to conform to SCAP requirements. Given SCAP's complexity, this formal testing is needed to ensure that products properly implement SCAP. Acquisition officials have already embedded requirements for SCAP-validated products in their procurements. For example, U.S. Office of Management and Budget (OMB) requires federal agencies and agency IT providers to use SCAP-validated Federal Desktop Core Configuration (FDCC) scanners for testing and assessing FDCC compliance.

To help automate security configuration verification, organizations can use National Vulnerability Database (NVD) to identify and obtain SCAP-expressed security configuration checklists relevant for their systems' operating systems and

Table 4: Standardization of Vulnerability and Related Knowledge

SCAP Component	Type	Description	Organization
Common Vulnerabilities and Exposures (CVE)	Dictionary	Dictionary of unique standard names of known vulnerabilities	CVE Editorial Board decides on assigning unique names to new vulnerabilities; MITRE Corporation maintains the dictionary; CVE records are the primary content of the NIST NVD
Common Platform Enumeration (CPE) schema	Schema	Definition of a schema for the dictionary of known products and the language for describing complex platforms	MITRE corporation maintains the schema
Common Platform Enumeration (CPE) dictionary	Dictionary	Dictionary of unique standard names of known software products, including IT systems, platforms and applications	MITRE corporation maintains the dictionary
CVE associated with CPE			NIST NVD maintains association between CVE records and their CPE descriptions
Common Vulnerability Scoring System (CVSS) schema	Specification	Specification for the common open vulnerability scoring system	Forum for Incidence Response and Security Teams (FIRST)
CVE associated with CVSS			NIST NVD maintains association between CVE records and their CVSS scores

applications. In some cases, a security configuration is mandated in policy (for example, the FDCC mandated for federal agency Windows XP and Vista hosts). In all other cases, selecting a checklist from the National Checklist Program (NCP) is highly recommended. Due to February 2008 modifications to Federal Acquisition Regulation (FAR) Part 39, federal agencies must procure IT products with relevant NCP checklists applied. NCP checklists are publicly vetted, and many offer manufacturer-endorsed methods of configuring and evaluating products.

Second, NIST SCAP facilitates separation of vulnerability knowledge from tools. This achieves two things: the openness of the ecosystem, and the possibility to assure the content. The NIST SCAP ecosystem emphasizes investment into the

Table 5: Automation of Configuration Checklists

SCAP Component	Type	Description	Organization
Extensible Configuration Checklist Description Format (XCCDF)	Specification and schema	Language for specifying checklists and reporting checklists results	NIST and National Security Agency (NSA)
Open Vulnerability and Assessment Language (OVAL)	Specification and schema	Language for specifying low-level testing procedures used by checklists	MITRE Corporation
Common Configuration Enumeration (CCE)	Dictionary	Dictionary of unique standard names of known configuration settings for few major IT platforms	MITRE Corporation

standard, rather than vendor lock-in into a proprietary "silo" tool and a proprietary vulnerability database. Information exchange between SCAP participants as shown below in the Figure 5 facilitates automation. The possibility of assuring the *content* in addition to running the automated tool is very important for building assurance case for security, as demonstrated in Chapters 2 and 3.

With a common agreed upon identifier of the vulnerability through defining CVE, all vulnerability databases and vulnerability management tools can reference this same object in their records and attach their unique additional facts to it. The alternative is very unattractive—pair-wise contracts for information exchanges between tools. CVE is a dictionary of unique, common names for publicly known software vulnerabilities. This common naming convention allows sharing of data within and among organizations and enables effective integration of services and tools.

Common identification of vulnerabilities is a critical first step in conceptual commitment for information exchanges of cybersecurity knowledge (see Figure 6). It allows cross-correlation between various units of knowledge that are of interest to the defender community. In particular, suppose a defender receives a security advisory for one Security Information Provider, which mentions a vulnerability involving a product from a vendor on a specific platform. A few days later, the vendor issues a security bulletin. Was the vendor referring to the same vulnerability? A search in another public vulnerability database lists several vulnerabilities for the same product. Is the initial vulnerability a new one? A few months later, the vendor releases a patch to a few vulnerabilities. Was the initial vulnerability fixed? The vulnerability scanner tool that is being used by the defender team has a separate database of signatures and assessment probes (checks that need to be performed to check for vulnerabilities). Does it cover the initial vulnerability? Another database is used by the Intrusion Detection Tool (IDS). Does it cover the initial vulnerability? Finally, the defender team wants to produce an enterprise-wide report to map the vulnerability to the host and network configuration, IDS

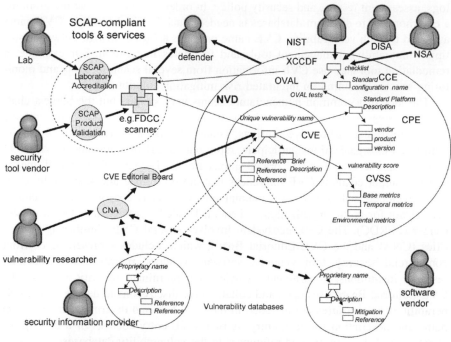

FIGURE 5 Information exchange between SCAP participants

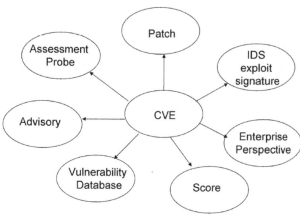

FIGURE 6 CVE associations

logs, assessment results, and security policy. In order to achieve these integrations, a common key to different databases is needed. Such key is the unique CVE name assigned to each vulnerability. CVE name provides a *logical bridge* between multiple vulnerability management tools and facilitates integration. For example, a remediation tool may use CVE information from several scanning tools and monitoring sensors, enabling an integrated risk mitigation solution.

The idea of a common nomenclature seems very simple, but the biggest challenge to its successful implementation is to motivate the tool vendors and to have a mechanism that will resolve conflicts. Today CVE is the de facto standard in the industry, 145 organizations participate, representing 261 products and services. 93 products and services from 51 organizations are "CVE-compatible," which means that the output contains CVE references that are up-to-date and searchable. CVE was developed and is currently maintained by MITRE corporation—a vendor-neutral not-for-profit organization, a Federal Funded Research and Development Center (FFRDC). The CVE ecosystem involves several CVE Numbering Authorities (CNA) and the CVE Editorial Board, which includes representatives from commercial security tool vendors, software vendors, members of academia, research institutions, government agencies, and prominent security experts. The CVE Editorial Board uses open and collaborative discussions to decide which vulnerabilities or exposures are included in the CVE List and determine the common name and description for each entry. A final CVE entry consists of a descriptive name, a brief description, and references to the vulnerability databases.

CVE as well as many other components of the SCAP were sponsored by the National Cyber Security Division of the US Department of Homeland Security. National Vulnerability Database (NVD) is the U.S. government repository of standards based vulnerability management data represented using the SCAP. This data enables automation of vulnerability management, security measurement, and compliance. NVD includes databases of security checklists, security vulnerabilities, misconfigurations, product names, and impact metrics.

Bibliography

Arbaugh, W., Fithen, W., McHugh, J. (2000) Windows of Vulnerability: A Case Study Analysis. *Computer*, Dec. 2000, vol. 33, no. 12.

NIST Special Publication SP800-126. *The Technical Specification for the Security Content Automation Protocol (SCAP). SCAP Version 1.0*, Quinn, S., Waltermire, D., Johnson, C., Scarfone, K., Banghart, J.

NDIA, *Engineering for System Assurance Guidebook.* (2008).

OSVDB, *The Open Source Vulnerability Database.* http://osvdb.org/.

Petroski, H. (1992). *To engineer is human: the role of failure in successful design.* Vintage Books.

CVE, *Common Vulnerabilities and Exposures (CVE).* http://cve.mitre.org/.

US-CERT, United States Computer Emergency Readiness Team. http://www.us-cert.gov/.

Vulnerability patterns as a new assurance content

I have now in my hands all the threads which have formed such a tangle.
—**Conan Doyle,** *The Study in Scarlet*

7.1 BEYOND CURRENT SCAP ECOSYSTEM

In many organizations, the internal security professionals are adept at finding and responding to information about the latest vulnerabilities to the commercial software products employed within business critical systems under their supervision. A great many security resources, both online and printed, are available from Security Information Providers, ready to help explain and address the potential vulnerabilities of the known products, or the off-the-shelf vulnerabilities, as described in Chapter 6. However, those who are responsible for the security and integrity of your systems face two problems: (1) the hit-or-miss disclosure of vulnerabilities in commercial software, and (2) presence of unknown vulnerabilities in the custom (in-house developed) applications that connect to and run on the top of commercial software.

Most organizations can do very little about the hit-or-miss disclosure of vulnerabilities in the off-the-shelf software deployed throughout the business. Your organization must rely on the software provider to have initiated appropriate quality controls and security testing, and provide bug-fixes or patches as necessary.

In the case of custom (in-house developed) applications, some organizations conduct a thorough security review of the system by performing a multi-tier assessment *application assessment* that consists of four levels: secure coding assessment, component-level assessment, security architecture assessment, and policy compliance assessment. Each level provides a progressively higher level of assurance. The organization selects which level best fits its assurance need.

A secure coding assessment focuses on the implementation layer of the application to identify code-level vulnerabilities. It tends toward more of an audit of coding practices (especially if the organization conducts manual reviews). While a coding assessment often initially appears to be more valuable, most organizations soon find that such a review often fails to identify most deployment issues.

Component-level assessment focuses on both the structural flaws that impact the security of an application's physical architecture and implementation security vulnerabilities that spread through key architectural/structural components affecting the application's architecture. To identify these flaws, component-level assessment performs the discovery of architectural components, applications entry points, data access points, third-party services (including the runtime platform), and data flows between them.

Security architecture assessment focuses on validating that safeguards are meeting security objectives. This assessment level utilizes and further deepens analysis of the previous two assessment levels to identify component-level threats, vectors of attack into application, and safeguards. The next step is to perform an analysis to uncover the adequacy and efficiency of identified safeguards.

Policy compliance assessment focuses on validating that the application and processes deployed to build applications are in compliance with outlined security polices. It validates that security engineering principles are followed in identifying security controls required by security polices, and by utilizing the previous three assessment levels it establishes traceability links to policies. Any discrepancy is marked as a possible vulnerability.

This four-level assessment approach focuses at detecting and eliminating vulnerabilities. The first three levels of the assessment deal with formal artifacts, such as the source and binary code, or the system in operation, and involve automated search for known *vulnerability patterns* either by analyzing code or by testing the system in operation. It is important to mention that these are not simple patterns of text; vulnerability patterns describe a unit of behavior that usually includes one or more statements and a pattern rule that describes constraints for a data-flow path connecting those statements. Patterns can describe desired or undesired units of behavior. A pattern that describes an undesired unit of behavior is very often referred to as an antipattern; however, an antipattern that has security implications is referred to as security weakness or a vulnerability pattern. An example of a desired pattern associated with security would be an "authentication pattern," while a vulnerability pattern from the same class would be an "authentication bypass." Vulnerabilities that can be described by a pattern that can be recognized in one of the system views were referred to in Chapter 6 as discernable vulnerabilities.

Knowledge of identifiable vulnerability patterns can be embedded into automated tools that provide deep analysis of the formal artifacts or interact with the system in operation and detect potential vulnerabilities. Improvements to the entire cyberdefence ecosystem can be achieved when the knowledge of vulnerability patterns is developed *independently* of the tools, as machine-readable vendor-independent *content* that is accumulated, updated, accredited, and then distributed to multiple vulnerability analysis tools.

The SCAP Ecosystem [NIST SP800-126] described in Chapter 6, successfully addresses the exchange of knowledge related to the off-the-shelf vulnerabilities that is simply a record of a certain security issue in a certain version of a commercially available product. The description of the problem itself in SCAP is *informal*. A larger ecosystem for vulnerability management (beyond the current SCAP) has to involve *machine-readable vulnerability patterns* as content that can be consumed by code

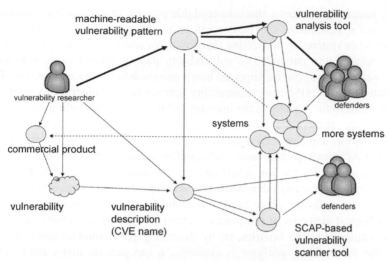

FIGURE 1 Potential expansion of SCAP to include vulnerability patterns

analysis tools and web scanning tools. As shown in Figure 1, SCAP could be extended to include formalized vulnerability patterns described in the following scenario:

- The researcher evaluates a system and locates vulnerability. Then the researcher describes this vulnerability (creates vulnerability knowledge). This knowledge includes identification of the product (product name, vendor, and version) and some description of the problem. Another kind of vulnerability is a misconfiguration of a certain product. Description of this kind of vulnerability additionally includes the particular configuration settings.
- More defenders can then apply this knowledge to other systems by searching for a product or its configuration with the version mentioned in the vulnerability using a standard product description (SCAP CPE) or configuration description (SCAP CCE).
- This knowledge can also be used to build a *vulnerability scanner tool* that will automatically search for affected products and generate a report. Ideally, the vulnerability description is an *input* to the vulnerability scanner. Vulnerability descriptions are stored in vulnerability databases. The vulnerability scanner can be used by more researchers, in a more systematic way, as well as faster and cheaper. The vulnerability description becomes a product. The vulnerability description format enables an *ecosystem* of vulnerability researchers and consumers. Additional meta-data can be associated with the vulnerability description, for example, the machine-readable description of (SCAP CVSS).

The above scenario describes the *current* SCAP, and is illustrated at the bottom part of Figure 1. The next step is to go deeper into the nature of the vulnerability and describe it in terms of identifiable system facts in the form of a machine-readable vulnerability pattern. This new scenario is illustrated at the top part of Figure 1.

The researcher creates a machine-readable pattern, describing the vulnerability in terms of system facts. This pattern can be used to search for the same vulnerability in other systems by inspecting their elements and looking for the occurrences of the vulnerability pattern. The vulnerability pattern can be made available to other researchers and can be imported into a *vulnerability analyzer tool*. The difference between a SCAP-based vulnerability scanner and a vulnerability analyzer is that the input to the scanner is the inventory of the system, including its configuration settings, while the input to the analyzer is an internal representation of the system, the implementation facts, or some logical model of the system. The SCAP OVAL language addresses vulnerability scanners by providing a common machine-readable format for describing off-the-shelf vulnerabilities that can be imported into scanner tools that determine versions of products and product configuration settings. On the other hand, vulnerability analyzers must understand the internal logical elements of the products either by parsing the source code, or by reverse engineering the binaries, or by dissecting the communication protocols. When the vulnerability analyzer is available, it can process many more systems systematically, regardless of whether these systems are off-the-shelf or in-house, already deployed or still under development, while the SCAP-based scanner can only deal with known off-the-shelf commercial products and their configurations.

7.2 VENDOR-NEUTRAL VULNERABILITY PATTERNS

There are multiple existing approaches to the classification of software vulnerabilities, but they all suffer from the fact that they do not enable automation. Rather than focusing on the high-fidelity description of systems traceable to the artifacts (code, binaries or protocols), they focus on informal descriptions of vulnerabilities themselves.

It is important to understand that vulnerability patterns are described in terms of the system facts. Since many automated vulnerability detection tools utilize a proprietary internal representation of the system under analysis, their vulnerability patterns are wedded to their proprietary internal formats, which creates a technical barrier to sharing vulnerability patterns. The key contribution of the OMG Software Assurance Ecosystem is the vendor-neutral standard protocol for exchanging system facts, described in Chapter 11. This protocol can be used as the foundation for the vendor-neutral formalization of vulnerability patterns. This chapter provides the introduction into formalization of vulnerability patterns as vendor-neutral machine-readable content for analysis tools, while further practical details of this approach are discussed in Chapters 9, 10, and 11.

Current SCAP lacks the protocol for exchanging machine-readable vulnerability patterns. In order to introduce such protocol, descriptions of vulnerabilities must be first generalized and then formalized as vendor-neutral machine-readable vulnerability patterns so that they can be turned into a commodity, unlocked from proprietary tools into a normalized, interconnected ecosystem.

The Common Weakness Enumeration (CWE) project led by MITRE [CWE], [Martin 2007] gathered and generalized many known off-the-shelf vulnerabilities,

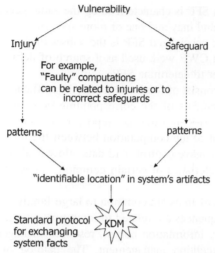

FIGURE 2 Vulnerability pattern and KDM

including informal descriptions of some vendor-specific patterns as well as the existing theoretical classifications of vulnerabilities into a comprehensive catalog of software weaknesses. Formalization of informal descriptions of vulnerabilities into machine-readable vulnerability patterns has started by the Department of Defense (DoD) research project focused on developing formal white-box vulnerability patterns (i.e. patterns that are based on system facts) and linking them to informal descriptions from the CWE catalog. These patterns are referred to as software fault patterns (SFPs). SFP is described as a faulty *computation*, where the computation is defined by system artifacts such as code, database schemas, and platform configuration and, formalized as a fact-oriented statement, focusing at the characteristic structural elements (identifiable locations in some system views or *footholds*) and the necessary conditions for the connecting elements of code (the *code path*) that can be systematically determined by data-flow analysis tools. Computations and the corresponding discernable vocabulary for various system views was described in Chapter 4.

The vendor-neutral protocol for system facts used in this approach is defined in ISO 19506 Knowledge Discovery Metamodel (KDM) [KDM 2006], [ISO 19506], described in Chapter 11. The project focused at the faulty computations that directly cause injury or those that are related to failed safeguards. Figure 2 shows how vulnerability patterns are using the Knowledge Discovery Metamodel.

7.3 SOFTWARE FAULT PATTERNS

The SFP is a generalized description of a family of faulty computations in the software. SFPs map to multiple elements of the CWE in such a way that each individual CWE element in the family can be defined as a specialization of the SFP.

A specialization of an SFP is characterized by the same generic foothold and same generic pattern rules, and may add one or more specific footholds and pattern rules. Thus the extent of the specialized SFP is the subset of the extent of the base SFP. The descriptions from CWE were used as a source of definitions of all the "faulty computations" in order to determine SFPs.

SFP descriptions consist of footholds (easily identifiable locations in the system that are necessary elements of the corresponding computations, and that can be detected by linear queries into the fact repository); and pattern rules (conditions that determine the rest of the computation between the footholds, and which typically require comprehensive control- and data- flow analysis to detect). Footholds are identifiable characteristics of certain common "steps" performed by software systems.

Certain sequences of steps are common to large families of systems. For example, such common sequences are related to input processing, authentication, access control, cryptography, information output, resource management, memory buffer management, and exception management. The catalog of faulty computations should focus on computations that are common to large families of systems. However, it should scale well to enable customization for a very targeted assessment. In order to express SFPs as identifiable footholds and associated pattern rules that enable grouping by specialization in a consistent, measurable, and comparable way, conceptual and logical models are developed that follow the fact-oriented approach described in Chapter 9 and focus on essential characteristics expressed as:

- Elements;
- Relations between elements;
- Rules describing relations.

Multiple physical models can be automatically derived from the logical model for selected implementation and imported into existing analyzer tools.

A conceptual model of an SFP is presented in Figure 3. The conceptual model facilitates white-box definitions of SFPs. It removes any ambiguity from the SFP and focuses on white-box discernable properties of the vulnerability traceable to the program elements. Each pattern has a start and an end statement connected by a path constrained by particular conditions. The start statement determines the source of data, while the end statement determines the data sink and the complete pattern describes any computation between the start and end statements that propagates certain data properties satisfying the given end-to-end data condition associated with the computation. The start- and/or end- statement contain at least one identifiable foothold.

The logical model expands on the conceptual model to show how the computation is presented in the code and also to show what properties are taken into account when the code path is computed. The logical model adds concrete details to the definition of a "computation" and a "property" in white-box terms. The logical model in Figure 4 shows how the SFP patterns are further formalized to

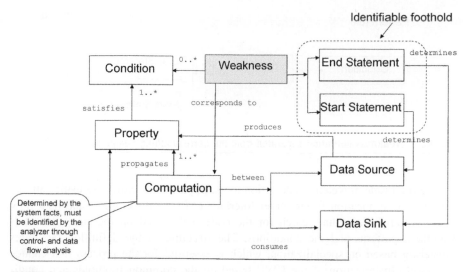

FIGURE 3 Weakness conceptual model

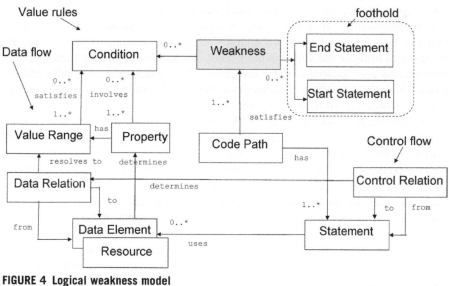

FIGURE 4 Logical weakness model

produce machine-readable SFPs by further mapping the corresponding elements to the standard protocol for representing system facts.

These models facilitate a certain structure of the definition of each weakness and provide a natural separation point between the definition of a weakness from the apparatus required to determine the corresponding computation (illustrated in Figure 5). This is the key to using weakness definitions as the common content

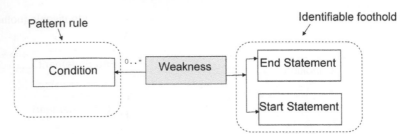

FIGURE 5 Weakness definition separated from the corresponding computation

for the multitude of weakness detection tools. In particular, Software Fault Patterns involve an Application Programmer Interface (API) to the control- and data flow analysis capabilities that search for the code path based on the start- and end-statement patterns and the conditions. The structure of the definition facilitates clustering based on specialization, which is essential for the process that creates a natural clusterization of the CWE based on the common footholds and conditions, outlined later in this chapter.

Vulnerability is defined as "a bug, flaw, weakness, or exposure of an application, system, device, or service that could lead to a failure of confidentiality, integrity, or availability." It can therefore be technically interpreted as a computation that can be exploited to produce injury. Certain computations in the system are designed to mitigate the vulnerabilities. These computations and the corresponding mechanisms and "locations" in the code are called "safeguards." A "faulty computation" is defined as either a computation that has direct injury or a computation that corresponds to an incorrect safeguard.

A "computation foothold" is an identifiable construct, an entry point, or an Application Programming Interface (API) call present at a specific location recognizable in the system's artifacts, which is a necessary element of the computation. Certain constructs in the code can directly cause injury under certain conditions. Such locations are footholds for the corresponding faulty computation sequences. Safeguards (as computation sequences) also have footholds related to the safeguard itself, as well as to the protected region. SFPs are elements of the catalog of the unique locations in the code associated with faulty computations that either directly cause injury or cause safeguards to be ineffective. Software Fault Patterns are parameterized by the concrete platform knowledge because the start- and end-statement often involve concrete system call signatures.

This viewpoint is constructive and systematic and therefore enables automation. A uniform viewpoint makes the SFP approach systematic and repeatable.

As the DoD research in this area is still on going, in the following sections of this chapter we present detailed views of a few SFPs arranged into natural clusters based on common footholds and conditions that could be further classified into two categories: safeguard and direct injury. The following sections illustrate the search for the identifiable footholds for the SFPs. The entire collection of 640

CWE elements was analyzed and grouped into clusters based on the common characteristics mentioned in the informal descriptions from CWE, then these characteristics were further analyzed to identify discernable footholds, if any.

7.3.1 Safeguard clusters and corresponding SFPs

The following three clusters of SFPs are examples of safeguard category.

7.3.1.1 Authentication

This cluster of software faults relates to establishing the identity of an actor associated with the computation, or the identity of the endpoint involved in the computation through a certain channel. The authentication cluster is closely related to access control, which focuses on resource access by an authenticated actor with appropriate access rights, as well as ownership of the resources by the authenticated actors.

The common characteristics of the authentication cluster include the following (see Figure 6):

- Authentication token, including password;
- Authenticated actor, its identity, and management;
- Authentication check;
- Management of actors;
- Guarded region of code where the access to resources or information assets is made.

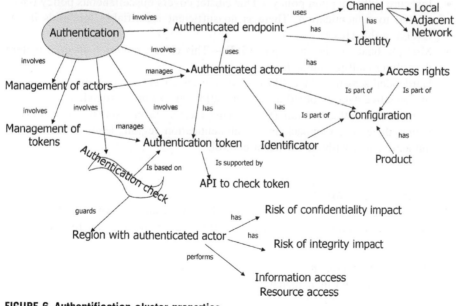

FIGURE 6 Authentification cluster properties

This cluster contains 43 CWEs. Only 14 CWEs contribute to SFPs. The major challenge of the authentication cluster is the lack of good footholds for the white-box description. The biggest challenge is to identify the boundaries of the authentication code that distinguishes it from the corresponding guarded region.

The authentication cluster includes the following nine secondary clusters. However, currently only six have contributed to extraction of SFPs (marked in the following list):

- Authentication bypass—This cluster covers situations related to incomplete authentication steps; there is no sufficient identifiable footholds in this cluster. However, once the statements of the Authentication code are identified by the analyst, it becomes possible to analyze authentication bypass.
- Faulty endpoint authentication (SFP)—This cluster covers scenarios involved in endpoint authentication; the foothold in this scenario is a certain condition that uses an inappropriate authentication mechanism.
- Missing endpoint authentication (SFP)—This cluster covers scenarios where the endpoint authentication is absent. The foothold of this scenario is the resource access or a critical operation.
- Digital certificate—This cluster covers specific authentication issues related to digital certificate management. There are no sufficient identifiable footholds in this cluster
- Missing authentication (SFP)—This cluster covers scenarios where the authentication is absent and the resource access or critical operation occurs at a code region where the corresponding actor is not authenticated.
- Insecure authentication policy—This cluster covers miscellaneous policy issues related to authentication. There is no sufficient identifiable footholds in the CWEs in this cluster.
- Multiple binds to the same port (SFP)—This cluster covers a specific pattern describing multiple binds to the same port.
- Hardcoded sensitive data (SFP)—This cluster covers various situations where the sensitive data involved in authentication checks are hardcoded.
- Unrestricted authentication (SFP)—This cluster covers specific situations in which there is a loopback in the authentication region, leading back to the authentication, without sufficient control.

7.3.1.2 Access control
This cluster of software faults relates to validating resource owners and their permissions. The common characteristics of this cluster include the following (see Figure 7):

- Authenticated actor, its identity, and management;
- Access rights and their management;
- Resource, protected resource;
- Resource ownership;

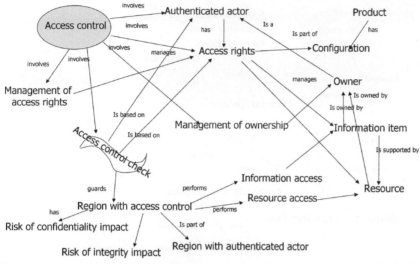

FIGURE 7 Access control cluster properties

- Access control check, guarded region;
- Resource access operation;
- Operation that sets access rights on a resource;

There are 16 CWEs in this cluster. Most CWEs in this cluster lack identifiable footholds.

The access control cluster includes the following three secondary clusters, however only one of these clusters helped create the SFP (marked in the following list):

- Insecure resource access (SFP)—This cluster covers situations related to the bypass of access control checks.
- Access management—This cluster covers various situations related to the management of resource owners and access rights. There is no sufficient white-box content in CWE descriptions for this cluster.
- Insecure resource permissions—This cluster covers various scenarios related to setting the permissions of the resources. The foothold of this scenario is the operation that sets resource permissions (such as resource creation, cloning, or explicit permission setting).

7.3.1.3 Privilege

This cluster of software faults relates to code regions with inappropriate privilege level. The common characteristics of this cluster include the following (see Figure 8):

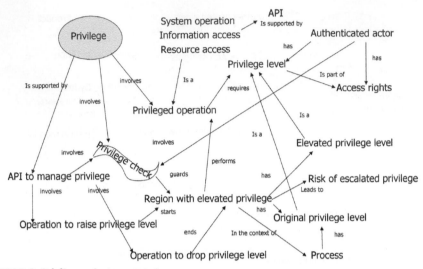

FIGURE 8 Privilage cluster property

- Privilege level;
- Privileged operation;
- Region with elevated privilege;
- Privilege check;
- Operations to change privilege.

There are 12 CWEs in this cluster. Most CWE descriptions do not have sufficient white-box content.

This cluster has only one secondary cluster that contributed to creation of the privilege SFP.

7.3.2 Direct injury clusters and corresponding SFPs

The following five clusters of SFPs are examples of this category.

7.3.2.1 Information leak

This cluster of software faults relates to the export of sensitive information from an application and several related issues. The common characteristics of this cluster include:

- Sensitive data is defined as data that flows from sensitive operations or flows into sensitive operations as the key parameter. "Sensitive" is the role that a data element plays in a certain context. It can be identified based on the APIs that are involved in producing/consuming/transforming the data element. If a data element was passed to a password management function, it can be assumed to be a password. If a data element is passed to a function that is known to require a private key, it is a private key.

- Information export operations (includes storing, logging, releasing as an error message, releasing as a debug message, as well as other exposures);

This cluster contains 94 CWEs. Most CWEs lack identifiable footholds, so only 37 contribute to SFPs.

The information leak cluster includes the following 12 secondary clusters. However, eight of them contribute to creation of SFPs (marked in the following list):

- Exposed data in motion (SFP)—This cluster covers various situations related to the data movements, which leads to information leaks, where there is corresponding code with sufficient foothold for a white-box description.
- Exposure through storing (SFP)—This cluster covers various situations related to the data at rest, which leads to information leaks, where there is corresponding code with sufficient foothold for a white-box description.
- Exposed data at rest (SFP)—This cluster covers various situations related to the data at rest, which leads to information leaks, as there is no corresponding code or no sufficient foothold for a white-box description.
- Exposure through logging (SFP)—This cluster covers various situations related to the data in use, which leads to information leaks through logging, where there is corresponding code with sufficient foothold for a white-box description.
- Exposure through debug message (SFP)—This cluster covers various situations related to the data in use, which leads to information leaks through debug messages, where there is corresponding code with sufficient foothold for a white-box description.
- Exposure through error message (SFP)—This cluster covers various situations related to the data in use, which leads to information leaks through error messages, where there is corresponding code with sufficient foothold for a white-box description.
- Inappropriate cleanup (SFP)—This cluster covers several buffer cleanup weaknesses.
- Insecure session management—This cluster covers several scenarios related to information leaks between sessions; CWEs in this cluster do not have sufficient white-box content.
- Programmatic exposures of data (SFP)—This cluster covers several scenarios related to miscellaneous constructs leading to information release.
- Other exposures—This cluster covers various miscellaneous scenarios leading to information leaks, not covered by the previous clusters. CWEs in this cluster do not have sufficient white-box content.
- State disclosure—This cluster covers various situations of state disclosure, which releases knowledge of some aspects of the internal state of the application. CWEs in this cluster do not have sufficient white-box content.
- Exposure through temporary files—This cluster covers scenarios related to temporary files management, in particular to their names. CWEs in this cluster do not have sufficient white-box content.

7.3.2.2 Memory management

This cluster of weaknesses relates to the management of memory buffers (as opposed to access to memory buffers). Common characteristics of this cluster include:

- Buffer, including stack and heap buffers; static and dynamic buffers;
- Buffer identity (pointer, name);
- Buffer allocation operation;
- Buffer release operation;
- Management of buffer identities.

This cluster contains six CWEs. All of the CWEs in this cluster are based on discernable properties and are therefore covered by few SFPs.

The memory management cluster includes the following two secondary clusters, both of which contribute to creation of SFPs:

- Faulty memory release (SFP)—This cluster covers various scenarios related to incorrect release of memory buffers. The foothold of this scenario is the buffer release operation.
- Failure to release memory (SFP)—This cluster covers various scenarios where the identity of a memory buffer is mismanaged, resulting in so-called memory leaks.

7.3.2.3 Memory access

This cluster of software faults is related to access to memory buffers. Common characteristics of this cluster include:

- Buffer, including stack and heap buffers; static and dynamic buffers;
- Buffer identity (pointer, name);
- Buffer access operations, including implicit buffer access (also known as string expansion);
- Operations involving buffer;
- Pointer uses, including pointer export.

This cluster contains 22 CWEs, 21 of which are based on discernable properties and are therefore covered by few SFPs.

The memory access cluster includes the following six secondary clusters, and all of them contribute in the creation of SFPs:

- Faulty pointer use (SFP)—This cluster covers common scenarios of using incorrect pointers to buffers.
- Faulty pointer creation (SFP)—This cluster is closely related to faulty pointer use, but focuses on the scenarios where faulty pointers are usually created (rather than the places where they are used).
- Faulty buffer access (SFP)—This cluster covers the common scenarios related to various buffer overflows, underflows, and related weaknesses.

- Faulty string expansion (SFP)—This cluster covers scenarios related to the use of certain API calls that involve implicit buffers and may lead to buffer overflows.
- Incorrect buffer length computation (SFP)—This cluster covers scenarios related to several known situations where the length of a buffer is incorrectly computed.
- Improper NULL termination (SFP)—This cluster covers scenarios related to several operations involving a buffer, which may lead to buffer overflows due to mismatch in data terminators within the data stored in the buffer.

7.3.2.4 Path resolution

This cluster of software faults is related to access to file resources using complex file names. The software faults in this cluster are related to the so-called path traversal functionality, which is provided by most file systems where the file system interprets the complex file name using a set of implicit rules. These faults are a common cause of security vulnerabilities. The common characteristics of this cluster include:

- File resources;
- File name, including special characters and their interpretation;
- File identity;
- Chroot jail (the mechanism to restrict interpretation of complex file names);
- Path equivalence.

There are 51 CWEs in this cluster. 43 CWEs in the cluster are based on discernable properties and are covered by few SFPs.

The path resolution cluster includes the following three secondary clusters, and all contribute to creation of SFPs:

- Path traversal (SFP)—This cluster covers the majority of patterns leading to path traversal vulnerabilities. The foothold of the corresponding SFP is the file access operation where the file name originates from the user input (is "tainted").
- Failed chroot jail (SFP)—This cluster covers a specific situation related to incorrect establishment of a chroot jail.
- Link in resource name resolution (SFP)—This cluster covers situations related to the use of symbolic links to file resources.

7.3.2.5 Tainted input

This cluster groups software faults related to injection of user-controlled data into various destination commands. This cluster focuses on data validation issues. The common characteristics of this cluster include:

- Destination command or construct;
- Data validation, special characters, and their interpretation;
- Tainted values;
- Channel (input channel);
- Input transformation (encoding, canonicalization, etc.);
- Input handling (processing complex input structures).

This cluster contains 137 CWEs, 74 of which contribute to SFPs and 63 are non discernable.

The tainted input cluster includes the following six secondary clusters from which four contribute in the creation of SFPs:

- Tainted input to command (SFP)—This cluster covers various scenarios that involve data validation, in particular the special characters for various destinations commands.
- Tainted input to variable (SFP)—This cluster covers scenarios where the destination of the tainted values is not an API call, but some construct, for example, a basic condition, a loop condition, and so on.
- Tainted input to environment (SFP)—This cluster covers scenarios where the tainted values affect various elements of the computation environment, which has an indirect effect on the computation itself.
- Faulty input transformation—This cluster covers several scenarios related to the transformation of input, such as encoding and canonicalization.
- Incorrect input handling—This cluster covers several scenarios related to the processing of complex input structures.
- Composite tainted input (SFP)—This cluster is introduced to describe vulnerabilities in which user-controlled input contributes to other weaknesses, for example, a buffer overflow in which the buffer length is tainted data.

Tainted input secondary clusters that have discernable properties consist of three types: Tainted Input to Command (TIC) Type, Tainted Input to Environment (TIE), and Tainted Input to Variable (TIV).

Many elements of the Common Weakness Enumeration (CWE) describe well-known code faults that however do not directly produce injury. For example, integer overflow is a serious implementation issue (a software bug), however it does not produce injury on its own, only if the faulty value is used in some other context, such as a loop header or a buffer operation. Additional SFPs do describe these issues as well, so that they can be used in combination with more pure vulnerability patterns, however in the system assurance context such conditions often contribute to false positive reports that are costly to process and eliminate. The objective of vulnerability patterns is to provide machine-readable content for code analysis tools that can generate evidence in support of a security assurance case, rather than simply detect implementation bugs.

7.4. EXAMPLE SOFTWARE FAULT PATTERN

To illustrate software fault patterns as machine-readable content we describe a single concrete SFP from the Tainted Input into Command (TIV) cluster. This SFP is a formalization of the CWE 134 "Uncontrolled Format String."

The description of this weakness available in CWE is very informal; it reads as follows: "The software uses externally-controlled format strings in printf-style functions, which can lead to buffer overflows or data representation problems."

The white-box content can be distilled from this description, under the guidance provided by the conceptual weakness model shown in Figure 3.

Distilled Whitebox Content
Definition: A weakness where the code path has:
1. start statement that accepts input
2. end statement that passes a format string to format string function where
    a. the input data is part of the format string and
    b. the format string is incorrectly validated

where "incorrectly validated" is defined through the following scenarios:

    a. not validated
    b. accepts elements that lead to a buffer overflow of the format string function

This content can be further formalized by the following statement in SBVR Structured English (further described in Chapter 10):

Uncontrolled Format String is a weakness where the code path has a start statement that accepts input and has an end statement that passes a format string to a format string function where the input is part of the format string and the format string is incorrectly validated.

Supporting Noun Concepts

weakness
statement
end statement
start statement
format string
input
format string function

Supporting Verb Concepts

code path has statement
code path has start statement
code path has end statement
statement accepts input
statement passes data element to function
data element is part of data element
input is incorrectly validated

The identifiable foothold of this pattern is:

Statement that *passes* format string *to* format string function

The condition of this patterns is:

Value *of* the data element that *is passed to* the format string function *includes incorrectly validated* input that *is accepted by* a statement.

Algorithmically, this pattern can be used to detect vulnerability as follows:

1. Locate statement that passes format string to a format string function.
2. Perform data-flow analysis to compute the set of possible values of the format string.
3. Check the value-set. The CWE 134 "Uncontrolled format string" is detected if the value-set contains a special value 'tainted,' which means that there exists a local code path on which the format string includes input from the user and the input is incorrectly validated.

These considerations, together with the guidance provided by the Logical Weakness Model (Figure 4), lead to the following statement in SBVR Structured English:

ControlElement *has* Uncontrolled Format String weakness *at* code path if the ControlElement *contains* an ActionElement and the ActionElement *passes* format string *to* format string function and the format string *satisfies uncontrolled format string condition in* the ControlElement *and* the ActionElement *at* the code path.

ControlElement and ActionElement are KDM terms, corresponding to a named unit of behavior (e.g., a function in the C programming language), and a statement, respectively.

Further,

Data Element *satisfies uncontrolled format string condition in* Control Element *and* ActionElement *at* code path if a Value *is a data-flow solution for* the Data Element *at* the ActionElement and the Value *is tainted* in which case the code path *corresponds to* the ControlElement *and* the ActionElement *for* the Data Element *and* the Value.

Here, the uncontrolled format string condition is defined in terms of the analysis tool API. On the other hand, the definition of an ActionElement that passes a format string to format string function can be done entirely based on the standard vocabulary provided by the Knowledge Discovery Metamodel (KDM).

We are using the SBVR Structured English, described in Chapter 10, to represent the formalization statements. SBVR defines the set of facts that is the meaning of these statements. SVBR also defines a canonical XML interchange format. Further details of this formalization are provided in Chapter 10.

Bibliography

CWE, Common Weakness Enumeration. http://cwe.mitre.org.

ISO/IEC 19506 Architecture Driven Modernization—Knowledge Discovery Metamodel. (2009).

KDM Object Management Group. (2006). *The Knowledge Discovery Metamodel (KDM).*

Martin, R. (2007). Being Explicit About Security Weaknesses, *CrossTalk. The Journal of Defense Software Engineering*, March.

NIST Special Publication SP800-126. *The Technical Specification for the Security Content Automation Protocol (SCAP). SCAP Version 1.0*, Quinn, S., Waltermire, D., Johnson, C., Scarfone, K., Banghart, J.

OMG software assurance ecosystem

> *Hercule Poirot: Remember, Monsieur Fraser, our weapon is our knowledge, but it may be a knowledge we do not know we possess.*
>
> —**Agatha Christie, The ABC Murders**

8.1 INTRODUCTION

Affordable cost-effective assurance requires efficiency in discovering system knowledge, exchanging knowledge, integrating knowledge from multiple sources, collating pieces of knowledge, and distributing the accumulated knowledge. Evidence of the effectiveness of the safeguards have to be specific to the system of interest. Therefore, there is a need to discover accurate knowledge about the system of and use it together with the general units of knowledge such as the off-the-shelf vulnerability knowledge, vulnerability patterns and threat knowledge.

The OMG Assurance Ecosystem involves a rigorous approach to knowledge discovery and knowledge sharing where individual knowledge units are treated as *facts*. These facts can be described using *statements*, in a controlled vocabulary of noun and verb phrases using structured English and represented in efficient fact-based repositories, or represented in a variety of machine-readable formats, including XML. This fact-oriented approach allows discovery of accurate facts by tools, integration of facts from multiple sources, analysis, and reasoning, including derivation of new facts from the initial facts, collation of facts, and verbalization of facts in the form of English statements. Generic units of knowledge can also be represented as facts and integrated with the concrete facts about the system of interest. This uniform environment industrializes the use of knowledge in system assurance - allows description of the patterns of facts, sharing patterns as content and using automated tools to search for occurrences of patterns in the fact-based repository. The key to the fact-oriented approach is the conceptual commitment to the common vocabulary which is the key contract that starts an ecosystem.

To better explain this industrialized approach to knowledge in the assurance context, let's consider a real-life example that most of us have experienced at one time or the other—security screening of bags at airports around the world. Luggage screening is a particular safeguard of the airport security program that utilizes

System Assurance: Beyond Detecting Vulnerabilities. DOI: 10.1016/B978-0-12-381414-2.00008-7
Copyright © 2011 Elsevier Inc. All rights reserved.

machinery, procedures, and security screeners to check each carry-on bag against anything that could be used as weapons on board the aircraft. The machinery consists of a conveyor belt for transporting bags to the inspection station, which involves electronic detection and imaging equipment and its operator, the screener. The equipment used is a variation of an X-ray machine that can detect explosives by looking at the density of the items being examined. The screening machine employs Computed Axial Tomography (CAT) technology originally designed for and used in the medical field to generate images (CAT scans) of tissue density in a "slice" through the patient's body. The screening machine uses a library of weapons and explosives *patterns* and produces a color-coded image to assist screeners with their threat resolution procedures. In other words, general knowledge about weapons and items that could be used as weapons is converted into patterns that these X-ray machines can automatically detect and display when applied to items in the bag. The conceptual commitment of the X-ray machine does not involve a full taxonomy of items in bags, for example, a clothing item, a personal care item, or a personal electronic device. The X-ray machine does not produce a listing of the items in the bag. Instead, the contents of a bag are describes as density slides of the material. The density slices of the bag is *the concrete knowledge* of all items in the bag, and when scanned by these special X-ray machines, the color-coded images are generated by applying patterns to the density slices. The X-ray machine produces a distilled color-coded image to the screener.

This is an illustration of merging general knowledge and concrete knowledge in a repeatable and systematic automated procedure. It is important to note that all elements of the luggage screening system, including the screening personnel, *commit* to the same predefined *vocabulary* of density slices (formed shapes with corresponding density of the item's material), so that *patterns* can be recognized and properly marked (e.g., metal knife vs. plastic knife, where the metal knife would be colored as a threat, while a plastic knife would be colored as neutral object according to the agreed upon color-coding schema). The resulting color-coded images are displayed on the monitor of the security screener, who reviews them and determines a course of action by applying a threat resolution procedure (e.g., bag passed inspection, further manual inspection is needed, bag needs to be removed). Manual screening is limited to situations where the automated images are inconclusive. Manual screening is informal but implies a different *conceptualization* (the screener looks at the real items around the area where an inconclusive image was produced) and a higher resolution (not just the shape based on the density of material, but the actual shape, color, weight, and so on, of the item).

In terms of system assurance, luggage screening is an operational safeguard that has technical and procedural elements. Understanding the effectiveness of this safeguard contributes to our confidence in the overall airport security posture. However, we use this example to illustrate systematic, repeatable, and fact-oriented inspection methods that involve collaboration based on shared *conceptual commitment*. The bag under inspection illustrates a system of interest where the concrete items in the bag need to be inspected (what are they?) and assessed (are they dangerous?).

There are many ways to conceptualize the bag contents, resulting in concrete *facts* of the system of interest. Concrete knowledge has to align with the general knowledge that we are using for assurance (such as the concepts of explosives and weapons as particular dangerous items). Our inspection must make repeatable and systematic decisions on whether the bag under inspection contains dangerous items.

Several things must be aligned in order to make this inspection cost effective: Machine-readable patterns of dangerous items must be available, the machine-readable descriptions of the concrete items in the bag under inspection (the concrete facts) must be available, and automatic pattern recognition must be done. All these components must agree on the same common conceptualization, so that the way security patterns are expressed match the concrete facts. The contents of the bag are therefore X-rayed and represented as shapes based on the density of the material. The library of dangerous items such as explosives and weapons (e.g., handguns, knifes, scissors, etc.) is based on the characteristics of these shapes. At this point, automatic pattern recognition is done, where patterns are used as *queries* to the normalized representation of the bag's contents. When a match is found between a pattern and facts from the normalized representation, the corresponding color-coded images are generated. The X-ray machine performs concrete *knowledge discovery*. Both units of knowledge, generic and concrete, are merged using the pattern-matching algorithms of the screening machine. The common conceptualization creates an *ecosystem* that:

- Integrates CAT technology, X-ray and imaging machines, procedures, and personnel (security screeners), and
- Unifies units of concrete knowledge (density slices of the items in the bag) and generic knowledge (predefined items and patterns in the form of shapes of the corresponding material density) as they are independently merged using certain technology, facilitating their processing to determine if the bag contains items that match given patterns.

Without such an ecosystem, security screeners would need to manually inspect every item in every bag, which would be intrusive to customers, time-consuming, unrepeatable, lengthy, and costly. Manual inspection would require that passengers send bags for inspection days before their scheduled departure.

8.2 OMG ASSURANCE ECOSYSTEM: TOWARD COLLABORATIVE CYBERSECURITY

An **ecosystem** is a community of participants who engage in exchanges of content using an explicit shared body of knowledge. An ecosystem involves a certain communication infrastructure, or *"plumbing,"* that includes a number of *standard protocols* implemented by using knowledge-management tools. Each protocol is based on a certain *conceptualization* that defines the corresponding interchange format. An ecosystem opens up a market where participants exchange tools, services, and content in order to solve significant problems. The essential characteristic of

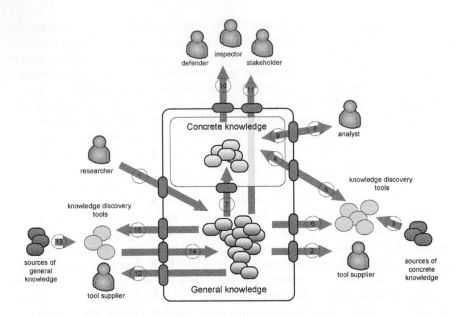

FIGURE 1 Knowledge exchange between assurance participants

an ecosystem is establishment of knowledge content as an explicit *product*, separated from producer and consumer tools, and delivered through well-defined protocols, in order to enable *economies of scale* and rapid accumulation of actionable knowledge. It is important to establish such an ecosystem for assurance in order to provide defenders of cybersystems with systematic and affordable solutions.

Figure 1 describes the key participants of the Assurance Ecosystem and the knowledge exchanges between them.

The purpose of the ecosystem is to facilitate the collection and accumulation of assurance knowledge, and to ensure its efficient and affordable delivery to the defenders of cybersystems, as well as to other stakeholders. An important feature of cybersecurity knowledge is separation between the general knowledge (applicable to large families of systems) and concrete knowledge (accurate facts related to the system of interest). To emphasize this separation, a certain area at the top of the ecosystem "marketplace" in the middle of the diagram represents concrete knowledge, while the rest represents general knowledge. Keep in mind that "concrete" facts are specific to an individual system. Thus, the "concrete knowledge" area represents *multiple* local cyberdefense environments, while the "general knowledge" area is the knowledge owned by the entire cyberdefense community. So the "defender," "inspector," and "stakeholder" icons represent people who are interested in providing assurance of one individual system.

Figure 1 also illustrates exchanges in the Assurance Ecosystem and the corresponding *protocols*. Exchanges are indicated by arrows. Participants in the ecosystem are shown by two kinds of icons. The first icon, the "actor" icon, represents a certain class of participants involved in the given information exchange. A single "actor" icon represents the entire class of real participants that can be involved in multiple concurrent interactions. The second icon—a grey oval—represents a tool. The ecosystem figure shows two clusters of knowledge discovery tools. As is true of participants, each cluster represents *multiple* real tools. Icons that look like a rectangle with rounded corners represent the *units of knowledge* either as the sources or as the results of exchanges within the ecosystem. Figure 1 illustrates important classes of information exchanges, differentiated by the classes of the ecosystem participants.

Let's see how the Assurance Ecosystem enables the defense team.

Knowledge delivery protocols. The purpose of the ecosystem, the tools, and the "plumbing," is to *deliver knowledge* to the defense team, as is illustrated by Flows #10 and #11. Flow #10 delivers concrete facts about the system and its environment, which constitutes the *evidence* of the assurance case. Flow #11 delivers general knowledge, which is used largely to develop the *argument*. The standards of the Assurance Ecosystem define the protocols for delivering the argument [ARM] and the evidence [SAEM].

System analysis protocols. Information Flows #9 and #8 illustrate the process of *system analysis*. This process is guided by the overall assurance argument and works with concrete facts about the system. The analyst starts with the top-level assurance claims and develops the subclaims, guided by analysis of the architecture of the system. The analyst *requests* a certain kind of analysis to be performed on the system in order to produce evidence to the subclaims. The analyst is also the source of some unique facts, such as the threat model and the value statements for the assets of the system. Usually, there is no machine-readable source of these facts, so the analyst's role is to collect this data. Flow #9 illustrates how these facts are added to the "concrete knowledge" repository.

General knowledge protocol. In the process of building the assurance case, general knowledge is utilized, as illustrated by Flow #7. For example, in order to build the threat model of the system, the analyst needs to know about recent incidents involving similar systems. The threat model is an example of concrete knowledge that is specific to the system of interest, while the database of security incidents searchable by the system features—the attacker's motivation, capability and the resulting injury—is an example of general cybersecurity knowledge. One of the central concerns addressed by the OMG Assurance Ecosystem is defining efficient mechanisms for utilizing general cybersecurity knowledge by the analyst and the defense team (Flow #7). Building shared conceptual committment in the form of a common vocabulary is described in Chapter 9.

Concrete knowledge discovery protocol. The majority of concrete cybersecurity facts are provided by automated tools, as indicated by Flow #4. The key protocol of the OMG Assurance Ecosystem is the standard protocol for exchanging system facts, called the Knowledge Discovery Metamodel (KDM), described in Chapter 11. There are several important scenarios here, all illustrated by Flow

#3, followed by Flow #4. Each scenario is characterized by a unique source of knowledge and the corresponding class of knowledge discovery tools.

1. Accessing *existing repositories* that contain facts required for assurance. The role of the knowledge discovery tool in this scenario is to provide an adaptor that will bridge the format of the existing repository to the format of the ecosystem facts. For example, the ITIL repository contains information related to the system's assets; the architecture repository contains operational and system views, as well as the data dictionaries; the human resources database contains information about personnel; business models contain information about the business rules; the problem report tracking system contains information about the vulnerabilities; and the network management system contains facts related to the network configuration of the system and configuration settings, such as the firewall configurations. Efficient assurance process must utilize any available units of data in order to avoid mistakes arising from incorrect interpretation of the manual data collection, access the latest snapshot, and be able to update during the subsequent assessments.

2. Discovering *network configuration*. The role of the "knowledge discovery tool" in this scenario is to scan the network and map the hosts, the network topology, and the open ports. The source of concrete knowledge is the network itself.

3. Discovering information from system artifacts, such as code, database schemas, and deployment configuration files. The role of the knowledge discovery tool is to perform *application mining*. This activity includes mining for basic behavior and architecture facts, as well as the automated detection of vulnerabilities, determined by known vulnerability patterns, also known as static code analysis. Some classes of application mining tools work with source code, while others work with machine code. The database structure can be discovered from accessing the data definition file (source code) or from querying the database itself.

4. Discovering facts from informal documents, such as requirements, policy definitions, and manuals. The role of a knowledge discovery tool in this scenario is to assist in *linguistic analysis* of the document and to extract the facts relevant to security assurance of the system.

Content import protocol. Knowledge discovery, especially the process of *detecting vulnerabilities*, is often driven by general knowledge (indicated as Flow #6). For example, a NIST SCAP vulnerability scanner tool is driven by vulnerability descriptions from the National Vulnerability Database (NVD). An antivirus tool is driven by virus patterns.

Integration protocol. Flow #5 represents the *integration* scenario, which is also quite central to the purpose of the Assurance Ecosystem. As you can see, the facts related to the security of the system can come from various sources, where each source described a partial view of the system. Integrating these pieces of knowledge into a single coherent picture facilitates system analysis.

The integration process is illustrated by Flow #5 followed by Flow #4 back into the repository. The role of the tool in this scenario is to identify common entities and to collate the facts from multiple sources. This is a form of knowledge discovery because integration produces new facts, describing the *links* between different views. Knowledge integration does not use any external sources of knowledge (Flow #3 is not utilized).

Knowledge refinery protocol. A similar process, also described by Flow #5 that is followed by Flow #4 back into the repository, is called *knowledge refinery*—the process of deriving new facts from existing facts. This process often involves general facts (Flow #6) as well as concrete facts (Flow #5) as inputs. The knowledge refinery process by which additional concrete facts are produced (Flow #4) from the primitive facts (Flow #5) and general patterns (Flow #6) by a knowledge refinery tool is one possible implementation of Flow #7.

Knowledge sharing protocol. The last but definitely not the least important information flow on the right side of the diagram is Flow #2, which describes how the Assurance Ecosystem influences tool suppliers to develop better and more efficient knowledge discovery tools. The direct benefit to the defense team comes from the use of efficient knowledge discovery tools, so the loop by which the general cybersecurity knowledge flows to the *suppliers* of the knowledge discovery tools is very important to the purpose of the Assurance Ecosystem.

Knowledge creation protocol. Moving to the left side of the Assurance Ecosystem diagram, the information Flow #1 describes the primary source of cybersecurity knowledge. All general knowledge is produced by *security researchers* through analysis of systems, security incidents, malware, experience reports, and so on. The role of the Assurance Ecosystem is to define efficient interfaces in support of Flow #1 and to enable the accumulation of content and its delivery to the consumers. The OMG Assurance Ecosystem builds upon the existing best practices of information exchanges within the cybersecurity community and brings modern technology to define the next generation of open-standards-based collaborative cybersecurity.

Flows #12, 13, 14, and 15 conclude the picture.

Bridging protocol. Existing sources of general cybersecurity knowledge include any existing repositories that do not comply with the "plumbing" standards of the Assurance Ecosystem. This includes the current NVD [NVD], [US-CERT] the Open Source Vulnerability Database [OSVDB], the Bugtraq list, proprietary repositories of the intrusion detection tools, risk management systems and their proprietary repositories, and the like. Information Flow #13, followed by #14, illustrates how this content is *bridged* into the Assurance Ecosystem. The role of the knowledge discovery tool in this scenario is to provide an *adaptor* between the formats.

Knowledge-sharing protocol. Flow #12 is the counterpart of Flow #2 and illustrates how the knowledge accumulated and distributed within the Assurance Ecosystem can influence *tool suppliers*, resulting in additional and more efficient data feeds into the Ecosystem.

Bridging protocol. Flow #15 concludes the picture. This flow illustrates how information from the Assurance Ecosystem can be distributed to outside communities, including tools that use proprietary formats and ecosystems built upon different information exchange standards.

Protocols of the Assurance Ecosystem are *contracts* that ensure interoperability between participants, including tools and people. An implementation of the Assurance Ecosystem provides the "plumbing" for the information exchanges and facilitates collaborations, leading to rapid accumulation of common knowledge. There is ample evidence that standards-based ecosystems jump-start vibrant communities and remove barriers to entry into the market of tools, services, and content, which attracts new talent. As a result, the information content is created and shared, while the quality of the content is rapidly improving through repeated use by tools and by competing peers. Exactly this kind of environment for cybersecurity is needed to close the knowledge gap between attackers and defenders. So, what is represented as a cluster of knowledge discovery tools in the Assurance Ecosystem diagram is a hub-and-spike knowledge-driven *integration architecture* that defines plug-and-play interfaces for tools. The interfaces are determined by the information exchange protocols (see Figure 2).

In a physical sense, the tools in the Assurance Ecosystem provide interfaces to people who work with tools. The Assurance Ecosystem defines the logical interfaces that are provisioned by the compliant tools (see Figure 3).

The purpose of the collaborations is to provide an integrated end-to-end solution to performing assessments of systems and delivering assurance to system stakeholders (see Figure 4).

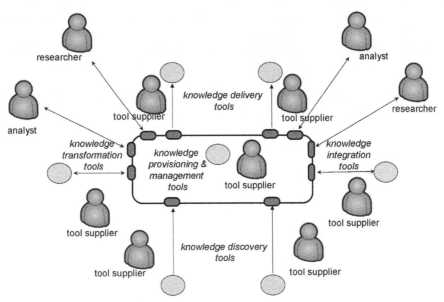

FIGURE 2 Knowledge-driven integration

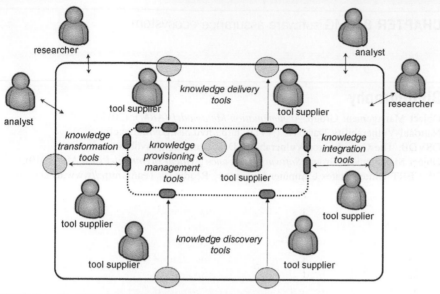

FIGURE 3 Logical interfaces provisioned by the compliant tools

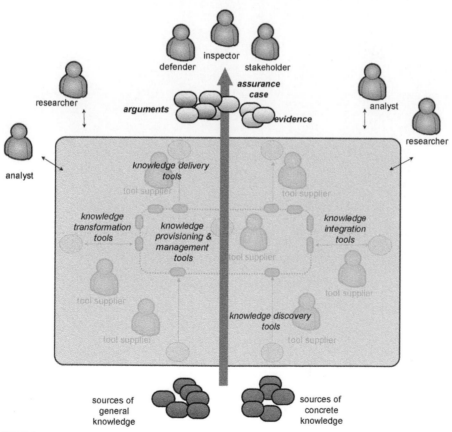

FIGURE 4 End-to-end solution delivering assurance to system stakeholders

Bibliography

Object Management Group, *Argumentation Metamodel (ARM)*. (2010).
National Vulnerability Database (NVD). http://nvd.nist.gov/home.cfm.
OSVDB, The Open Source Vulnerability Database. http://osvdb.org.
Object Management Group, *Software Assurance Evident Metamodel (SAEM)*. (2010).
US-CERT United States Computer Emergency Readiness Team. http://www.us-cert.gov.

Common fact model for assurance content

The first step in wisdom is to know the things themselves; this notion consists in having a true idea of the objects; objects are distinguished and known by classifying them methodically and giving them appropriate names. Therefore, classification and name-giving will be the foundation of our science.
—Carolus Linnaeus. Systema Naturae

The Name that can be named is not the constant Name.
—Tao Te Ching

9.1 ASSURANCE CONTENT

In order to assess the system's security, you need to collect information related to both the internal and external factors that contribute to the security posture, as well as information related to the *data-collection process* itself, which together provide evidentiary support for the assurance case. In particular, you need to understand the system's *entry points*: How can the attacker access the system? And how do you know that all entry points have been considered? You need to understand the *assets*: What are the things that need to be protected? What is their criticality? And how do you know that all assets have been considered? These questions can be particularly challenging because of the *interdependencies* not only between parts of the same system within the agreed upon scope of the assessment, but also between various systems. For example, a seemingly insignificant asset can be a critical protection element or something that can be used as a stepping-stone for a multi-stage attack. You need to understand the *impacts:* What are the undesired events that need to be protected against? How do you know that all impacts have been taken into account? You need to understand *security controls*: What are the countermeasures proposed for the system?

You also need to understand the *threats* to the system. The process of developing a credible assessment of threats must be guided by the information available in the community. What are the threats to similar systems? You need to understand what this system is doing that has been done before, so that you can tap into the existing experiences, historic data, and statistics. What are the common threats?

System Assurance: Beyond Detecting Vulnerabilities. DOI: 10.1016/B978-0-12-381414-2.00009-9

What attack methods have been used? What traps can you walk into, operationally? What common components are used? What is the security posture of the common components? How do they contribute to attacks? What is the experience with using these components?

Vulnerability is where internal factors meet external ones. Eventually you will need to detect vulnerabilities in the system. The starting point is to look for vulnerabilities in the off-the-shelf components; this information is available in the public vulnerability databases. But then you will look for the unique implementation and architecture vulnerabilities of the system under assessment. This search can be guided by knowledge of *vulnerability patterns*: What are the common problems in the code "like that"? Your assurance tool can be very efficient if it can download relevant and up-to-date vulnerability patterns and detect them in the code.

When internal factors are considered, your questions eventually turn into *requests for evidence collection* from the system artifacts and the development team. When it comes to external factors, the questions turn into *requests for information* that is required as a particular input into building the assurance case.

Assurance *content* is a collection of facts about the system of interest and its operating environment, and these facts need to be gathered, managed, accumulated, and shared.

Establishing standard protocols is critical in order to efficiently manage the information exchanges between the owners and producers of the information (including automated tools) and the consumers of the information:

- Establishing the common vocabulary to information exchange, which deals with the question: How do you express a request for information so that it is understood by the owner of the information and you obtain accurate data? Or when there is an existing information feed, like an online database, or a tool for information gathering, how do you correctly query that information feed to obtain accurate data? Inevitably, some of the exchanges are point-to-point, and the transformation between vocabularies must be established on the fly, on an as-needed basis. Fortunately, however, as the industry matures, more information feeds become available, and standard vocabularies can be developed to avoid point-to-point negotiations of the vocabulary.
- Integrating the information items once they become available. Efficient management of the information implies use of automated tools and stipulates the use of some sort of machine-readable format for the exchanges.
- Aligning the general-purpose knowledge available off the shelf with the system-specific knowledge of the system under assessment.

The OMG Software Assurance Ecosystem provides the infrastructure for collaborative cybersecurity in the form of standard protocols that define information exchange contracts between the participants of the ecosystem. The first step toward achieving this goal is to agree on the set of discernable concepts in order to build the *conceptual commitment*. The second step is to represent all segments of information in a *common format* in which information can be distributed, managed, integrated, transformed, refined, and analyzed. We start by describing the fact-oriented approach, based on normalized common vocabularies. A fact model is a combination of a conceptual schema, and for one specific system, a set of facts, defined using only the concepts of the conceptual schema. Conceptual schema is a combination of concepts and statements of what is possible, necessary, permissible and obligatory in each possible world. Fact models focus on simple factual statements that assert the existence of individual objects/things and individual relations between these objects/things. In the next chapter we introduce the OMG standard called Semantics of Business Vocabularies and Business Rules (SBVR) [SBVR], which extends the fact-oriented approach by defining linguistic models that focus on conceptual schemes and especially the statements of what is necessary, permissible and obligatory in a world described by a vocabulary of concepts. The OMG Assurance Ecosystem uses linguistic models for describing advanced assurance content using structured English.

9.2 **THE OBJECTIVES**

As we demonstrated in Chapters 4–7, system assurance involves multiple viewpoints, each described by its own vocabulary. Thus there are multiple fact models involved. The issue of designing a common vocabulary and establishing interoperability in the form of standard protocols is a recurring issue in system assurance. The Common Fact Model provides the foundation for the protocols of the OMG Software Assurance Ecosystem, described in Chapter 8. The Common Fact Model has the following objectives:

- To facilitate exchanges of cybersecurity knowledge for building assurance arguments at an affordable cost by introducing standard information exchange protocols.
- To facilitate development of vendor-neutral machine-readable cybersecurity content that automated tools can use to implement the information exchange protocols.
- To facilitate collaboration in the area of cybersecurity in order to accumulate and distribute cybersecurity content for assurance. Such content must be based on the common vocabulary defined by the information exchange protocol, rather than on some proprietary representation. The information exchange protocols are used to import the common protocol into proprietary tools.
- To facilitate a common terminology for system assurance.

These objectives are *interdependent*. Exchange of assurance content within the framework of collaborative cybersecurity requires *uniform terminology*; ad hoc point-to-point integrations are too costly; handling prose as the format for collaboration is too costly, since it requires significant effort for interpretation and leads to misunderstandings, and is not easily consumed by automated tools, so some machine-readable format is required. In order to achieve automation, a formal contract is needed to specify facts that can be produced by automated tools, so the content must be unambiguous and discernable. On the other hand, in order to separate producer and consumer tools, achieve *economies of scale*, and open up the market for content, the content must be made independent from tools, un-locking the proprietary representations used by individual tools.

Ambiguous terminology is one of the barriers to collaboration in the area of cybersecurity. Cybersecurity is a young and rapidly evolving discipline. It is somewhat famous for its inconsistent terminology, which contributes to insufficient interoperability at the machine-readable level. Multiple authors and organizations have proposed varying definitions of the basic cybersecurity terms, such as threat, attack, asset, countermeasure, vulnerability, and risk. Within each area, taxonomies are being suggested one after another, but none seems to take hold, while some of the taxonomies are believed to "resist automation." The lack of traceability of terminology to the agreed upon system facts makes it difficult to establish whether two definitions are for the same concept and whether two statements have the same *meaning*. It also makes it difficult to map one taxonomy onto another or to take the report produced by one tool and collate it with the report from a different tool. The Common Fact Model addresses this issue by focusing on discrenable concepts and providing a uniform machine-readable representation.

As a result, the Common Fact Model enables collaborative development of the common content for industrialization in system assurance.

9.3 DESIGN CRITERIA FOR INFORMATION EXCHANGE PROTOCOLS

An information exchange protocol implicitly defines a common vocabulary to which the proprietary vocabularies of the participants of the information exchange are mapped. The primary concern of designing an information exchange protocol is to adequately *design* this common vocabulary. When we choose how to represent something in a common vocabulary, we are making design decisions. To guide and evaluate our designs, we need objective criteria such as the following:

1. **Clarity**: A common vocabulary should effectively communicate the intended meaning of defined terms. Definitions should be objective. While the motivation for defining a concept might arise from social situations or computational requirements, the definition should be independent of social or computational context. Formalism is a means to this end. When a definition can be stated in logical axioms, it should be. Where possible, a complete definition (a predicate defined by necessary and sufficient conditions) is preferred to a partial definition (defined by only necessary or sufficient conditions). All definitions should be documented with natural language.
2. **Coherence**: A common vocabulary should be coherent: That is, it should allow inferences that are consistent with the definitions. At the least, the defining axioms should be logically consistent. Coherence should also apply to concepts that are defined informally, such as those described in natural language documentation and examples. If a sentence that can be inferred from the axioms

contradicts a definition or an example given informally, then the common vocabulary is incoherent.

3. **Extendibility**: A common language should be designed to anticipate the uses of the shared vocabulary. It should offer a conceptual foundation for a range of anticipated tasks, and the representation should be crafted so that one can extend and specialize the vocabulary monotonically. In other words, one should be able to define new terms for special uses based on the existing vocabulary, in a way that does not require revising existing definitions.

4. **Minimal encoding bias**: The conceptualization should be specified at the knowledge level without depending on a particular symbol-level encoding, such as an XML schema. An encoding bias results when representation choices are made purely for the convenience of notation or implementation. Encoding bias should be minimized because knowledge-sharing agents may be implemented in different representation systems and styles of representation.

5. **Minimal conceptual commitment**: A common vocabulary should require the minimal number of concepts sufficient to support intended knowledge-sharing activities. A common vocabulary should make as few claims as possible about the world being modeled, allowing the parties committed to the vocabulary freedom to specialize and instantiate the vocabulary as needed. Since conceptual commitment is based on consistent use of vocabulary, conceptual commitment can be minimized by specifying the most general discernable concepts and defining only those terms that are essential to the communication of knowledge.

Successful common vocabularies are usually also:

- Mutually exclusive—classifying in one category excludes all others because categories do not overlap.
- Collectively exhaustive—taken together, the categories include all possibilities.
- Unambiguous—clear and precise so that classification is not uncertain, regardless of who is classifying.
- Repeatable— repeated applications result in the same classification, regardless of who is classifying.
- Accepted—logical and intuitive so that categories could become generally approved.
- Useful—can be used to gain insight into the field of inquiry.

9.4 TRADE-OFFS

Design of common vocabularies, like most design problems, often requires making trade-offs among the criteria. However, the criteria are not inherently at odds. For example, in the interest of clarity, definitions should restrict the possible interpretations of terms. Minimizing conceptual commitment, however, means specifying a small set of general concepts, admitting many possible interpretations. These two goals are not in opposition. The clarity criterion talks about definitions of terms, whereas conceptual commitment is about the collection of discernable concepts being described. Having decided that a distinction is worth making, one should give the tightest possible definition of it.

Another apparent contradiction is between extendibility and conceptual commitment. A common vocabulary that anticipates a range of tasks need not include concepts sufficient to express all the knowledge relevant to those tasks (requiring an increased commitment to that larger vocabulary). An extensible vocabulary may specify few very general concepts and may also include the representational machinery needed to define the required specializations.

Both extendibility and conceptual commitment include a notion of sufficiency or adequacy. A common vocabulary serves a different purpose than a *knowledge base*. A shared vocabulary supports making statements about a domain, whereas a knowledge base may include the facts needed to solve a problem or answer arbitrary queries about the individual things/objects of a particular system of interest within this domain.

9.5 INFORMATION EXCHANGE PROTOCOLS

The following considerations will guide you in designing efficient information interchange protocols:

1. Identify the real tangible things that are involved in the communications. Provide concrete examples. This will greatly help establish mapping from the proprietary vocabulary of each participant to the common format. Figure 1 illustrates the process of building a common vocabulary. This process is based on the BORO methodology used by the IDEAS Group [McDaniel 2008] to build a common vocabulary for the interchange of enterprise architecture information within the NATO coalition forces. The input into the process is the existing vocabularies that are already used by the potential participants in information exchanges.

2. Focus on how you are going to identify the same individual thing that is referenced in two or more communications. This is the key to integrating multiple statements about the same object.

3. Identify relationships between these things. These relationships determine the facts being exchanged.

4. Recognize that the result of this process is a normalized common vocabulary, which facilitates mappings from the existing tools and repositories that already collect the facts in the area where you want to enable interoperability.

5. Select a speech community, for example, an English-speaking community. Focus on defining the vocabulary: the noun concepts, as well as the verb concepts involved in expressing the facts you have identified. This is the key deliverable. Make sure your concepts are sharply defined and are discernable. Exchanging prose that is not based on a set of well-defined concepts introduces a layer of inefficiency that can kill most of the interoperability efforts. A well-understood statement is one that you can fully *deconstruct* and that can guide

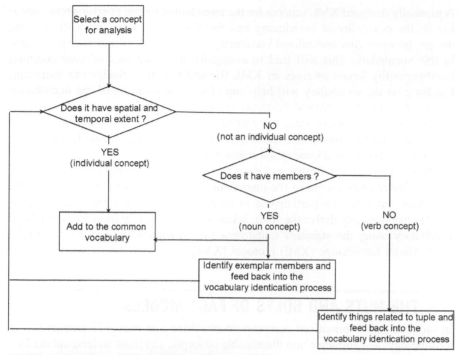

FIGURE 1 The process of building a common vocabulary

you in deciding whether or not it is true in any given situation. This means that you should be able to deconstruct the statement to elementary facts; use only well-defined ways of constructing statements from elementary facts; and have an efficient way to supply the elementary facts, so that the correctness of each statement can be validated. It is this combination of selecting the set of elementary facts, and the way of constructing larger statements from the elementary facts, that facilitates interoperability.

6. Only then select some *canonical expression* for your facts. Exchanging XML files is fine and is a good compromise in achieving a quick win because of the ubiquity of XML technology. So you can specify the canonical XML schema that defines the XML documents. XML documents express the facts that you identified and described in your vocabulary. This approach is beneficial for the developers who will need to implement adaptors for their existing tools, exporting and importing the new common format, since they are allowed a more natural "grasp" of what meanings are exchanged using XML; they will therefore be more efficient in identifying these meanings in their system. The extra level of "encoding" is removed, so the entire approach leaves fewer places to inconsistencies.

7. Allow for multiple alternative expressions of the facts defined by the common vocabulary. Remember, that you are defining meanings, not syntax.

A manually designed XML schema for the interchange format is error-prone, opening up the possibility of introducing new implicit facts during the XML schema design, between your normalized vocabulary and the XML files that express facts in this vocabulary. This will lead to ambiguity when the user of your common interoperability format receives an XML file and tries to verbalize the statement. Focusing on the vocabulary will help you clarify the meaning of the interchange format. Statements in natural language are understood by many, so they can be used to validate the XML. Manually crafted XML schema may lead to ambiguities. Interchange formats based on manually crafted XML schemes usually violate the principle of the minimal conceptual commitment.

You can go one step further and insist that it is your vocabulary of concepts that is the primary embodiment of the interchange specification (defining the possible meanings that you want participants to exchange). To achieve this end you may want to mechanically derive the XML schema [XML] directly from the normalized vocabulary using the standard transformation algorithms defined by the OMG XML Model Interchange (XMI) protocol [XMI].

9.6 THE NUTS AND BOLTS OF FACT MODELS

In order to build normalized common vocabularies that reconcile ambiguities in terminology, and eliminate non discernable concepts, you must understand the fundamentals of the fact-oriented approach, such as noun and verb concepts, objects and facts, and how they build conceptual commitment [Halpin 2008], [Ross 2003], [Ross 2009]. Let's consider some concrete examples. We'll need a few nuts, bolts, and washers from the nearest hardware store.

9.6.1 Objects

The first step in building a common vocabulary is to identify the tangible things in the domain of interest. Grab a nut. Feel its weight on your palm; toss it into a pond and watch the ripples. Our objects have nothing to do with object-oriented programming. An object has spatial (or sometimes a temporal) extent and identity, that's all. You must be able to *discern* an object from the background, as well as from other objects. A synonym of an "object" is a "thing." Figure 2 is an illustration of an "object." You can refer to this object as "this thing" or "my favorite nut" or "the nut n-2." At this point the *conceptual commitment* is to agree to discern this object, agree on its boundaries, and agree on how to identify it.

FIGURE 2 Ilustration of the Object "Nut N-2"

There are many ways to refer to an object, including words, pictures, gestures, and sounds. Some of the references include the *concept* of the object.

Now take a handful of nuts. A *collection* has some characteristics of an individual thing. It has weight. It produces ripples when tossed into a pond. It has spatial or temporal extent. Collection has a few additional characteristics. You can count the elements of the collection. You can add more things to your collection. You can check if your favorite nut is in the pile. Figure 3 is an illustration of a collection of several similar things.

FIGURE 3 Illustration of collection of objects

9.6.2 **Noun concepts**

Now, let's perform a mental exercise. Let's imagine a glass jar full of nuts, an infinite supply of 1¼ inch stainless steel nuts. Whenever we need a nut (for example, to toss it into the pond and watch the ripples), we can grab one from the nut jar. This jar illustrates a concept "nut" – an unit of knowledge that corresponds to the entire collection of similar things with unique combination of characteristics. The nut on the palm is called a "member" of the concept "nut" (one nut from the jar full of similar nuts). When I say "a nut makes more elegant ripples than a pebble," I am referring to an anonymous member of the concept "nut." When I say "I am tossing 10 nuts into the pond," I am referring to particular 10 members of the concept "nut." A concept has an "extent" that is the collection of objects considered to be members of that concept. The extent of the concept "nut" is the collection of all 1¼ inch stainless steel nuts. The trick is that this collection is only mentally associated with the concept. In other words, you cannot throw the concept of a nut into the pond.

Figure 4 is an illustration of a concept "nut."

Usually in order to recognize an object, you must know *what* it is. A concept is "discernable" when you can tell with confidence when a certain object is a member of this concept. The concept "nut" is discernable in this sense. Whenever you need to make a statement about an individual nut, you "instantiate" the concept (by taking one nut out of the imaginary jar). When you verbalize your thought, you use an agreed upon word, such as the word "nut" to refer to the individual member of the concept (that you took from the jar). The consumer of your statement must match the word back to the concept, as if the physical object materializes so that it can be sensed, and then tossed back into the corresponding jar where it belongs.

FIGURE 4 Illustration of concept "nut"

Communication is possible when both parties share the same *meaning* (the concept) as well as the particular *expression*.

The concept "nut" is an example of a noun concept; it is represented by nouns or noun phrases. In our example we will also use concepts "bolt", and "washer".

At this point the *conceptual commitment* is to agree on the ability to discern (at least in principle) any object in the extent of the noun concept and to use the corresponding noun phrase in statements. In particular, we agree that there may exist other objects that share some characteristics with the object that is already part of the conceptual commitment (for example, "the nut n-2"). Noun concepts allow making statements about the common characteristics of objects and relationships between objects without the reference to individual objects.

9.6.3 Facts about the existence of objects

In order to *state* facts, it is very important to agree on how we are referring to objects. The *identifier* of the object is used as a reference to it when stating the facts. Figure 5 illustrates the identifiers of objects.

We assume a unique reference schema for each hardware item by means of a canonical identifier, such as a serial number. In practice, a particular object can be referred to in more than one way, and the canonical identifier is not always feasible. You will find examples of indirect references later in this section.

Once we have an agreed upon reference schema, we can state some facts. Our first set of facts states the existence of several uniquely identifiable objects. The following four facts describe Figure 5:

- There exists a bolt identified as "b-25."
- There exists a nut identified as "n-2."
- There exists a washer identified as "w-7a."
- There exists a washer identified as "w-7b."

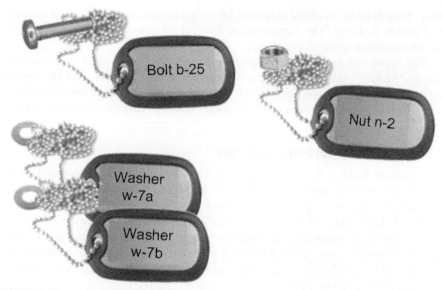

FIGURE 5 Illustration of the identifiers of objects

The above four facts are called *existential facts* because they assert the existence of certain objects that belong to a certain concept. It may seem obvious, but you must have the agreed upon set of concepts before you can assert the existence of any objects. Common conceptualization is the contract between the parties that attempt exchanging information.

9.6.4 Individual concepts

An individual concept corresponds to a single object. Figure 6 is an illustration of the individual concept alongside with the thing "the nut n-2". You can toss the thing denoted by the name "Nut n-2" into a pond, and this thing ceases to exist (in a practical sense, at least). However, you cannot toss the concept "Nut n-2" into the pond. We need this concept to discuss the potential properties of the individual

FIGURE 6 Illustration of individual concept

thing, regardless of its actual existence (at the given moment). Individual concepts give names to things. The corresponding *conceptual commitment* is the agreement on the canonical name of the object.

The name and the canonical identifier do not have to be same. For example, strings "SPAIN," "ESPAGNE," the ISO canonical identifier ES, and the expression "the country that won the 2010 FIFA World Cup" all refer to the same object, which is a particular instance of the concept "country" and has the name Spain.

9.6.5 Relations between concepts

Each concept is also a *thing* (a rather intangible one). We can talk about collections of concepts and relations between concepts. For example, one concept can be *more general* than another concept (think about jars inside other jars). The general concept behind "nut," "bolt," and "washer" is the concept "hardware item." We can talk about the (very general) concept "concept." A verb concept is a relation between noun concepts, while a fact is a relation between individual objects. We will describe concepts and relationships between them in more detail in Chapter 10 that describes linguistic models.

9.6.6 Verb concepts

Verb concepts describe relationships between things and are represented by verbs and verb phrases. In the same way that objects are instances of the noun concepts, *facts* are instances of verb concepts. For example, the verb concepts are "nut is screwed onto bolt" or "washer is fastened onto bolt." Some corresponding facts are illustrated in Figure 7. We assume the existence of objects "bolt b-26" and "bolt b-27."

- Nut "n-2" is screwed onto bolt "b-25."
- Washer "w-7a" is fastened onto bolt "b-26."
- Washer "w-7b" is fastened on bolt "b-27."

The above three facts define instances of the verb concepts "nut is screwed onto bolt" and "washer is fastened onto bolt." The identity of objects is important for the correct statement of facts. Facts state the existence of an association between

FIGURE 7 Illustration of facts based on verb concepts

several individual things, so facts are basically *tuples* (ordered lists of identities of participating objects). A verb concept is discernable when you can tell with confidence if the corresponding relationship exists.

The corresponding *conceptual commitment* is the agreement to recognize the relationship between any individual objects and use the corresponding verb phrase in statements.

The relationship between objects may have temporal aspects that need to be considered when you examine the existence of relationships, or when relationships change over time. For example, earlier we stated that the nut n-2 is screwed onto bolt b-25. You may need to say that this was true from Monday until Friday afternoon, when the nut went off. The next chapter, which is dedicated to linguistic models, will describe some examples of building complex statements like the one above. The present chapter is dedicated to facts that correspond to elementary statements in an agreed upon vocabulary. We must therefore agree to use a more complex verb phrase, such as "nut is screwed onto bolt since date1 until date2." Instead of representing a binary relationship (a binary fact type) between a nut concept and a bolt concept, this verb phrase represents a relationship between four concepts: a nut, a bolt, and two dates. A "date" is a concept too, and an individual instance of this concept is identified, for example, as "Monday, July 12, 2010."

Observe that using verbs to represent relationships between things results in readable statements (verbalizations) of facts. Failure to consider elementary verb concepts as the basic blocks of meaningful information exchanges is the primary root cause of the terminology confusion, as will be explained in more detail later in this chapter when we introduce complex situational concepts.

9.6.7 Characteristics

The previous example illustrated *binary* relationships, in which two objects are involved. Some relationships involve a single object. Such relationships are called *unary* relationships (relationships with a single participant), or *characteristics*. Let's consider an example of a characteristic. "Hardware item has thread" is an example of a characteristic. Here "thread" is not a new concept. Instead, "having a thread" is a discernable characteristic that allows one to group concepts. For example, "hardware items" can be divided into two groups: one group containing the "nut" and "bolt" (since they are hardware items that have thread), and the second one containing the "washer" (since this is a hardware item that does not have thread). You cannot easily deprive a nut of "having a thread." Such verb concepts are called "essential characteristics" or "properties." Every nut has a thread, which is so important to the nature of the nut that without it the nut will be something else, a ring, perhaps.

Other characteristics that are essential for the "nuts and bolts" example are the following.

- Hardware item is cylindrical.
- Hardware item has hole.
- Hardware item is flat.

Some people believe that concepts are defined by the process of "name-giving." However, names are only *expressions* of concepts within a given speech community. A definition of a concept can be built by providing the general concept and a set of essential characteristics, for example:

A washer is a hardware item that is flat and has a hole and does not have thread.
A nut is a hardware item that is cylindrical and has a hole and has thread.

9.6.8 Situational concepts

One cause of ambiguous terminology is that some concepts are less *tangible* than others. Grab a bolt, a nut, and two washers, and assemble them together, as illustrated at the right side of Figure 8. The left side of the figure shows the four things involved in the assembly.

FIGURE 8 Illustration of "nut-and-bolt assembly"

On one hand, all the things remain the same after the assembly operation. On the other hand, the new situation is that the four original things are now related. The new relationships are described by the verb phrases: "a nut is screwed onto a bolt," "a washer is fastened onto a bolt," and "washer1 is above washer2." What makes this situation different from the one described previously is that it involves the same "bolt" thing.

- Nut "n-2" is screwed onto bolt "b-25."
- Washer "w-7a" is fastened onto bolt "b-25."
- Washer "w-7b" is fastened on bolt "b-25."
- Washer "w-7a" is above washer "w-7b."

The new situation is that now all four things act as a unit (for example, you cannot toss them into the pond individually without first disassembling). Linguistically, this situation is often handled by using a new concept to describe this unit: in our case, a noun concept "nut-and-bolt assembly" (see Figure 9). This new concept works exactly like the previous noun concepts: The assembly has weight and can be tossed into a pond. However, the difference between the original concepts "nut," "bolt," and "washer" is that the "nut-and-bolt assembly" is not quite so real: It exists only as long as the member things are related. So we say that the new concept "nut-and-bolt assembly" is an *objectification* of the relations between the original things.

Each component now plays a specific *role* in the new *situation*, for example, the "top washer of the nut-and-bolt assembly." As you can see, identifying a role has created yet another concept—a "top washer." This concept is *contextualized*:

FIGURE 9 Illustration of noun concept "nut-and-bolt assembly"

We can talk about a "top washer" only in the context of some "nut-and-bolt assembly." "Top washer" is a role concept. Contextualized concepts are often used as reference schemes: You can refer to the washer "w-7a" as "the top washer of the nut-and-bolt assembly that involves bolt b-25."

You can choose to assert the existence of the assembly: "There exists a nut-and-bolt assembly identified as 1." Then instead of facts above, you will have different facts corresponding to the new part-of verb phrases:

- Bolt "b-25" is the bolt of the nut-and-bolt assembly "1."
- Nut "n-2" is the nut of the nut-and-bolt assembly "1."
- Washer "w-7a" is the top washer of the nut-and-bolt assembly "1."
- Washer "w-7b" is the bottom washer of the nut-and-bolt assembly "1."

In free-form communications, supported by linguistic models, you may want to use both verbalizations. However, efficient information exchanges require commitment to one particular conceptualization.

Failure to recognize elementary verb concepts as the foundation of complex situational concepts often leads to terminology confusion when different communities choose overlapping (yet different) situational concepts that are based on the same set of elementary verb concepts, especially when the physical boundary of the situation in not obvious. For example, consider situations where the following elementary verb concepts are involved:

- A threat agent attacks the system;
- the attack involves a sequence of data packets;
- each data packet uses a certain entry point;
- some data packets cause certain events in the system;
- one event causes another event;
- some event is undesired;
- the undesired event causes injury to an asset;
- some event is the consequence of another event.

Further, it is possible that the undesired event is caused by multiple sequences of data packets.

Elementary verb concepts create complex chains of facts linked through common objects that participate in multiple facts. This leaves far too many possibilities for ambiguity in associating derived situational concepts with different segments of this chain. For example, one community may use the situational concept "threat" to refer to the entire family of attacks that cause same injury to a certain asset, regardless of the threat agent that causes the attack. This community will then use the derived verb concepts "threat is caused by threat agent" and "threat has consequence" to address the remaining segments of the original chain. Another community may choose to use the same concept "threat" to refer to just the central undesired event. The second community will use the derived verb concepts "threat is caused by event," "event is a consequence of threat," and "threat causes injury." When indirect attacks are considered, the extent of the rival definitions of "threat" will be drastically different, leading to severe interoperability problems. The guidelines for building information exchange protocols presented in Figure 1 describe how to analyze the use of potentially ambiguous situational concepts and help focus on the elementary verb concepts.

9.6.9 Viewpoints and views

A collection of noun and verb phrases representing a set of concepts is called a *vocabulary*. Vocabulary determines a *viewpoint* for describing a system. Such descriptions are always partial because of the preselection of the agreed-upon concepts (the viewpoint) that determines the kinds of facts in the description of the particular system (the view). A viewpoint determines what facts are available in the view of the system. Figure 10 illustrates a view that is based on a "nuts-and-bolts" viewpoint. The four jars illustrate the concepts "nut," "bolt," "washer," and "nut-and-bolt" assembly (as a shortcut for several relations between the noun concepts). Figure 10 shows a "nuts-and-bolts" view of some system—in this example, the system is the demo installation of an iBrick device at the head office of the Cyber Bricks Corporation. The tray illustrates the *scope* of the view—the system for which the view is produced. The view only contains facts about nuts, bolts, washers, and

FIGURE 10 Illustration of a view that is based on a "nuts-and-bolts" viewpoint

relationships between them. It does not include any information about any other parts of the iBrick device because they are not part of the viewpoint.

Each view has a certain scope: In this example, the view describes the nuts and bolts of the iBrick device from Cyber Bricks, collected on July 12, 2010. Another part of the conceptual commitment that is essential for using fact-oriented views is *completeness* of a particular view: Does this view include facts about all nuts and bolts within the scope, or only some of them? In other words, does the tray contain all nuts, bolts, and washers extracted from the iBrick device from Cyber Bricks? Completeness is not a property of the viewpoint but of an individual view. Understanding completeness is very important when facts are used as evidence in support of assurance claims, which may involve a positive or negative statement about the entire system, for example, "all bolts are such that ... ", or "there is no nut-and-bolt assembly such that ...." The completeness claim for the view is essential for analyzing the facts and presenting the findings of the analysis as evidence.

The scope of the view provides the context that may lead to creation of a few new concepts. For example, how do we define a "loose nut"? In the context of a particular view, a "loose nut" is a nut that is not screwed onto any bolt. Yet talking about "loose nuts" without the traceability to the particular vocabulary and a particular repository of facts may lead to some terminological ambiguities.

9.6.10 **Information exchanges and assurance**

Let's imagine that you are responsible for security assessment of the "iBrick device at the Cyber Bricks Corporation." In order to understand the "iBrick device," you *request* the "nuts and bolts" view of the "iBrick device." You agreed that the "nuts-and-bolts" vocabulary is defined by the verb phrases "nut is screwed onto bolt," "washer is fastened onto bolt," "washer is above washer," and the noun concepts "bolt," "nut," and "washer." The "nuts-and-bolts" viewpoint defines the *contract* between the producer of the "nuts and bolts" view and the consumer of the view (yourself). The "nuts-and-bolts" vocabulary guides you in understanding the structure and the meaning of the "nuts and bolts" view. This view is delivered to you in some physical representation, such as a photo, a prose report, an XML file, a SOAP message, or an SQL query response. Once the "nuts-and-bolts" view is available, you can use alternative noun and verb phrases such as the "nut-and-bolt assembly" and the "top washer" to make more readable statements about this view for the consumers of your report.

At some point you *request* that the "loose nuts" analysis be performed on the "nuts and bolts" view of the "iBrick device." The "loose nuts" analysis is the process that derives "nut is loose" facts using the original "nuts and bolts" view as the input. This process produces facts in the extended vocabulary that adds the characteristic "nut is loose" to the original "nuts-and-bolts" vocabulary. The extended vocabulary is the contract between you and the producer of the new facts, However, the "nut is loose" concept is not part of the contract with the producer of the original facts. Since the new facts refer to things from the original viewpoint, the derived facts can be easily integrated with the original facts.

Suppose that some fictitious *Handbook for Justifiable Cyber Bricks Security* mentions that "it is obligatory that a secure iBrick device does not have loose nuts." You can directly use the derived facts as evidence to substantiate the claim, that "the target iBrick device does not have any loose nuts," and later use this evidence to support the argument to justify that "the target iBrick device" is secure. In addition, the assurance case needs to be warranted by an argument related to the accuracy of the primary fact collection as well as the accuracy of the "loose nuts" analysis.

We used the formal definition of the concept "nut is loose" as a *query* into the "nuts-and-bolts" repository of facts to produce facts in the new vocabulary that is aligned with the vocabulary used in the *Handbook*.

9.6.11 Fact-oriented integration

Suppose we have another vocabulary that corresponds to the supply chain viewpoint, including the following concepts:

- Order
- Warehouse
- Shipping company
- Date
- Hardware item is part of order
- Order is delivered by shipping company from warehouse on date

The new "supply chain" view of the "iBrick device" includes the following facts:

- Bolt "b-25" is part of order "hw145."
- Nut "n-2" is part of order "hw146."
- Washer "w-7a" is part of order "hw145."
- Washer "w-7b" is part of order "hw145."
- Order "hw145" is delivered by "UPS" from "warehouse A" on 01-05-2009.
- Order "hw146" is delivered by "FedEx" from "warehouse A" on 02-05-2009.
- Bolt "b-26" is part of order "hw147."
- Order "hw147" is delivered by "UPS" from "warehouse B" on 03-06-2010.

To integrate this view with the original "nuts-and-bolts" view, you first need to match the objects, which are described by the corresponding existential facts. In case the two sets of facts do not use the same identities for the things that they reference, the integration needs a translation table that establishes correspondence between the things involved in the two views. This correspondence of the existential facts is an important part of any information exchange contract. The original "nuts-and-bolts" view and the "supply chain" view agree on the identities of the hardware items, so they can be easily integrated. The two sets of facts reference the same objects, so the two sets can be simply merged. As a result, you can trace nuts and bolts to assemblies, and also track nuts and bolts to orders, warehouses, and dates.

9.6.12 **Automatic derivation of facts**

The primitive facts are usually discernable and can be discovered by automated tools in a fully objective, systematic, and repeatable way. However, they are usually too low level and insignificant to be directly linked with any of the assurance claims. In order to be useful for assurance, more interesting facts must be *derived*. Aggregation is a simple automatic operation that uses the "part-of" facts to derive relationships for some high-level concepts. For example, assuming all iBricks facts introduced so far, it is reasonable to derive the following new facts:

- Since bolt "b-25" is part of order "hw145" and "bolt-25" is part of the assembly "1," we can derive the fact that assembly "1" *depends on* order "hw145."
- Assembly "a" also *depends on* order "hw146," based on the fact that "nut n-2" is part of assembly "1" and "nut n-2" is part of order "hw146."
- Dependency between assembly "1" and order "hw145" is stronger than the relationship between that assembly and order "hw146," since the first relationship is based on three primitive facts (bolt and two washers), while the second relationship is based only on a single fact (nut n-2).
- Based on the available facts, assembly "1" *does not depend on* order "hw147."

Since the "nut-and-bolt assembly 1" is part of the "iBrick device," you can also derive the following facts:

- "iBrick device" *depends on* "order "hw145."
- "iBrick device" *depends on* order "hw146."
- Based on the available facts, the "iBrick device" *does not depend on* order "hw147."

A variation of the "is part of" relationship is called "is implemented by." This relationship is essential for traceability between high-level domain-specific concepts and their implementations by the low-level programming language-specific concepts. For example, the concept "customer" is implemented by the class "client," variable "current client," and the relational tables "customers" and "customer details," and the html forms "add customer" and "browse customer."

Finally, the same mechanism of aggregating relationships can be used to derive more facts:

- Since order "hw145" "originated in" "warehouse A" and "bolt "b-25" is part of order "hw145," bolt "b-25" *depends on* warehouse "A."
- Further, the iBrick device *depends on* warehouse "A."
- Also, based on the available facts, the iBrick device *does not depend on* warehouse "B."
- Similarly, based on the available facts, the iBrick device *does not depend on* any "order shipped in 2010."

Primitive relationships lose some of their flavor during the aggregation. However, the resulting dependencies are still discernable, and provided the primitive facts are comprehensive, allow nontrivial and accurate reasoning about the high-level objects. They therefore can contribute to evidence in support of assurance claims, involving external factors for cybersecurity.

9.7 THE REPRESENTATION OF FACTS

The next step in building an information exchange protocol is to select a representation of the facts. There are numerous options. You can represent facts as prose using some natural language, such as English, or use more formal languages, such as XML, text files, SQL, RDF [Leuf 2006], or Prolog. You can use an API such as CORBA IDL, or SOAP, or you can define facts using one of the programming languages, such as C, Java, or Python. You can represent facts graphically, for example, in UML.

In this section we discuss representation of facts using XML and Prolog.

9.7.1 Representing facts in XML

XML technology is often used as the basis for common interchange formats. However, simply selecting XML technology as the basis for interoperability is insufficient because there are multiple approaches to using XML. In this section we illustrate several design patterns for using XML to represent facts.

The **first** pattern illustrates the "noun-based approach." This example uses explicit XML elements to represent "things" corresponding to the primitive concepts, and uses the objectified version of the relationship. Here we see an explicit element for the nut-and-bolt assembly concept and explicit XML attributes for the corresponding roles, such as "the bolt of the nut-and-bolt assembly," the "nut of the nut-and-bolt assembly," and so on. These properties reference the corresponding primitive objects.

```xml
<?xml version="1.0"?>
<NutsAndBolts name="iBrick device from Cyber Bricks corp">
    <Nut id="n-2"/>
    <Bolt id="b-24"/>
    <Washer id="w-7a"/>
    <Washer id="w-7b"/>
    <NutAndBoltAssembly id="1" bolt="b-24" top-washer="w-7a" bottom-washer="w-7b" nut="n-2" />
</NutsAndBolts>
```

The benefit of this pattern is that the elements are explicitly recognizable in the XML file, and their names are coordinated with the original vocabulary. The top XML element NutsAndBolts corresponds to the scope of the view; all other elements are nested in the scope. This is a natural way to represent part-of facts.

Here is the XSD schema for this example:

```
<xsd:schema xmlns:xsd="http://www.w3.org/2001/XMLSchema"
        targetNamespace="http://www.example.com/nutsandbolts"
xmlns:nab="http://www.example.com/nutsanbbolts"
  <xsd:complexType name="NutsAndBolts">
    <xsd:choice maxOccurs="unbounded" minOccurs="0">
    <xsd:element name="Nut" type="nab:Nut" />
    <xsd:element name="Bolt" type="nab:Bolt" />
    <xsd:element name="Washer" type="nab:Washer" />
    <xsd:element name="Assembly" type="nab:NutAndBoltAssembly" />
  </xsd:choice >
    <xsd:attribute name="name" type="string" use="required" />
  </xsd:complexType>

  <xsd:complexType name="Nut">
    <xsd:attribute name="id" type="string" use="required" />
  </xsd:complexType>
  <xsd:complexType name="Bolt">
    <xsd:attribute name="id" type="string" use="required" />
  </xsd:complexType>
  <xsd:complexType name="Washer">
    <xsd:attribute name="id" type="string" use="required" />
  </xsd:complexType>
  <xsd:complexType name="NutAndBoltAssembly">
    <xsd:attribute name="id" type="string" use="required" />
    <xsd:attribute name="bolt" type="nab:Bolt" use="required" />
    <xsd:attribute name="topWasher" type="nab:Washer" use="required" />
    <xsd:attribute name="bottomWasher" type="name:Washer"
    use="required" />
    <xsd:attribute name="nut" type="nab:Nut" use="required" />
  </xsd:complexType>
</xsd:schema>
```

The schema introduces an XSD type for each noun concept in the original vocabulary. XSD offers certain means to describe constraints for schemas. In the above example we constrained the number of elements that are part of a nut-and-bolt assembly. As you can see, the schema does not allow a bolt with only one washer, or a bolt with three washers but no nut. The order of elements of the assembly is not constrained, since the schema only represents their roles, so we had to distinguish between the top washer and bottom washer as explicit roles.

The **second** pattern emphasized the part-of facts even further: The elements of the nut-and-bolt assembly are nested within the assembly, so instead of the attributes, the complex type NutAndBoltAssembly declares nested elements.

```
<?xml version="1.0"?>
<NutsAndBolts name="iBrick device from Cyber Bricks corp">
  <NutAndBoltAssembly id="1" />
      <Bolt id="b-24"/>
          <Washer id="w-7a"/>
          <Washer id="w-7b"/>
          <Nut id="n-2"/>
  </NutAndBoltAssembly/>
</NutsAndBolts>
```

Here is the corresponding fragment of the XSD schema illustrating this approach. First we define the NutAndBoltAssembly as an XSD sequence of elements, thus constraining their order. This example allows multiple washers, no washers, and, at most, one nut at the bottom of the assembly.

```
<xsd:complexType name="NutAndBoltAssembly">
 <xsd:sequence>
    <xsd:element name="bolt" type="nab:Bolt" minOccurs="1"
maxOccurs="1" />
    <xsd:element  name="Washer"  type="nab:Washer"  minOccurs="0"
maxOccurs="unbounded"/>
    <xsd:element name="nut" type="nab:Nut" minOccurs="0" maxOccurs=
"unbounded" />
  </xsd:sequence>
  <xsd:attribute name="id" type="string" use="required" />
</xsd:complexType>
```

Here we define the nested elements as an unordered collection, similar to the definition of the original NutsAndBolts element.

```
<xsd:complexType name="NutAndBoltAssembly">
  <xsd:choice maxOccurs="unbounded" minOccurs="0">
      <xsd:element name="bolt" type="nab:Bolt" />
      <xsd:element name="topWasher" type="nab:Washer" />
      <xsd:element name="bottomWasher" type="nab:Washer" />
      <xsd:element name="nut" type="nab:Nut" />
  </xsd:choice>
  <xsd:attribute name="id" type="string" use="required" />
</xsd:complexType>
```

The **third** pattern demonstrates the "verb-based approach." Instead of using the objectified noun concept for the nut-and-bolt assembly, which introduces the explicit roles of the primitive things with respect to the assembly and thus restricts the possible combinations, we can build an XML representation based on the original verb concepts that describe the individual relationships between things (prior to the objectification). Here is the XML view of the facts:

```
<?xml version="1.0"?>
<NutsAndBolts name="iBrick device from Cyber Bricks corp">
  <Nut id="n-2"/>
  <Bolt id="b-24"/>
  <Washer id="w-7a"/>
  <Washer id="w-7b"/>
  <IsScrewedOnto nut="n-2" bolt="b-24"/>
  <IsSecuredOn washer="w-7a" bolt="b-24"/>
  <IsSecuredOn washer="w-7b" bolt="b-24"/>
  <IsAbove washer1="w-7a" washer2="w-7b"/>
</NutsAndBolts>
```

The XSD scheme for this example is very similar to the first pattern. However, instead of the type for the noun concept nuts-and-bolt assembly, it introduces explicit types for the verb concepts that are designated by the terms "is screwed onto," "is secured on," and "is above." The benefit of this approach is that it makes a close match to the original vocabulary and does not restrict the multitude of combinations, beyond just the bolt with two washers and a nut. The disadvantage is that the selected XSD types do not include the objectified noun concept of a nut-and-bolt assembly.

We have demonstrated the most common patterns of representing a fact view as an XML document (and at the same time, representing the vocabulary as XML schema). Many more variations are possible. To conclude we will introduce another pattern that demonstrates how an XSD schema can be normalized.

The **fourth** pattern can be called the "role-based approach." Instead of explicitly representing the primitive concepts of the vocabulary, such as "Bolt," "IsScrewedOnto" or "NutAndBoltAssembly," this approach focuses at the *meta-level* concepts. A meta-level concept is in some ways similar to a general concept: What is the common general concept of "bolt," "nut," and "washer"? A "hardware item." General concept describes certain characteristics that are shared by all specialized concepts. The meta-level concept addresses the question: What are "bolt," "nut," and "washer" *instances* of? "Bolt," "nut," and "washer" are instances of a "noun concept." "IsScrewedOnto" and "IsAbove" are instances of a "verb concept." Together they are instances of the "concept." From this perspective, a "nut" is a "noun concept" that plays the role of a nut in a nuts-and-bolts viewpoint. This offers a different way to structure the XML document. Instead of defining an explicit element "Nut," "Bolt," and so on, we can define a single element "Object" with an attribute "role." Then the nuts-and-bolts view will use the roles "nut," "bolt," and the like. This approach is illustrated below:

```
<?xml version="1.0"?>
<Scope id="s1" type="NutsAndBolts" name="iBrick device from Cyber
Bricks corp">
  <Object type="Nut" id="n-2"/>
```

```
<Object type="Bolt" id="b-24"/>
<Object type="Washer" id="w-7a"/>
<Object type="Washer" id="w-7b"/>
<Fact type="NutAndBoltAssembly" id="1" />
    <RoleBinding id="f1" role="bolt" subject="1" object="b-24"/>
    <RoleBinding id="f2" role="nut" subject="1" object="n-2"/>
    <RoleBinding id="f3" role="top washer" subject="1" object="w-7a"/>
    <RoleBinding id="f4" role="bottom washer" subject="1"
object="w-7b"/>
</Scope>
```

The same meta-level elements can be used to represent the verb concepts:

```
<Fact type="washer1 is above washer2" id="r1" />
    <RoleBinding id="f5" role="washer1" subject="r1" object="w-7a"/>
    <RoleBinding id="f6" role="washer2" subject="r2" object="w-7b"/>
```

Here is the XSD schema for this example:

```
<xsd:schema xmlns:xsd="http://www.w3.org/2001/XMLSchema"
        targetNamespace="http://www.example.com/nutsandbolts"
            xmlns:nab="http://www.example.com/nutsandbolts"
<xsd:complexType name="Scope">
  <xsd:attribute name="id" type="string" use="required" />
  <xsd:attribute name="name" type="string" use="required" />
  <xsd:element name="type" type="nab:type" minOccurs="0"
maxOccurs="unbounded" />
</xsd:complexType>

<xsd:complexType name="Object">
  <xsd:attribute name="id" type="string" use="required" />
  <xsd:element name="type" type="nab:noun" minOccurs="0"
maxOccurs="unbounded" />
</xsd:complexType>

<xsd:complexType name="Fact">
  <xsd:attribute name="id" type="string" use="required" />
  <xsd:element name="type" type="nab:verb" minOccurs="0"
maxOccurs="unbounded" />
</xsd:complexType>
<xsd:complexType name="RoleBinding">
  <xsd:attribute name="id" type="string" use="required" />
  <xsd:attribute name="role" type="nab:role" use="required" />
  <xsd:attribute name="subject" type="Object" use="required" />
  <xsd:attribute name="object" type="Object" use="required" />
</xsd:complexType>
```

```
<xsd:simpleType name="noun">
  <xsd:Restriction base="xsd:NCName">
     <xsd:enumeration value="bolt"/>
     <xsd:enumeration value="nut"/>
     <xsd:enumeration value="washer"/>
  </xsd:Restriction>
</xsd:simpleType>

<xsd:simpleType name="verb">
  <xsd:Restriction base="xsd:NCName">
     <xsd:enumeration value="nut and bolt assembly"/>
     <xsd:enumeration value="washer1 is above washer2"/>
  </xsd:Restriction>
</xsd:simpleType>

<xsd:simpleType name="role">
  <xsd:Restriction base="xsd:NCName">
    <xsd:enumeration value="bolt"/>
    <xsd:enumeration value="nut"/>
    <xsd:enumeration value="top washer"/>
    <xsd:enumeration value="bottom washer"/>
  </xsd:Restriction>
</xsd:simpleType>
</xsd:schema>
```

The benefit of this approach is that the schema is separated from the vocabulary. The schema becomes *common* for all vocabularies that we want to represent, so it supports integration of facts from different vocabularies.

9.7.2 Representing facts and schemes in Prolog

Let's consider a few more illustrations of how facts can be represented in a machine-readable format. Prolog language is very closely aligned with the fact-oriented approach. Here is an illustration of the nuts-and-bolts facts, represented in Prolog.

```
nut('n-2').
bolt('b-24').
washer('w-7a').
washer('w-7b').
scope('s1','iBrick device from Cyber Bricks corp').
nutAndBoltAssembly('1','b-24','n-2','w-7a','w-7b').
contains('s1','b-2').
contains('s1','b-24').
contains('s1','w-7a').
contains('s1','w-7b').
contains('s1','1').
```

Observe that the scope of the nuts-and-bolts is represented as an explicit object "scope" and several "contains" relationships, while in the XML examples we used nesting of the elements for that purpose. Prolog allows nesting of facts, but this is already beyond the scope of what we intend to show in this section. Instead, let us demonstrate the role-based approach in Prolog:

```
object('n-2','Nut').
object('b-24','bolt').
object('w-7a','washer'),
object('w-7b','washer').
object('s1','scope').
fact('s1','name','iBrick device from Cyber Bricks corp').
object('1','nutAndBoltAssembly').
fact('s1','part-of','b-2').
fact('s1','part-of','b-24').
fact('s1','part-of','w-7a').
fact('s1','part-of','w-7b').
fact('s1','part-of','1').
fact('1','bolt','b-24').
fact('1','nut','n-2').
fact('1','top washer','w-7a').
fact('1','bottom washer','w-7b').
object('r1','washer1 is above washer2').
fact('r1','washer1','w-7a').
fact('r1','washer2','w-7b').
```

Observe that only two Prolog predicates are used—"object" and "fact"—to support the integration of facts from different vocabularies. Attributes are represented as explicit relationships: The name of the nuts-and-bolts view is represented as an explicit fact.

9.8 THE COMMON SCHEMA

This section introduces a simple common schema for exchanging facts. We assume that the vocabulary has been developed, and focus only on the ground facts. The fact model references the elements of the vocabulary, which are assumed to be defined externally and are identifiable via a URL. This ground fact model was introduced in the OMG specification Software Assurance Evidence Metamodel [SAEM]. Ground facts are assumed to comply with the constraints of the corresponding vocabulary. Constraints for the vocabulary are also assumed to be defined externally.

The Object element represents an instance of a noun concept. The Fact element represents an instance of a verb concept. A Fact references one or more Subjects, where each subject plays a certain unique Role in the Fact. Facts and objects are arranged into a Segment.

Here is the XSD schema for the common fact model:

```xsd
<xsd:schema xmlns:xsd="http://www.w3.org/2001/XMLSchema"
       targetNamespace="http://www.omg.org/CommonFactModel"
              xmlns:cfm="http://www.omg.org/CommonFactModel"
<xsd:complexType name="Segment">
    <xsd:attribute name="id" type="string" use="required" />
    <xsd:element name="type" type="nab:type" minOccurs="0"
maxOccurs="unbounded" />
</xsd:complexType>

<xsd:complexType name="Object">
    <xsd:attribute name="id" type="string" use="required" />
    <xsd:element name="type" type="string" minOccurs="0"
maxOccurs="unbounded" />
</xsd:complexType>
<xsd:complexType name="Fact">
<xsd:sequence>
     <xsd:element name="role" type="cfm:RoleBinding" minOccurs= "1"
maxOccurs="1" />
  </xsd:sequence>
    <xsd:attribute name="id" type="string" use="required" />
    <xsd:attribute name="type" type="string" use="required" />
</xsd:complexType>

<xsd:complexType name="RoleBinding">
  <xsd:choice maxOccurs="unbounded" minOccurs="1">
    <xsd:attribute name="role" type="string" use="required" />
    <xsd:attribute name="object" type="cfm:Object" use="required" />
  </xsd:choice>
</xsd:complexType>
</xsd:schema>
```

9.9 SYSTEM ASSURANCE FACTS

System Assurance requires facts that are related to the several external and internal viewpoints that contribute to security of the system. Traditionally, these viewpoints are grouped into the following areas:

- System facts
- Assets
- Consequences (impacts, injuries)
- Threat agents

- Threats and risks
- Countermeasures
- Vulnerabilities

We added another viewpoint called vulnerability patterns.

As we presented these viewpoints in the first part of the book, each viewpoint defines its own preferred type of assurance argument. A comprehensive and defendable assurance argument must use all viewpoints and, in addition, must consider the layered defense argument. Each kind of argument is based on certain vocabulary of noun and verb concepts. Usually, the corresponding views of the system are built independently. The conceptualization of each viewpoint defines the contract between the producer of the view and the consumer of the view (the analyst building the assurance case). It is possible to request an "asset view" of the target system, or the "threat view." However, in order to build the overall assurance case, multiple views must be collated; therefore integration of the views is required.

The Common Fact Model includes eight vocabularies that support the six kinds of assurance arguments. The Common Fact Model also includes two vocabularies for building assurance cases: the Argumentation vocabulary [ARM] and the Evidence vocabulary [SAEM]. Furthermore, the Common Fact Model includes the common vocabulary for system facts, known as the Knowledge Discovery Meta-model (KDM), described in Chapter 11. Table 1 illustrates how cybersecurity arguments are supported by the evidence derived from various viewpoints.

Table 1 List of Type of Arguments and Supporting Evidence

Kind of Argument	Facts
Vulnerability argument	Vulnerability facts, system facts
Vulnerability pattern argument	Vulnerability patterns, system facts
Threat event argument	Threat agent facts, Threat event facts, Threat facts
Asset argument	Asset facts, system facts
Countermeasure argument	Countermeasure facts, system facts
Entry point argument	Entry point facts, system facts
	Argument facts
	Evidence facts
	System facts

The Common Fact Model addresses the so-called *conceptual* level of system description [Bridgeland 2009], [Olive 2007], [Halpin 2008]. At least four levels of system descriptions are used during system development (illustrated in Figure 11):

- Conceptual level
- Logical level
- Physical level
- Implementation level

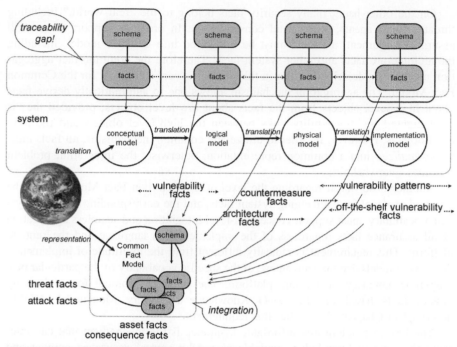

FIGURE 11 Closing the traceability gap with the common fact model

Each level involves a certain *resolution* of facts and involves a certain conceptualization, represented by a *conceptual schema* (a vocabulary together with the statements of what is necessary, permissible or obligatory). For example, at the implementation level the conceptualization is determined by a programming language (e.g., Java), the data definition language (e.g., SQL), the user interface definition language (e.g., JSP and HTML), and the runtime platform (e.g., J2EE). The facts at each level are determined by the corresponding conceptualization, so at the implementation level there are Java facts (such as classes, Java expressions, and Java predefined types), J2EE facts (such as the use of ThreadPoolExecutor class), SQL facts (such as the select statement), and so on. The logical level may involve SysML conceptualization and the corresponding facts. System development involves translations between levels, where the meaning of the "real world" is first represented as conceptual facts; then these conceptual facts are translated into the logical facts determined by the selected logical model; next the logical facts are translated into the physical facts determined by the physical model; and so on. Different development teams use different methodologies for each level. Therefore two teams developing the same system will likely produce completely different implementation-level facts. Multiple translations between methodologies often result in the *traceability gap* between the facts that belong to different levels.

On the other hand, many security facts belong to the "real world," including threats, threat agents, assets, and consequences. In order to support the overall assurance argument, all facts must be integrated into a single model, including the architecture facts and other system facts. Therefore the common fact aggregation mechanism described earlier in this chapter is very important for the Common Fact Model. The aggregation mechanism allows one to automatically derive facts about high-level objects from the facts about low-level objects, provided the "is implemented by" traceability links between the high-level objects and the low-level objects. However, in order to utilize any common mechanisms, all facts must be *normalized* into a common representation; otherwise, the integration problem becomes overwhelming.

Another observation regarding the level of the Common Fact Model is that the standard protocol for exchanging system facts, and the corresponding common System Vocabulary, must support conceptual-level integration and seamless aggregation of all assurance facts regardless of the implementation language and the runtime platform. This requirement is radically different from the multitude of implementation-level models that take advantage of the specific vocabulary of the particular programming language or runtime platform. The standard protocol for exchanging system facts based on the OMG Knowledge Discovery Metamodel (KDM), described in Chapter 11, satisfies this requirement.

The key to efficient and affordable assurance is the mechanism that can integrate the general knowledge available as vendor-neutral assurance content and the concrete facts about the target system. The general cybersecurity knowledge corresponds to large families of systems. However, each individual assurance project deals with a single system of interest. The common vocabularies are part of the general cybersecurity knowledge, as well as particular classes, enumerations, and checklists, such as the enumerations of common threat activities, common threat agent classes, and common vulnerabilities. However, each system uses additional, very specific vocabularies, related to its mission, its architecture, its operations, and its implementation. These system-specific vocabularies and the corresponding facts are important because they are involved in some of the claims and evidence. Therefore, the Common Fact Model must be open-ended and support efficient extension with the system-specific vocabularies because this tailoring has to be done during each individual assessment. This approach is the source of efficiency because the entire assurance "plumbing" is reused from project to project. Once the "last mile" of the assurance plumbing is provided when the system-specific viewpoints are identified and integrated with the common ones, then large amounts of machine-readable assurance content can start flowing to the assurance team from the Assurance Ecosystem.

The Common Fact Model defined in this chapter is an open framework for developing standard information exchange protocols for various assurance areas in such a way that:

1. A uniform expression format is provided.
2. A multitude of interoperable physical representations is possible.

3. The common vocabularies do not limit the addition of new vocabularies, and facilitate integration by establishing links across multiple vocabularies.
4. Vocabularies can be extended to address specific information exchange needs to the participants. (This is just another way of saying that this approach gives you an efficient means to link your own content to the common facts.)
5. The common format is aligned with linguistic models.
6. The common format is efficient for integration transformation and analysis.

Bibliography

Object Management Group. (2010). *Argumentation Metamodel (ARM) 1.0*.

Bridgeland, D. M., & Zahavi, R. (2009). *Business Modeling: A Practical Value to Realizing Business Value*. Burlington, MA: Morgan Kaufmann Publishers.

Halpin, T., & Morgan, T. (2008). *Information Modeling and Relational Databases*. Burlington, MA: Elsevier Morgan Kaufmann Publishers.

Object Management Group. (2006). *Knowledge Discovery Metamodel (KDM) 1.2*.

Bo Leuf. (2006). *The Semantic Web: Crafting Infrastructure for Agency*. Hoboken, NJ: John Wiley & Sons.

McDaniel, D. (2008). Analyzing and Presenting Multi-Nation Process Interoperability Data for End-Users: the International Defence Enterprise Architecture Specification (IDEAS) project. In *Proc. Integrated EA Conference*. London, UK. http://www.integrated-ea.com.

Olive, A. (2007). *Conceptual Modeling of Information Systems*. Berlin, Heidelberg: Springer.

Ross, R. G. (2009). *Business Rules Concepts, Business Rules Solutions* (3rd ed.). Houston, TX: Business Rule Solutions, LLC.

Ross, R. G. (2003). *Principles of the Business Rules Approach*. Boston, MA: Addison-Wesley.

Object Management Group. (2010). *Software Assurance Evidence Metamodel (SAEM) 1.0*.

Object Management Group. (2009). *Semantics of Business Vocabularies and Rules (SBVR) 1.1*.

Object Management Group. *XML Model Interchange (XMI)*.

W3C. (2008). *Extensible Markup Language (XML) 1.0* (5th ed.). W3C Recommendation.

Linguistic models

-The name of the song is called 'Haddock' Eyes'.
-Oh, that's the name of the song, is it?
-No, you don't understand. That's what the name is called. The name really is 'The Aged Aged Man'.
- Then I ought to have said 'That's what the song is called'?
- No, you oughtn't; that's quite another thing! The song is called "Ways and Means': but that's only when it's called, you know!
- Well, what is the song, then? said Alice, who was by this time completely bewildered.
-I was coming to that, the Knight said. The song really is 'A-sitting On A 'Gate': and the tune's my own invention.

—**Lewis Carroll,** *Through the Looking-Glass*

10.1 FACT MODELS AND LINGUISTIC MODELS

Linguistic models deal with statements as they are used to express meanings. While fact models focus on simple operational meanings within a given conceptual commitment (existence of objects, discernability of objects as representatives of certain concepts, characteristics of individual objects and relationships between objects), linguistic models focus on meanings corresponding to the conceptual commitment itself, regardless of the actual objects, such as what are the characteristics of concepts, how concepts are defined in terms of other concepts, and what relationships between concepts are necessary, permissible or obligatory. Thus statements in fact models describe individual views while statements in linguistic models describe viewpoints. Linguistic models focus at the definitions of new meanings, therefore they facilitate unconstrained communications where new meanings are defined on-the-fly. The flexibility of unrestricted linguistic communication comes with a price: the intended meaning needs to be unraveled from the expression, and the more complex the meaning, the more complex is the unraveling process. The key challenge of unrestricted linguistic communication is not so much in parsing a natural language sentence (which can be quite complex) but rather in dealing with complex meanings that are defined on-the-fly by some sentences and are used in the follow-up sentences. For example, we can say:

System Assurance: Beyond Detecting Vulnerabilities. DOI: 10.1016/B978-0-12-381414-2.00010-5

"Remember the nuts-and-bolts illustrations from the previous chapter? Did you notice that there are a total of 35 nuts visible in these figures?" While humans routinely deal with the dynamic updates to the conceptual commitment, it is a barrier for machine-to-machine information exchanges.

Fact models, on the other hand, facilitate constrained communications in which the vocabulary is preselected; the forms of expressing this meaning are preselected, and consequently the range of meanings is bounded. Fact models do not define new meanings on-the-fly. Instead, they simply express meanings from the preselected set defined by the vocabulary. These boundaries (the vocabulary, the form of expressing meanings, and the intended range of meanings) become the *contract* between the participants of the information exchange. This contract is essential for repeatable information exchanges, which is a two-phase process: First, the scope of communications is bounded and the contract is established, and then the actual exchanges start flowing. Linguistic models are efficient in the first phase, but fact models are used for the second phase. Each fact model is tailored to a specific contract. Although it is tempting to say that a fact model is the contract itself, there are several more aspects of interoperability in addition to the exchanged meanings and the agreed upon form of expression of meaning. These additional aspects include locations, responsible contact points, trust, monetization, quality, and so on. It is not surprising that the fact models are also used for conceptual definition of the information systems.

Figure 1 compares linguistic models to fact models and ontologies. Ontology is a branch of philosophy that deals with questions concerning what entities exist or

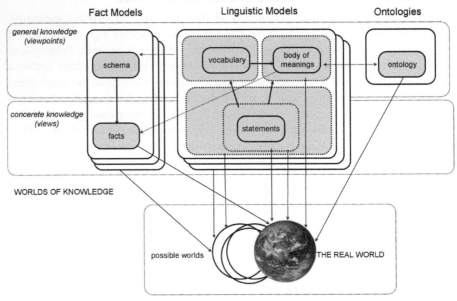

FIGURE 1 Linguistic models and fact models

can be said to exist, and how such entities can be grouped, related within a hierarchy, and subdivided according to similarities and differences. However, recently this word has been commonly used in a more applied sense as a formal representation of the knowledge of a particular domain by a set of concepts and the relationships between those concepts. Linguistic models as well as fact models describe entities and their relationships in the real world, or in any possible world, regardless of whether these entities and relationships exist or could potentially exist. Fact models separate concrete (operational) knowledge of the actual things and relationships between them (known as facts), and the general knowledge of what kinds of things and kinds of relationships can be described (known as the conceptual schema). Linguistic models do not make this distinction, instead they focus on concepts and those relationships that are necessary, permissible or obligatory between concepts regardless the instances of these concepts or the instances of the relationships. This is the reason why linguistic models provide the foundation for describing business rules, i.e. the statements of behavior guidance.

Linguistic models involve a body of meanings and a vocabulary to express meanings, as well as a mechanism to construct statements that can define new meanings based on the initial ones. This mechanism makes linguistic models unbounded compared to fact models.

10.2 BACKGROUND

The **Semantics of Business Vocabularies and Business Rules (SBVR)** is a publicly available specification from the Object Management Group (OMG) [SBVR]. It was developed by 17 organizations in 7 countries and adopted by OMG in September 2005. It was published as a formal OMG specification in January 2008. The word "business" emphasizes the fact that SBVR focuses on conceptual models that directly represent the operational vocabulary of systems, related to the business mission of the system, as opposed to any implementation views used by the downstream stages of the system life cycle. The terms *business model* and *conceptual model* are often used as synonyms [Ross 2003], [Ross 2009], [Halpin 2008], [Olive 2007], [Bridgeland 2009].

SBVR provides the provides the following means for building linguistic models:

- Defining vocabularies as a cohesive set of interconnected concepts, not just a list of terms and definitions;
- Defining behavioral guidance (policy, rules, etc.) that govern the actions of subject of the conceptualization that is defined by means of a vocabulary;
- Exchanging vocabulary definitions, rules, and patterns.

The OMG Assurance Ecosystem uses SBVR to analyze and represent cybersecurity knowledge as formal machine-readable content that can be directly used by assurance tools but at the same time allow human readable statements in structured

English as well as other controlled natural languages. Another use of SBVR within the Assurance Ecosystem is to define *patterns* as fragments of interconnected concepts that can be used as queries and matched against fact models.

10.3 OVERVIEW OF SBVR

The SBVR provides the means to build linguistic models, including propositions, questions, rules, and corresponding conceptual schemes and vocabularies. The SBVR specification consists of six major parts (illustrated at Figure 2):

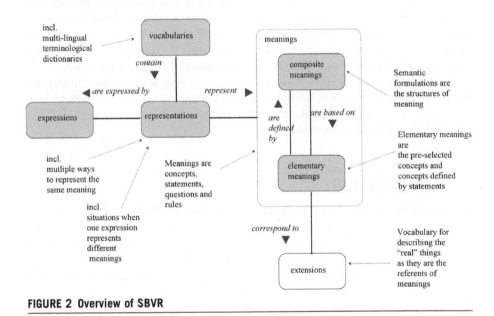

FIGURE 2 Overview of SBVR

- **Elementary meanings** (vocabulary for describing elementary meanings, including the conceptual schema)
- **Composite meanings** (vocabulary for defining new meanings including propositions, questions and rules, based on elementary meanings)
- **Expressions** (very small vocabulary dedicated to the building blocks of written communications that are commonly used to express meanings)
- **Representations** (the building blocks of vocabularies that bring together expressions and their meanings)
- **Vocabularies** (a very small vocabulary for defining vocabularies as collections of representations)
- **Extensions**, or the "things that are meant by meanings" (a very small vocabulary to describe the referents of concepts, the "objects" and the "facts")

SBVR captures business concepts and business rules that may be expressed either informally or formally. Business rule expressions are formal only if they are expressed purely in terms of the preselected conceptual schema for the business domain and *semantic formulations*, including certain logical and mathematical operators, logical quantifiers, and so on. Formal rules can be exchanged as content with other rules-based software tools [Leuf 2006]. Informal rules may be exchanged as uninterpreted comments.

The SBVR specification defines a standard protocol for exchanging vocabularies, rules, and patterns, including an XML Schema [XML].

10.4 HOW TO USE SBVR

Let's look at some practical uses of SBVR. First, we will see how SBVR is used to define a simple conceptual scheme based on well-known, informally defined terms. Then we will look at how to formalize propositions using the SBVR vocabulary. Finally, we will show how propositions are used to define new elements of the vocabulary.

10.4.1 Simple vocabulary

Before we can make any meaningful statements, we need to agree on a conceptual schema that includes some noun and verb concepts as well as some individual concepts. Concepts are defined and expressed as terms and other symbols, and they are represented as vocabulary entries in SBVR Structured English. Below is an example of the nuts-and-bolts vocabulary from Chapter 9 in SBVR.

```
Nut
    Definition:    a hardware fastener item that has threaded hole
                   into which an appropriate bolt can be screwed to
                   fasten things together.
    Source:  based on wikidedia (english)
    Concept type:  noun concept
    Note:  this is an informal definition of a noun concept
    Reference scheme:  id of nut
Bolt
    Definition:    threaded pin that screws into a nut and is used to fasten
                   things together
    Source:  New Oxford American Dictionary 2nd edition, 2005
    Reference scheme:  id of bolt
Washer
    Definition:    a small ring made of metal, rubber or plastic fixed under
                   a nut or the head of the bolt to spread the pressure
                   when tightened or between two joining surfaces as a
                   spacer or seal
    Source:  New Oxford American Dictionary 2nd edition, 2005
    Reference scheme:  id of washer
```

<u>Nut</u> *is screwed onto* <u>bolt</u>
    Definition: the actuality **that** nut is fastened onto bolt
    Concept type: verb concept
    Note: this is an informal definition of a verb concept
<u>Washer</u> *is fastened on* <u>bolt</u>
    Definition: the actuality that washer is fixed onto bolt
<u>Washer$_1$</u> *is above* <u>washer$_2$</u>
    Definition: the actuality that <u>washer$_1$</u> and <u>washer$_2$</u> are fastened
                    on the same *bolt* in such order that <u>washer$_1$</u> is closer
                      to the head of the <u>bolt</u> than <u>washer$_2$</u>
    Synonymous form: <u>washer$_2$</u> *is below* <u>washer$_1$</u>
<u>Nut</u> *has* <u>id</u>
    Concept type: characteristic
<u>Bolt</u> *has* <u>id</u>
    Concept type: characteristic
<u>Bolt</u> *has* <u>head</u>
    Concept type: characteristic
<u>Washer</u> *has* <u>id</u>
    Concept type: characteristic
<u>Nut n-2</u>
    Definition: the <u>nut</u> **that** *has* <u>id</u> "n-2"
    Note: this is a definition of an individual concept
<u>Bolt b-25</u>
    Definition: the <u>bolt</u> **that** *has* <u>id</u> "b-25"

10.4.2 Vocabulary entries

A vocabulary is described in a document (or document section) that features glossary-like entries for concepts that have representations in the vocabulary. Each entry starts with a primary representation, which is either a designation or a template of expression for the concept and is followed by several captioned details for the concept. Neither the order of vocabulary entries nor the order of caption details inside the entry is significant. Here is a skeleton of a vocabulary entry with captions.

Primary representation
    General concept: *designation of the general concept*
    Definition: *statement or text*
    Description: *text*
    Dictionary basis: *text of the citation for externally defined terms*
    Source: *vocabulary reference for externally defined terms*
    Example: *text*
    Note: *text*
    See: *reference to the preferred representation*

Synonym: *alternative designation*
Synonymous form: *alternative designation*

A typical primary representation of a noun concept is its designation. The primary representation for a verb concept (fact type) is a template of expression with a placeholder for the roles. A subscript on each placeholder can be given in cases where the same designation is used for more than one placeholder, so that references to the roles within the entry are unambiguous (see verb concept "washer-1 is above washer-2" in the nuts-and-bolts vocabulary). Designations usually do not include quantifiers (including articles) and logical operators.

The following list describes some simple captions. More advanced captions are introduced later in this chapter.

- **Source** caption cites an external source that relates to a concept's meaning. The source's designation for the concept (which might not match the entry's primary representation) is given in square brackets and is quoted after the name of the source. The keywords "based on" indicate that the definition of the concept is largely derived from the given source but had some modification.
- **Example** caption provides examples involving the entry concept.
- **Note** caption is used to label explanatory notes that do not fit within the other captions.
- **Synonym** describes another designation that can be substituted for the primary representation of a noun concept. It is a designation for the same concept.
- **See** provides a caption that introduces the preferred representation where the primary representation is not a preferred representation for the entry concept. No definition is given in this case.
- **Synonymous Form** is an alternative template of expression for the same verb concept; for example, the synonymous form can be a passive form of the primary representation or one that reverses the order of roles. The meaning of two templates of expression being synonymous is that the two represent the same verb concept.

10.4.3 **Statements**

Statements are expressions of propositions, questions, and rules. SBVR defines the so-called SBVR Structured English notation that uses English vocabulary to state propositions, questions, and rules (and not graphical diagrams, not a formal logical language, like Prolog, and not XML).

Here are some examples of statements using the above nuts-and-bolts vocabulary:

<u>Nut n-2</u> *is screwed onto* <u>Bolt b-25</u>
<u>Nut n-2</u> is not a <u>bolt</u>
<u>Nut n-2</u> has <u>id</u> "n-2"
Some <u>nut</u> *is screwed onto* <u>Bolt b-25</u>
Each <u>nut</u> *is screwed onto* some <u>bolt</u>

Exactly one <u>nut</u> *is screwed onto* <u>Bolt b-25</u>

It is not the case that <u>2 nuts</u> *are screwed onto* <u>Bolt b-25</u>

It is prohibited that <u>2 nuts</u> *are screwed onto* a <u>bolt</u>

It is possible that more than one <u>washers</u> *are fastened on* a <u>bolt</u>

10.4.4 Statements as formal definitions of new concepts

Each SBVR vocabulary is created for a particular *speech community*. Since this book is written in English, all our examples assume an English language speech community. SBVR separates the meaning from its expression, so that when the SBVR vocabulary is exchanged, new expressions can be associated with the given meanings, for example in German, creating a vocabulary for the different speech community. Two vocabularies can share the same structure of meanings. Thus a particular meaning is defined not by a particular word, but rather by the structure of the meaning, including the verb concepts and the unique characteristics of the concept, regardless of the language in which they are expressed. SBVR defines a large set of these structures of meaning, called *semantic formulations*, illustrated at the end of this chapter.

10.4.4.1 Definition of a noun concept

A common pattern of definition begins with a designation for a more general concept followed by the keyword "that" and then an expression of necessary and sufficient characteristics that distinguish a thing of the defined concept from other things of the more general concept. Another, less used pattern also leads with a designation for a more general concept but then uses the word "of" with another expression.

Two kinds of information are formally expressed by a fully formal definition.

1. A fact that the concept being defined is a category of a particular more general concept.
2. A closed projection that defines the concept.

Only the first kind of information is formally expressed by a partially formal definition. A partially formal definition leads with a styled designation that is for a more general concept. That designation is generally followed by the keyword **that** and then an informal expression of necessary and sufficient characteristics.

Definitions of the individual concepts nut n-2 and bolt b-25 above are fully formal. Other definitions are partially formal or informal.

Another style of formal definition is extensional. Usually the extensional style uses disjunction to combine a number of concepts.

10.4.4.2 Definition of a verb concept

A definition given for a verb concept (fact type) is an expression that can be substituted for a simple statement expressed using a template of expression of the fact type. The definition must refer to the placeholders in the template of expression. This is done in order to relate the definition to the things that play a role in instances of the fact type. Whether or not the definition is formal, each reference to a placeholder appears in the "noun concept" font and is preceded by the definite article, "the".

10.4.4.3 The general concept caption

The General Concept caption can be used to indicate a concept that generalizes the entry concept. This is not needed if there is a definition that starts with the general concept, but it is helpful in cases where a definition is not provided, such as is often the case for individual concepts (named things) or concepts taken from a source.

10.5 SBVR VOCABULARY FOR DESCRIBING ELEMENTARY MEANINGS

SBVR itself is defined as several vocabularies. The noun concepts of the SBVR vocabulary for defining elementary meanings are illustrated in Figure 3.

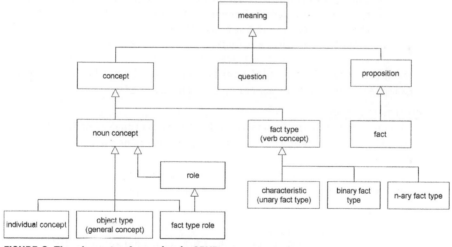

FIGURE 3 The elements of meaning in SBVR: noun concepts

The following fragment illustrates the original definition of SBVR in SBVR:

```
Meaning
    Definition:  what is meant by a word, sign, statement, or descrip-
                 tion; what someone intends to express or what someone
                 understands
Concept
    Source:  ISO 1087-1 (English) (3.2.1) ['concept']
    Definition:  unit of knowledge created by a unique combination of
                 characteristics
```

General Concept: meaning
Reference Scheme: a designation of the concept

Noun concept

Definition: concept that is the meaning of a noun or noun phrase
Reference scheme: a closed projection that defines the noun concept

Object type

Definition: noun concept that classifies things on the basis of
              their common characteristics
Source: based on ISO 1087-1 (English) (3.2.3) ['general concept']
Synonym: general concept
Necessity: the set of characteristics that are incorporated by an
            object type is not the set of characteristics that
            are incorporated by another object type
Note: an object type incorporates a set of characteristics which are
        a unique combination that distinguishes this object type
        from all other object types. (See 'concept incorporates
        characteristic'). If an object type A and an object type B
        have the very same incorporated characteristics, they are
        the same concept. If they have the very same necessary char-
        acteristics, they are logically equivalent and they denote
        the same things in all possible worlds.
Example: the concept 'nut' corresponding to the hardware fastener
Example: the concept 'number', the concept 'person'

Individual concept

Source: ISO 1087-1 (English) (3.2.2) ['individual concept']
Definition: concept that corresponds to only one object [thing]
General concept: noun concept
Necessity: No individual concept is an object type
Necessity: No individual concept is a fact type role

Characteristic

Definition: fact type that has exactly one role
Source: ISO 1087-1 (English) (3.2.4) ['characteristic']
Definition: Abstraction of a property of an object [thing] or
              a set of objects.
Synonym: unary fact type
Note: A characteristic always has exactly one role, but it can be
        defined using fact types having multiple roles
(in SBVR formatting):

Fact type

Definition: concept that is the meaning of a verb phrase that
              involves one or more noun concepts and whose
              instances are states of affairs
Synonym: verb concept
Note: For each instance of a fact type, each role of the fact type is
        one point of involvement of some object in that instance
Necessity: Each fact type has at least one role

The concept "characteristic" is an abstraction of some property intrinsic to each instance of the concept; the collection of essential characteristics makes up the concept. Two definitions can describe the same object by producing the same set of incorporated characteristics. Noun concepts were informally introduced in Chapter 9. Unique characteristics of the concept allow discerning the objects of this concept.

Some relationships between the SBVR concepts are illustrated at Figure 4.

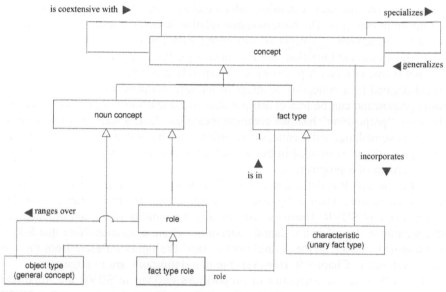

FIGURE 4 The elements of meaning in SBVR: verb concepts

The role is an abstraction of a thing involved in an instance of the verb concept. The verb concept with the designation '<u>verb concept</u> *has* <u>role</u>' identifies the set of roles for another verb concept (a fact type is a synonym for a verb concept) the inverse relation is described by the verb concept '<u>fact type role</u> *is in* <u>fact type</u>'.

Roles are related to the characteristics of the concept (an object type, to be precise). The verb concept '<u>Role</u> *ranges over* <u>object type</u>' identifies the corresponding characteristic. For example, the role 'company' of the verb concept 'company employs person' ranges over the object type 'company'.

The verb concept '<u>Concept</u>$_1$ *specializes* <u>concept</u>$_2$' is the key to developing intentional definitions. This verb concept is defined by the following statement: '<u>Concept</u>$_1$ incorporates each characteristic that is incorporated by the <u>concept</u>$_2$ plus at least one differentiator.' A synonymous form for this verb concept has the designator '<u>Concept</u>$_2$ *generalizes* <u>concept</u>$_1$.'

For example, the noun concept 'whole number' specializes the noun concept 'integer,' the differentiator being that whole numbers are nonnegative. As another example, the individual concept 'Cyber Bricks' specializes the concept 'company,' the differentiator being that Cyber Bricks is one particular fictitious company used in the case study for this book.

Semantic integrations often involve recognizing where different concepts (having different intentional definitions) have the same extensions in all possible worlds. Also, it is possible that concepts employing different methods of conceptualization have the same extension in all cases. For example, the individual concept defined as 'the owner of the Clicks2Bricks system' is coextensive with an object type defined as 'the companies featured in the case study of this book.' The two companies have the same extension (which includes only 'Cyber Bricks'), but they are different concepts. The corresponding relation between concepts is represented using the designator 'Concept1 *is coextensive with* concept2.'

Propositions and Questions are also meanings. Proposition is defined as meaning that is true or false. A proposition corresponds to a state of affairs in a possible world defined by a collection of things of interest and possibly a time frame. The same proposition can be true in one possible world and false in another. Note that the word "proposition" has two common meanings: first, a statement that affirms or denies something, and second, the meaning of such a statement. The SBVR concept 'proposition' is defined in the second sense and should not be confused with the statement of a proposition.

A Fact in SBVR is defined as a proposition that is taken as true. How one ascertains what is true, whether by assertion, observation, or other means, is outside of the scope of SBVR. However, ascertaining the validity of certain propositions (the assurance claims) is the central concern of system assurance. Note that SBVR is a linguistic model, so the definition of a 'fact' is slightly different from the one we introduced in Chapter 9. However, the two definitions are in alignment.

The following characteristics of propositions defined in SBVR are important for assurance:

Proposition *is necessarily true*—The proposition always corresponds to an actuality; a proposition is considered to be necessarily true if it is true by definition—the definitions of relevant concepts make it logically impossible for the proposition to be false.

Proposition *is possibly true*— It is possible that the proposition corresponds to an actuality.

Proposition*is obligated to be true*—The proposition corresponds to an actuality in all acceptable worlds.

Proposition *is permitted to be true*—The proposition corresponds to an actuality in at least one acceptable world.

Question is defined as the meaning of an interrogatory. Note that the word "question" has two common meanings: first, a written or spoken expression of inquiry, and second, the meaning of such an inquiry. By the second definition, a single question can be asked in two languages. But by the first definition, using two languages results in two expressions, and therefore, two questions. The SBVR concept "question" is defined in the second sense (meaning) and should not be confused with the expression or representation of a question.

10.6 SBVR VOCABULARY FOR DESCRIBING REPRESENTATIONS

The following definitions tie together the three major areas of SBVR:

Expression *represents* meaning
    Definition: the expression portrays or signifies the meaning
Representation
    Definition: the actuality that a given expression represents a given meaning
    Necessity: each expression has exactly one meaning
    Necessity: each representation represents exactly one meaning
Representation *has* expression
Representation *represents* meaning
    Synonymous form: meaning has representation
    Synonymous form: representation has meaning

The noun concepts of the SBVR vocabulary for defining representations are illustrated in Figure 5.

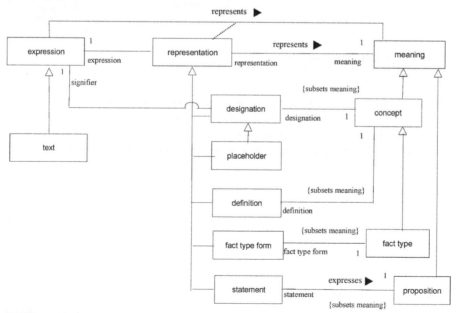

FIGURE 5 The elements of representation in SBVR

A <u>Designation</u> in SBVR is a representation of a concept by a sign that denotes it. (This may include a specific namespace that includes the designation to allow disambiguation of terminology when integrating statements from different communities.) Designation involves a <u>signifier,</u> which is the expression of the designation. For example, the concept '<u>nut</u>' has a signifier, which is a string produced by concatenating the characters "n," "u," and "t." The signifier exists only in the context of a designation, so the string "nut" on its own may be interpreted in many diverse ways.

A <u>Definition</u> in SBVR is a representation of a concept by a descriptive statement (expression), which serves to differentiate it from related concepts. A fully formal definition uses one of the semantic formulations, and its meaning is interpreted unambiguously.

Figure 6 illustrates the organization of the designators for verb concepts.

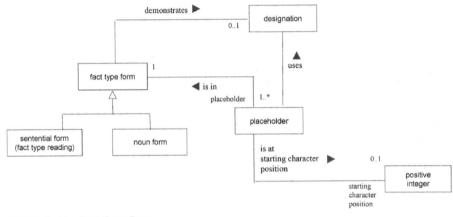

FIGURE 6 The Fact Type Form

A <u>Fact type form</u> in SBVR is a representation of some verb concept by a template of expression. For example, the fact type form 'product of company' demonstrates a designation 'of' and has two placeholders—one using the designation 'product' at the starting position 1 and the other using the designation 'company' at the starting position 12.

<u>Sentential form</u> (also known as a fact type reading) is a fact type form that is a template that can be used for starting a proposition based on a fact type.

<u>Noun form</u> is a fact type form that acts as a noun rather than forming a proposition. A noun form can have a placeholder for each role of a fact type, in which case the noun form result comes from the role the first placeholder serves. A noun form can have one less placeholder than there are roles, in which case the noun form result comes from the role that no placeholder is for. An example is 'bolt of the nut-and-bolt assembly' for the fact type 'nut-and-bolt assembly has bolt.' This noun form refers to the bolt. Another example of a noun form is 'screwing nut' for the fact type 'nut is screwed onto bolt.' This noun form yields the screwing act, which is an action.

Gerunds are used in noun forms like this for actions, events, and states. They are used in sentences like this: 'A nut must be screwed onto bolt after fastening the washer."

SBVR distinguishes between the following three kinds of designation:

- <u>Term</u>—verbal designation of a general concept in a specific subject field (typically a common noun or noun phrase)
- <u>Name</u>—verbal designation of an individual concept (typically a proper noun)
- <u>Icon</u>—nonverbal designation whose signifier is a picture

<u>Expression</u> is defined as something that expresses or communicates, but is independent of its meaning (such as a sequence of characters, a sequence of sounds, a diagram, or an XML file). A <u>Signifier</u> is an expression that is a linguistic unit or pattern, such as a succession of speech sounds, written symbols, or gestures, used in a designation of a concept. Two particularly important kinds of expression are Text and Uniform Resource Identifiers (URI).

10.7 SBVR VOCABULARY FOR DESCRIBING EXTENSIONS

Earlier in this chapter we discussed the differences between linguistic models and fact models. SBVR provides the means for building linguistic models (including the definition of a conceptual schema for the fact model and stating what is necessary, permissible or obligatory in the world described by the conceptual schema). SBVR does not focus on statements of existence of the objects and relationships between the objects. The concept 'individual concept' is a point of alignment between fact models and linguistic models. However, the SBVR vocabulary includes terminology for describing the referents of concepts because this terminology is required to build statements and rules that define the semantics of other SBVR concepts. The linguistic perspective on the fact models defined in Chapter 9 is illustrated in Figure 7.

<u>Extension</u> is the totality of objects to which a concept corresponds. SBVR defines a concept 'Thing' (based on the ISO 1087-1 term 'object'), as anything perceivable or conceivable. Every other concept in SBVR implicitly specializes the concept thing.

The concept 'State of affairs' is key to understanding verb concepts and their meaning. A <u>state of affairs</u> is any event, activity, situation, or circumstance. A state of affairs can be possible or impossible. Some of the possible ones are <u>actualities</u> (they occur in the actual world). A state of affairs is what is denoted by a proposition. A state of affairs either occurs or does not occur, whereas the proposition is either true or false. A state of affairs is not a meaning. It is a thing that exists and can be an instance of a concept, even if it does not happen. Conceptual commitment in the form of a vocabulary determines our viewpoint on what state of affairs we can consider.

10.8 REFERENCE SCHEMES

A reference scheme defines the chosen way of identifying instances of a given concept. Understanding reference schemes is critical for integrating facts from

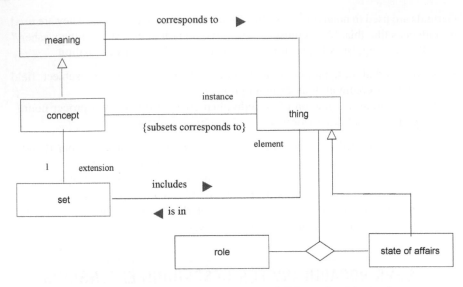

FIGURE 7 The elements of extension in SBVR

multiple sources during information exchanges. A reference scheme is a way of referring to instances of a concept through related things that are either lexical or are otherwise identifiable. A reference scheme usually uses one or more fact type roles of binary types in order to identify an instance of a concept from facts about the instance. A reference scheme can also use one or more characteristics. A reference scheme can be partial or complete. It is complete if it can always be used to refer to every instance of a concept. An overall complete reference scheme for a concept can result from there being multiple partial reference schemes for that concept, its more general concepts, and its categories. For example, the concept <u>nut</u> involves a characteristic <u>id</u> that is used to identify instances of this concept, for example 'nut <u>n-2</u>'. Alternatively, a particular nut instance can be identified using its relationship to some other concept—for example, 'the <u>nut</u> of the <u>nut-and-bolt assembly</u> that *involves* <u>bolt</u> <u>b-52</u>.'

The semantics of the reference scheme is illustrated in Figure 8.

10.9 SBVR SEMANTIC FORMULATIONS

Communications between humans generally use natural language to express propositions, although some technical propositions are at times expressed in a formal language, such as XML, C, or Prolog, or even graphically, such as a UML model. SBVR provides a means for describing the *structure of the meaning* of the

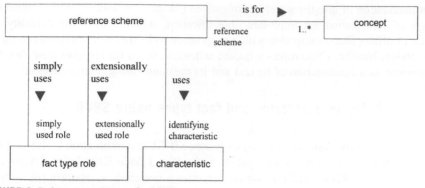

FIGURE 8 Reference schemes in SBVR

proposition expressed in the natural language that business people use. SBVR calls this "semantic formulation." Semantic formulations are not expressions or statements. They are *structures* that make up meaning. SBVR provides a vocabulary for describing them. By using SBVR, the meaning of a definition or statement is communicated as *facts* about the semantic formulation of the meaning, not as a restatement of the meaning in a formal language.

Semantic formulations contribute to SBVR Structured English through defining all keywords, as follows:

- **Quantification keywords** (each, some, at least one, at least n, at most one, exactly one, exactly n, at least n and at most m, more than one)
- **Logical operations keywords** (it is not the case that, and, or, or but not both, if then, if, if and only if, not both, neither nor, whether or not).
- **Modal operations keywords** (it is obligatory that, it is prohibited that, it is necessary that, it is impossible that, it is possible that, it is permitted that)
- **Other** keywords (the, a, an, another, a given, that, who, is of, what)

Semantic formulations make distinctions between expression, representation, meaning, and extension. Note how phrase 'session hijacking is a threat to a web applications' is interpreted differently in each of the following examples.

1. Expression (literal text): John did a Google search for 'session hijacking is a threat to a web application.'
2. Representation (quoting a statement): Ron said, 'session hijacking is a threat to a web application.'
3. Meaning (nominalization of a proposition): Ron said that session hijacking is a threat to a web application.
4. Extension (objectification of a proposition): Assessment disregarded that session hijacking is a threat to a web application.

SBVR provides a kind of formulation for nominalization of propositions, which makes a proposition to be an object of discourse as in (3). SBVR also supports nominalization of questions and interrogatives ("what," "whether," etc.). A separate kind of formulation accomplishes objectification, which makes the actuality or state of affairs that corresponds with a proposition to be an object of discourse as in (4) above. Number (2) involves a quoted statement, so its formulation identifies the statement as a combination of its text and its meaning (using nominalization).

10.9.1 Defining new terms and fact types using SBVR

SBVR provides the capability to define new terms and facts using semantic formulations. The OMG Assurance Ecosystem uses SBVR in combination with the standard protocol for exchanging system facts (the OMG Knowledge Discovery Metamodel, or KDM), [KDM] which describes a common vocabulary for system facts to define vendor-neutral assurance patterns. KDM is presented in Chapter 11 in more detail.

The following example uses SBVR to provide a formal definition of a new pattern—a statement that passes a format string to a format output function, which corresponds to the family of formatted output statements, like printf(). This definition was used in Chapter 7 in the example of the *vulnerability pattern*.

SBVR Structured English:
Action Element *passes* format string to *format output function* if an Action Element *calls* a Control Element *with* Name and the Action Element *reads* the format string *at* position and the Name *is a format string function at* that position.

Supporting KDM noun concepts:
ActionElement
Control Element
Name
Position

Supporting platform-specific concepts:
Format String Function
Name *is a format string function for* Position

Supporting KDM verb concepts:
Action Element *calls* Control Element
Action Element *reads* Data Element *at* position
Control Element *has* Name

SBVR semantic formulation outline:
The verb concept "Action Element *passes* Format String *to format string function*" is defined by an **sbvr:setprojection** (1)
    The projection 1 is on the variable "Stmt"
      The variable "Stmt" ranges over the noun concept "Action Element"
    The projection 1 is on the variable "Fmt"
      The variable "Fmt" ranges over the noun concept "Format String"

The projection is constrained by an **sbvr:existentialquantifica-tion** (1)
  The existential quantification 1 is on the variable "F"
    The variable "F" ranges over the noun concept "Control Element"
  The existential quantification 1 scopes over **sbvr:existential-quantification** (2)
    The existential quantification 2 is on the variable "FN"
      The variable "FN" ranges over the noun concept "Name"
    The existential quantification 2 scopes over **sbvr:existential-quantification** (3)
      The existential quantification 3 is on the variable "Pos"
        The variable "Pos" ranges over the noun concept "Position"
      The existential quantification 3 scopes over **sbvr:conjunction** (1)
        The logical operand 1 of the conjunction 1 is **sbvr:atomicformulation**
          The atomic formulation is based on the verb concept "Action Element *calls* Control Element"
              The role "Action Element" is bound to the variable "Stmt"
                The role "Control Element" is bound to the variable "F"
        The logical operand 2 of the conjunction 1 is **sbvr:conjunction** (2)
          The logical operand 1 of the conjunction 2 is **sbvr:atomicformulation**
            The atomic formulation is based on the verb concept "Control Element *has* Name"
              The role "Control Element" is bound to the variable "F"
              The role "Name" is bound to the variable "FN"
          The logical operand 2 of the conjunction 2 is **sbvr:conjunction** (3)
            The logical operand 1 of the conjunction 3 is **sbvr:atomicformulation**
              The atomic formulation is based on the verb concept "Action Element *reads* Data Element *at* Position"
                The role "Action Element" is bound to the variable "Stmt"
                The role "Data Element" is bound to the variable "Fmt"
                The role "Position" is bound to the variable "Pos"
            The logical operand 2 of the conjunction 3 is **sbvr:atomicformulation**
              The atomic formulation is based on the verb concept "Name *is a format string function at* Position"
                The role "Name" is bound to the variable "FN"
                The role "Position" is bound to the variable "Pos"

This can be further represented as the following Prolog rule:

```
StatementThatPassesFormatStringToFormatFunction(Stmt, Fmt ) :-
where
Arguments:
    input Stmt - CallableUnit which is the scope of the trigger
    output Fmt - Format String that is being passed to a format
                    string function
Rule definition:
Calls(Stmt,F),
Feature(F,name,FN),
Reads(Stmt,Fmt,Pos),
isFormatStringFunction( FN, Pos )
```

Bibliography

Bridgeland, D. M., & Zahavi, R. (2009). *Business Modeling: A Practical Value to Realizing Business Value*. Burlington, MA: Morgan Kaufmann Publishers.

Halpin, T, & Morgan, T (2008). *Information Modeling and Relational Databases*. Burlington, MA: Elsevier Morgan Kaufmann Publishers.

Object Management Group, (2006). *Knowledge Discovery Metamodel (KDM) 1.2*.

Leuf, B. (2006). *The Semantic Web: Crafting Infrastructure for Agency*. Hoboken, NJ: John Wiley & Sons.

Olive, A. (2007). *Conceptual Modeling of Information Systems*. Berlin, Heidelberg: Springer.

Ross, R. G. (2009). *Business Rules Concepts, Business Rules Solutions* (3rd ed.) Business Rule Solutions, LLC, Houston, TX.

Ross, R. G. (2003). *Principles of the Business Rules Approach*. Boston, MA: Addison-Wesley.

Object Management Group. (2009). *Semantics of Business Vocabularies and Rules (SBVR) 1.1*.

Object Management Group *XML Model Interchange (XMI)*.

W3C. (2008). *Extensible Markup Language (XML) 1.0* (5th ed.). W3C Recommendation.

Standard protocol for exchanging system facts

The principle difficulty in your case lay in the fact of there being too much evidence. What was vital was overlaid and hidden by what was irrelevant. Of all the facts which were presented to us we had to pick those which we deemed to be essential, and then piece them together in their order, so as the reconstruct this very remarkable chain of events.

—Arthur Conan Doyle, *The Adventure of the Naval Treaty*

Facts that are concealed acquire a suspicious importance. Facts that are frankly revealed tend to be regarded as less important than they really are.

—Agatha Christie, *Thirteen at Dinner*

11.1 BACKGROUND

Knowledge Discovery Metamodel (KDM) is a publicly available specification from the Object Management Group (OMG) [KDM]. The initial proposals for the specification were provided by several companies in the software modernization space, including IBM, Unisys, and Electronic Data Systems (now a division of Hewlett-Packard). The specification was developed during the years 2003–2006 by a group of 12 companies. The KDM specification was adopted by the OMG in 2006 and is maintained by a dedicated revision task force. The current version of the KDM specification is KDM 1.3. It is being adopted by ISO as ISO/IEC 19506 [ISO 19506].

KDM was designed as OMG's common foundation for "modeling in reverse," that is, performing fact-oriented analysis of *existing* software-intensive systems for the purposes of software modernization and software assurance. KDM standardizes existing approaches to knowledge discovery in software engineering artifacts, or software mining. The key requirement for "modeling in reverse" is a model of system artifacts that can be built bottom-up, normalizing the differences in programming languages and vendor-specific runtime environments.

KDM provides such a common representation for existing software systems and their operating environments and defines a body of shared meanings required for exchanging facts about systems during diverse assessment projects involving existing software intensive systems.

KDM defines a standard protocol for exchanging system facts that allows interoperability between existing software analysis and modernization tools, services, and their respective proprietary formats. KDM protocol is the foundation for the OMG Assurance Ecosystem, as described in Chapter 8. More specifically, KDM defines a common vocabulary and an interchange format that facilitates the exchange of data that is currently contained within proprietary programming language-specific and vendor-specific models. The metamodel represents the physical and logical elements of systems as well as their relationships at various levels of resolution.

KDM arranges facts about existing systems into several viewpoints each of which corresponds to an ISO 42010 architectural viewpoint. Following the fact-oriented approach, KDM focuses on the entities and their relationships that are essential for each viewpoint, formalizing the common vocabulary for the viewpoint (the viewpoint language). A KDM representation of a given software system—KDM views—is a collection of *facts* about that system. KDM supports the Common Fact Model, described in Chapter 9, in such a way that the KDM elements are standard "locations" of the system of interest, to which information from additional non-KDM vocabularies can be easily integrated. KDM views become part of the complete architectural description of the system, as defined by ISO 42010.

KDM views are represented as XML documents conforming to the KDM XMI schema. KDM uses OMG's Meta-Object Facility (MOF) to define an XMI interchange format [XMI] between tools that work with existing software as well as an application programmer's interface (API) for the next-generation assurance and modernization tools.

11.2 ORGANIZATION OF THE KDM VOCABULARY

The central part of KDM is its common vocabulary for representing and exchanging facts about systems. Other parts that together comprise the standard protocol for exchanging system facts include guidance for generating KDM facts from the system artifacts and specification of mapping into XML for exchange [XML].

The common vocabulary for system facts, defined by the Knowledge Discovery Metamodel, consists of 12 packages arranged into four layers (represented as concentric circles in Figure 1). Most KDM packages define a language for one of the viewpoints. KDM implementations may choose individual packages for compliance.

11.2.1 Infrastructure layer

The KDM Infrastructure Layer consists of the **Core**, KDM, and Inventory packages, which provide a small common core for all other packages, define Inventory views of the artifacts of the system, and provide full traceability between

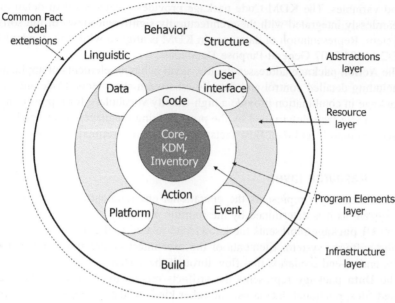

FIGURE 1 KDM Layers

the metamodel elements as links back to the artifacts (in software-intensive systems many of these links point to source code or binary code). The Core package defines a uniform extensibility mechanism, which is utilized to attach diverse attributes to the standard KDM entities, so that KDM becomes the foundation for the Common Fact Model, described in Chapter 9. KDM is defined as a *metamodel* that uses MOF, which defines the physical information exchange protocol for KDM using the OMG MOF to XML mapping. In addition, the KDM Core is aligned with the Resource Description Framework (RDF), which ensures that KDM can be efficiently mapped to RDF triples. Use of standard OMG technologies based on MOF allows a multitude of conforming physical representation for KDM facts. For example, one conforming implementation may define a set of Java classes to represent KDM facts in memory, and another implementation may choose to store KDM facts in an RDF triple-store, such as OpenRDF or Oracle. Both implementations can interoperate by exchanging standard KDM XML files built according to the KDM XML schema, defined in the KDM specification.

11.2.2 Program elements layer

The Program Elements Layer consists of the Code and Action packages.

- The **Code package** represents programming elements as determined by programming languages—for example data types, procedures, classes, methods, and variables. The KDM Code package provides greater level of detail and is seamlessly integrated with the architecturally significant views of the software system. Representation of datatypes in KDM is aligned with ISO standard ISO/IEC 11404:2007 General-Purpose Datatypes.

- The **Action package** addresses the low-level behavior elements of applications, including detailed control and data flow between statements. Code and Action package in combination provide a high-fidelity vocabulary for representing and exchanging facts determined by the programming languages, with emphasis on precise control- and data-flow facts, as they are determined by code.

11.2.3 Resource layer

The Resource Layer represents the operational environment of the existing software system as it is determined by the runtime platform.

The **UI package** represents the knowledge related to the user interfaces of the existing software system. Elements of the user interface are important endpoints for the end-to-end scenarios that flow through the system.

The **Data package** represents the artifacts related to persistent data, such as indexed files, relational databases, and other kinds of data storage. These artifacts are key to enterprise software as they represent the enterprise metadata. The KDM Data package is aligned with another OMG specification, called Common Warehouse Metamodel (CWM).

The **Platform package** represents the operating environment of the software, related to the operating system, middleware, and the like, including the control flows between components as they are determined by the runtime platform, such as callbacks and interprocess communication. The Platform package also includes the vocabulary for describing network nodes and the allocation of software components to network nodes. This network view of a system is important for system assurance.

The **Event package** represents the knowledge related to events and state-transition behavior of the existing software system. These facts complement control and data flows defined in the application code in situations when the software system uses dynamic state machine management code, and when some of the control flow is available as state-transition handlers that are dispatched by the state machine manager. Representing these facts is critical for establishing end-to-end scenarios, as they are defined by code and supported by the runtime platform.

11.2.4 Abstractions layer

The Abstraction Layer is a gateway into the Common Fact Model, described in Chapter 9. The purpose of this layer is to support the Integrated System Model for the entire duration of the system assurance project by supporting fact-oriented integration with other vocabularies identified for the OMG Assurance Ecosystem, such as the system architecture vocabulary described in Chapter 4, the threats and risks vocabulary described in Chapter 5, and the specific vocabulary of the system of interest. The mechanism of the Abstraction Layer supports identification of an object, for example, a particular *asset* of the system of interest, which can be done either externally or by mining the underlying KDM facts, entering the object as an element of the Integrated System Model, and establishing horizontal links to related objects and the vertical traceability links to the underlying KDM objects.

The **Conceptual package** consists of Linguistic and Behavior viewpoints as follows:

- **Linguistic Viewpoint** represents business domain knowledge and business rules. These facts can be mined from the underlying KDM facts, or identified externally, imported into the KDM repository of facts, and integrated with the underlying KDM facts by re-creating the vertical traceability links. The linguistic part is aligned with the Common Fact Model, described in Chapter 9, and the OMG Semantics of Business Vocabulary and Business Rules (SBVR) specification, [SBVR] described in Chapter 10.
- **Behavior Viewpoint** represents operational and system functions. These facts can be mined from the underlying KDM facts, or identified externally, imported into the KDM repository of facts, and integrated with the underlying KDM facts by re-creating the vertical traceability links. The input to the behavior facts are some of the operational and system views described in Chapter 4.

The **Structure package** describes the vocabulary for representing the logical organization of the software system into subsystems, layers, and components. These facts can be mined from the underlying KDM facts, or identified externally, imported into the KDM repository of facts, and integrated with the underlying KDM facts by re-creating the vertical traceability links.

The **Build package** represents the integration and supply chain views of the software system.

11.3 THE PROCESS OF DISCOVERING SYSTEM FACTS

KDM provides the foundation for the Integrated System Model. The high-level overview of the activities involved in establishing this model is provided in the description of the system assurance process in Chapter 3. In particular:

- Activity 2.3: **Establish system model** of the Project Preparation phase of the system assurance project focuses at establishing the so-called *baseline system model*.
- Activity 4.1: **Discover system facts** of the Architecture Security Analysis phase enhances the baseline model with the architecture facts about the system components, their functions, system entry points, security policy of the system, as well as the specific vocabulary of the system as described in Chapter 4.
- Activity 4.2: **Identify threats** of the Architecture Security Analysis phase enhances the integrated system model with the facts from the cybersecurity

vocabulary related to threats described in Chapter 5 (assets, injuries, threat events, threats, risk measures, etc.).

- Activity 4.3: **Identify safeguards** of the Architecture Security Analysis phase enhances the integrated system model with the facts from the cybersecurity vocabulary related to safeguards (their identity, category, location within the system, and relation to threats that they mitigate). Safeguards were briefly discussed in Chapter 5.
- Activity 4.4: **Detect vulnerabilities** of the Architecture Security Analysis phase enhances the integrated system model with the facts from the cybersecurity vocabulary related to detected vulnerabilities as described in Chapters 6 and 7.

As a result of these activities, the integrated system model of the system of interest contains the facts corresponding to all relevant system assurance viewpoints, interconnected with vertical traceability links as well as horizontal relationships, including relationships across different vocabularies. This is illustrated in Figure 2. Traceability links are one of the key mechanisms of the KDM protocol. Their major benefit is that they enable integration between high-level system facts, such as the systems and operational views, risk views, supply chain views, and life-cycle processes views with the high-fidelity facts extracted directly from various

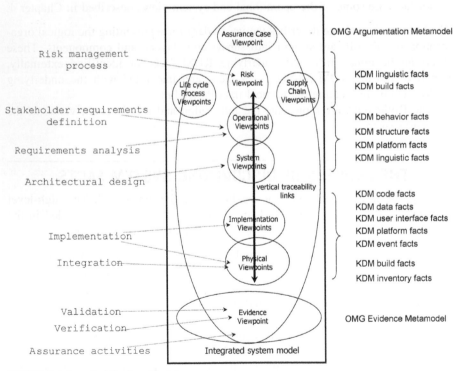

FIGURE 2 Integrated System Model

machine-readable artifacts of the implementation of the system (including source and binary files of the applications, network configuration, runtime platform configuration, and database descriptions). Details of the fact-oriented integration and vertical traceability links were provided in Chapter 9.

The system assurance case developed during Phase 3 of the system assurance process is also integrated with the system model. Other phases of the system assurance process, described in Chapter 3, analyze the integrated system model and gather evidence in support of the claims of the assurance case.

The process of building the baseline system model starts with the physical views defined by the KDM Inventory and Build viewpoints. The initial models are analyzed to understand the details of the programming languages and machine code formats used, the runtime platform used, and so on. At this point the proper KDM extractor tools for implementing the system of interest must be acquired. The process of building the baseline model continues by applying the KDM extractor tools to produce KDM *code facts* from the code of various applications; the *user interface facts*; the *data facts* related to the organization of persistent data; the *platform facts* related to the network configuration and deployment; and the facts related to the use of runtime resources and interprocess communications. This phase usually involves several iterations. Usually the KDM code facts are extracted first and then they are used as one of the inputs for extracting the user interface, data, platform, and event facts, because resource management supported by the runtime platform is controlled through the application programming interfaces (APIs) used in the code. From the perspective of the code, these API calls look like calls to library functions; while the resource views link these API calls to the KDM elements that represent specific *resources,* dynamically managed by the runtime platform.

Extraction of the physical and implementation views is a bottom-up process (see Figure 2). However, the process of enhancing the baseline system model with high-level facts, corresponding to systems and operational viewpoints, risk viewpoints, supply chain viewpoints, and process viewpoints, can be top-down, bottom-up, or any combination. The particular arrangement depends on how the system assurance process is integrated into the overall system life cycle and on the availability of high-fidelity machine-readable content to import into the system model.

Ideal integration of system assurance into the system life cycle and utilization of modeling techniques for system engineering enable the top-down process of completing the integrated system model by importing systems and operational views from the existing architecture repository, as well as importing the risk facts from the existing risk management system. When the machine-readable artifacts are not available, they can be entered manually from existing documentation and integrated with the baseline system model. However, when the artifacts are not available—for example, when a third-party security evaluation is performed during the transition into operation—the corresponding facts are identified during the security evaluation project bottom-up using the baseline system model.

The rest of this chapter provides a brief description into each KDM viewpoint as they are utilized in the System Assurance process.

11.4 DISCOVERING THE BASELINE SYSTEM FACTS

11.4.1 Inventory views

The very first step in building the baseline system model is to enumerate the available *artifacts*. The Inventory package defines a set of noun and verb concepts whose purpose is to represent the physical artifacts of the existing system, such as source files, images, configuration files, and resource descriptions. The Inventory view of the system of interest contains the corresponding objects and facts. The inventory facts also include traceability links between other KDM elements and the regions of source and binary code; this is used to link a logical view of a module to the corresponding physical file.

The nature of the "source code" represented by a particular KDM inventory element is indicated by the "language" attribute and is not specified as part of the KDM vocabulary. Thus, when several years from now some system of interest involves a source file "foo.bas" in a language called visual basic 2020, the KDM Inventory view will represent this artifact as something like: <SourceFile id="sf0056" name=" foo.bas" language="visual basic 2020"/>. On the other hand, in order to extract the program element facts corresponding to the logical organization of the file "foo.bas," the KDM extractor for the "visual basic 2020" must be acquired. These considerations position the Inventory view extractor at the initial phase of the fact gathering process. The Inventory view is investigated to determine the need for additional extractors. The Inventory view is utilized to calculate the *metrics* related to the effort of the system evaluation project. The artifacts are one of the well-known *"locations"* in the system, to which other facts can be linked. For example, vulnerabilities detected by a static analysis tools are often linked to a particular source file.

The Inventory package defines an Inventory viewpoint. It is determined by the entire software development environment of the existing software system. This viewpoint is defined as follows:

Concerns

- What are the artifacts (software items) of the system?
- What is the general role of each artifact (for example, is it a source file, a binary file, an executable, or a configuration description)?
- What is the organization of the artifacts (into directories and projects)?
- What are the dependencies between the artifacts?

Analytic methods

The Inventory viewpoint supports the following kinds of analysis:

- What artifacts depend on the given artifact?
- What are all unique programming languages used by the system?
- Are there any identifiable third-party components in the system? This analysis is based on the known signatures of the third-party packages, such as the open-source components, the header files for the third-party libraries, and APIs.

- What runtime platform elements are used by the system?
- What are the key measurements, related to the estimated effort, such as the total count of source files, the total count of the lines of code, and the distribution of the lines of code per each unique programming language used?

The Inventory views in combination with other KDM views support analysis to determine the original artifacts that correspond to a given KDM element providing the vertical traceability links all the way down to the regions of the source code.

Construction methods

- Inventory views are usually constructed by directory scanning tools, which identify files and their types.
- Construction of an Inventory view is determined by the particular development and deployment environments of the existing software system.
- Construction of an Inventory view is determined by the semantics of the environment as well as the semantics of the corresponding artifacts, and it is based on the mapping from the given development environment to KDM. In particular, the Inventory view extractor tool may use the "fingerprints" of the known programming languages to guess the file type.

Inventory views provide the foundation for the initial investigation of the system of interest and for building the baseline system model. Later in the process of enhancing the integrated system model, KDM Inventory views are used as standard locations to integrate various pieces of assurance information from non-KDM vocabularies, especially metrics and *vulnerability findings* from third-party vulnerability detection tools as described in Chapters 6 and 7.

11.4.1.1 *Inventory viewpoint vocabulary in SBVR*

This section describes the concepts of the KDM Inventory viewpoint vocabulary. Several definitions in SBVR Structured English are included to demonstrate how KDM vocabulary is defined as a vocabulary in SBVR [SBVR]. Figure 3 illustrates the noun concepts of the KDM Inventory viewpoint. The six InventoryItem elements—SourceFile, ExecutableFile, BinaryFile, Image, Configuration, and ResourceDescription—are the common elements selected in KDM to describe software artifacts. Directory and Project elements provide a hierarchical organization to lists of software artifacts.

```
Inventory View
    Definition:      A KDM view that represents facts about the physical
                     artifacts of the existing software system
    Source:     based on Knowledge Discovery Metamodel 1.2 (11.3.1)
                ['InventoryModel']
    General concept:    KDM view
    Reference schema:    id of KDM view
```

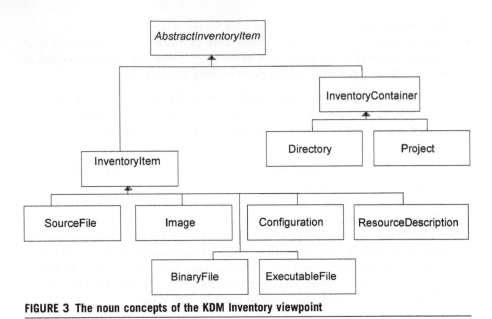

FIGURE 3 The noun concepts of the KDM Inventory viewpoint

Source File

    Definition: a text file that contains instructions in a programming language

    Source: based on Knowledge Discovery Metamodel 1.2 (11.3.5) ['Source File']

    General concept: Inventory Item

    Reference schema: id of KDM Entity

Source File *has* Language

    Definition: the programming language that determines the logical organization of the source file.

    Reference schema: Language of Source File

Source File *has* encoding

    Definition: the encoding that determines the interpretation of the source file.

    Reference schema: Encoding of Source File

Figure 4 represents the verb concepts of the KDM Inventory viewpoint.

Abstract Inventory Element$_1$ *depends on* Abstract Inventory Element$_2$

    Definition: the constraint of an inventory.

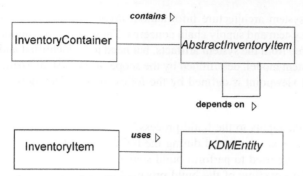

FIGURE 4 The verb concepts of the KDM Inventory viewpoint

Source: based on <u>Knowledge Discovery Metamodel 1.2</u> (11.5.1)
             ['DependsOn']

Concept type: <u>Abstract Inventory Relationship</u>

Reference schema: <u>id</u> of a <u>KDM Relationship</u>

<u>Inventory Container</u> *contains* <u>Inventory Element</u>

Definition: describes a hierarchy of inventory elements

Concept type: <u>KDM built-in Relationship</u>

Reference schema: <u>Inventory Element</u> of <u>Inventory Container</u>

<u>Inventory Element</u> *uses* <u>KDM Entity</u>

Definition: an underspecified <u>relationship</u> between a <u>inventory
               element</u> and a <u>KDM Entity</u> and that can be further
               extended through <u>stereotyping</u>

Source: based on <u>Knowledge Discovery Metamodel 1.2</u> (11.8.2)
              ['InventoryRelationship']

Concept type: <u>Abstract Inventory Relationship</u>

Reference schema: <u>id</u> of a <u>KDM Relationship</u>

11.4.2 Build views

The second step in building the baseline system model is to understand the *role* of the artifacts in the system. The artifacts are enumerated earlier as part of the Inventory Views. The Build view establishes the links between artifacts according to their role in the system life cycle. The process of identifying these relationships starts from the physical build instructions for the system (for example, make files, deployment scripts). The KDM Build package defines noun and verb concepts that represent the common vocabulary of facts involved in the build process of the given software system (including but not limited to the engineering transformations of the "source code" to "executables"). However, this process continues to consider the system architecture information, involving other life-cycle processes and enabling system and supply chain concerns. These concerns cannot be automatically discovered from the system artifacts, but need to be identified and added to the integrated system model, determined by the scope of the system assurance project.

The Build viewpoint is defined by the following considerations:

Concerns
- What are the inputs to the build process?
- What artifacts are generated during the build process?
- What tools are used to perform build steps?
- What is the workflow of the build process?
- Who are the suppliers of the source artifacts?

Analytic methods
- Supply chain analysis (what are the artifacts that depend on a given supplier?)

Construction methods
- Build views are initially constructed by analyzing build scripts and build configuration files for the given system. These inputs are specific to the development environment of the system of interest. The Build extractor tool uses knowledge of the semantics of the build environment to produce one or more Build views as output.
- Construction of the Build view is determined by the semantics of the build environment, and it is based on the mapping from the given build environment to KDM. Such mapping is specific only to the build environment (for example, the format of the build configuration files, etc.) and not to a specific software system.

Build views are used in combination with Inventory views to establish the baseline system model. Later in the process of enhancing the integrated system model, KDM Build views are used as standard *locations* to integrate various pieces of assurance information from non-KDM vocabularies, especially the information related to life-cycle processes and the supply chain.

Figure 5 illustrates the noun concepts of the Build viewpoint vocabulary.

Figure 6 illustrates the verb concepts of the Build viewpoint. The build process is described as the graph of *transformation steps*, represented by BuildStep elements that consume build elements and produce build elements, such as Library, BuildComponent, and BuildProduct. These three elements are containers for various other KDM elements, in particular the elements of the Inventory model. The hierarchy is created through the "*is implemented by*" relationship from BuildComponent, and so forth, to the elements that are considered an implementation of the BuildComponent.

11.4.3 Data views

The KDM Data package defines a set of noun and verb concepts to describe the organization of persistent data in software systems. Facts in the Data viewpoint are

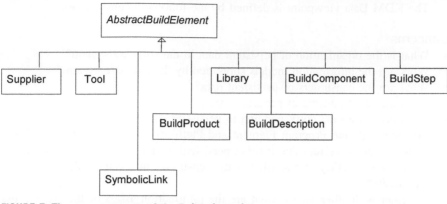

FIGURE 5 The noun concepts of the Build viewpoint

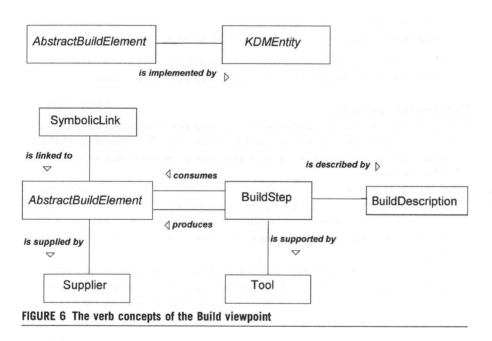

FIGURE 6 The verb concepts of the Build viewpoint

usually determined by Data Description Languages (for example, SQL) but may in some cases be determined by the code elements. KDM Data views use the elements of the Code package related to simple datatypes. KDM Data views describe organizations of complex data repositories, such as record files, relational databases, structured data stream, XML schema, and XML documents.

The KDM Data viewpoint is defined by the following considerations:

Concerns
- What is the organization of persistent data in the software system?
- What are the information models supported by the software system?
- What are the consumers of persistent data?
- What are the producers of persistent data?
- What are the events corresponding to persistent data?
- Together with the Program Element and Platform views, what are the critical scenarios in the system that involve persistent data as source or as target?
- Together with other views, what is the sensitivity of the individual persistent data items?
- Together with other views, what are the information assets of the system and how do they map to physical data?
- Together with other views, what are the threats to information assets?

Analytic methods
The Data architectural viewpoint supports the following kinds of analysis:

- Data aggregation (the set of data items accessible from the given ColumnSet by adding data items through foreign key relationships to other tables).

Construction methods
- Data views are usually constructed by analyzing Data Definition Language artifacts for the given data management platform. The Data extractor tool uses knowledge of the data management platform to produce one or more Data views as output.
- As an alternative, for some languages like Cobol, in which some elements of the Data are explicitly defined by the language, the Data views are produced by compiler-like tools that take artifacts of the system as the input and produce one or more Data views as output (together with the corresponding Code views).
- Construction of the Data view is determined by the semantics of the data management platform and is based on mapping from the given data management platform to KDM. Such mapping is specific only to the data management platform and not to a specific software system.

Data views are used in combination with Code views and Inventory views. Later in the process of enhancing the integrated system model, KDM Data views are used as standard *locations* to integrate various pieces of assurance information from non-KDM vocabularies, especially information related to *information assets* and their sensitivity.

Figure 7 illustrates the noun concepts of the KDM Data viewpoint vocabulary.

Catalog, RelationalSchema, and ColumnSet elements are containers for data elements; RelationalSchema may also contain CodeItem (for example, to represent

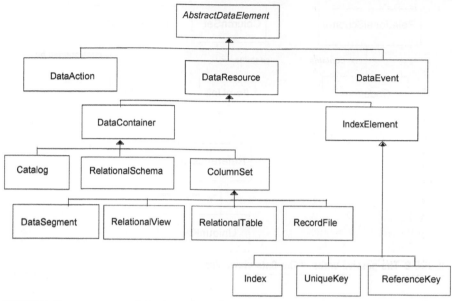

FIGURE 7 Noun concepts of the Data viewpoint

stored procedures); and ColumnSet may contain ItemUnit (to represent database fields). All elements may contain DataEvent and DataAction elements, to represent specific behaviors associated with persistent data operations. Various IndexElements define another hierarchy on top of ItemUnit, using the "*is implemented by*" relation, to represent how groups of fields contribute to private and foreign keys and indices of the database. '*References*' relationship is the link between a foreign key and the corresponding primary key. The passive verbs that define the structural relationship of Data views are illustrated in Figure 8.

Figure 9 illustrates the active verbs of the Data viewpoint, which are part of the common vocabulary supporting analysis of system functions and behaviors. DataActions are units of behavior associated with DataResource elements. Why is it important? Persistent data management systems determine some of the control and data flow for the application through various mechanisms such as callbacks, exceptions, and implicit assignments to variables. For the end-to-end analysis of the system of interest, all control- and data-flow facts must be accounted for, and assurance evidence regarding the soundness of the analysis must be collected. DataActions and DataEvents provide the common vocabulary and mechanism for the knowledge extractor tools to adequately represent the semantics of the runtime platform of the system of interest. Further explanations are provided later in this chapter, in the section dedicated to the KDM Platform viewpoint.

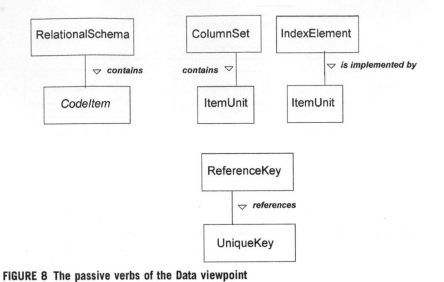

FIGURE 8 The passive verbs of the Data viewpoint

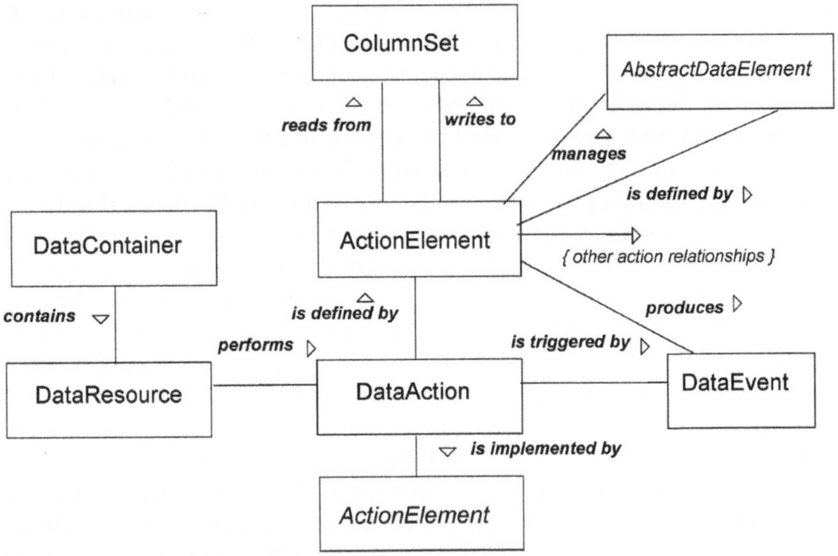

FIGURE 9 The active verbs of the Data viewpoint

Figure 10 illustrates a fragment of a KDM Data view. The left side of the picture shows two relational tables and a fragment of the corresponding description in SQL. The right side of the picture shows the key KDM facts involved in describing these tables, and the verbalization of these facts in Structured English using the noun and verb concepts of the Data viewpoint.

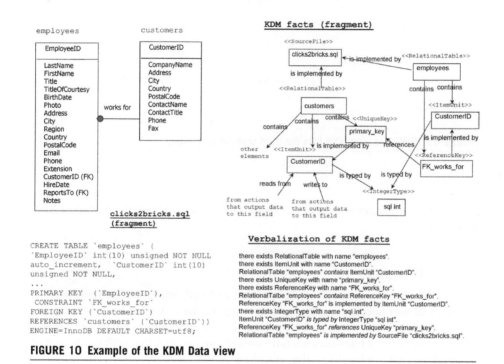

FIGURE 10 Example of the KDM Data view

The next diagram, Figure 11, illustrates the Data view at a lower (less detailed) resolution. The view shows a tool-generated KDM view, where each node is a RelationshipTable element. These elements show the 12 tables of the Clicks2-Bricks relational schema (this is a system described as the case study in Chapter 12). Dependencies between data elements are the so-called KDM aggregated relationships. They summarize all data facts that involve a pair of relational tables. The nodes named "ENV:SRC" and "ENV:SNK" represent the rest of the system (any elements that are not in the current view). These nodes are the endpoints for the aggregated relationships that summarize the uses of the 12 main elements of the view by the rest of the system (relationships from the ENV:SRC node) and how these elements use the rest of the system (relationships to the ENV: SNK node). Relationships between tables are determined by the foreign keys from one table to another. Uses of relational tables are determined by the data actions

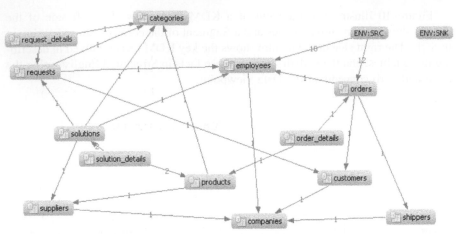

FIGURE 11 KDM Data view at a less detailed level of resolution

and the use of relational data in the application code, for example, SQL SELECT statements.

11.4.4 UI views

The KDM UI package defines a set of noun and verb concepts that represent the elements of user interfaces, such as screens, reports, and their fields; their composition, sequence of operations, and, of course, their relationships to the other elements of the systems. User interfaces are notorious for involving a tremendous amount of detailed attributes related to color, positions of the elements, and various minute properties affecting the behavior and appearance of the graphical widgets. These details are highly specific to a particular graphical framework, such as the Java AWT, Microsoft Windows, and the X windows. The KDM common vocabulary for the user interface includes a very small number of terms because KDM focuses on the user interfaces only as the conceptual endpoints for various end-to-end scenarios and functionality of the system of interest. The KDM User Interface viewpoint is defined by the following considerations:

Concerns
- What are the distinct elements of the user interface of the systems?
- What is the organization of the user interface?
- How does the user interface use artifacts of the system (for example, images)?
- What data flows originate from the user interface?
- What data flows output to the user interface?
- What control flows are initiated by the user interface events?

Analytic methods

The UI architectural viewpoint supports the following kinds of analysis:

- Data flow (for example, what scenarios read from a given UI element; what scenarios write to a given UI element; what scenarios manage a given UI element?)
- Control flow (for example, what action elements are triggered by events in a given UI element; what scenarios operate on a given UI element?)
- Workflow (for example, what UI elements will be displayed after the given one; what UI elements are displayed before the given one?)

Construction methods

- UI views are usually constructed by analyzing Code views for the given system as well as the UI-specific configuration artifacts. The UI extractor tool uses knowledge of the API and semantics for the given runtime platform to produce one or more UI views as output.
- As an alternative, for some languages like Cobol, in which the elements of the UI are explicitly defined by the language, the UI views are produced by the parser-like tools that take artifacts of the system as the input and produce one or more UI views as output (together with the corresponding Code views).
- Construction of the UI view is determined by the semantics of the UI platform, and it is based on mapping from the given UI platform to KDM. Such mapping is specific only to the UI platform and not to a specific software system.
- UI views are used in combination with Code views and Inventory views. During the Architecture Security Analysis phase, KDM UI views enable understanding of the functionality of the system of interest.

Figure 12 illustrates the noun concepts of the UI viewpoint. UIResource elements Screen and Report are containers for UIField elements. The corresponding "*contains*" relationship determines the structure of the UI views. In addition

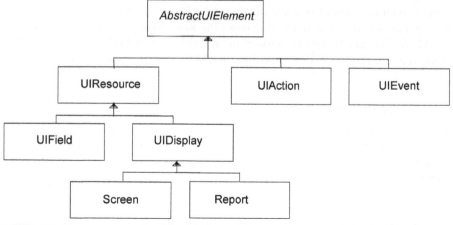

FIGURE 12 The noun concepts of the UI viewpoint

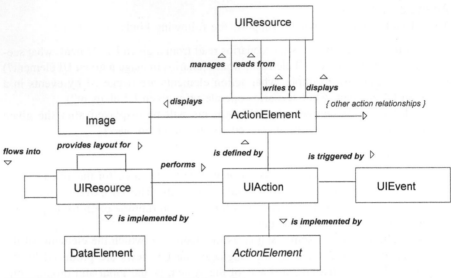

FIGURE 13 The verb concepts of the UI viewpoint

UIResource elements can contain UIAction and UIEvent elements to represent control and data flows determined by the UI part of the runtime platform. This is further explained in the section dedicated to the Platform views.

Figure 13 illustrates the verb concepts of the UI viewpoint. Specific relationships between UI elements are "UIResource *flows into* UIResource" and "UIResource *provides layout for* UIResource." Other verb concepts describe control and data flows between code and the elements of the user interface.

Figure 14 illustrates the KDM UI views. The left side of the picture shows a typical Web page with fields and buttons and a fragment of its description in Java Server Pages (JSP). The right side shows the key elements of the corresponding KDM UI view and the verbalization of the KDM facts in SBVR Structured English using the noun and verb concepts of the KDM UI common vocabulary.

11.4.5 Code views

The Code viewpoint defines a large set of elements whose purpose is to provide a language-independent vocabulary for various constructs determined by common programming languages. The Code viewpoint is defined by the following considerations:

Concerns
- What are the computational elements of the system?
- What are the modules of the system?

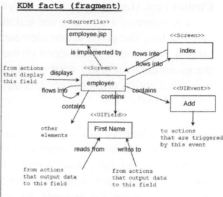

KDM facts (fragment)

Verbalization of KDM facts

there exists Screen with name "employee".
there exists UIField with name "First Name".
Screen "employee" *contains* UIField "First Name".
there exists UIEvent with name "Add".
Screen "employee" *contains* UIEvent "Add".
there exists Screen with name "index".
Screen "index" *flows into* Screen "employee".
Screen "employee" *flows into* Screen "index".
Screen "employee" *flows into* Screen "employee".
there exist SourceFile with name "employee.jsp".
Screen "employee" *is implemented by* SourceFile "employee.jsp".

```
<h2>Personal Information</h2>
  <form method="get" action="employee">
    <table>
      <tr>
        <td> First Name: </td>
        <td>
          <input type="text"
              name="first_name"
              value="${employee.firstName}" />
        </td>
      </tr>
      . . .
  <input type="submit" name="action" value="Add" />
```

employee.jsp
(fragment)

FIGURE 14 Example of the KDM UI view

- What is the organization of the computational elements?
- What are the datatypes used by the computational elements?
- What are the elementary units of behavior of the system?
- What are the relationships between the code elements? In particular what are the control-flow and data-flow relationships?
- What are the important noncomputational elements?
- How are computational elements and modules related to the physical artifacts of the system?

Analytic methods

The Code viewpoint supports the following main kinds of analysis:

- Composition (for example, what code elements are owned by a Compilation-Unit, SharedUnit, or a CodeAssembly; what action elements are owned by a CallableUnit?)
- Data flow (for example, what action elements read from a given StorableUnit; what action elements write to a given StorableUnit; what action elements create dynamic instances of a given Datatype; what action elements address a particular StorableUnit; what data elements are being read as actual parameters in a call?)

- Control flow (for example, what CallableUnit is used in a call; what action element is executed after the given action element; what action elements are executed before the given action element; what data element is used to dispatch control flow from a given action element; what action element is executed after the given element under what conditions; what is the exceptional flow of control; what action elements are executed as entry points to a given module or a CallableUnit?)
- Datatypes (for example, what is the datatype of the given storable unit; what is the base datatype of the given pointer type; what is the base datatype of the given element of the record type; what is the signature of the given CallableUnit?)
- Analysis of the interfaces, templates, and pre-processor. All relationships defined in the Code model are nontransitive. Additional computations are required to derive, for example, all action elements that can be executed after the given action element, or all CallableUnits that a given action element can dispatch control to.

The KDM mechanism of aggregated relationship is used to derive relationships between KDM elements that own or reference various Code elements (usually, Module and CodeAssembly) based on the low-level relationship between individual Code elements.

Construction methods

- Code views that correspond to the KDM Code viewpoint are usually constructed by parser-like tools that take artifacts of the system as the input and produce one or more Code views as output.
- Construction of the Code view is determined by the syntax and semantics of the programming language of the corresponding artifact, and it is based on the mapping from the given programming language to KDM. Such mapping is specific only to the programming language and not to a specific software system.
- The mapping from a particular programming language to KDM may produce additional information (system-specific, programming language-specific, or extractor tool-specific). This information can be attached to KDM elements using stereotypes, attributes, or annotations.

11.4.5.1 Code views: elements of structure

The Code package defines the so-called *code item* elements—the named elements determined by the programming language, the so-called symbols, definitions, and so on—and structural relations between them. Code items are further categorized into ComputationalObject, Datatypes, and Modules. The Action package defines behavioral elements and various behavioral relationships, which determine the control and data flows between code items.

Description of the Code viewpoint is further subdivided into the following parts:

- Code Elements representing Modules
- Code Elements representing Computational Objects

- Code Elements representing Datatypes
- Code Elements representing Preprocessor Directives
- Miscellaneous Code Elements

Data representation of KDM is aligned with the International Standard ISO/IEC 11404:2007 (General-Purpose Datatypes). In particular, KDM provides distinct metamodel elements for "data elements" (for example, global and local variables, constants, record fields, parameters, class members, array items, and pointer base elements) and "datatypes." Each data element has a property "type" that links the data element to its corresponding datatype element. KDM distinguishes primitive datatypes (for example, Integer, Boolean), complex user-defined datatypes (for example, array, pointer, sequence), and named datatypes (for example, a class, a synonym type). KDM metamodel elements corresponding to datatypes are subclasses of a generic class Datatype. KDM metamodel elements corresponding to data elements are subclasses of a generic class DataElement.

KDM code elements represent existing artifacts determined by a programming language. KDM elements provide sufficient coverage for most common datatypes and data elements, common to the mainstream programming languages. KDM also provides several powerful generic extensible elements that can be further used with stereotypes to represent uncommon situations.

The taxonomy of the noun concepts of the Code viewpoint is illustrated in Figure 15.

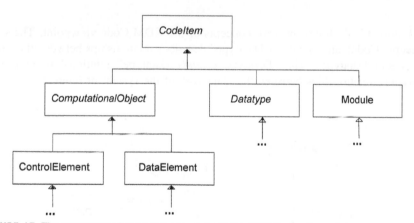

FIGURE 15 The taxonomy of the noun concepts of the KDM Code viewpoint

The next diagram, Figure 16, illustrates the entire organization of the KDM Code viewpoint. Most of the top-level elements are decomposed into another level, with the exception of the Datatype element, which contributes to over the half of the number of elements in the KDM Code vocabulary.

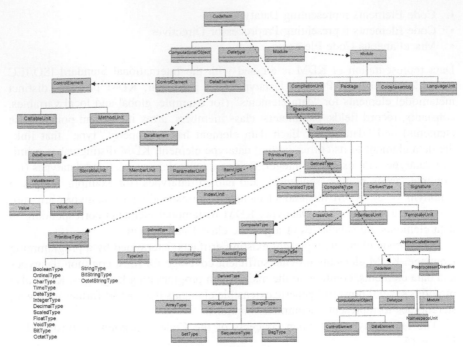

FIGURE 16 Complete taxonomy of the noun concepts of the Code viewpoint

Figure 17 illustrates the verb concepts of the KDM Code viewpoint. The verb concept "CodeItem *is typed by* Datatype" describes relationships between the Code items and Datatypes. The "Datatype *extends* Datatype" relationship represents subtyping relationships between the Datatypes of the system of interest.

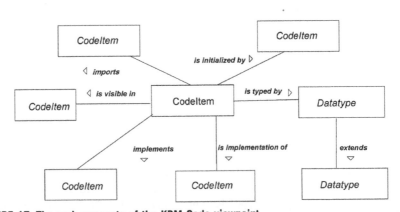

FIGURE 17 The verb concepts of the KDM Code viewpoint

Figure 18 illustrates the Code view: The left side of the picture shows a code fragment (in Java). In the middle of the picture is the decomposition of the code example according to the constructs defined by the Java language. Above each element is guidance for the mapping into KDM. Thus, the element s1 that corresponds to the Java file with the name "Main.java" is mapped to the KDM CompilationUnit element. Figure 18 also illustrates several relationships that are implicit in the code fragment (elements e1-e4). The right side of the picture shows a small fragment of the KDM code view.

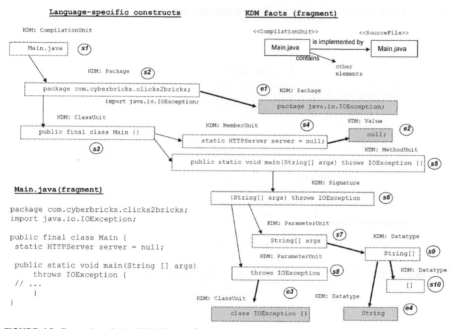

FIGURE 18 Example of the KDM Code view

11.4.5.2 Code views: elements of behavior

The Action package defines the elements of behavior—the statements and various control- and data-flow relationships between statements and code items. Figure 19 illustrates the noun concepts from the common vocabulary of behavior elements of the Code viewpoint. The key element is ActionElement. It represents a statement in the application code (sometimes a collection of statements or a part of the original statement). A BlockUnit represents blocks of statements in the original application code.

The next diagram, Figure 20, illustrates the verb concepts that describe the elementary data-flow relationships within the application code. The corresponding facts are illustrated in Figure 21, using an example code fragment.

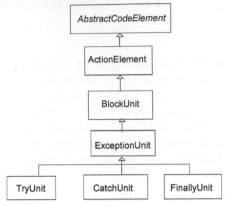

FIGURE 19 The noun concepts of the Code viewpoint: actions

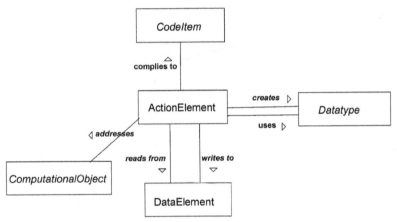

FIGURE 20 The verb concepts of the Code viewpoint: data flow

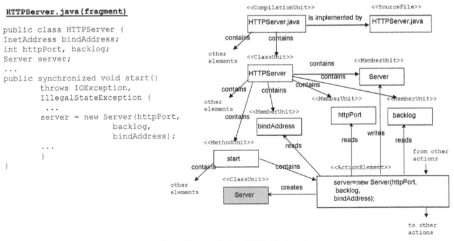

FIGURE 21 Example of the data-flow facts of the KDM Code views

The next two diagrams, Figures 22 and 23, illustrate the elementary control flow relations.

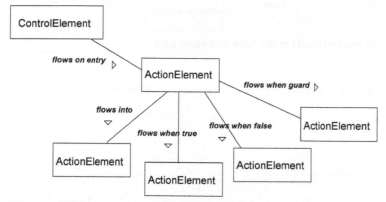

FIGURE 22 The verb concepts of the Code view: control flow

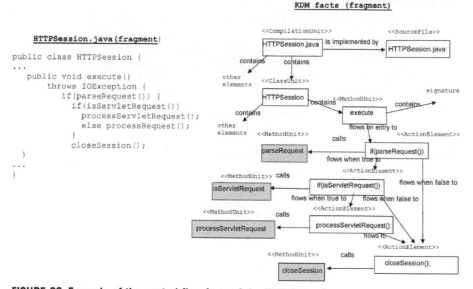

FIGURE 23 Example of the control flow facts of the KDM Code views

The next two diagrams, Figures 24 and 25, illustrate the call relationships.

Figure 26 illustrates the Code facts at a less granular level of resolution. The picture shows a tool-generated view, where six nodes represent classes of the Clicks2Bricks application and the last node represents a Java package "servlet." Relationships between nodes are the KDM aggregated relationships that

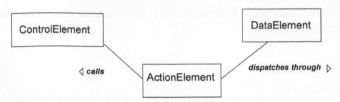

FIGURE 24 Verb concepts of the Code viewpoint: calls

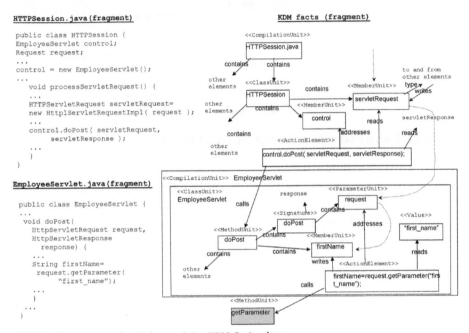

FIGURE 25 Example of call facts of the KDM Code views

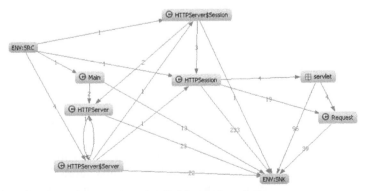

FIGURE 26 KDM Code view at a less detailed level of resolution

summarize all facts existing between each pair of nodes, including the two ENV nodes that represent the rest of the system.

11.4.5.3 Micro KDM

The KDM specification defines a separate compliance point for each viewpoint. The ordinary compliance point for the Code viewpoint does not specify the granularity of ActionElement. It is the responsibility of the supplier of the knowledge extractor tool to select appropriate resolution. Usually this decision is made based on the level of resolution of the existing proprietary representation. Regardless of the selected resolution the resulting KDM views are useful for architecture evaluation because they support fact-based integration, the vertical traceability links, and aggregated relations to the architecture significant levels, which are of lower resolution anyway. However, at the detailed level, the scope of the action element may lead to ambiguities in interpreting the precise semantics of the control and data flows. This is illustrated in the next picture (left side) in Figure 27, where one ActionElement represents a complex statement. The pattern of relationship is ambiguous.

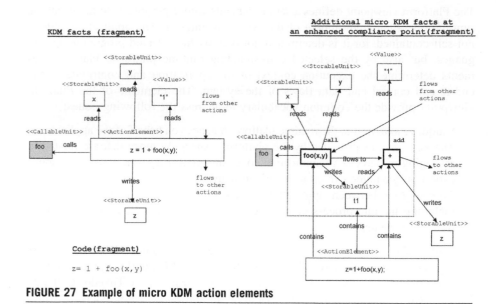

FIGURE 27 Example of micro KDM action elements

To support high-fidelity analysis (including full static analysis) of KDM views, the KDM specification defines an enhanced compliance point, which involves precise definitions of high-resolution ActionElements (called micro action). This compliance point is referred to as micro KDM. The specification of micro KDM actions essentially defines a "virtual machine" for KDM. The micro KDM representation of the same example is illustrated at the right side of Figure 27. The two micro actions involved are "Call" and "Add."

Micro KDM actions are grouped into the following 11 categories (the total number of micro actions in each group is given in parentheses):

- Comparison actions, based on ISO 11404 (10)
- Operations on primitive numeric types, based on ISO 11404 (7)
- Bitwise operations on primitive datatypes, based on ISO 11404 (7)
- Control actions (13)
- Access to Derived Datatypes, based on ISO 11404 (13)
- Conversions between Datatypes (4)
- Operations on StringType, based on ISO 11404 (5)
- Operations on SetType, based on ISO 11404 (8)
- Operations on SequenceType, based on ISO 11404 (5)
- Operations on BagType, based on ISO 11404 (6)
- Resource actions (4)

11.4.6 Platform views

The Platform viewpoint defines a set of elements whose purpose is to represent the runtime operating environment of the system of interest. The application code is not self-contained, for it is determined not only by the selected programming languages, but also by the selected corresponding runtime platform. Platform elements determine the execution context of the application and contribute to the end-to-end control and data flows of the system. The elements of the Platform viewpoint provide the common vocabulary to address the following issues:

- Unique *resources* that the runtime platform manages on behalf of the applications.
- The key *services* provided by the platform, especially those that are related to managing resources. An application code calls platform services using an application programmer's interface (API) to manage the life cycle of a resource.
- *Control flow* between application components determined by the platform, including the interprocess communication, and error handling across application components.

Examples of Platform elements include UNIX OS File System, UNIX OS process management system, Windows 2000, OS/ 390, Java (J2SE), Perl language Runtime support, IBM CICS TS, IBM MQSeries, Jakarta Struts, BEA Tuxedo, CORBA, HTTP, TCP/IP, Eclipse, EJB, JMS, Database middleware, Java Servlets, and Java Threads.

The Platform viewpoint is defined by the following considerations:

Concerns
- What unique resources are used by the software system?
- What elements of the runtime platform are used by the software system?
- What behavior is associated with the resources of the runtime platform?

- What control flows are initiated by the events associated with the runtime resources?
- What control flows are initiated by the runtime environment?
- What are the bindings between the code and runtime environment?
- What are the deployment configurations of the software system?
- What are the dynamic/concurrent threads of activity within the software system?

Analytic methods

The Platform viewpoint supports the following kinds of analysis:

- Data flow (for example, what action elements read from a given resource; what action elements write to a given resource; what action elements manage a given resource; including indirect data flow using a MarshalledResource or a MessagingResource where a particular resource is used to perform a data flow between the "send" action element and the "receive" action element?)
- Control flow (for example, what action elements are triggered by events in a given resource; what action elements operate on a given resource?)
- Identify resource instances based on resource handles and their use in various modules.

Construction methods

- Platform views that correspond to the KDM Platform architectural viewpoint are usually constructed by analyzing Code views for the given system as well as the platform-specific configuration artifacts. The platform extractor tool uses knowledge of the API and semantics for the given runtime platform to produce one or more Platform views as output.
- As an alternative, for some languages such as Cobol, in which the elements of the runtime platform are explicitly defined by the language, the Platform views are produced by the parser-like tools that take artifacts of the system as the input and produce one or more Platform views as output (together with the corresponding Code views).
- Construction of the Platform view is determined by the semantics of the runtime platform and is based on mapping from the given runtime platform to KDM. Such mapping is specific only to the runtime platform and not to a specific software system.

Platform views are used in combination with Code views and Inventory views. The purpose of Platform views is to complete the control and data flows of the end-to-end system scenarios.

The next two diagrams, Figures 28 and 29, illustrate the noun and verb concepts of the KDM Platform viewpoint.

Figures 30–32 illustrate the behavior determined by the runtime platform and shows how KDM facts represent this behavior to ensure end-to-end control and data flows through applications with assurance of the soundness of the cause-and-effect analysis performed using the KDM views. Figure 30 illustrates three

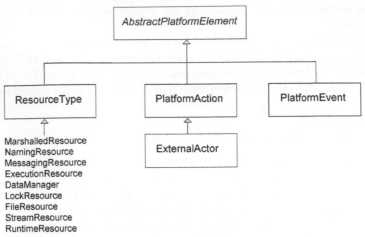

FIGURE 28 The noun concepts of the Platform viewpoint

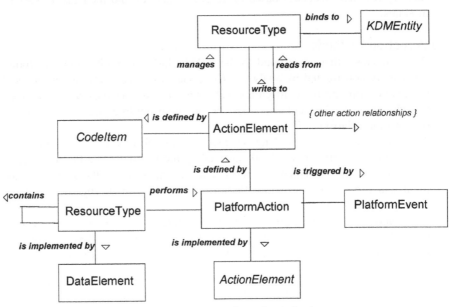

FIGURE 29 The verb concepts of the Platform viewpoint: behavior

Java classes from the Clicks2Bricks system. The code uses the so-called Thread-PoolExecutor API of the standard Java runtime platform. The key relationships determined by this mechanism are illustrated next. Basically, the ThreadPoolExecutor object launches Java threads (using an internal pool of threads). The new thread executes method "call" of the class, submitted to the executor.

```
public synchronized void start() throws IOException, IllegalStateException {
  if(isRunning())
    throw new IllegalStateException();
  System.err.println("Ready.");
  server = new Server(httpPort, backlog, bindAddress);
  executor =
    new ThreadPoolExecutor(0, maxConnections + 1, 60L, TimeUnit.SECONDS,
                           new SynchronousQueue<Runnable>());
  executor.submit(server);
}
```

```
class Server implements Callable<Void> {
  ServerSocket socket;

  public Server(int port, int backlog, InetAddress address)
    throws IOException
  {
    if(address != null)
      socket = new ServerSocket(port, backlog, bindAddress);
    else
      socket = new ServerSocket(port, backlog);
  }

  public Void call() throws Exception {
    try {
      while(true) {
        Socket client = socket.accept();

        if(getConnectionCount() >= maxConnections) {
          // Ungracefully close connection.
          client.close();
          continue;
        }

        executor.submit(new Session(new HTTPSession(documentRoot,
                                      client.getInputStream(),
                                      client.getOutputStream())));

      }
    } finally {
      return null;
    }
  }
}
```

```
final class Session implements Callable<Void> {
  HTTPSession session;

  Session(HTTPSession session) {
    this.session = session;
  }

  public Void call() throws Exception {
    incrementConnectionCount();
    session.execute();
    decrementConnectionCount();
    return null;
  }
}
```

FIGURE 30 Platform behavior in KDM Platform views: code example

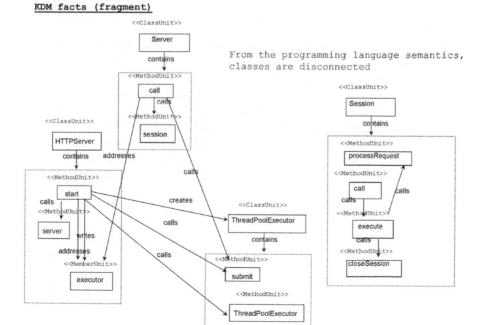

FIGURE 31 Platform behavior: The KDM Code view is not enough

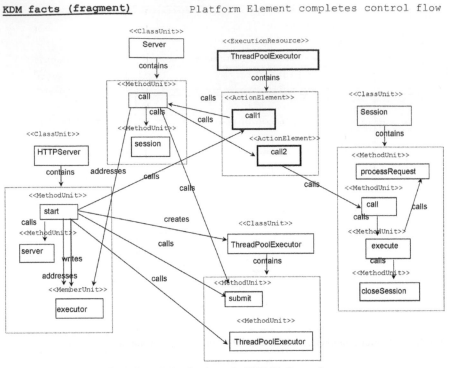

KDM facts (fragment)   Platform Element completes control flow

FIGURE 32 Example of Platform behavior facts in KDM Platform view

From the pure code perspective (determined by the Java language), however, there are no calls to the methods with name "call" in classes "Server" and "Session." There are no relationships from the class HTTPServer to the class Server and from the class Server to the class Session. However, classes HTTP-Server and Server have relationships to the methods of the class ThreatPoolExecutor. The code perspective does not show an end-to-end scenario of elementary control-flow relationships between classes HTTPServer, Server, and Session (see Figure 31). The knowledge that is required to have an end-to-end control and data flow in the system model is related to the semantics of the Java runtime platform, in particular the semantics of the ThreadPoolExecutor API.

Once the additional platform-specific knowledge is imported into the platform extractor tool, it can generate several facts that restore the end-to-end scenario. The new facts are illustrated at Figure 32. Note that now the combined KDM view (Code + Platform) shows an end-to-end scenario from the method "start" to method "Call" in "Server" class, to method "Call" in the class "Session," to method "processRequest" in the class "Session". This is the key functional scenario of the Clicsk2Bricks system. Note that the KDM facts in this example are aggregated to a less detailed level of resolution: Entire methods are shown as the sources of the "calls" relationships. However, the elementary "Calls" relationship is defined as having an ActionElement as the source.

The same mechanism of "platform actions" representing abstracted behavior of the system's runtime platform based on knowledge of the corresponding APIs is used in KDM Data, UI, and Event views. Additional actions can be associated with the DataResources, UIResources, and the elements of KDM state transition view to provide a high-fidelity representation of end-to-end control and data flows through the applications and through the entire system.

Figure 33 illustrates the noun concepts of the KDM Platform viewpoint describing the elements of deployment. The deployment views show how relationships between machine nodes on the network and the software components are deployed to these nodes. The verb concepts of Platform viewpoint are illustrated at Figure 34.

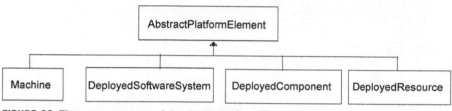

FIGURE 33 The noun concepts of the Platform viewpoint: deployment

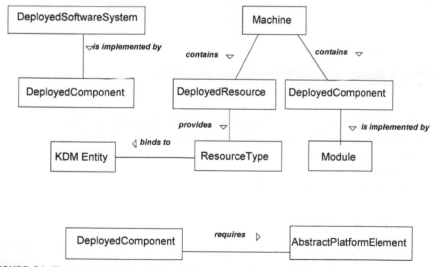

FIGURE 34 The verb concepts of the Platform viewpoint: deployment

The Machine element is a container for the DeployedResource and Deployed-Component elements allocated to the corresponding machine node. On the other hand, the DeployedSoftwareSystem element gathers the entire set of components of a single system. A single machine node may host components of different systems, so both groupings are needed.

Figure 35 illustrates the deployment configuration for the network diagram of the Clicks2Bricks system, provided in the concept of operations description in Chapter 12. The purpose of the deployment elements is to extend the set of *"locations"* in the system available for the analysis and integration with other non-KDM vocabularies.

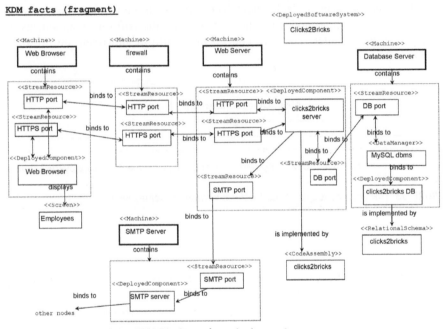

FIGURE 35 Example of the KDM Platform view: deployment

Figure 36 illustrates the additional noun and verb concepts related to concurrency in code. Knowledge of the API to the runtime platform is required to generate these views. However, once extracted, these facts are seamlessly integrated with other KDM facts.

Figure 37 illustrates the KDM facts related to concurrency.

11.4.7 Event views

The Event viewpoint defines a set of elements whose purpose is to represent the high-level behavior of systems in terms of event-driven state transitions. Elements of the KDM Event viewpoint represent states, transitions, and events. States can be

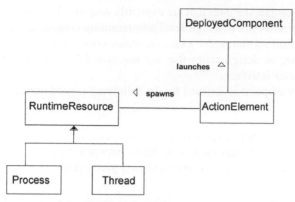

FIGURE 36 The concepts of the Platform viewpoint: concurrency

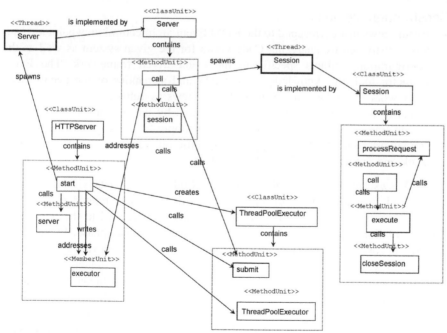

FIGURE 37 Example of the KDM Platform view: Concurrency

concrete, for example, the ones that are explicitly supported by some state-machine-based runtime framework or a high-level programming language, such as CHILL, or can represent abstract states, for example, states corresponding to the operational or system views, or design states that are associated with a particular algorithm, resource, or a user interface.

The Event viewpoint is defined by the following considerations:

Concerns
- What are the distinct states involved in the behavior of the software system?
- What are the events that cause transitions between states?
  - What action elements are executed in a given state?

Analytic methods
The Event architectural viewpoint supports the following main kinds of analysis:

- Reachability (for example, what states are reachable from the given state?)
- Control flow (for example, what action elements are triggered by a given state transition; what action elements will be executed for a given traversal of the state transition graph?)
- Data flow (for example, what data sequences correspond to a given traversal of the state transition graph?)

Construction methods
- Event views that correspond to the KDM Event architectural viewpoint are usually constructed by analyzing Code views for the given system as well as the configuration artifacts specific to the event-driven framework. The Event extractor tool uses knowledge of the API and semantics of the event-driven framework to produce one or more Event views as output.
- Construction of the Event view is determined by the semantics of the event-driven framework, and it is based on the mapping from the given event-driven framework to KDM. Such mapping is specific only to the event-driven framework and not to a specific software system.

Event Views are used in combination with Code views, Data views, Platform views, and Inventory views to represent high-fidelity facts related to complete control flows of the system of interest, especially ones related to the underlying runtime platform. During the Architecture Security Analysis phase, Event views are used in combination with the Behavior views to represent relevant system architecture views and establish vertical traceability links to the system facts at the implementation level. In this capacity the event entities are used as standard locations to integrate various pieces of assurance information from non-KDM vocabularies, especially the information related to functions of the system of interest.

The next two diagrams, Figures 38 and 39, illustrate the noun and verb concepts of the KDM Event viewpoint vocabulary. These elements are further illustrated at Figure 40 by showing example facts.

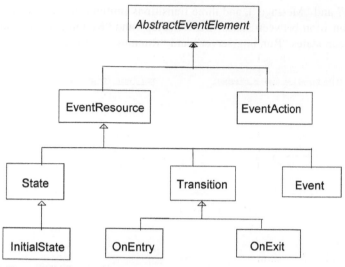

FIGURE 38 The noun concepts of the Event viewpoint

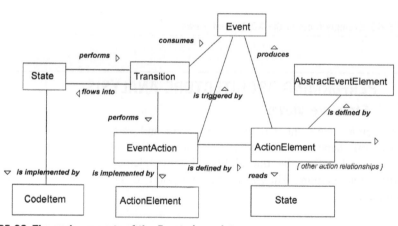

FIGURE 39 The verb concepts of the Event viewpoint

For example, the Clicks2Bricks Web server may have first go through an initialization, then enter a state in which it awaits a connection, and then spawn a session in which it processes the request and sends a message back. According to the viewpoint language of KDM event models, this example involves three entities of kind "state" (state "Server initialization," state "Running server," and state "Running session"), three entities of the kind event (events "Connection,"

"Request," and "Message"), and three transitions (initial transition to state "Server setup," transition between states "Server setup" and "Running server," and transition between states "Running server" and "Running session").

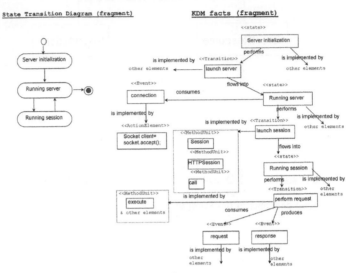

FIGURE 40 Example facts of the KDM event views

11.5 PERFORMING ARCHITECTURE ANALYSIS

11.5.1 Structure views

The Structure viewpoint defines several noun and verb concepts that represent architectural elements of the system of interest, such as subsystems, layers, and packages, and define the traceability of these elements to other KDM facts for the same system. The Structure viewpoint is defined by the following considerations:

Concerns
- What are the structural elements of the system, and what is the organization of these elements?
- What software elements compose the system?
- How are the structural elements of the system related to the computational elements?
- What are the connections of these elements based on the relationships between the corresponding computational elements?
- What are the interfaces of the structural elements of the system?

Analytic methods

The Structure architectural viewpoint supports the following kinds of analysis:

- Dependencies (are components properly connected?)
- Coupling and cohesion (the number of internal relationships within a component compared to the number of relationships to other components)
- Efferent and afferent relationship (uses of a component by other components and uses of other components by the given component)
- Interfaces (what is the required and provided interface of the given component?)

Construction methods

- Structure views that correspond to the KDM Structure architectural viewpoint are usually constructed by analyzing the architecture models of the given system. The Structure extractor tool uses knowledge of the architecture models to produce one or more Structure views as output.
- As an alternative, Structure views can be produced manually using the input from the architect of the system and architecture documentation.
- Construction of the Structure view is determined by the architectural description of the system.
- Construction of the Structure views corresponding to a particular architectural description may involve additional information (system-specific or architecture-specific). This information can be attached to KDM elements using stereotypes, attributes, or annotations.

The organization of the system may be presented as a single Structure view or as a set of multiple Structure views showing layers, components, subsystems, or packages. The reach of this representation extends from a uniform architecture to an entire family of module-sharing subsystems.

The Structure model owns a collection of StructuralElement instances.

Packages are the leaf elements of the Structure model, representing a division of a system's Code modules into discrete, nonoverlapping parts. An undifferentiated architecture is represented by a single Package.

The StructuralGroup recursively gathers StructuralElements to represent various architectural divisions. The Software System subclass provides a gathering point for all the system's packages directly or indirectly through other Structure elements. The packages may be further grouped into Subsystems, Layers, and Components, or Architecture views.

Structure views are used in combination with Code views, Data views, Platform views, UI views, and Inventory views. Structure elements are the main "locations" of the system of interest for the purpose on integrating various non-KDM vocabularies, in particular the operational and system views, threats, and risks.

Figures 41 and 42 illustrate the noun and verb concepts of the KDM Structure viewpoint.

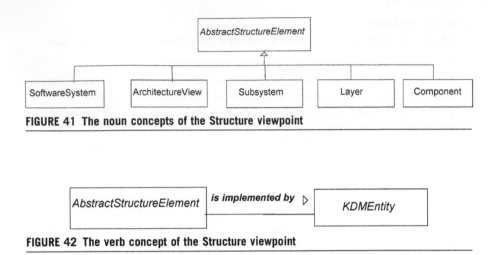

FIGURE 41 **The noun concepts of the Structure viewpoint**

FIGURE 42 **The verb concept of the Structure viewpoint**

Relationships of the Structure views are entirely defined by the mechanism of aggregated relations. The only relationship defined in the Structure view established the vertical traceability links between the system elements (instances of the noun concepts of the Structure vocabulary) and other KDM elements. The next diagram, Figure 43, illustrates an architecture significant Structure view of the Clicks2Bricks system (from the case study that is described in Chapter 12).

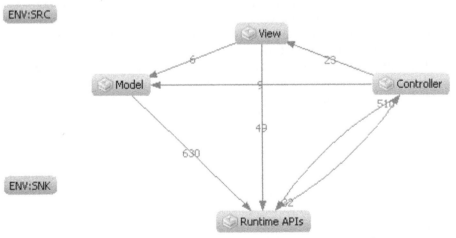

FIGURE 43 **Example of the Structure view at a less detailed level of resolution**

The view at Figure 43 maps the entire code base of the Clicks2Bricks into the elements of the Model-View-Controller architecture pattern. The facts in Figure 43 can be verbalized using the SBVR Structured English as follows:

There exists Subsystem with name "View."
There exists Subsystem with name "Controller."
There exists Subsystem with name "Model."
Subsystem "View" *depends on* Subsystem "Model."
Subsystem "View" *depends on* Subsystem "Runtime Paltform APIs."
Subsystem "Model" *depends on* Subsystem "Runtime Paltform APIs."
Subsystem "Controller" *depends on* Subsystem "View."
Subsystem "Controller" *depends on* Subsystem "Model."
Subsystem "View" *depends on* Subsystem "Runtime Paltform APIs."

Figure 43 shows that Subsystems "Model," "View," "Controller," and "Runtime Platform APIs" cover an entire set of system facts. This is based on the absence of relations to ENV nodes and from ENV nodes (to and from the rest of the system), as well as on the understanding that the KDM system model is a closed system that contains all known facts about the system of interest (within the scope of the model). Under these assumptions, the above view is evidence for the claim that the Subsystem "Model" depends *only* on the entities inside the subsystem "Runtime Platform APIs."

11.5.2 Conceptual views

The Conceptual viewpoint defined in the KDM Conceptual package provides constructs for creating a linguistic and behavior models during the analysis phase of knowledge discovery from the existing code.

The Conceptual viewpoint is defined by the following considerations:

Concerns
- What domain concepts are implemented by the system?
- What are the behavior elements of the system?
- What business rules are implemented by the system?
- What scenarios are supported by the system?

Analytic methods
The Conceptual viewpoint supports the following main kinds of checking:

- Conceptual relationships (what are the relationships between conceptual entities, based on their implementation by the Code and Data entities?)
- Scenario flow (what are the control-flow relationships between the two scenarios based on the flow between action elements referenced by each scenario?)
- BehaviorUnit coupling (what are the control-flow and data-flow relationships between two behavior units based on the action elements referenced by each behavior unit?)

- Business Rule analysis (what is the logic of the business rule based on the action elements referenced by the business rule?)

Conceptual views are used in combination with Code views, Data views, Platform views, UI views, and Inventory views.

Construction methods

- Conceptual views can be produced manually using the input from the information analysis and the architect of the system and architecture documentation.
- Construction of the Conceptual view is determined by the domain model and the architectural description of the system.
- Construction of the Conceptual views corresponding to a particular architectural description may involve additional information (system-specific or architecture-specific). This information can be attached to KDM elements using stereotypes, attributes, or annotations.

The Conceptual Model enables mapping of KDM compliant model to models compliant to other specifications. Currently, it provides "concept" classes—TermUnit and FactUnit facilitating the mapping to SBVR specification, described in Chapter 10.

KDM TermUnit is a representation of the SBVR noun concept or SBVR individual concept as a first-class citizen on a KDM view. This element can be further connected to its implementation by lower-level KDM elements for the Code, Data, UI and Platform views by the vertical traceability links using the "is implemented by" relationships. This is the key to mechanism for using KDM as the nucleus of the Common Fact Model and importing the vocabularies, defined in Chapters 4–7 in a KDM-compliant tool for the purpose of establishing the integrated system model.

Similarly, a KDM FactUnit is a representation of the SBVR verb concept in the integrated fact model. KDM RuleUnit element is the representation of the SBVR elements of behavior guidance.

The Conceptual Model also provides "behavior" types—BehaviorUnit and ScenarioUnit that support mapping to various external models, including but not limited to activities/flow chart and swim lane diagrams, and use case scenarios. The following explains the difference between these "behavior" types:

- BehaviorUnit represents a behavior *graph* with several paths through the application logic and associated conditions. The "implementation" of this graph is provided by the ActionElements connected with Flow relations, from the Program Elements KDM layer. The graph can be as small as a single ActionElement. BehaviorUnit is an "abstraction" of ActionElements since it provides a modeling element for representing a collection of ActionElements that is meaningful from the application domain perspective, and further manipulates with this representation as a first-class citizen of the ConceptualModel of KDM.
- ScenarioUnit represents a *path* (or multiple related paths) through the behavior graph. For example, ScenarioUnit corresponds to a trace through the systems,

or a "use case." ScenarioUnit can own an entire collection of BehaviorUnits, connected with ConceptualFlow elements, and can thus represent a slice of the original behavior graph in implementing the software system. The conditions responsible for navigation between alternative paths within the graph can be represented as RuleUnits.

- RuleUnit represents a *condition*, a group of conditions, or a constraint. RuleUnit is a representation for some meaningful navigation conditions within behavior graphs represented by several BehaviorUnits.

11.5.2.1 Linguistic viewpoint

The purpose of Linguistic elements is to provide a bridge between low-level, physical, and implementation viewpoints and high-level policy documents describing the business rules of the system of interest. Also, systematic traceability from domain-specific vocabulary terms all the way down to the individual code elements provides an efficient way of navigating the system and allows assurance of certain evaluation activities.

Figure 44 illustrates the noun concepts of the KDM Linguistic viewpoint.

The next diagram, Figure 45, illustrates the verb concepts of the Linguistic viewpoint.

Figure 46 illustrates KDM linguistic facts for a fragment of the Conceptual Model for Clicks2Bricks system, described in more detail in Chapter 12.

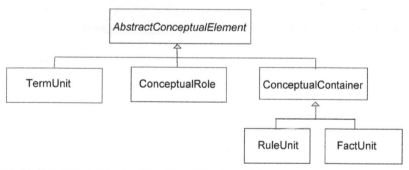

FIGURE 44 The noun concepts of the Linguistic viewpoint

11.5.2.2 Behavior viewpoint

The purpose of Behavior elements is to provide a bridge between low-level, physical, and implementation viewpoints and high-level functional views of the system of interest. Also, systematic traceability from the system functions all the way down to the individual code elements provides an efficient way of navigating the system and allows assurance of certain evaluation activities.

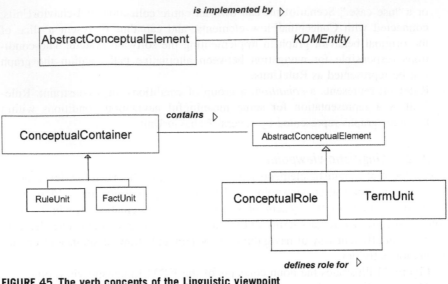

FIGURE 45 The verb concepts of the Linguistic viewpoint

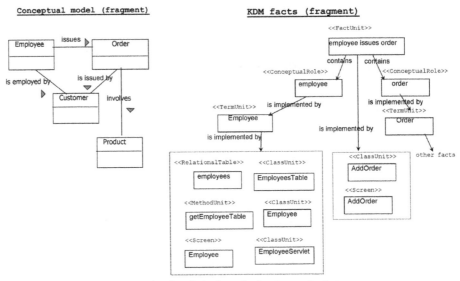

FIGURE 46 Example of the KDM linguistic facts in the Conceptual view

The next two diagrams, Figures 47 and 48, illustrate the concepts of the KDM Behavior viewpoint.

BehaviorUnit is a named unit of functionality, defined by the vertical traceability links to other KDM elements (for example, to ActionElements). In addition, direct "flows into" facts involving BehaviorUnits can be generated if needed.

Figure 49 illustrates KDM BehaviorUnits by using a fragment of the Data-Flow Diagram describing Clicks2Bricks system from Chapter 12.

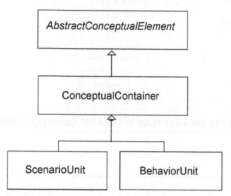

FIGURE 47 The noun concepts of the Conceptual viewpoint: behavior

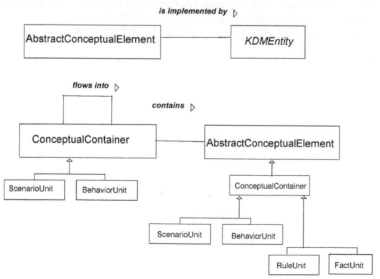

FIGURE 48 The verb concepts of the Conceptual view: behavior

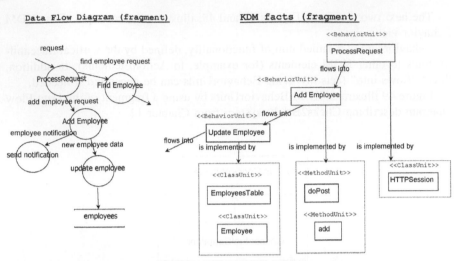

FIGURE 49 **Example of the behavior facts in the KDM Conceptual view**

Bibliography

ISO/IEC 19506 *Architecture Driven Modernization—Knowledge Discovery Metamodel.* (2009).

Object Management Group. (2006). *Knowledge Discovery Metamodel (KDM) 1.2.*

Object Management Group. (2009). *Semantics of Business Vocabularies and Rules (SBVR) 1.1.*

Object Management Group. *XML Model Interchange (XMI).*

W3C. (2008). *Extensible Markup Language (XML) 1.0* (5th ed). W3C Recommendation.

Case study

12

No data yet—It is a capital mistake to theorize before you have all the evidence. It biases the judgment.

Arthur Conan Doyle, *A Study in Scarlet*

It was easier to know it than to explain why I know it. If you were asked to prove that two and two made four, you might find some difficulty, and yet you are quite sure of the fact.

Arthur Conan Doyle, *A Study in Scarlet*

12.1 INTRODUCTION

In this chapter we use a single case study to illustrate some of the activities of a system assurance evaluation, highlighting the exchanges of content and managing pieces of cybersecurity knowledge in an *integrated system model* throughout the entire system assurance project. We illustrate the concept documents: the system Concept of Operations (CONOP) document and the definition of the system security policy based on the full vocabulary in SBVR [SBVR]. These documents are the key inputs to the project definition phase of the system assurance project. We then illustrate some of the activities involved in building the *baseline system model*. Many examples provided in Chapter 11, illustrating the key ideas of the standard protocol for exchanging system facts [ISO 19506] were also derived from this case study. We outline the common content that describes various runtime platforms. Affordable system evaluations depend on the availability of such content for import into the project preparation phase in order to build a comprehensive baseline system model with sufficient assurance that all the primitive system facts have been correctly recognized.

Then we illustrate how the baseline system model is enhanced with the *system architecture information* and how *traceability links* are created between the cybersecurity content, such as the elements representing the information assets of the system of interest, and the baseline system facts, such as the tables in the relational database that implement some of the information assets.

We illustrate the development of the assurance case and focus on specific goals describing the evaluation of one security functional requirement, the so-called

System Assurance: Beyond Detecting Vulnerabilities. DOI: 10.1016/B978-0-12-381414-2.00012-9

unobservability property that corresponds to several specific security threats. We show how the goals of the assurance case are systematically developed based on the characteristics of the property, and we consider how they guide the security analysis and evidence collection for the assurance case. The online appendix to this book contains further examples of analysis and evidence gathering for the case study, using KDM-compliant tools.

12.2 BACKGROUND

The system of interest is called Clicks2Bricks. It is a fictitious system developed by a fictitious company called Cyber Bricks Corporation. Here is the background information. Cyber Bricks is a privately owned company whose business is in the area of the innovative devices called cyber bricks. Cyber Bricks Corporation offers innovative products and services. Their flagship product is iBrick. Cyber Bricks is also the supplier of the iBrickWall product. The RoadToBricks service is another very successful offer by Cyber Bricks. The online iMortar store is closely integrated with both the iBrick and the iBrickWall products and has gained significant popularity over the last nine months.

In order to establish leadership in this new application of cyber bricks, the company decided to launch a website to support the growing online community of suppliers and clients. The new system, called Clicks2Bricks, will work as a marketplace for the suppliers and clients to keep track of the current products and needs. The community will also include service providers who can deliver value-added services based on products. The objective of Cyber Bricks is to promote interoperability between available solutions, identify the gaps, and publish value-added content related to cyber bricks, publish this content on the dedicated interactive website, and support the online user community. The initial version has *limited functionality*, and focuses on the quality content related to the benefits of the entire cyber bricks community.

12.3 CONCEPTS OF OPERATIONS

This section contains the CONOPS for the Clicks2Bricks interactive Web information system, version 1.0.

12.3.1 Executive summary

This section provides basic information regarding the operation of the Clicks2-Bricks interactive Web system, developed by the Cyber Brick Corporation. This section includes a description of the Clicks2Bricks system, including connection details; data sensitivity information; access limitation to the Clicks2Bricks software and hardware; the user community for the Clicks2Bricks system and its related equipment; and personnel or positions responsible for the operation, administration, and maintenance of the Clicks2Bricks system. This document is the basis for security recommendations.

12.3.2 Purpose

The purpose of the Clicks2Bricks system is to support the needs of the growing online community of users. The Clicks2Bricks system will facilitate information exchanges within the cyber bricks community. This initial version of the Clicks2Bricks system has limited functionality. The system allows a user to create an online profile (which includes a login and associated used data). The Clicks2Bricks system allows users to read the online content, allows customers to search for available products and service offerings, allows suppliers to input information about their products and service offerings, and allows service providers to input information about their services. The customer can enter a request for certain capabilities, and the suppliers will describe a portfolio of products and services to match his or her unique needs. The customer can then place an order to acquire the desired capabilities. The Clicks2Bricks system allows adding value-added content to the Clicks2Bricks system. The administrator of the Clicks2Bricks community manages content and users. The information processed and generated by Clicks2Bricks systems is unclassified. The system collects information about the registered users; this information is designated protected.

The diagram shown in Figure 1 provides a high-level illustration of the operations of Clicks2Bricks. The numbers represent the typical sequence of the transaction flows through the system.

12.3.3 Locations

The Clicks2Bricks system will consist of a server located in the Marketing Department Area of the Cyber Bricks Office Building A, with a dedicated database server located in the Data Center Area, Building A. Users will access the system through the dedicated fiber optics line provided to the Building A by Jolly Byte Stream Internet Service Provider. The SMTP server is located in the Data Center Building A. Employees of Cyber Bricks access Clicks2Bricks system from desktop and laptop computers through connections in the Marketing Department Area, Building A. Users access Clicks2Bricks over the Internet.

12.3.4 Operational authority

The Operational Authority for this system is the Marketing Department of Cyber Bricks Corporation. The server software and hardware are owned, maintained, and managed by the Department of Engineering of Cyber Bricks Corporation.

The Information System Security Office (ISSO) for the Clicks2Bricks system is designated by the Chief Security Officer of Cyber Bricks. The responsibilities of the Clicks2Bricks ISSO are identified in Cyber Bricks Security Policy.

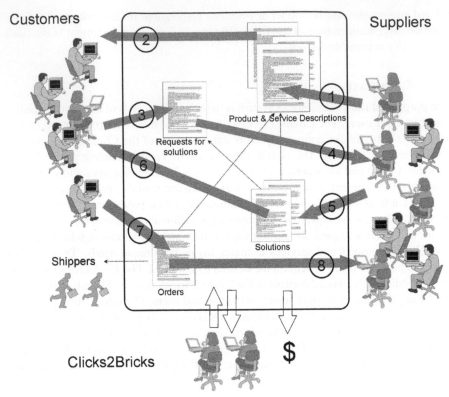

FIGURE 1 The operational concept for Clicks2Bricks system

12.3.5 System architecture

The Clicks2Bricks system consists of a Web server running a Clicks2Bricks application and the dedicated database server (See Figure 2). The server will run on the Linux operating system. The unstructured online content is stored in the local directory managed by the Web server. The structured data will run off a dedicated database server running open source database management system MySQL on the Linux operating system. The system will be connected to the Internet through a firewall.

12.3.5.1 Clicks2Bricks Web server

The Web server processes requests from users of the Clicks2Bricks system through the listening HTTPS port. Clicks2Bricks provides limited services to anonymous unregistered users over the HTTP port, which allows them to browse the Welcome page and some general-purpose content stored at the local disk of the Web server. The Web server processes login requests from registered users and establishes

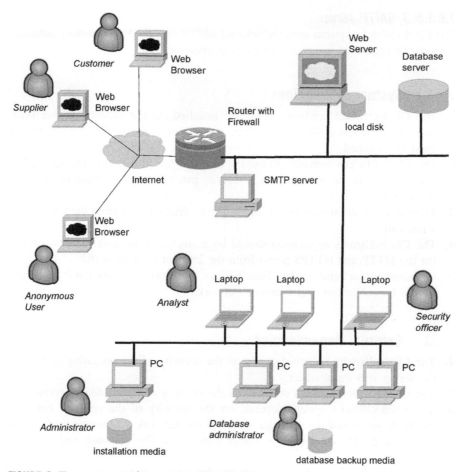

FIGURE 2 The system architecture for Clicks2Bricks

secure sessions during which multiple requests are processed. The registered user is allowed to browse subscription content and add subscription content, based on the registered user's access rights. Requests for the subscription content are processed by the database server.

12.3.5.2 Database server

The database server of the Clicks2Bricks system processes requests for subscription content and allows modification of the subscription content. The database server also contains personal information about the registered users of the Clicks2Bricks system.

12.3.5.3 SMTP server

The Clicks2Bricks system uses the internal SMTP server to send e-mail notifications to the registered users, and to the administrator.

12.3.6 System assumptions

1. The Clicks2Bricks application will be installed on the server that has been secured to current industry guidelines. Current security patches for the server must be installed.
2. The Clicks2Bricks website will use the database server that has been secured to current industry guidelines. Current security patches to the database server must be installed.
3. The database server should be protected from direct access from the Internet by a firewall.
4. The Clicks2Bricks application should be protected from direct access (except for the HTTP and HTTPS ports) from the Internet by a firewall.
5. Communication between the Clicks2Bricks Web server and the database server should be conducted over a private network.

12.3.7 External dependencies

1. The Clicks2Bricks system depends on the security of the operating system of the server it is installed on.
2. The Clicks2Bricks system depends on the security of the database server.
3. The Clicks2Bricks system depends on the security of the network between the Web server and the database server. If the network is compromised, sensitive data could be viewed or direct attacks on the database server could be made.
4. The Clicks2Bricks system depends on the session management of the Web server being secure. If the Web server's session management is not secure, an attacker might be able to hijack another user's session.
5. The Clicks2Bricks system depends on the external Simple Mail Transfer Protocol (SMTP) server to deliver notifications to users and administrators.

12.3.8 Implementation assumptions

1. Clicks2Bricks will use the open-source BareHttp Web server and will extend it with servlets to implement the business logic.
2. Clicks2Bricks system will not address any of the legal, contractual, and financial aspects of the information exchanges. These issues will be resolved by the other departments of Cyber Bricks. Clicks2Bricks will use an external SMTP server to deliver notifications that will integrate into the business processes of the corresponding departments.

12.3.9 **Interfaces with other systems**

1. The Clicks2Bricks system is connected to the Internet via the Jolly Byte Stream Internet Service Provider.
2. Clicks2Bricks uses the external SMTP server maintained by another department of Cyber Bricks Corporation.
3. Clicks2Bricks system is using the power supply of the Cyber Bricks Office Building.

12.3.10 **Security assumptions**

1. Personnel security: All employees and contractors of Cyber Bricks have passed through background checks. The Clicks2Bricks user community consists of the employees of the companies working in the cyber bricks industry. Users of the Clicks2Bricks system do not share a common requirement for access rights to the information.
2. Physical security: The servers, desktop computers, routers, and firewall are all located within the confines of Cyber Bricks establishments and are protected under local security orders. Servers, routers, and the firewall are located in the area with restricted access. The laptops used by several key personnel are mobile and can be used anywhere in the world. Use of these laptops and the information stored in them is protected by a password scheme. The installation media and backup media are stored in a secure off-site facility.
3. Procedural security: Information System Security Officers (ISSOs) are appointed for the overall system where the assets are installed and information is processed. The role of the ISSO is to provide security advice, to produce and maintain the security assurance case of the system, to coordinate security incident response, and to respond to security direction from the Chief Security Officer (CSO) of Cyber Bricks Corporation.
4. Information Technology security—The following highlights individual security features of the implemented Clicks2Bricks system's ITSEC facets.
   Registration for the Clicks2Bricks system. Any user can submit a registration request; approval of the registration request follows a three-step process. First, the domain of the user needs to match the domain name of the company that the user claims to be employed by. Second, the dedicated contact person for the company is notified and has to confirm the identity of the user and the need to access information. Third, the administrator of the Clicks2Bricks system must grant access rights to the new user. Registration of the new companies subscribing to the Clicks2Bricks system is done manually by the administrator of the Clicks2Bricks system upon request and upon completion of the service contract. Employees of the Cyber Bricks Corporation are authorized to access the Clicks2Bricks system by the administrator and the ISSO of Clicks2Bricks. In each case, formal access right approval is enforced.
   Registered users are required to have login credentials that include a username and a password.

Transmission Security—Communication with the Clicks2Bricks system is performed over Secure Socket Layer.

12.3.11 External security notes

1. The Clicks2Bricks system has no password quality enforcement. Users and authors must choose strong passwords that are hard to guess or discover by brute force.
2. The Clicks2Bricks system must support HTTPS.

12.3.12 Internal security notes

1. All queries to the database are done using only one set of credentials—that of the Web server identity.
2. The Clicks2Bricks system makes use of an SMTP server on the internal network of Clicks2Bricks.

12.4 BUSINESS VOCABULARY AND SECURITY POLICY FOR CLICKS2BRICKS IN SBVR

The specific security requirements for the Clicks2Bricks system are determined by the following policy statements:

1. It is prohibited that the Clicks2Bricks system disclose any subscription content to an unregistered user.
2. It is prohibited that the Clicks2Bricks system disclose order items to an unauthorized user.
3. It is prohibited that the Clicks2Bricks system disclose the identity of a Clicks2Bricks customer to an unauthorized user.
4. It is prohibited that the Clicks2Bricks system accept content from an unregistered user.

Some context is required in order to understand these statements. This context can be defined by a *linguistic model* for Clicks2Bricks. Linguistic models introduced in Chapter 10 define the noun and verb concepts selected as a conceptualization of some possible worlds; they also state facts of what is necessary, permissible or obligatory in these worlds. Linguistic models provide the conceptual schema for a set of concrete facts, defining one possible world. This section shows the full description of Clicks2Bricks in SBVR, including the vocabulary of the terms specific to the operations of Clicks2Bricks and definitions of the security policy as business rules on top of the Clicks2Bricks vocabulary. The security requirements use the specific vocabulary that is shared by the semantic community of the Clicks2Bricks system. This is the community of interest that includes the stakeholders of Clicks2Bricks, people who are involved with Clicks2Bricks in a multitude of ways. This vocabulary is expressed in English (as presented in this example). However, there is another version of the Clicks2Bricks vocabulary that expresses the same set of concepts in German. It is used by the German-speech subcommunity of the Clicks2Bricks semantic community. The German version of the vocabulary that expresses the same set of concepts is likely to be included in the German language edition of this book.

Cyber brick
   Definition: a fictitious product
   Note: for many a cyber brick is simply a pile of zeros and ones, but when installed professionally it turns into the most powerful information systems in cyberspace
   Description: identified for the purpose of this case study as the foundation of a vibrant business ecosystem

Cyber Bricks Corp
   Definition: a fictitious company whose business is related to cyber bricks

Company
   Definition: a legally recognized organization designed to provide goods or services, or both, to consumers, businesses and governmental entities
   Source: Steven M. Sheffrin (2003). Economics: Principles in action. Upper Saddle River, New Jersey 07458: Pearson Prentice Hall. pp. 29. ISBN 0-13-063085-3
   Reference scheme: name *of* the company

Company *has* name

Company *has* address

Company *operates at* location

Company *employs* person
   Synonym: person *is employed by* company

Product *is acquired by* company
   Note: the common usage of this verb phrase also includes acquisition of products by persons or by noncommercial organizations

Person
   Definition: an individual human being **that** has legal rights and duties
   Reference scheme: name *of* the person
   Reference scheme: name *of* the person **and** birthdate *of* the person
   Reference scheme: name *of* the person **and** address *of* the person
   Reference scheme: name *of* the person **and** email address *of* the person

Person *has* name
Person *has* address
Person *has* birthdate
Person *has* email address

Product
  Definition: an article or substance **that** is related to cyber
                     bricks **and** is manufactured or refined for sale
  Synonym: goods
  Reference scheme: product-id
Product *is manufactured by* company
  Synonym: company *manufactures* product
  Note: for the purposes of this case study, this also
                     includes transforming raw material into products
                     or refining products for the purpose of selling
                     them
Product *is supplied by* company
  Synonym: company *supplies* product
  Note: a product may be supplied by a different company
                     than the manufacturer of the product
Product *is shipped by* company
  Synonym: company *ships* product
  Note: a product may be shipped by a different company
                     than that the supplier of the product
Product *is supplied to* company
  Synonym: product *is sold to* company
  Synonym: company *acquires* product
  Note: the common usage of this verb phrase also
                     includes sale of products to persons or to
                     noncommercial organizations
  Note: acquisition of product is beyond the scope of
                     this vocabulary

Company *orders* product
  General concept: Operation
  Note: Usually, the order of product by a company causes
                     the delivery of the product to the company. The
                     product is supplied by the supplier of the
                     product and is delivered by the shipper

Note: Usually, the shipment is associated with the
                         transfer of ownership to the product from the
                         supplier to the company that acquired the product
                         and the remuneration from the acquirer of the
                         product to the supplier.

Note: The remuneration to the shipper is done either by
                         the supplier or by the acquirer of the product

<u>Manufacturer</u>

Definition: a <u>company</u> **that** *manufactures* <u>product</u>

<u>Supplier</u>

Definition: a <u>company</u> **that** *supplies* <u>product</u>

<u>Shipper</u>

Definition: a <u>company</u> **that** *ships* <u>product</u>

<u>Customer</u>

Definition: a <u>company</u> **that** *orders* <u>product</u> **or** *acquires* <u>product</u>

<u>Acquirer</u>

Definition: a <u>company</u> **that** *acquires* <u>product</u>

<u>Employer</u>

Definition: a <u>company</u> **that** *employs* <u>person</u>

<u>Employee</u>

Definition: a <u>person</u> **that** *is employed by* <u>company</u>

<u>Document</u>

Definition: a piece of written, printed, or electronic matter
                         that provides information or evidence or that
                         serves as an official record.

<u>Product listing</u>

Definition: a <u>document</u> **that** *describes* <u>product</u>

Reference schema: <u>item-id</u>

<u>Product</u> *is listed by* <u>supplier</u>

Synonym: <u>Product</u> *is listed on behalf of* <u>supplier</u>

Synonym: <u>Supplier</u> *lists* <u>product</u>

Necessity: the <u>product listing</u> **that** is *listed on behalf of* a
                         <u>supplier</u> *is supplied by* **the** <u>supplier</u>

<u>Product listing</u> *describes* <u>product</u>

<u>Product listing</u> *has* <u>item-id</u>

<u>Product</u> *is listed by* <u>person</u> *on behalf of* <u>supplier</u>

Synonym: <u>Person</u> *lists* <u>product</u> *on behalf of* <u>supplier</u>

Necessity: the person that *lists* a product *on behalf of* supplier *is employed by* the supplier

Request for solution

Definition: a document that describes a business need and enumerates the list of requirements that should be satisfied by a solution

Reference scheme: request-id

Request for solution *has* request-id

Request for solution *is issued by* customer

Synonym: customer *issues* request for solution

General concept: Operation

Request for solution *is issued by* person *on behalf of* customer

Synonym: person *issues* request for solution *on behalf of* customer

Necessity: the person that *issues* a request for solution *on behalf of* a customer *is employed by* the customer

Solution

Definition: a document that is issued by a supplier in response to a request for solution and that enumerates the set of products that address the need of the customer

Reference scheme: solution-id

Solution *has* solution-id

Solution *addresses* request for solution

Possibility: Request for solution *is addressed by* zero or more solutions

Solution *includes* solution item

Solution item *involves* business item

Solution *is issued by* supplier

Synonym: supplier *issues* solution

General concept: Operation

Solution *is issued by* person *on behalf of* supplier

Synonym: Person *issues* solution *on behalf of* supplier

Necessity: the person that *issues* a solution *on behalf of* a supplier *is employed by* the supplier

Order
    Definition: a <u>document</u> **that** *is issued by* a <u>customer</u> **that** *involves* the set of *products* **that the** <u>customer</u> *intends to acquire*
    Reference scheme: <u>order-id</u>
    Possibility: <u>order</u> *involves* **zero or more** <u>products</u>
    Necessity: <u>order</u> *involves* **at least one** <u>product</u>
<u>Order</u> *includes* <u>order item</u>
    Synonym: <u>order item</u> *is part of* <u>order</u>
<u>Order item</u>
    Definition: <u>document</u> **that** *is part of* an <u>order</u> **and that** *involves* a <u>product</u> **that the** <u>customer</u> **that** *issued* **the** <u>order</u> *intends to acquire*
<u>Order item</u> *is delivered to* <u>location</u>
<u>Order item</u> *involves* <u>business item</u>
<u>Order item</u> *is shipped by* <u>shipper</u>
<u>Order</u> *is issued by* <u>customer</u>
    Synonym: <u>Customer</u> *issues* <u>order</u>
    General concept: <u>Operation</u>
<u>Order</u> *is issued by* <u>person</u> *on behalf of* <u>customer</u>
    Synonym: <u>person</u> *issues* <u>order</u> *on behalf of* <u>customer</u>
    Necessity: **the** <u>person</u> **that** *issues* **an** <u>order</u> *on behalf of* **a** <u>customer</u> *is employed by* **the** <u>customer</u>

<u>Notification</u>
    Definition: a <u>document</u> **that** *notifies* the <u>recipient</u> *about* a <u>business event</u>
<u>Person</u> *receives* <u>notification</u>
    Synonym: <u>notification</u> *has* <u>recipient</u>
<u>Person</u> *is notified about* <u>business event</u>
<u>Designated contact person</u>
<u>Company</u> *has* <u>designated contact person</u>
<u>Product listing notification</u>
    Definition: <u>notification</u> *about* <u>listing</u> a <u>product</u> *by* a <u>supplier</u>
    General concept: <u>Notification</u>

It is obligatory that the <u>designated contact person</u> *of* a <u>company</u> *is notified* if a <u>product</u> *is listed on behalf of* the <u>company</u>

<u>Issuing solution</u>

Definition:	<u>business event</u> that *corresponds to* the <u>actuality</u> that a <u>solution</u> *is issued by* a <u>supplier</u>
General concept:	<u>business event</u>

<u>Solution notification</u>

Definition:	<u>notification</u> *about* <u>issuing solution</u> by a supplier
General concept:	<u>Notification</u>

It is obligatory that the <u>designated contact person</u> *of* the <u>company</u> *is notified on* <u>issuing solution</u> that *addresses* the <u>request for solution</u> that *is issued by* the <u>company</u>

<u>Ordering</u>

Definition:	<u>business event</u> that *corresponds to* the <u>actuality</u> that an <u>order</u> *is issued by* a <u>customer</u>
General concept:	<u>business event</u>

<u>Ordering</u> *involves* <u>business item</u>

Definition:	<u>order</u> *involves* an <u>order item</u> and the <u>order item</u> *involves* <u>business item</u>

<u>Order notification</u>

Definition:	<u>notification</u> *about issuing* an <u>order</u> *by* a <u>customer</u>
General concept:	<u>Notification</u>

It is obligatory that the <u>designated contact person</u> *of* a <u>company</u> *is notified on* <u>ordering</u> that *involves* a <u>business item</u> that *is supplied by* the <u>company</u>

<u>Clicks2Bricks</u>

Definition:	a fictitious <u>information system</u> that *is developed by* <u>Cyber Bricks Corp</u>

<u>Employee of Cyber Bricks</u>

Definition:	a <u>person</u> that *is employed by* <u>Cyber Bricks</u>
General concept:	<u>person</u>
Concept type:	<u>role</u>

<u>Administrator</u>

Definition:	an <u>employee of Cyber Bricks</u> that *is responsible for the operations of* <u>Clicks2Bricks</u>
Concept type:	<u>role</u>

Analyst

Definition: an employee of Cyber Bricks that *analyzes* subscription content of Clicks2Bricks **and** *maintains* open pages

Concept type: role

Database administrator

Definition: an employee of Cyber Bricks that *manages* the database server of Clicks2Bricks

Concept type: role

Security officer

Definition: an employee of Cyber Bricks that *manages security of* Clicks2Bricks

Concept type: role

registered Customer

Definition: company **that** *is registered to* Clicks2Bricks *as customer*

General concept: company

Note: it is assumed that there is no need for a company to play both roles

It is prohibited that a company that *is* a registered Supplier *is* a registered Customer

Registered customer *has* identity

Identity *of a* registered customer

Definition: any document that identifies a registered customer by disclosing the characteristics of the company

General concept: Document

Identity *of* registered customer *involves* name *of* **the** customer

Identity *of* registered customer *involves* address *of* **the** customer

Identity *of* registered customer *involves* location at **which the** customer *operates*

registered Supplier

Definition: company **that** *is registered to* Clicks2Bricks *as supplier*

General concept: company

Note: it is assumed that there is no need for a company to play both roles

It is prohibited that a company that *is* a registered Customer *is* a registered Supplier

<u>User</u> *interacts with* <u>Clicks2Bricks</u>

<u>User</u>

Definition:	a <u>person</u> **or** a <u>computer system</u> **that** *interacts with* the <u>Clicks2Bricks</u>
General concept:	<u>thing</u>
Concept type:	<u>role</u>

<u>Anonymous user</u>

Definition:	a <u>user</u> **that** *has not presented* <u>login credentials</u> *to* <u>Clicks2Bricks</u>
General concept:	<u>user</u>

<u>User</u> *registers to* <u>Clicks2Bricks</u>

<u>Registration notification</u>

Definition:	<u>notification</u> *about* a <u>registration</u> *by* a <u>user</u>
General concept:	<u>Notification</u>

<u>Registering</u>

Definition:	a <u>business event</u> **that** *corresponds to* the <u>actuality</u> **that** a <u>user</u> *registers to* <u>Clicks2Bricks</u>
General concept:	<u>business event</u>

It is obligatory that <u>administrator</u> *is notified on* <u>registering</u> *by* a <u>user</u> *to* <u>Clicks2Bricks</u>.

It is obligatory that <u>designated contact person</u> *of a* <u>company</u> *is notified* **if a** <u>user</u> *registers to* <u>Clicks2Bricks</u> **and** <u>user</u> *claims to be employed by* the <u>company</u>.

<u>Person</u> *approves* <u>registration</u>

Definition:	<u>person</u> **that** *is a designated contact person for a* <u>company</u> *approves* <u>registration</u> *of* **any** <u>user</u> **that** *claims to be employed by* the <u>company</u>

<u>Registration</u> *is approved*

Definition:	the <u>actuality</u> **that** <u>person</u> *approves* the <u>registration</u>

<u>User</u> *receives* <u>login credentials</u>

It is obligatory that <u>user</u> *receives* <u>login credentials</u> **if** the <u>registration</u> of the <u>user</u> is approved

<u>Registered user</u>

Definition:	a <u>person</u> **that** *has* <u>login credentials</u> for <u>Clicks2Bricks</u>
General concept:	<u>person</u>

Note: registered user is associated with employer

Necessity: registered user is associated with exactly one
                         employer

Note: the actions of a registered user may be performed
                         on his behalf by a computer system. Nevertheless
                         these actions are attributed to a particular
                         person and the employer of this person

Registered user *has* identity

Identity *of a* registered user

  Definition: any document that identifies the user by
                         disclosing the characteristics of the person

  General concept: Document

Identity of registered user *involves* name

Identity of registered user *involves* address

Identity of registered user *involves* birthdate

Identity of registered user *involves* email address

Subscription content

  Definition: document **that** *is issued to* Clicks2Bricks *by* a
                         registered customer **or a** registered supplier

Open pages

  Definition: document **that** *is issued to* Clicks2Bricks *by* an
                         analyst

User *issues* document *to* Clicks2Bricks

User *is qualified to issue* document

  Definition: user *is qualified to issue* document *to*
                         Clicks2Bricks **if the** user *is registered* **and the**
                         user *is* a registered supplier **and the** user *issues*
                         a product listing **or a** solution **or the** user *is* a
                         registered customer **and the** user *issues* a request
                         for solution **or an** order

Unqualified user

  Definition: user **that** *is* **not** *qualified to issue* a document

Clicks2Bricks *accepts* document *from* user

   It is prohibited that Clicks2Brick *accepts* document *from* an
unqualified user

User *accesses* document *from* Clicks2Bricks

  Synonym: document *is disclosed to* user

Content *is issued by* user

Definition: document *is issued by* user1 if user1 *added* the document *to* Clicks2Bricks or some user2 *added* the document *to* Clicks2Bricks and user2 *is employed by* a company and user1 *is a designated contact person of* the company.

User *is authorized to access* document

Definition: user *is authorized to access* document if the user *is registered* and

the document *is issued by* user or

the document *is* a solution or

the document *is* a product listing or

the document *is* a request for solution or

the document *is* an order item that *involves* a product that *is supplied by* the employer *of* the user

Clicks2Bricks *discloses* document *to* user

Unauthorized user

   Definition: user that *is* not *authorized to access* document

Unregistered user

   Definition: user that *is* not a registered user

It is prohibited that Clicks2Bricks *disclose* any subscription content *to* an unregistered user.

It is prohibited that Clicks2Bricks *disclose* identity *of* a registered customer *to* an unauthorized user.

It is prohibited that Clicks2Bricks *disclose* identity *of* a registered user *to* an unauthorized user.

The SBVR description of the operational vocabulary and rules for Clicks2-Bricks identifies the vocabulary of the system-specific facts to describe operational snapshots of the Clicks2Bricks (descriptions of the business objects, actors, and business operations). The full linguistic model usually defines a larger set of concepts than required for the operational fact model, but it includes the operational conceptual schema as a subset because many statements about the system refer to its business entities and operations (but many also include other concepts, in particular those related to the management and governance life-cycle processes). When the operational conceptual schema is identified, the formal SBVR descriptions can be used to automatically build a rough prototype of the system because formal SBVR definitions contain enough information to generate the database structure to store the snapshot of the operational facts, the stored procedures for the operational queries and updates corresponding to the operation, and even a prototype user interface. This process is valuable for the stakeholder requirements definition phase and the requirements analysis phase. This use of SBVR is outside the scope of this book. Later in this chapter we will show how the Clicks2Bricks vocabulary is imported into the integrated system model to support security analysis and evidence gathering for the assurance case. The vocabulary of Clicks2Bricks is part of the system facts, in addition to the operational and systems viewpoints, introduced in Chapter 4. Other viewpoints relevant for assurance where introduced in Chapters 5–7 and summarized at the end of Chapter 9. SBVR was used to describe these viewpoints at various degrees of formality. SBVR linguistic models describe all relevant system views, from business/operational facts that correspond to business transactions, to the facts describing the behavior and structure of the business processes, to behavior and structure of the systems that enable the business processes. SBVR descriptions focus on the conceptualizations and statements of what is necessary, permissible and obligatory in the worlds described by the conceptualization. So, SBVR is used to express all common vocabularies for cybersecurity, introduced in this book.

12.5 BUILDING THE INTEGRATED SYSTEM MODEL

The process of building the system model has been described in Chapter 3 and Chapter 11. In this section we provide some highlights of how this process is applied to Clicks2Bricks. We will use the fact-oriented process and assume a KDM-compliant fact-based repository to store the views of the system [ISO 19506].

12.5.1 Building the baseline system model

The first step in building the baseline system model is to create the KDM Inventory view of the system. This is a purely physical view of the system's artifacts without any regard to their logical organization. Elements of the Inventory view provide the initial set of "locations" in the system of interest. This view is essential to assure completeness of the baseline models, since the coverage of other views can be validated against the Inventory view. Next we show a fragment of standard KDM XML representation of the inventory facts described in Chapter 11. This XML file [XMI] can be used as a further illustration of the methodology of developing information exchange protocols for the OMG Assurance Ecosystem, described in Chapter 8 involving a seamless transformation between a vocabulary in SBVR, its illustrations using conceptual UML diagrams, and the physical XML format for exchanging facts.

```
<?xml version="1.0" encoding="UTF-8"?>
<kdm:Segment xmi:version="2.1"
xmlns:xmi="http://schema.omg.org/spec/XMI/2.1"
xmlns:kdm="http://schema.omg.org/spec/KDM/1.2/kdm"
```

```
xmlns:source="http://schema.omg.org/spec/KDM/1.2/source"
name="Clicks2Bricks Inventory Fragment">
        <model xmi:id="id.0" xmi:type="source:InventoryModel">
        <inventoryElement xmi:id="id.1" xmi:type="source:Directory"
name="clicks2bricks">
        <inventoryElement xmi:id="id.2" xmi:type="source:Directory"
name="org">
        <inventoryElement xmi:id="id.3"
xmi:type="source:Directory" name="savarese">
        <inventoryElement xmi:id="id.4"
xmi:type="source:Directory" name="barehttp">
        <inventoryElement xmi:id="id.5"
xmi:type="source:SourceFile" name="HTTPServer.java"
language="java 1.5" encoding=UTF=8"/>
        <inventoryElement xmi:id="id.6"
   xmi:type="source:SourceFile" name="HTTPSession.java"
   language="java 1.5" encoding="UTF-8"/>
        <inventoryElement xmi:id="id.7"
   xmi:type="source:SourceFile" name="Main.java"
   language="java 1.5" encoding="UTF-8"/>
        <inventoryElement xmi:id="id.8"
   xmi:type="source:SourceFile" name="Request.java"
   language="java 1.5" encoding="UTF-8"/>
        <inventoryElement xmi:id="id.8"
   xmi:type="source:SourceFile" name="overview.html"
   language="generic html" encoding="UTF-8">
        <inventoryRelation xmi:id="id.10"
   xmi:type="source:DependsOn" to="id.4" from="id.8"/>
        </inventoryElement>
      </InventoryElement>
     </InventoryElement>
    </InventoryElement>
  </inventoryElement>
 </model>
 </kdm:Segment>
```

Additional relations between the artifacts and their role in the system are understood when the *build instructions* for the system of interest are identified and analyzed, resulting in the creation of Build views. All KDM views beyond the Inventory view describe the logical and conceptual organization of the system, so they require compiler-like knowledge extraction tools that understand the syntax and semantics of the system artifacts. For example, the Build view is often created by analyzing the so-called makefiles for the Unix "make" utility. Several other build automation utilities are available, each supporting its own format of the build configuration files. Affordable system assurance relies on the availability of knowledge extractor tools supporting various off-the-shelf and proprietary formats and languages, so that the baseline model can be assembled in a timely fashion. The OMG Assurance Ecosystem emphasizes a standard protocol in which compiler-like tools can export relevant system facts for the purpose of integration into the system model.

The next steps in building the baseline system model involve identification of the programming languages (or machine code formats), the data description languages, and the user interface elements. As a result, the Program Elements, Data, and UI views are created. Several examples of these views are provided in Chapter 11.

The last phase of creating the baseline system model involves identifying elements of the runtime platform and creating the Platform views. Usually, Platform views are created by using the Program Element views as one of the inputs to analyze the platform APIs and libraries, and to apply the platform patterns for generating the corresponding facts that complete the control and data flows of the system of interest. This is a critical step that usually requires a backing assurance argument, since it is responsible for the soundness of the security analysis, as described in Chapter 3, and defined in the generic assurance case goals.

Several examples of Platform views have been provided in Chapter 11. Let's consider the "ThreadPoolExecutor" example. Chapter 11 illustrated potential loss of important facts, and the corresponding loss of soundness of the analysis from insufficient consideration of the control flows defined by the runtime platform. When only the semantics of the Java programming language was considered, the classes HTTPServer, Server, and Session appeared disconnected, and the "Call" methods of classes Server and Session appeared unused. Only when the additional platform resource and the corresponding platform actions are identified and added to the model does it become possible to identify system behaviors and functions, as illustrated in Chapter 11 in the sections on the Event viewpoint and Behavior viewpoint. Otherwise, the system model is not sound for the detailed cause and effect analysis, required for the Architecture Security Analysis, described in Chapter 3.

The particular situation involving the ThreadPoolExecutor is described by the following informal pattern:

- Library: java.util.concurrent
- API: ThreadPoolExecutor, ThreadPoolExecutor::submit
- Maps to KDM resource: ExecutionResource ThreadPoolExecutor (the full identity of this element is determined by the call to the constructor of the class)
- Each call to the submit method must be supported by a unique ActionElement (referred to as an "abstracted action") contained in the corresponding ThreadPoolExecutor resource, a Calls relationship from the original submit ActionElement to the abstracted action, and another Class relationship from the abstracted action to the method "call" of the class, that is submitted to the ThreadPoolExecutor as the first actual parameter

These patterns represent valuable content for building system models both cost-efficiently and with sufficient assurance. Guidance on using SBVR to formalize such patterns on top of the standard protocol for exchanging system facts was provided in

Chapter 10 on Linguistic Models. These patterns are then imported into generic platform knowledge discovery tools to build the Platform views for the system of interest. In Chapter 8 this import was described as the content import protocol of the OMG Software Assurance Ecosystem. Further assurance for the soundness of the system model is provided by cross-analyzing the Inventory views, the Program Element views, and the platform patterns applied, to validate the coverage of all libraries and APIs used in the code of the system.

12.5.2 Enhancing the baseline model with the system architecture facts

The baseline system model, consisting of the Code views, Data views, User Interface views, and Platform views, must be further enhanced to match the level of granularity at which the assurance case is formulated and at which most of the cybersecurity knowledge exists. Within the framework of the standard protocol for exchanging system facts, this is done by adding the corresponding elements of the KDM Abstraction Layer into the integrated system model and establishing the vertical traceability links from the new elements to the existing low-level elements of the baseline system model. The system fact discovery phase includes five steps: adding structure elements, adding functional elements, identifying entry points, adding linguistic elements, and adding rule elements. Enhanced system facts use KDM Structure views, KDM linguistic views, KDM behavior views, and KDM event views. Several examples have already been provided in Chapter 11, when the corresponding KDM views were presented.

System structural elements (subsystems, architectural layers, components, etc.) are identified in the CONOPS document and more detailed architecture description documents. There is a growing trend for system engineering projects to use machine-readable architecture repositories (this is one of the reasons we used DoDAF as an example in Chapter 4). Machine-readable architecture artifacts, such as SysML models, can be imported into the integrated system model and then linked with the baseline facts. In Chapter 8 this import was described as the concrete knowledge discovery protocol. Note, that a SysML or a UML architecture model, while machine-readable, is not fact-oriented, as its foundation is a class with properties and attributes. In order to import information from a SysML or a UML model into a fact-based repository, the corresponding vocabulary of noun and verb concepts must be identified, as described in Chapter 4, and then the properties of classes must be decomposed into elementary verb concepts. The noun concepts of the fact-oriented approach do not have any attributes. Alternatively, high-level structure components can be discovered in the code by a bottom-up process—modeling in reverse—where the analyst reviews the system using the baseline views, rationalizes the organization of elements, and identifies high-level subsystems. This way, the implementations of subsystems are identified first, the new KDM elements are entered second, and the traceability links are established last. When existing machine-readable architecture elements are imported, the new KDM elements are created first, then the analyst identifies their implementations and creates traceability links. The latter is a more efficient process. On the other hand, there are various elements of guidance to identification of the high-level structure in the Inventory and Code views themselves.

Similar notes apply to the functional elements and linguistic elements. SBVR vocabulary can be imported into the integrated system model. In particular, the key terms of the SBVR vocabulary, the ones corresponding to the operational conceptual schema subset of the full linguistic model, are represented as KDM TermUnit and FactUnit elements and connected to the implementation elements by the vertical traceability links. The resulting facts are illustrated in Chapter 11, in the section on Linguistic views.

Let's first look at an example of how a structure model, like the one presented in Chapter 11, in the section on the Structure viewpoint, can be *discovered* bottom-up by using the baseline model. To begin with, the Code view already contains initial information about the structure of the system, which makes review and manipulation of the Code view very efficient, but which may or may not be relevant to the logical architecture of the system. We are talking about the physical organization of files into directories and packages. The KDM Code view captures these facts. You have already noticed that the KDM views involve many facts with the designator "*contains*" and "*is implemented by.*" These facts define the *hierarchies* of system elements. For example, Figure 3 illustrates what the top elements of the Code view from the baseline model for Clicks2Bricks look like. The nodes at the diagram are KDM Package elements, corresponding to the top-level Java packages. The nodes with the names "ENV:SRC" and "ENV:SNK" represent the rest of the system (the environment of the current diagram).

The entire hierarchy can be reviewed one level at a time (see Figure 4). Here, the "org" package contains two packages: "apache" and "savarese", and the "savarese" package contains individual classes (the class diagram at the third level of the hierarchy is presented in Chapter 11; see the section on the Code viewpoint).

So, even when the analyst is working bottom-up to discover high-level elements of software systems, he works with a manageable hierarchically organized model.

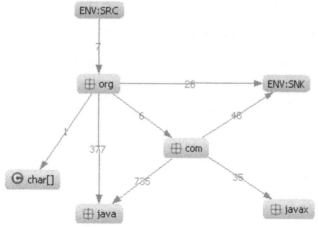

FIGURE 3 A view of the top-level Java packages in Clicks2Bricks

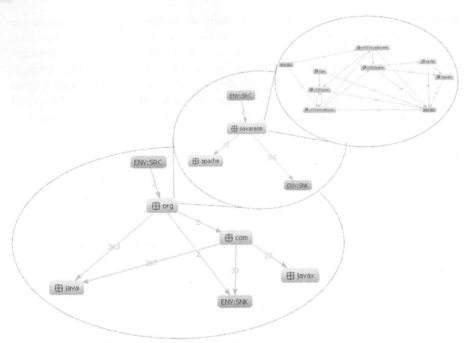

FIGURE 4 The Hierarchy of Java packages in Clicks2Bricks

One can make a query to the KDM fact repository to select all leaf packages (the ones that do not contain further packages) and show them in one view. This view is illustrated in Figure 5. Each node represents a leaf package (containing no further packages). The four highlighted nodes are application packages.

This view strongly suggests that the Clicks2Bricks system uses a Model-View-Controller architecture, based on the names of the packages and the fabric of relationships to the platform packages, such as "net," "apache," "servlet," "io," and "sql."

The hierarchy of the baseline Code view is defined by the "contains" facts, which identifies the single parent "defining" hierarchy of each Code element (e.g., a MethodUnit is contained in one and only one ClassUnit). On the other hand, the new view is an ArchitectureView element in a Structure view which uses "*is implemented by*" facts that are many-to-many relationships between different levels of granularity. As a result, the "barehttp" package can be linked to mutiple hierarchies. For the above illustration we have created a new Structure view called "All leaf packages" with a single ArchitectureView element with the name "package view." The elements in the above diagram are "implementations" of the "package view." Let's create another view called "application packages," containing only application packages (see Figure 6).

The package "barehttp" is related to the new element "application packages" as "*is implemented by*" relationship (not visible at the diagram, and only available in the KDM fact base).

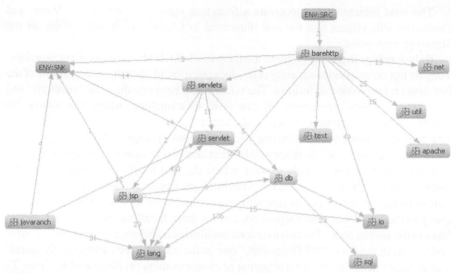

FIGURE 5 A view of all leaf Java packages in Clicks2Bricks

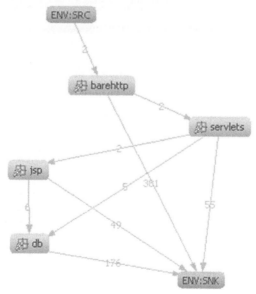

FIGURE 6 View of the application packages in Clicks2Bricks

The next logical step is to create a Structure view with the Model, View, and Controller subsystems like the one illustrated in Chapter 11 in the section on the Structure viewpoint.

Relationships in the above views are the so-called KDM *aggregated relationships*. They do not correspond to separate verb concepts; instead, they are aggregations of the low-level relationships as follows. The relationship between the node "barehttp" and the node "servlets" represents all low-level relationships, where the source "*is contained*" in the "barehttp" node, and the target "*is contained*" in the "servlets" node. The "*is implemented by*" relationship also determines aggregated relationships, in the same way as "*contains*." In other words, there are two unique locations in the entire code base of the Clicks2Bricks system, where the first location is in one of the elements (transitively) contained in the "barehttp" package and where the second location is in one of the elements (transitively) contained in the "servlets" package. A query to the KDM fact-based repository can list these locations by using the standard links to the source code. The two locations are illustrated below as fragments of source code, both in the class "HTTPSession," one in the method "processServletRequest" and another one in the static initialization of class members (as illustrated at Figure 7).

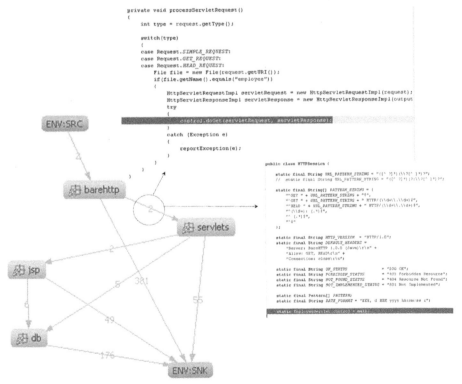

FIGURE 7 Aggregated relationships provide traceability links

KDM views support assurance analysis through the mechanism of "environment." All KDM views are "closed" and contain information about the entire fact base in the following sense: Each KDM view is capable of showing the aggregated relationships to the nodes within the current view from the rest of the system (ENV: SRC) and from the nodes of the current view to the rest of the system (ENV:SNK). Thus, the above diagram supports the claim that "package servlets" is not used by any other package except the package "barehttp." KDM has the following important property: not only an aggregated relationship in a KDM view is the evidence of a dependency between two elements, but also the absence of an aggregated relationship is the evidence of the lack of dependency between the two elements.

12.6 MAPPING CYBERSECURITY FACTS TO SYSTEM FACTS

The next step in the assurance project is to identify cybersecurity elements such as trust levels (the categories of external actors), assets, threat events, and threats and to map them to the system model by creating the new elements and establishing the traceability links to existing elements of the integrated system model. Cybersecurity elements are represented by a separate vocabulary described in Chapter 5 that is not part of the standard protocol for exchanging system facts. However, the system facts are the "*locations*" with which the assets, threat events, and other components of the "security threat" are *associated*. Adding these elements to the integrated system model is the process of fact-based integration.

Here are some *information assets* for Clicks2Bricks:

```
A1-1. User's login credentials
   Description:    The user's login credentials: username and password
   Trust level:    TL2 Remote user with login credentials
A1-4. Customer's identity
   Description:    According to the Clicks2Bricks security policy,
                   customer's identity shall be available only to
                   supplier through order addressed to that supplier or to
                   the employees of the customer. Identify of the customer
                   includes the name of the company, the email address,
                   the address, the requests issued by the particular
                   customer, the user names of the registered users that
                   are the employees of the particular customer and the
                   orders issued by the particular customer.
   Trust level:    TL3 Supplier
A1-6. Employee's personal data
   Description:    The personal data that the user enters such as contact
                   information, the employer, etc.
```

```
Trust level:        TL2 Remote user with login credentials (only the user,
                    the administrator and the designated contact person
                    for the employer of the user)

A1-9. Orders
Description:        Order is a document issued by customer. The order
                    contains the list of products and services that the
                    customer intends acquiring. Orders shall be available
                    only to the corresponding suppliers.
Trust level:        TL3 Supplier
```

These elements are added to the integrated system model by creating a new KDM Conceptual view importing each asset element as a new TermUnit, and creating relationships to the trust levels and the corresponding physical elements that implement each asset. Note that for some of the elements (such as "Order") we only need to link it to the corresponding linguistic element, already imported from the SBVR vocabulary. TermUnits representing assets are collected in a separate Conceptual view with the name "assets." More elaborate vocabulary integration can be achieved by establishing "*is an instance of*" relationships from each asset TermUnit to a TermUnit with the name "asset" representing the concept "asset."

Here are some *threat events* for Clicks2Bricks:

```
C-1. Disclosure of User's login credentials
Description:
Asset:              A1-1 User's login credentials

C-5. Disclosure of User's personal data
Asset:              A1-6 User's personal data
Consequences:       privacy, illegal in some jurisdictions; possible
                    litigation; potential damage to the reputation of Cyber
                    Bricks

C-6. Disclosure of Orders
Asset:              A1-9 Orders
Consequnces:        violation of the contract with customers; possible loss
                    of customer; possible loss of revenue; possible
                    litigation
```

These elements are also added to the integrated system model as KDM Term-Units and linked with the corresponding assets. Then a systematic analysis of the functional views of the system can be performed to identify the locations that can produce these threat events and "*is implemented by*" links established to the "threat event" elements.

Here are some *threats* to Clicks2Bricks:

Threat 2: Disclosure of Login Information

Name:	Adversary acquires another user's login credentials
Descriptions:	If an adversary obtains the login credential of another user, he can perform any task that user can.
Consequence:	Information disclosure, Elevation of privilege, Tampering
Entry points:	Login page, database stored procedures
Assets:	User's login data
Threat agent:	Hacker

Threat 3: Session Hijacking

Name:	Adversary acquires the session ID of another user
Description:	If an attacker acquires the session ID of a logged-in user, he can perform any task that user can
Consequence:	Elevation of privilege
Entry points:	Web server listening ports (HTTP, HTTPS)
Assets:	Login session
Threat agent:	Hacker

Threat 4: User Data Disclosure

Name:	Adversary retrieves another user's personal data
Description:	Disclosing another user's personal data raises privacy issues. Furthermore, the Clicks2Bricks would not be perceived as trustworthy.
Consequence:	Spoofing, Information disclosure
Entry points:	Web server listening ports (HTTP, HTTPS)
Assets:	User's personal information
Threat agent:	Hacker

The "threat" elements are also added to the integrated system model as KDM TermUnits and linked with the corresponding assets, entry points, threat events, and threat agent elements. Once all threat and risk elements have been identified, a systematic analysis and validation of threats can be performed through the integrated system model using the combination of the assurance strategies outlined in Chapter 5.

Exactly the same approach is performed to identify *safeguards*.

As a result, the integrated system model contains all cybersecurity elements and can be used to *manage* all system assessment facts. The Common Fact Model and the standard protocol for exchanging system facts provide a uniform extensible and scalable environment for managing facts during the entire assessment project and making these facts available for efficient reevaluations and incremental operational risk analysis.

Information exchanges play an important role in making threat and risk identification systematic and efficient; these exchanges also allow additional assurance of the correctness of the results. The general content for the identification of the threats and risks is available in the form of risk analysis checklists, including asset categories, common injuries, threat classes, threat activities, threat agent categories and safeguard classes. This content, when made machine-readable, can be imported into the integrated system model to organize the individual entities (assets, threat events, threats, specific threat agents, and safeguards) into containers based on the generic categories.

The threat model is determined by the concept of operations, so the corresponding content can be developed concurrently with building the baseline system model. In Chapter 8, this was described as the general knowledge protocol of the OMG Assurance Ecosystem. However, the threat model and the baseline system model must be connected, because of the need to provide assurance that all system-specific threats have been addressed. This connection is established by the systematic architecture-driven threat identification approach, described in Chapter 5. On the other hand, vulnerability detection also connects the generic threat model to the baseline system model, as described in Chapters 6 and 7. Chapter 8 described this connection as the knowledge refinery protocol. In addition, system analysis is driven by the assurance claims and provides further connections between the baseline system model and the threat model by deriving intermediate facts that link the claims, and in particular the safeguard effectiveness claims, which use the vocabulary of the threat model, to the evidence, which eventually uses the vocabulary of the baseline system model. These considerations are essential to understanding of the general structure of the assurance case, described in Chapter 3 and its elaboration in the next section.

12.7 ASSURANCE CASE

This section illustrates security assurance case [ARM], [SAEM] for Clicks2Bricks as an illustration to Phase 3 of the System Assurance process described in Chapter 3. Figure 8 provides a simplified version of the top claim focusing on the satisfaction of the identified security requirements. In this case study we focus on a single security requirement, called the "unobservability" which is stated as follows: "the system shall ensure that all users/subjects are unable to observe any operation on any object/resource by any other user/subject". Figure 9 presents the results of our linguistic analysis of this property to identify the noun and verb concepts involved to provide guidance to the development of the assurance case for this property. The first tier simply lists the original noun and verb concepts used in the formulation of the Unobservability property. The second tier maps these concepts onto the

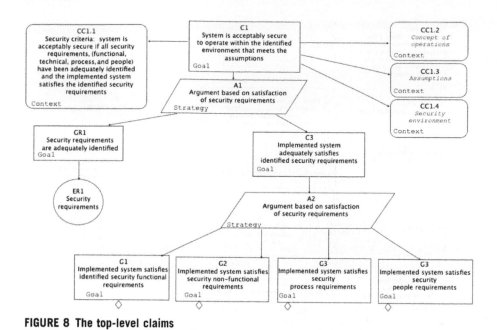

FIGURE 8 The top-level claims

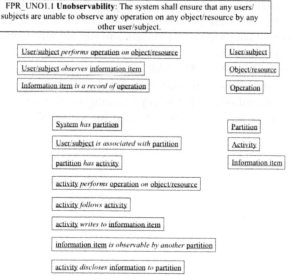

FIGURE 9 Analysis of the unobservability property

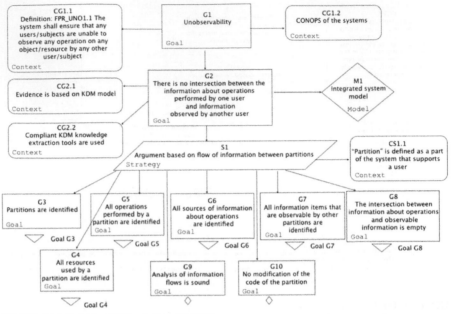

FIGURE 10 Unobservability claims: G1-G10

concepts available in the integrated system model. Figure 10 describes the top level assurance case for Unobservability. Figures 11–16 elaborate the argument outlined in Figure 10 and provide the guidance for analysis of the system and evidence gathering. The online appendix to the book provides advanced technical examples of how the OMG Software Assurance Ecosystem tools are used to analyze the integrated system model and collect evidence to support this assurance case.

The process of building confidence in security posture of cyber systems is a knowledge-intensive process. The OMG Software Assurance Ecosystem approach focuses at what knowledge is needed, how it is described, collected and exchanged in order to build confidence. Knowledge sharing is essential to the productivity of the organizations performing assessments, for the simple reason that it allows division of labor.

Assurance case organizes system analysis into several systematic, and coordinated goal-based activities. The elements of the assurance case are facts that are based on a certain conceptual commitment, involving a vocabulary of noun and verb phrases as well as statements of what is necessary, permissible or obligatory. The decomposition of the assurance claims into subclaims coincides with the refinement of this vocabulary, until the vocabulary of the leaf sub-claims is aligned with the vocabulary of the facts available in the integrated system model. System analysis supports this refinement of the vocabulary as it derives more comprehensive facts from the low-level system facts. In practice, the assurance case offers a semi-formal justification because the goals of the assurance case guide the analyst

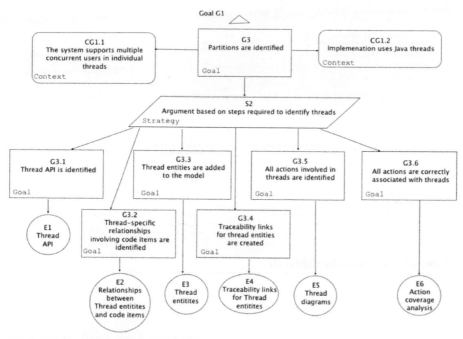

FIGURE 11 Unobservability claims: G3

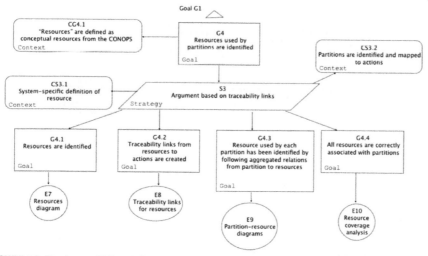

FIGURE 12 Unobservability claims: G4

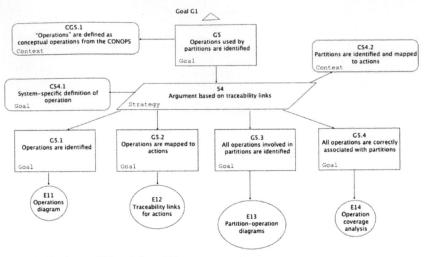

FIGURE 13 Unobservability claims: G5

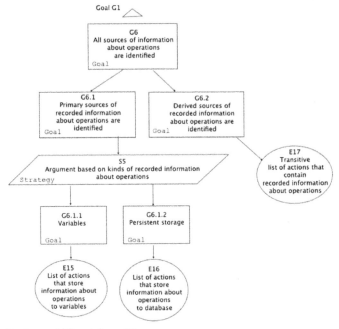

FIGURE 14 Unobservability claims: G6

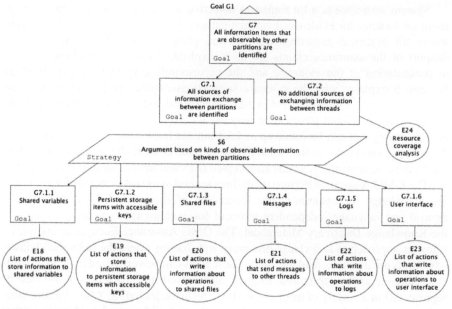

FIGURE 15 Unobservability claims: G7

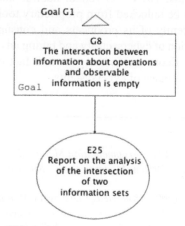

FIGURE 16 Unobservability claims: G8

to perform the remaining system analysis to bridge the gap between the sub-claims and the elementary facts in the repository, rather than always work as fully-formal queries into the repository. So, assurance case is a practical tool to manage the system analysis process and communicate its results to the system stakeholders in a clear, comprehensive and defendable way.

System assurance is a lot similar to detective work, where most of the effort is spent on looking for evidence. Evidence gathering is guided by the assurance case where all evidence gathering activities are planned and their contributions to support of the assurance claims are made explicit. Assurance case brings clarity to presentation of the evidence and the corresponding system analysis findings because it explains why the evidence supports assurance claims. Assurance case is used to manage evidence items as they are gathered, explains any counter evidence and provides a rational justification why the security posture of the system is adequately strong and can be relied upon. Last but not least, assurance case documents the assumptions made, so that when the operational context changes, a re-evaluation can be done incrementally, so that all accepted risks will not accumulate unreasonably.

The OMG Assurance Ecosystem defines several standard protocols for exchanging knowledge for assurance. The foundation of these standards is the vendor-neutral and language-independent protocol for exchanging facts about systems – the Knowledge Discovery Metamodel. The OMG Assurance Ecosystem involves a rigorous approach to knowledge discovery and sharing where the individual knowledge units are machine-readable facts. These facts can be verbalized by human-readable statements in structured English and stored in efficient repositories or represented in a variety of machine-readable formats, including XML. Vendor-neutral protocol for describing system facts allows building and exchanging other machine-readable content for assurance, such as vulnerability patterns or descriptions of common platforms. The OMG vendor-neutral standards enable machine-readable content that can be unlocked from proprietary tools and can be developed and exchanged independently of its producers and consumers to allow evolution towards the industrialization of cybersecurity and taking advantage of the economies of scale. OMG Assurance Ecosystem is a step towards fact-oriented, repeatable, systematic and affordable assurance of cybersystems.

Bibliography

Object Management Group. (2010). *Argumentation Metamodel (ARM)*.

ISO/IEC 19508 *Architecture Driven Modernization—Knowledge Discovery Metamodel*. (2009).

Object Management Group. (2006). *Knowledge Discovery Metamodel (KDM) 1.2*.

Object Management Group. (2010). *Software Assurance Evidence Metamodel (SAEM)*.

Object Management Group. (2009). *Semantics of Business Vocabularies and Rules (SBVR) 1.1*.

Object Management Group. *XML Model Interchange (XMI)*.

W3C. (2008). *Extensible Markup Language (XML) 1.0* (5th ed). W3C Recommendation.

Index

Note: Page numbers followed by *f* indicate figures and *t* indicate tables.

Printed and bound by CPI Group (UK) Ltd, Croydon, CR0 4YY

03/10/2024

01040322-0007